Legal Accounting

SECOND EDITION

Jacqueline Asselin

Keri Nisbet

emond ▪ Toronto, Canada ▪ 2019

Emond Montgomery Publications Limited
1 Eglinton Avenue E, Suite 600
Toronto ON M4P 3A1
http://www.emond.ca/highered

Printed in Canada.

We acknowledge the financial support of the Government of Canada.

Canadä

PCLaw® Screen Shots used with permission from LexisNexis. LexisNexis and the Knowledge Burst logo are registered trademarks of RELX Inc. PCLaw® is a registered trademark of LexisNexis Canada Inc. Copyright 2018 LexisNexis. All rights reserved.

Vice president, publishing: Anthony Rezek
Publisher: Lindsay Sutherland
Director, development and production: Kelly Dickson
Developmental editor: Vicki Austin
Production manager: Laura Bast
Copy editor: Dina Theleritis
Typesetter: Tom Dart
Permissions editor: Monika Schurmann
Proofreaders: Kristy Hankewitz, Geoff Graves
Indexer: Kristy Hankewitz
Cover image: Atstock Productions/Shutterstock

Library and Archives Canada Cataloguing in Publication

Asselin, Jacqueline, author
    Legal accounting / Jacqueline Asselin, Keri Nisbet. — Second edition.
    (Working with the law)
Includes bibliographical references and index.
ISBN 978-1-77255-404-5 (softcover)

    1. Lawyers—Ontario—Accounting—Textbooks. 2. Textbooks. I. Nisbet, Keri, author II. Title. III. Series: Working with the law

HF5686.L35A77 2019   657'.834   C2018-905679-7

To Allan
—JA

To my family and my dad, David MacPhee
—KLMN

Brief Contents

Contents   vii

Preface.   xv

About the Authors   xvii

1   Role of the Law Society of Ontario   1

2   Introduction to Bookkeeping   19

3   Keeping Books and Records.   39

4   Posting and Trial Balance   73

5   Preparing Financial Statements   99

6   Special Journals   117

7   Trust Accounting   157

8   Adjusting Accounts for Financial Statements.   197

9   Final Steps in the Accounting Cycle   221

10   Banking Procedures and Accounting for Cash   255

11   Accounting for GST/HST, Payroll, and Income Tax.   283

12   Computerized Time and Money Management   305

Appendix: By-Law 9, Financial Transactions and Records   321

Glossary.   335

Index   349

Contents

Brief Contents   v
Preface   xv
    Chapter Features   xvi
    Acknowledgments   xvi
About the Authors   xvii

1   Role of the Law Society of Ontario — 1

Introduction   2
Requirement for Books and Records in Legal Firms   2
Forms of Business Organization in Legal Services Firms   3
    Sole Proprietorship   3
    Partnership   4
    Limited Liability Partnership   4
    Multi-Discipline Practice or Affiliation   4
    Professional Corporation   4
Insurance Requirements   6
Importance of Maintaining Proper Records   6
Retainers   7
Bank Accounts in a Legal Services Firm   7
    General Bank Account   8
    Mixed or Pooled Trust Bank Account   8
    Separate Interest-Bearing Trust Account   10
Financial Institutions for Mixed Trust Accounts   10
Interest on Trust Accounts   11
Review Questions   15

2 Introduction to Bookkeeping ... 19

What Is Accounting? ... 20
Accounting Standards for Private Enterprises ... 21
Categories of Accounts ... 22
The Accounting Equation ... 24
Preparing an Opening Balance Sheet ... 26
Expanded Accounting Equation ... 26
    Classifying Expenses ... 29
Review Questions ... 31
Practice Exercises ... 32

3 Keeping Books and Records ... 39

Accounting Period ... 40
The Accounting Cycle ... 41
    Transactions ... 42
    Journal Entries ... 42
    Posting ... 42
    Trial Balance ... 42
    Worksheet ... 42
    Adjusting Journal Entries ... 43
    Financial Statements ... 43
    Closing the Books ... 43
Basic Rules of Debit and Credit ... 43
    Debits and Credits ... 44
Business Transaction Source Documents ... 46
Analyzing the Transaction ... 47
Recording Transactions Using the Basic Accounting Equation ... 48
    Other Types of Entries ... 49
Examples of Transactions ... 49
The General Journal ... 59
    Post Reference Column ... 59
Recording the Opening Balance Sheet in the Firm's Records ... 59
Review Questions ... 62
Practice Exercises ... 63

4 Posting and Trial Balance 73

General Ledger   74
Posting   75
Preparing the Trial Balance   80
    Finding Errors in the Trial Balance   81
    Common Mistakes   82
Review Questions   85
Practice Exercises   85

5 Preparing Financial Statements 99

Preparing the Income Statement   100
    Steps in Preparing the Income Statement   101
    Interpreting Information from the Income Statement   102
Preparing the Statement of Owner's Equity   105
    Interpreting Information on the Statement of Owner's Equity   106
Preparing the Balance Sheet   106
    Interpreting Information from the Balance Sheet   108
Review Questions   111
Practice Exercises   111

6 Special Journals 117

Why Use Special Journals?   118
Client Billing   118
Billing Out Time on a Client File   119
    Docketing Time and Preparing Invoices   119
Disbursements   120
Expense Recovery   120
Client Trust Ledger   120
Fees Book   123
    Posting from the Fees Book   124
Recording Payment of an Invoice   124
Accounts Receivable Journal   124
Other Specialized Journals   125
Recording Transactions in Specialized Journals   125
    General Receipts Journal   127
    General Disbursements Journal   129
    General Journal Entries   130

Posting from Special Journals 131
Analysis of Each Transaction in November 131
Completed Journal and Ledgers to November 30 134
Review Questions 141
Practice Exercises 141

7

Trust Accounting 157

Difference Between a General Account and a Trust Account 158
Deposits and Withdrawals from Trust 159
Cash Receipts 160
Trust Bank Journal 161
Book of Original Entry 162
Steps in Using the Trust Bank Journal 162
Recording Debits and Credits in the Trust Bank Journal 162
Posting from the Trust Bank Journal 165
Proving That Debits Equal Credits 167
Possible Error 167
Trial Balance 168
Matter-to-Matter Trust Transfer Journal 169
Valuable Property Record 171
Practice Audits 171
Review Questions 176
Practice Exercises 176

8

Adjusting Accounts for Financial Statements 197

Adjusting Entries 199
Preparing a Worksheet 199
Types of Adjusting Entries 201
Prepaid Expenses 201
Amortization or Depreciation 201
Work in Progress 203
Accrued Expenses 204
Accrued Revenues 204
Preparing Adjusting Entries 204
Adjusting Entries for Year-End 204
Adjustment (A): Prepaid Expenses 205
Adjustment (B): Office Supplies 207
Adjustment (C): Depreciation 208

Adjustment (D): Personal Loan 208
Adjustment (E): Accrued Salaries Expense 209
Checking the Adjusting Entries 210
Adjusted Trial Balance Column 210
Looking for Errors 210
Income Statement and Balance Sheet Columns 210
Completing the Worksheet 211
Calculating Net Profit or Loss 211
Completing the Balance Sheet Portion of the Worksheet 211
Review Questions 215
Practice Exercises 215

9 Final Steps in the Accounting Cycle 221

The Income Statement 223
The Statement of Owner's Equity 223
The Balance Sheet 224
Recording the Year-End Adjustments 225
Preparing Closing Entries 226
Step 1: Closing the Income (Revenue) Accounts 226
Step 2: Closing the Expense Accounts 227
Step 3: Closing the Income Summary Account 227
Step 4: Closing the Drawings Account 228
Preparing the Post-Closing Trial Balance 229
General Ledger Accounts at the End of the Fiscal Year 230
Review Questions 237
Practice Exercises 237

10 Banking Procedures and Accounting for Cash 255

Petty Cash 256
Establishing a Petty Cash Account 256
Recording Petty Cash Entries 257
Replenishing a Petty Cash Account 257
Cash Short and Over 258
Banking Procedures and Handling of Money 259
Cheque Endorsement 259
Cheques 260
Reconciling a Bank Account 260
How to Reconcile the General and Trust Bank Balances 260

Reconciling the Mixed Trust Bank Account 266

    Reviewing the Trust Bank Reconciliation 271

Maintenance and Retention of General and Trust Records 271

    General Bank Records 271

    Trust Bank Records 272

    Dormant Accounts 272

Review Questions 274

Practice Exercises 275

11 Accounting for GST/HST, Payroll, and Income Tax 283

Goods and Services Tax 284

    Remitting GST/HST to the Receiver General 284

    Maintenance of Records 285

    Methods for Calculating GST/HST Remittance 285

    Remitting GST/HST 288

Payroll 288

    The Payroll Process 288

    TD1 Form 289

    Payroll Calculator 289

    Vacation Pay and Vacation Time 291

    Taxable Benefits 292

    T4 Information Return 292

Income Tax 292

    Legal Requirements for Keeping Records 292

    The Six-Year Requirement 293

    Types of Operating Expenses 293

    Deductions and Remittances 298

    Capital Gains 298

Review Questions 301

Practice Exercises 302

12 Computerized Time and Money Management 305

Getting Started with Legal Accounting Software 307

Setting Up the Firm 307

Creating Opening Entries 307

    Managing Client Files 307

    Type of Law 307

    Conflict of Interest Search 308

    Closing Client Files 308

Time Entries and Billing 308
    Recording Time Entries 309
Trust Receipts and Disbursements 310
Recording Receipts and Disbursements 311
    Recovering Client Costs 312
Billing Requirements 312
End-of-Period Functions 312
Maintaining Electronic Records 312
Review Questions 314

Appendix: By-Law 9, Financial Transactions and Records 321
Glossary 335
Index 349

Preface

The idea of learning legal accounting can be intimidating—all that math! As instructors, we often tell our students that we are not doing math, just some simple arithmetic.

Legal Accounting introduces students and legal professionals to basic accounting concepts so that they will gain an understanding of what bookkeeping and record-keeping are all about. It is important for licensed paralegals to understand the by-laws and requirements of the Law Society of Ontario (LSO) as they relate to record-keeping in a law firm. An understanding of these requirements is also useful for law clerks, who often see the financial dimensions of client files.

The primary goals of this text are:

- to explain the LSO's bookkeeping and record-keeping requirements as found in the *Law Society Act*, LSO by-laws, and the *Paralegal Rules of Conduct*;
- to explore the common bookkeeping issues that arise in a legal services firm;
- to demonstrate how to analyze and record transactions, prepare various adjusting entries, identify and complete the steps in the financial cycle;
- to explain the basics of financial accounting so that students can create, read, and understand simple financial statements;
- to provide insight into the financial, banking, and tax reporting aspects of a legal services firm; and
- to demonstrate how stakeholders use financial statements in decision-making.

The text uses the example of Justin Case, a paralegal who opens his own firm, to show how to create records at the start of the business and maintain them through the accounting cycle. The firm's books are opened with Justin's initial investment in the firm and continue through the accounting cycle to the preparation of financial reports and closing accounts to start the new year. The examples demonstrate how to comply with LSO by-laws, especially those with respect to accounting for trust funds received from clients.

The text explains the process of double-entry bookkeeping, and how to record debits and credits, so that students will be able to summarize business transactions in a manner acceptable to the Law Society and meet requirements under the *Income Tax Act*.

The text also explores legal accounting software and shows how it can be used to manage client files, record transactions, and prepare reports.

The skills taught in this text are transferable, so students who start their own business, in any area, will know how to record and interpret financial information.

The text provides general advice regarding common bookkeeping issues; it does not cover every possible situation that can arise in a firm. If you have questions about the by-laws, you can call the Law Society Practice Management Helpline at 416-947-3315 or toll-free in Ontario at 1-800-668-7380, ext. 3315. You can also check the Law Society's website at <https://lso.ca/>. If you have specific bookkeeping, accounting, or tax questions, we suggest that you consult an accountant, financial adviser, or lawyer who practises in these areas.

Chapter Features

Learning Outcomes

To guide the learning process, the learning outcomes at the beginning of each chapter identify the concepts being covered in the chapter.

Potential Paralegal Pitfalls

Each chapter highlights potential pitfalls and the consequences if proper procedures are not followed, along with recommendations for resolving issues.

Chapter Summary

The chapter summary explains why the information presented in the chapter is important. It provides examples of how the information can be applied and how pitfalls can be avoided.

Key Terms

Key terms are boldfaced throughout the chapter. Detailed definitions of all key terms are included in the glossary at the end of the text.

 ## Practice Exercises

True-or-false questions allow students to test their knowledge of what has been covered in the chapter and help them focus on important concepts. Short-answer questions require students to apply what they have learned. Accounting is best learned by doing; the longer exercises at the end of the chapter give students an opportunity to put theory into practice.

Put It into Practice

Case examples featuring Ann Litigate's paralegal practice are used to demonstrate chapter concepts. Through these examples, instructors can generate discussion and ensure that students have grasped the material presented in the chapter.

Acknowledgments

We wish to thank the reviewers of the text for their valuable feedback:

    Kent Peel, Seneca College
    Amy Maycock, Fleming College
    Trudie Robertson, Loyalist College

We would also like to thank the Emond Publishing team—Lindsay Sutherland, Kelly Dickson, Laura Bast, and the team members behind the scenes—for their full support at all stages of the project.

Jacqueline Asselin, B Admin, LLB, thanks her husband, Allan, for his patience and support, and her co-author, for the practical experience she brought to the project. Jacqueline also thanks Barb Asselin who has taught the course for a number of years and who offered suggestions for improvement.

Keri Nisbet, CPA, thanks her husband, Ryan, and her sons, Cole, Jake, and Troy, for their encouragement and enthusiasm while she wears her many hats each day. Keri also appreciates her co-author and Emond Publishing for inviting her into this amazing opportunity.

About the Authors

Jacqueline Asselin was called to the Ontario Bar in 1979 after completing her LLB and Bachelor of Administration degrees at the University of Ottawa. She opened her own law firm in Ottawa in 1979 and was initially engaged in a sole private practice. She later expanded her firm under the name J. Asselin & Associates. She remained with her firm until 2009, practising in the areas of residential real estate, family law, and wills and estates. She was a full-time faculty member at Algonquin College of Applied Arts and Technology in Ottawa from 2003 until 2017 in the Law Clerk and Paralegal programs. She taught legal accounting, residential real estate, and estates administration and procedures, as well as property relationships, introduction to law, and landlord and tenant law. In 2013, Jacqueline was appointed by the Council for the Township of McNab/Braeside to the sit on the Property Standards Committee which deals with by-law infractions and the Committee of Adjustments which hears severance and minor variation applications. Jacqueline retired from Algonquin College in June 2017 and devotes her time to travelling and to managing Tallyho Inc., a foundation that helps students meet their educational goals. She is vice-chair of the Arnprior Regional Health Foundation and Pension Concerns representative for district 21 of the Retired Teachers of Ontario.

Keri Nisbet graduated from Wilfrid Laurier University in 2000 and continued on to obtain her Chartered Accountant designation in 2003, while working in assurance at KPMG LLP in Hamilton. She has since earned experience in manufacturing within Canada and the United States and in health care. Keri is now a CPA and has been a professor at the McKeil School of Business, Mohawk College, since 2008.

1

Role of the Law Society of Ontario

Introduction. 2

Requirement for Books and Records in Legal Firms 2

Forms of Business Organization in Legal Services Firms 3

Insurance Requirements 6

Importance of Maintaining Proper Records. 6

Retainers 7

Bank Accounts in a Legal Services Firm. 7

Financial Institutions for Mixed Trust Accounts 10

Interest on Trust Accounts 11

Chapter Summary 14

Key Terms 14

Further Reading. 14

Review Questions 15

Put It into Practice. 17

After reading this chapter, you should be able to:

LO1 Describe the Law Society of Ontario's rules of conduct for lawyers and paralegals.

LO2 Explain the requirements in by-law 9 of the Law Society dealing with financial transactions and records.

LO3 Define various forms of business organization.

LO4 Describe the ethical and professional responsibilities of paralegals as they pertain to maintenance of books and records in the management of a legal services firm.

LO5 Compare bank accounts in a Legal Services Firm in PCLaw®.

[LO1] Introduction

The **Law Society of Ontario (LSO)** regulates the Ontario legal profession to ensure that legal professionals conduct themselves in a competent and ethical manner pursuant to the *Law Society Act*[1] and regulations made under the Act. A **licensee**—any paralegal or lawyer who is licensed to practise by the LSO—must meet the professional and ethical obligations imposed by the LSO. Infractions can result in disciplinary action, including but not limited to suspension of the licensee's privileges.

[LO2] Requirement for Books and Records in Legal Firms

The LSO requires licensees to keep books and records that reflect the financial activities carried out by them. Licensees have the added duty to maintain accurate records of all their financial activities because of the duty owed by them to their clients.

The record-keeping requirements of the LSO are set out in part V of its by-law 9.[2] Every licensee is required to maintain financial records to track all money and other property received and disbursed in connection with the licensee's professional business. The goal of this book is to assist paralegals in understanding the type of financial records required to meet their obligations and to learn how to keep the necessary records. The focus is on a small practice; examples of transactions a licensee is likely to encounter will be used for demonstration purposes. Law clerks who perform their duties under the supervision of a lawyer should also be aware of record-keeping requirements to assist the lawyer or law firm in meeting the LSO's obligations.

A paralegal who is not confident of being able to do his or her own accounting will want to hire a **bookkeeper** to maintain the firm's books and records. Bookkeepers record day-to-day transactions in the appropriate accounting journals. Samples of these tasks include entering bills from vendors, paying vendors, processing employee payroll, issuing invoices to clients, recording receipts from clients, and reconciling bank accounts. The bookkeeper records financial transactions and summarizes the transactions using general and trust ledgers. A bookkeeper will usually bring the books to the trial balance stage of the accounting process.

A **chartered professional accountant (CPA)**, who has a university degree and completes a professional education program, takes over where the bookkeeper leaves off. Chartered professional accountants prepare adjusting entries to correct the balances in accounts to reflect items

---

1   RSO 1990, c L.8.

2   Made under s 62(0.1), para 6 of the *Law Society Act*.

such as prepaid expenses and depreciation. Once the adjusting entries are completed, the accountant prepares the firm's financial statements, which include the income statement, statement of owner's equity, and balance sheet. These statements are required for income tax purposes, and the accountant can complete the tax returns for the firm. An accountant will ensure that the firm's financial records reflect relevant professional accounting standards.

Why do paralegals need to learn **bookkeeping** if bookkeepers and accountants are able to do the job for them? Ultimately, it's the paralegal who is responsible to ensure that the persons hired maintain the records in an acceptable manner. This book introduces paralegals to the essentials of legal accounting and explains why and how books and records need to be kept so that they conform to the requirements of the LSO.

Other reasons to know basic bookkeeping and accounting principles:

- As a business owner, it is in the paralegal's best interest to be able to analyze financial information for the purpose of making financial decisions in their own practice.
- Paralegals might have to understand a client's financial records in the course of litigation when financial statements are relevant to the case.
- As a community volunteer, paralegals may become a member of a board of directors and be presented with financial statements for review and approval by the board.

The following organizations require that proper records are maintained:

- The **Canada Revenue Agency (CRA)** requires the filing of income tax, payroll, and GST/HST remittances. The CRA is the agency responsible for administering the tax laws for the Government of Canada and most of Canada's provinces and territories.
- The LSO requires the filing of annual reports and performs audits to ensure that records are correct and, in particular, that all trust funds are properly accounted for. Licensed paralegals who fail to file their Paralegal Annual Report with the LSO on time are subject to a $100 late fee, as well as potential administrative suspension.
- The **Law Foundation of Ontario (LFO)** requires the filing of an annual report with the LSO. First created in 1974, the LFO is a non-profit organization that aims to help people understand the law and use it to improve their lives.

 # Forms of Business Organization in Legal Services Firms

By-law 7 of the LSO sets out several ways lawyers and paralegals in Ontario may carry on the practice of law and the provision of legal services, respectively. The form of business organization used is often determined by income tax implications as well as bookkeeping issues.

Basic forms of business organization include sole proprietorships, partnerships, limited liability partnerships, multi-discipline practices or affiliations, and professional corporations. The various modes of practice are set out in more detail on the LSO website[3] and should be referred to as needed.

Sole Proprietorship

A **sole proprietorship** is a business carried on by one individual who is the owner. The sole proprietor usually makes all management decisions and is personally responsible for all the

---

3   Law Society of Ontario, *Business Structures*, online: <https://lso.ca/lawyers/practice-supports-and-resources/business-structures>.

debts of the business. Many small firms are sole proprietorships. The owner pays personal income taxes on the profit made by the firm. When net profits reach higher levels, there may be tax advantages in switching to a corporate form of ownership.

Partnership

A **partnership** is a business carried on by two or more individuals as owners. Two or more persons may find it worthwhile to combine their talents and money to form a partnership. They may own the business in equal or unequal shares, and their shares of the profits or losses in the business are usually proportionate to their capital investment in the business, as documented in the partnership agreement. All the partners are equally liable for all the debts of the business. General partnerships have unlimited personal liability for business debts. The net income or loss of the business is allocated to the members of the partnership, who then pay personal income taxes on their share of the profits.

Limited Liability Partnership

A **limited liability partnership** is one in which partners have limited personal liability for the debts of the business, and no partner is responsible or liable for other partners' misconduct or negligence. The name of the limited liability partnership must be registered under the *Business Names Act*,[4] and the name must include the words "limited liability partnership" or "société à responsabilité limitée," or the abbreviations "LLP," "L.L.P.," or "s.r.l." as the last words or letters of the firm's name.

Multi-Discipline Practice or Affiliation

In a **multi-discipline practice (MDP)** or **affiliation**, lawyers and licensed paralegals work with other professionals—such as accountants, tax consultants, trademark and patent agents, or others—who support or supplement their practice of law or provision of legal services. When a licensee and another professional enter into a formal partnership agreement, it is considered a multi-discipline partnership, which must be approved by the LSO by way of application. Licensees are responsible for the actions of professional partners and must maintain professional liability insurance for all professional partners.

Professional Corporation

In a **professional corporation**, lawyers or licensed paralegals carry on the practice of law or the provision of legal services through an incorporated entity. Corporations operate under a government charter and are owned by shareholders. All the shareholders of a professional corporation must be lawyers or licensed paralegals who are entitled to practise law in Ontario. Incorporation does not affect the professional liability of the shareholders, and they are jointly and severally liable with the corporation for all professional liability claims against the company.

Lawyers and licensed paralegals may not practise law or provide legal services through a professional corporation until the company has received a certificate of authorization from the LSO. Certain tax advantages can be gained by incorporating because the corporation is taxed separately on its profits at corporate taxation rates, which are lower than the personal tax rate after a certain level of income is achieved.

---

4   RSO 1990, c B.17.

Taxation Legislation

Canada first collected federal income tax in 1917, at which time it was intended to be a temporary tax to fund the First World War. This temporary measure evolved into the Canada Revenue Agency in 1927 and has become the largest form of income available to the Canadian government. The CRA administers the tax laws for the government of Canada, including the administration and enforcement of the *Income Tax Act*,[5] and for most provinces and territories. Income tax is collected from individuals and businesses by the CRA for the federal government and the provinces and territories. The Canadian tax system is also based on self-assessment, which places the responsibility on Canadian residents to ensure they have paid their taxes according to the requirements of the *Income Tax Act*.

Unincorporated Practices

Sole Proprietorships

The income or loss of a sole proprietorship must be included on the personal tax return of the sole proprietor for the year in which the income was earned. The net profit is taxed at the same rates that apply to individuals. These rates are progressive and increase with income. Sole proprietors are also required to make Canada Pension Plan (CPP) payments on self-employed earnings when their personal income tax return is filed each year. Any person claiming an income tax refund, an HST credit, or the Canada child tax benefit must file a return. Provincial tax credits may also be available. A sole proprietor may be required by the CRA to pay income tax by installments. Financial statements for the licensee's practice must be included with the personal tax return.

Partnerships

The income or loss of the business carried on in partnership is determined at the partnership level and then allocated to the partners in accordance with their share, usually based on the terms of a partnership agreement. A partnership by itself does not pay income tax on its operating results and does not file an annual income tax return. Instead, each partner includes a share of the partnership income (or loss) on his or her personal tax return. The share of the income earned is taxed whether or not it has actually been received personally by the partner. Each partner must file a copy of the financial statements of the partnership with his or her return. The partnership may also be required to register for and collect GST/HST on behalf of the CRA.

Expenses, capital cost allowance, and other deductions are subtracted from the income of the partnership to determine whether the business has a net income or loss. The resulting income or loss is divided among the partners, prorated to each partner's contribution or as otherwise stipulated in the partnership agreement. Each partner's share of the income or loss is then included in the calculation of that partner's individual income from all sources for tax purposes.

Each partner is taxed at the rate applicable to individuals under the *Income Tax Act*, as is a sole proprietor. Like the sole proprietor, a partner must aggregate his or her share of net income or loss with income or losses from all other sources.

Incorporated Practices

A professional corporation is a separate legal entity that is separately taxed on its profits at corporate taxation rates.

A corporation may have some of the following features:

- It has a perpetual existence, since ownership shares can be sold to new shareholders.
- It can generally raise larger amounts of capital more easily than a sole proprietorship or partnership.
- The shareholders cannot personally claim any loss the corporation sustains.

When forming a corporation, the business owners can transfer money, assets, or services to the corporation in exchange for shares. The owners are referred to as shareholders. The owners may also transfer liabilities to the corporation that relate to the assets contributed. For instance, if the owner contributes a photocopier that has a loan outstanding, both the asset (photocopier) and the liability (associated loan) become the responsibility of the corporation. Shares can be bought and sold without affecting the corporation's existence. A corporation continues to exist unless it winds up, amalgamates, or surrenders its charter for reasons such as bankruptcy. Because a corporation has a separate legal existence, it must pay tax on its income, and therefore must file its own income tax return. The corporation may also be required to register for, collect, and remit GST/HST on behalf of the CRA.

---

5 RSC 1985, c 1 (5th Supp), as amended.

A corporation must file a corporation income tax return (T2) within six months of the end of every tax year, even if it does not owe taxes. It also has to attach complete financial statements and the necessary schedules to the T2 return. A corporation usually pays its taxes in monthly or quarterly installments.

A licensee who incorporates will receive a salary or take dividends from the corporation as payment for his or her services. These payments will be included on the licensee's individual tax return. An accountant should be consulted to determine whether there is a benefit to incorporating to take advantage of the lower corporate tax rates.

LO4 Insurance Requirements

Licensees who provide legal services to the public must carry professional liability insurance in accordance with by-law 6, part II, section 12 of the LSO. A policy limit for each single claim of not less than $1 million and an aggregate policy limit for all claims of not less than $2 million per year are required. In the case of a limited liability partnership, coverage must be maintained for each partner in the amount required for individual licensees. Some exemptions are allowed, such as when a paralegal is working under the supervision of a lawyer who has professional liability insurance through the LSO and the paralegal is covered under the lawyer's policy. Licensees must provide written proof of compliance with their insurance requirements before they begin providing legal services and annually thereafter.

Importance of Maintaining Proper Records

In addition to keeping books and records that reflect their financial activities, lawyers and paralegals have an added obligation to maintain accurate records because they hold funds in trust for their clients. The LSO regulates the Ontario legal profession to ensure that paralegals and lawyers conduct themselves in a competent and ethical manner pursuant to the *Law Society Act* and regulations made under the Act. The LSO has the role of protecting the public, and one way it fulfills this responsibility is by auditing the records kept by law firms. An audit is an inspection of the books and records of a company, usually by an independent third party. Licensees who fail to meet the professional and ethical obligations imposed by the LSO are subject to its complaints process, which can result in disciplinary action, including suspension of their privileges.

Failure to maintain proper records can result in errors and an inability to meet financial obligations as they come due. For example:

- Failure to record accounts payable as bills are received results in an overstatement of income and may result in an inability to pay bills when they are due.
- Failure to stay on top of accounts receivable may result in insufficient funds in the general bank account, resulting in an inability to pay operating expenses.
- Failure to track trust receipts and disbursements in the correct client ledger could result in errors, with a trust account getting overdrawn for a particular client.
- Failure to maintain trust records can result in an inability to meet obligations incurred on a client's behalf and to account to clients for any funds received on their behalf.
- Failure to track income and expenses and properly report to the CRA may result in assessments and/or audits, with severe penalties and interest being charged if taxes were not properly remitted.

- Inability to know where the firm stands financially impairs good management decision-making regarding day-to-day operations, expansion, addition of staff, and other such matters.
- Failure to maintain financial statements may result in lenders refusing applications for loans or lines of credit because lenders require financial statements in order to assess interest rates imposed on loans and qualification for loans.
- The LSO conducts regular audits of licensees. Failure to maintain up-to-date trust records can result in suspension or other action by the LSO.

Retainers

A **retainer** is an agreement between a client and a legal services provider for the engagement of legal services. The form of retainer can vary and be customized for each situation. Because clients can believe that they have retained the legal services provider based on an oral conversation, it is important to observe client identification protocols and to document any conversation in writing.

It is a good practice to get monetary retainers from clients to ensure that there will not be any difficulty getting paid once work has started or a task is completed. The cash flow in an office is important, and having to worry about paying bills can interfere with a legal services provider's ability to focus on providing excellent service to clients.

Firms usually require that clients provide a **monetary retainer** when the paralegal–client relationship is entered into. This is usually obtained when the client signs a retainer agreement, with the firm setting out the scope of the work to be performed and the hourly rate that will be charged by the paralegal primarily responsible for the file, as well as the rate charged by other persons who will work on it. The retainer agreement should also set out the firm's billing policies.

The money received from the client must be deposited into the firm's mixed trust account (described below) by the end of the next banking day after funds are received. Money includes, by definition, cash, cheques, bank drafts, credit card sales slips, post office orders, and express and bank money orders.

A **general monetary retainer**, which is described in by-law 9, section 8(2)1 of the LSO, does not need to be deposited into the trust account. This is money received for which the paralegal is not required either to account to the client or to provide services. A general retainer should be evidenced by a written agreement with the client. As an example, it might be used when a paralegal is asked to do all collections for a client at a fixed monthly rate and to which the firm agrees to do all the collections and will be paid whether or not the client submits any claims in a particular period. This type of retainer is not common in small practices and is carefully scrutinized by the LSO.

Bank Accounts in a Legal Services Firm

At the very least, most law firms have one general bank account and one mixed trust account. It is important to understand which transactions require use of the general bank account and which require the use of the trust bank account. Mixing trust funds, which are funds that belong to the client, with general firm funds, which are funds that belong to the firm, is not allowed.

General Bank Account

Just as individuals have a bank account that they use for their day-to-day deposits and disbursements, a business must have a **general bank account** for making deposits and for payment of bills. The general bank account will be opened in the name of the firm. If the firm is a sole proprietorship, the bank account will be in the name of the owner. Corporations will open such accounts in the name of the corporation. The types of funds that will be deposited into the general bank account include:

- funds that belong to the firm;
- funds invested into the firm by the owner;
- funds received by the firm for payment on bills sent to the client; and
- other receipts, such as interest income earned on the general bank account and miscellaneous income.

Regardless of the accounting system being used, care must be taken to ensure that the correct bank account is used when making deposits and disbursements. Firms often use different coloured cheques for their general and trust bank accounts so there is a visual cue for the person writing a cheque, to be sure disbursements are made from the appropriate account.

Mixed or Pooled Trust Bank Account

A **mixed** or **pooled trust bank account** is a bank account into which money received from clients for certain purposes is deposited. This account is called "mixed" or "pooled" because the firm opens one bank account into which money for many clients will be deposited. The funds must be deposited into the mixed trust account because the money does not belong to the firm. It belongs to the client and is to be used for specific purposes (for example, to pay court fees on behalf of the client or to be applied to a bill sent to the client). How will one know what amount belongs to which client? A separate client summary called a ledger must be kept for each client, so that firms always know how much money is in the trust account for each one. It is important to note that only firms who hold client money need a trust account.

EXAMPLE

The table in Figure 1.1 illustrates a list of funds in the trust account that are pooled. Why a record is required for the amount held for each client is explained below.

Justin Case is a paralegal who has three clients. He has received a retainer from each client and has made payments out of the mixed trust account for some clients. The bank balance for the mixed trust account is $5,950. Justin needs to know that he has $250 left in trust for Client A, $700 for Client B, and $5,000 for Client C. The best way to track this information is to have a separate client trust ledger sheet for each individual client that shows all the transactions for each client with a running balance at all times.[6]

If Justin did not have proper records and wrote another cheque in the amount of $300 from the trust account to pay for a disbursement on behalf of Client A, the trust ledger account for Client A would be overdrawn by $50 ($250 less $300). However, the cheque would still go through the bank because there was $5,950 in the pooled account before the $300 cheque was written. Errors like this must be reported to the LSO when submitting the annual report, with an explanation as to why the error occurred.

The financial records required to be maintained for trust accounts must be entered in the account journal and **posted** (recorded) in each client's ledger so as to be current at all times.

The LSO's *Rules of Professional Conduct*[7] dictate that trust accounts are to be used only for clients' money.

---

6   By-law 9, s 22(1).

7   Law Society of Ontario, *Rules of Professional Conduct* (1 October 2014; amendments current to 25 January 2018), online: <https://lso.ca/about-lso/legislation-rules/rules-of-professional-conduct>.

If a legal service provider does not receive retainers from clients, it may not be necessary to open a trust account. Trust accounts can never be used for the personal or office use of the business owner.

Justin knew he would have to send a cheque to the CRA every quarter to remit the HST he collected. So he deposited money in the trust account to cover the potential HST he would have to pay. However, LSO rules dictate that this action is not allowed for the purpose of remitting HST at the end of each quarter. HST funds must be accumulated in the firm's general bank account.

Client	Receipts	Payments	Balance
Client A	300	50	250
Client B	800	100	700
Client C	5,000	0	5,000
Totals	6,100	150	5,950

FIGURE 1.1 Summary of clients and balance held in trust

Overdraft in Trust Account

It is a good practice to place a hold on trust funds received from clients (unless paid in cash, money order, or certified cheque) to make sure there are sufficient funds in the client's bank account to cover the cheque. Firms should confirm with their financial institution how many days it takes a cheque to clear. If a cheque from a client is returned by the bank for insufficient funds (NSF), and the licensee has written a cheque against that amount, the trust ledger for that client will be overdrawn. In addition, bank charges may be taken out of the trust account because of the NSF transaction. The bank should be directed to charge any service fees against the trust account to the firm's general account instead.

Paralegals are personally responsible to ensure that any overdraft in a client's trust account is corrected as soon as an error is discovered. This can be done by having the client bring in funds to deposit into the account, or by the paralegal depositing their personal funds into the trust bank account to make up for the deficiency.

With experience, paralegals develop an instinct for knowing which funds should go into the mixed trust account and which funds should go into the general bank account. If ever unsure, paralegals should refer to by-law 9 to determine whether or not the funds belong in the trust account. The table in Figure 1.2 shows which bank account must be used for different types of deposits.

Mixed Trust Account	General Account
Funds that must be deposited to the trust account:	Funds that must be deposited to the general account:
• money received on behalf of the client • money received for future client disbursements • money received for future or unbilled legal services • an overpayment of billed services—the excess payment must be either returned to the client or held in the trust account if the client instructs you to do so	• money paid on account of a bill previously sent to the client • reimbursement for expenses paid on behalf of the client • lawyer/paralegal's or firm's money • general money retainer

FIGURE 1.2 Accounts for depositing funds

Separate Interest-Bearing Trust Account

Another type of trust account can be set up to hold funds for only one client. This may be done on the client's written instructions when a large amount is to be held in trust for an extended period of time. For example, if a client deposits $20,000 with a firm to hold until a case settles, and it is anticipated that the case may go on for an extended period, the client may want the interest on the account to accrue to herself. If a client wants interest on the trust funds that a firm holds for her, her written instructions to deposit such funds into a **separate interest-bearing trust account** must be obtained—for example, a guaranteed investment certificate (GIC), term deposit, or other savings account—in the firm's name in trust for that client.[8]

Opening a separate interest-bearing account for a client requires additional paperwork and bookkeeping for the paralegal and is not usually done unless the return on investment is significant. Bank charges on this account would be charged to the separate interest-bearing trust account and noted as a disbursement to the client.

Separate interest-bearing trust accounts must be reconciled and included in the monthly trust comparison.[9] If a client instructs his legal service provider to put his funds in an interest-bearing account, some additional information may be required from him, such as his social insurance number or corporation number, if applicable, as well as how the interest is to be allocated for income tax purposes. This is especially important when the funds being held are in dispute.

Financial Institutions for Mixed Trust Accounts

The following institutions are approved for opening a mixed trust account for all client funds, or a separate account for one client:

- a chartered bank, such as RBC, TD, Scotiabank, BMO, or CIBC;
- a provincial savings office, a government-run banking institution;
- a credit union, a member-owned financial cooperative;
- a league to which the *Credit Unions and Caisses Populaires Act, 1994*[10] applies; and
- a registered trust corporation.

The institution in which the account is opened must have an agreement with the LFO for the payment of interest on mixed trust accounts. The institution must also provide monthly bank statements and the originals or copies of the front and back of returned cheques, including certified cheques. Any time a mixed trust account is opened, the LFO must be notified by sending a letter to the Foundation (Form 2: Report on Opening a Mixed Trust Account, available on the LFO's website).

---

8 By-law 9, s 8(1).

9 By-law 9, s 18(8).

10 SO 1994, c 11.

- **Potential pitfall:** Not keeping accurate, complete, and up-to-date books and records.
- **Possible fallout:** In 2017, a Canadian legal firm was fined $25,000 for failing to provide documents to the Law Society of Ontario in a timely manner. In 2013, the LSO made five attempts to obtain certain documents from the firm, which the firm failed to do in a reasonable amount of time.
- **Proposed recommendation:** Set aside time to complete the bookkeeping of your firm. Make an appointment in your calendar to remind you to get the work done. If you can't keep up on your own, consider hiring a bookkeeper on contract or a part-time basis.

TAX TIP

Registering for GST/HST

Paralegals just starting a business will probably begin as a **small supplier**, exempt from collecting GST/HST. An individual is deemed to be a small supplier if their total annual revenues from taxable supplies (before expenses) from all of their businesses are $30,000 or less in a fiscal year. Once their revenues exceed the $30,000 threshold over a period of twelve consecutive months, they must register and start collecting and remitting GST/HST.

Business owners can register for GST/HST voluntarily before they have reached the $30,000 threshold and may want to do so in order to recover the GST/HST that they pay when starting up the business.

Once registered, they are required to charge, collect, and remit GST/HST on all invoices sent to clients and to file GST/HST returns monthly, quarterly, or annually depending on the level of revenues. Business owners must stay registered for at least one year before they can request to cancel their registration. If the business is small, and the business owner chooses not to register for GST/HST voluntarily, the business owner cannot collect GST/HST from clients and cannot claim back the income tax credits paid on business purchases.

Obtaining a Business Number

Before a business owner can register for GST/HST, a **business number (BN)** needs to be obtained from the CRA. Registering for a business number can be done online at the CRA website. This number conveniently identifies business owners to the government for all business purposes, including remittances of GST/HST, corporate income tax remittances, and payroll remittances.

Informing Clients

Business owners must let clients know if GST/HST is being charged on fees. The invoice sent to the client should show the total amount charged for fees and disbursements and the rate and amount charged for GST/HST. The GST/HST registration number must also appear on the invoice. The amount collected from clients will be recorded as GST/HST payable in accounting journals and ledgers, as the money collected for GST/HST from clients will be owed to the CRA on the next GST/HST return.

Interest on Trust Accounts

Section 57 of the *Law Society Act* states that interest earned on a mixed trust account must be remitted to the LFO by the financial institution in which the account is located.[11] This is done by signing a letter of direction regarding interest on a mixed trust account, which directs the financial institution to forward interest on the account to the LFO (see Figure 1.3).

It is the paralegal's responsibility to ensure that the financial institution where the mixed trust account is to be opened pays interest at a rate approved by the trustees of the LFO. Most financial institutions have an agreement with the LFO and are accustomed to remitting the

---

11 RSO 1990, c L.8, s 57(1).

interest as required. The LFO uses these funds to carry out its mandate, which is to promote access to justice.

An annual report must be sent to the LSO and to the LFO by March 31 each year.

To: The Manager

Name of Bank: [Name of chartered bank, provincial savings office, registered trust company, credit union, or caisse populaire]

Branch: _____

Address: _____

Re: The Law Foundation of Ontario and Account No.

The above account is in: _____ my name

                                 _____ the name of the firm with which I am associated

In accordance with Section 57 of the *Law Society Act*, I direct you, until further notice, to compute the amount earned by applying to the balance in the above account the rate of interest approved from time to time by the Trustees of The Law Foundation of Ontario. Please pay into an account held in your main office in Ontario in the name of The Law Foundation of Ontario amounts so calculated and give written notice to me at the address shown on the above account and to The Law Foundation of Ontario, 20 Queen Street West, Suite 3002, Box #19, Toronto, Ontario, M5H 3R3, when each such payment is made. This notice should show, as applicable as per the terms of the interest agreement between the LFO and your financial institution, the amount of the payment, the amounts of the daily/monthly balances, and the rates of interest used in computing the payment.

Dated: the day of   _____, _____, 20_____

Signature

Firm Name: _____

Address: _____

FIGURE 1.3   **Letter of direction**

Source: Law Foundation of Ontario. Used with permission.

LO5

PCLAW®

Bank Accounts in a Legal Services Firm

Legal software is useful in ensuring that the firm's books comply with by-law 9, which requires a licensee to maintain financial records. A good legal accounting system incorporates mandatory bank accounts and other features required to facilitate compliance. Typically, the application will include at least one General Bank Account and one Trust Account, as shown in Figure 1.4. When deposits and cheques are entered into a bank account, the system shows the entry in the bank account as well as in a corresponding ledger account that summarizes the entries. One big advantage of a legal accounting computer program is that the amount held for each client in trust will be shown in the client's trust ledger account; this way, the licensee always knows exactly how much is held in the mixed trust account for each client.

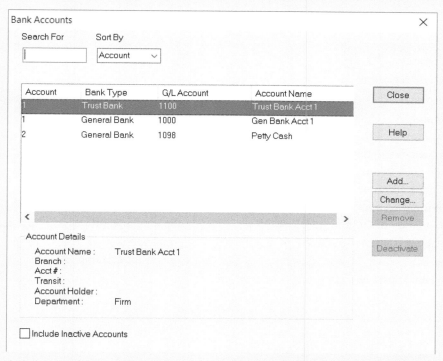

Bank accounts included with PCLaw® include one General Bank Account, one Trust Bank Account, and one Petty Cash Account (which is considered a General Bank Account).

Use this feature to add, change, or remove the pre-set accounts provided in PCLaw®.

FIGURE 1.4   Bank accounts included with PCLaw® legal accounting software

POTENTIAL PARALEGAL PITFALLS

- **Potential pitfall:** Advertising your paralegal firm in a way that is not in accordance with the professional conduct of the LSO.
- **Possible fallout:** You may be fined by the LSO and may need to spend more money remarketing your business.
- **Proposed recommendation:** Be honest, professional, and accurate when marketing your business. Do not oversell yourself or claim to be better than other paralegals or legal professionals.

CHAPTER SUMMARY

Whether you decide on a career as a paralegal working alone or in association with other licensees, you need to have an understanding of record-keeping. Although you may not be directly involved in preparing bookkeeping entries and financial statements, you will be accountable to clients and must protect their interests. It is your responsibility to ensure that the firm you work with acts ethically and with integrity. Even when working in association with other paralegals, a licensee often maintains his or her own trust account and is required to account for funds received in trust.

You will be required to submit annual reports to the LSO, the LFO, and the CRA. Having proper systems in place makes it easier to comply with all these obligations.

KEY TERMS

bookkeeper, 2
bookkeeping, 3
business number (BN), 11
Canada Revenue Agency (CRA), 3
chartered professional accountant (CPA), 2
general bank account, 8
general monetary retainer, 7
Law Foundation of Ontario (LFO), 3
Law Society of Ontario (LSO), 2
licensee, 2
limited liability partnership, 4

mixed or pooled trust bank account, 8
monetary retainer, 7
multi-discipline practice (MDP) or affiliation, 4
partnership, 4
posted, 8
professional corporation, 4
retainer, 7
separate interest-bearing trust account, 10
small supplier, 11
sole proprietorship, 3

FURTHER READING

The Law Foundation of Ontario, "Reporting Mixed Trust Accounts," online: <http://www.lawfoundation .on.ca/our-revenue-sources/interest-on-mixed-trust-accounts/>.

Law Society of Ontario, *The Bookkeeping Guide for Paralegals* (Toronto: LSO, December 2015), online: <https://lawsocietyontario.azureedge.net/media/lso/media/legacy/pdf/p/paralegal_bookkeeping_ guide_final-s.pdf>.

REVIEW QUESTIONS

True or False

_____ 1. A separate interest-bearing trust account should be opened for each client. **(LO4)**

_____ 2. A general monetary retainer does not need to be deposited into the trust account. **(LO4)**

_____ 3. It is a mandatory requirement for a legal professional (for example, a lawyer or paralegal) to open and maintain a trust account. **(LO4)**

_____ 4. Lawyers and paralegals may operate a legal practice with unlicensed professionals who provide other non-legal services. **(LO3)**

_____ 5. By-law 9 of the LSO deals with the form of business organization. **(LO3)**

_____ 6. Income taxes payable to the CRA in a partnership are paid by the partnership itself. **(LO3)**

_____ 7. Understanding basic bookkeeping and accounting principles is useful only for the legal professional's reporting requirements to the LSO. **(LO1)**

_____ 8. Moneys received from a client for services not yet rendered should be deposited into the trust bank account. **(LO4)**

_____ 9. A cheque received from a supplier as a refund for goods returned would be deposited in trust. **(LO4)**

Fill in the Blanks

1. Refer to *Law Society of Upper Canada v Sam*, 2014 ONLSTH 140, and then fill in the blanks in the following quotation from the case: "[T]he Respondent ... b) failed to immediately deposit those funds into a trust account, contrary to By-Law 9, section _____, or alternatively, contrary to By-Law 9, section _____." **(LO4)**

2. Refer to by-law 9 of the LSO and fill in the blanks: Section _____ of by-law 9 requires licensees to maintain financial records to record all money and other property _____ and _____ in connection with the licensee's professional business and, at a minimum, the _____ described in sections _____ to _____. **(LO2)**

3. A retainer is considered a _____ retainer when it is deposited in a trust account and when there is an agreement between the paralegal/lawyer and the client regarding legal services. **(LO4)**

Short Answer

Give a full answer for each question.

1. What is the difference between the role played by a bookkeeper and that played by an accountant? (LO2)

2. What business structure is most likely to be used by a paralegal opening an office who plans to work from home? (LO3)

3. Assume a firm has two bank accounts—a general bank account and a mixed trust account. Indicate whether the following transactions would involve a deposit or cheque, and the bank account that would be used. (LO4)

Transaction	General Bank Account	Trust Bank Account
Paralegal pays rent for the month	(General) Cheque	
Paralegal receives a retainer in the amount of $1,000 from a new client, Jane Phillips		
Paralegal invests $5,000 into the firm		
Paralegal pays court filing fees of $150 on the Jane Phillips file		
Paralegal pays telephone bill		
Paralegal withdraws money for personal expenses		
Paralegal prepares an invoice on the Jane Phillips file and writes a cheque in payment of invoice		

4. What happens to interest earned on a mixed trust account? (LO4)

5. In what circumstances should a paralegal maintain a separate interest-bearing trust for a client? (LO4)

6. Look up the Law Foundation of Ontario online. What is its mandate? (LO1)

PUT IT INTO PRACTICE

Case Example: LSO Rules

Ann Litigate is currently operating her legal services firm under the business name "Ann Litigate Paralegal Services." If Ann is interested in transitioning her legal services practice from a sole proprietorship to a corporation, what steps will she need to take? What are the advantages and disadvantages of Ann establishing her legal services practice as a corporation? Discuss.

2 Introduction to Bookkeeping

What Is Accounting? 20

Accounting Standards for Private Enterprises 21

Categories of Accounts 22

The Accounting Equation 24

Preparing an Opening Balance Sheet 26

Expanded Accounting Equation 26

Chapter Summary 30

Key Terms 30

Further Reading 30

Review Questions 31

Practice Exercises 32

Put It into Practice 37

After reading this chapter, you should be able to:

LO1 Understand the basic terminology used in accounting.

LO2 Identify the generally accepted accounting principles (GAAP) and understand the accounting standards for private enterprises.

LO3 Define the categories of accounts—assets, liabilities, owner's equity, income, and expenses—and classify accounts by category.

LO4 Create an opening balance sheet for a firm.

LO5 Demonstrate an understanding of the expanded accounting equation.

You probably have some experience with basic bookkeeping if you keep track of the balance in your personal chequing account. However, using such a simple method in a business would be inadequate because it does not provide the information needed for making daily business decisions. Your business records must show where money came from and how it was spent in much more detail. Throw into the mix a trust account with money that belongs to your clients, and you will quickly see the importance of a good system of record-keeping. With the increased popularity of electronic banking and the use of debit cards, it is easy to lose track of funds received and funds paid out.

As a legal professional, you do not want to have cheques returned by your bank for insufficient funds. You always need to know what is going in to and coming out of your bank accounts on a regular basis. Remember that the bank balance you view online might not accurately reflect how much money you have in the bank, because some cheques may not yet have cleared and some deposits may not yet be recorded. Keeping accurate records will not only help track your actual bank balance, but it will also help you plan your spending over the next period.

LO1 What Is Accounting?

Accounting is the language of business. Business owners may wish to communicate financial information about their business to various **stakeholders**, each of whom has a different interest:

- **Internal users** are interested in managerial accounting. People working in the business need to have financial information for making management decisions. Is the business profitable? Can the business afford to expand? Can we hire another person for the office? The user wants information that is as accurate as possible to help make appropriate decisions.
- **External users** are interested in financial accounting. People who lend money to the business will want to review its financial statements to assess the risks associated with a loan. Usually, business owners have a natural bias to make the business appear that it is doing very well and is profitable. The LSO uses the information generated by the firm to complete audits and to ensure that its by-laws are being followed.
- **Government users** are interested in tax accounting, and businesses are required to submit income tax returns annually. Usually, business owners have a natural bias to present less profit on its financial statement in order to minimize its tax liability.

Business owners communicate information using financial statements prepared in accordance with generally accepted accounting principles, described in the next section.

LO2 Accounting Standards for Private Enterprises

As of January 1, 2012, accounting was restructured to move away from a single financial reporting framework, formerly known as generally accepted accounting principles, to implement a variety of rules for different types of organizations. For example, Canada adopted the **international financial reporting standards (IFRS)**, which is a set of international accounting rules imposed on corporations whose shares are listed on a stock exchange. In the case of not-for-profit organizations, the standards for these entities are set out in part III of the *CPA Canada Handbook: Accounting.*

Given the nature of ownership in legal and paralegal firms, paralegals are concerned with the standards set out in part II of the handbook regarding **accounting standards for private enterprises (ASPE)**. Financial statements must present fairly—and in accordance with Canadian **generally accepted accounting principles (GAAP)**—the financial position, results of operations, and cash flows of an entity.

These standards apply to sole proprietorships and small private enterprises, with the aim of ensuring that bookkeeping records and financial statements are prepared using acceptable accounting practices. The standards ensure that everyone prepares and interprets financial reports the same way. Such consistency enables users of the information—including paralegals, lawyers, lenders, auditors, and regulators such as the CRA and the LSO—to rely on the financial statements and information presented.

Some examples of common accounting standards that paralegals must adhere to include the following principles:

- *Business entity principle.* Every business should be treated as a separate unit for the purpose of keeping accounting records. Paralegals should not mix personal and business transactions. Separate bank accounts should be used for personal activities and business activities. Personal expenses should not be recorded as expenses of the business and vice versa. It is good practice to have separate credit cards for the business and for personal expenses, for record-keeping purposes. For example, it would be a breach of this principle to take a spouse out to a movie and charge it to the business credit card and claim it as a business expense.
- *Conservatism principle.* A business should report moderate and realistic financial information to prevent overvaluation.
- *Consistency principle.* The same accounting methods must be used period after period, unless a reason for a change in accounting methods is justifiable.
- *Going concern principle.* A business is presumed to continue its operations for the foreseeable future.
- *Cost principle.* Assets purchased are recorded at their actual cost. Take for example a painting purchased at a yard sale: even though a painting that is believed to be worth $1,000 was purchased at a yard sale for $10, the business records should show the painting's value at the amount that was actually paid.
- *Revenue recognition principle.* Revenue is recorded when it is earned, regardless of whether or not payment has been received; expenses are recorded when incurred, regardless of whether or not they have been paid. This method of accounting is referred to as the **accrual basis of accounting** and is the one used by paralegals as required

under the *Income Tax Act*.[1] The **cash basis of accounting** recognizes revenue only when the cash is actually received, and expenses only when payment has actually been made.

In the event that a client does not pay for fees billed, the firm would have to write the invoice off as a bad debt if it had already been included in income. Income recorded in the firm's records is taxed when it is earned, not when the client pays the bill, consistent with the accrual basis of accounting.

- *Matching principle*. Expenses must be reported in the same period as the revenues that were earned as a result of those expenses.

TAX TIP

Work in Progress

Lawyers and accountants receive special treatment when dealing with work in progress (WIP) under the *Income Tax Act*.[2] When lawyers file their first tax return, they can file an election with the CRA to report WIP only after it has been billed; then, work that is in progress at the end of the fiscal period cannot be included in income. When this election is made, revenue is considered to have been earned when the bill is sent to the client and not before. The value of work done on a file is not included for tax purposes.

At the time of this printing, the *Income Tax Act* had not been amended to permit paralegals to file this election. The Act requires paralegals to include the value of WIP, even if the time spent on a file has not yet been billed to the client at the end of the fiscal period.

LO3 ## Categories of Accounts

The books of a business are set up using three main categories of accounts: assets, liabilities, and owner's equity. Two further categories are revenue (or income) and expenses. Each category will have individual accounts listed under it.

In simple terms, transactions are recorded in a **general journal** and are then posted to each individual account in a *general ledger*. (The general journal and the general ledger will be covered in more detail in Chapters 3 and 4.) Each account is listed in the general ledger, and the totals from the individual general ledgers are used to prepare the financial statements. There are separate accounts for each of the elements of the accounting equation (described in the paragraphs that follow)—assets, liabilities, owner's equity, income, and expenses. These accounts are used to record increases and decreases in each category.

Assets are items of value that are owned by a business or a person. Assets are often broken down into current assets and fixed or capital assets. **Current assets** are assets that will be converted into cash or used up within one year. Examples of current assets are cash in bank accounts, including trusts; accounts receivable; and prepaid expenses such as supplies, rent, or insurance. **Fixed** or **capital assets** are assets that are expected to provide a benefit for longer than one year. Examples of fixed or capital assets are land, buildings, equipment, and vehicles. Assets are not always purchased with cash. They often are purchased using *debt* (for example, by charging the purchase to a credit card).

---

1 RSC 1985, c 1 (5th Supp).

2 Made under s 34.

Liabilities are debts owed to others by a business or a person. Examples of liabilities are personal or bank loans, accounts payable (if supplies or assets are purchased on account), and taxes payable. In a firm, the money held in trust for clients is also shown as a liability. Should the owner decide to close the business, liabilities must be paid off before the owner can receive a return on investment from the firm. Companies that are owed money are referred to as *creditors*.

Owner's equity represents the value of assets remaining after all liabilities have been deducted. The owner's net worth is represented by owner's equity. The amount of the investment by an owner in a firm is often referred to as *capital*. The equity account in an incorporated company is identified as **shareholder's equity**. Capital does not always refer to cash; it may refer to the value of assets other than cash that an owner has invested in the firm.

Income is a subcategory of owner's equity and is revenue earned by the firm. Examples of income accounts are legal fees earned, interest income on bank account balances and investments, and expense reimbursement. Income increases the firm's owner's equity.

Expenses are also a subcategory of owner's equity and represent the costs of doing business. The CRA allows the deduction of any reasonable current expense paid, or an expense that will have to be paid, for the purpose of earning business income. Examples include insurance, rent, supplies, wages, and administrative expenses. Expenses decrease the firm's owner's equity.

The **chart of accounts** is a numbered list of all the business accounts used in a particular firm. A sample chart of accounts is printed on the inside cover of this textbook and shows the account names used in the book. Five categories of accounts are broken down into account names and individual accounts are assigned an account name and an account number.

Note that the account categories each have an account number range. The table in Figure 2.1 shows how numbers might be assigned to each category and the **normal balance** for each. (Debits and credits will be briefly discussed later in this chapter and will be more fully covered in Chapters 3 and 4.)

Account Name	Account Number Begins with	Normal Balance
Assets	1	Debit
Liabilities	2	Credit
Owner's equity	3	Credit
Income (revenue)	4	Credit
Expenses	5	Debit

FIGURE 2.1 Categories of accounts

The accounts are numbered to make it easier to locate each account quickly. In other words, when an account is numbered 300, the account is listed under owner's equity. If the account number is 500, it is clear that the account is an expense account. It should also be noted that the list may skip over some numbers. This allows the insertion of additional accounts if the bookkeeper decides that a new account is needed.

PCLAW®

Accounts in PCLaw®

PCLaw® software provides a list of accounts commonly used in legal firms. Users are able to add or delete accounts as they require. In this system the numbering of asset accounts begins at 1000, liabilities accounts start at 2000, equity accounts start at 3000, revenue accounts start at 4000, and expense accounts start at 5000 (see Figure 2.2). The account number in PCLaw® is called the account's "nickname."

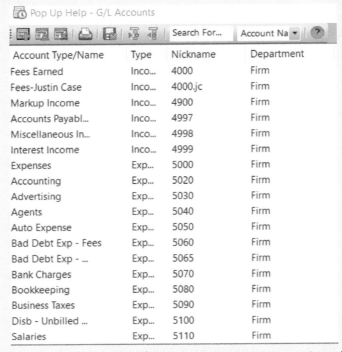

FIGURE 2.2   Accounts commonly used by legal firms, shown in PCLaw® accounting software

The Accounting Equation

The financial position of a business is stated in the form of the **accounting equation**. All transactions are analyzed using this fundamental accounting equation. The terms *debit* and *credit* will be encountered as part of the accounting equation. *Debit* refers to the left side of the equation; *credit* refers to the right side of the equation. More about the terms *debit* and *credit* will be covered in Chapters 3 and 4. Debit and credit do not mean increase or decrease. To keep things simple, a paralegal should get used to thinking of these terms as meaning "left side" (debit) and "right side" (credit), and nothing more.

Assets = Liabilities + Owner's Equity

In simple terms, the accounting equation tells us that everything we own (our assets) was obtained by either borrowing for it (our liabilities) or by investing our own money (owner's equity).

An essential component of the accounting system is **double-entry bookkeeping**. This system of **internal controls** requires that there be a check and a balance of the debits and the credits. There must be at least two accounts affected for every transaction—one entry must be a debit entry and the other a credit entry.

The following example introduces the application of the accounting equation by using the paralegal firm of Justin Case.

EXAMPLE

Justin Case has decided to open his own paralegal practice as a sole proprietor. He plans to start the business by investing the following:

Cash that he received as a graduation present	$1,000
Money borrowed from his father	4,000
Total cash he has to deposit in the bank	$5,000
His credit card debt (used to purchase assets)	$500
Computer and printer that he bought for school; now valued at	$900
Desk and office chair valued at	$150

STEP 1

To apply the accounting equation to Justin's situation, list his assets in the accounts for cash, computer equipment, and office furniture.

Assets	
General Bank Account (cash)	$5,000
Computer Equipment	900
Office Furniture	150
Total Assets	$6,050

STEP 2

Calculate Justin's total liabilities by listing the accounts for the personal loan and credit card debt.

Liabilities	
James Case (father), Loan	$4,000
Credit Card Debt	500
Total Liabilities	$4,500

Calculating Owner's Equity

STEP 3

Calculate owner's equity by deducting the total liabilities or debts owed to creditors from the total assets. As you can see, the calculation yields an answer of $1,550 for owner's equity.

$$\text{Assets} - \text{Liabilities} = \text{Owner's Equity}$$
$$6{,}050 \quad\; 4{,}500 \quad\quad ?$$

STEP 4

Check to ensure that the accounting equation is balanced.

Justin's assets are worth $6,050 and are equal to his liabilities plus owner's equity, which also equal $6,050.

We have included the cash borrowed from Justin's father in the listing of cash assets. Realistically, Justin has the cash; he also has a corresponding debt that is owed to his father and a credit card debt. Because he has total debts of $4,500, his equity in the firm is only $1,550.

In the event that Justin were to sell all his assets at the value shown in his books and he were to pay off all his debts, he would be left with $1,550.

Depending on which variable you are trying to calculate, the accounting equation can be stated in three ways:

$$\text{Assets} - \text{Liabilities} = \text{Owner's Equity}$$
$$6{,}050 \quad\; 4{,}500 \quad\quad 1{,}550$$

$$\text{Assets} = \text{Liabilities} + \text{Owner's Equity}$$
$$6{,}050 \quad\; 4{,}500 \quad\quad 1{,}550$$

$$6{,}050 = 6{,}050$$

$$\text{Assets} = \text{Liabilities} + \text{Owner's Equity}$$

$$\text{Assets} - \text{Liabilities} = \text{Owner's Equity}$$

$$\text{Assets} - \text{Owner's Equity} = \text{Liabilities}$$

Accounting Software

Accounting software also uses the double-entry system of bookkeeping. All the principles that apply to manual record-keeping apply when using computer software.

Even though most accounting software is designed to detect errors, this does not mean that every transaction is always correct. Understanding accounting basics will help to locate errors regardless of what system is used.

LO4 Preparing an Opening Balance Sheet

The **opening balance** is the balance for each account at the beginning of each accounting period. The balance is taken from the ending or **closing balance** of that account from the last period.

Justin Case, Paralegal				
Opening Balance Sheet				
Oct. 1, 20**				
Assets			**Liabilities**	
General Bank Account (cash)	$5,000		Personal Loan	$4,000
Computer Equipment	900		Credit Card Debt	500
Office Furniture	150		Total Liabilities	$4,500
			Owner's Equity	
			Justin Case, Capital	1,550
Total Assets	$6,050		Total Liabilities and Owner's Equity	$6,050

FIGURE 2.3   Opening balance sheet

The **capital account** (here called Justin Case, Capital) refers to the investment by the owner in the business. Capital is not always cash; it can be any assets that the owner chooses to invest in the business. The capital account includes the owner's beginning investment plus the profits or minus the losses of the firm. Any withdrawals by the owner will also reduce the amount in Justin Case's capital account.

LO5 Expanded Accounting Equation

The **expanded accounting equation** takes into account three categories of accounts, in addition to assets, liabilities, and owner's equity:

1. **Withdrawals** refers to amounts taken out of the business for the personal use of the owner.
2. Income, as previously defined, refers to all earnings for the firm. In a paralegal firm, the main source of income is fees billed to clients. When clients are billed for services rendered, the amount of fees billed is entered immediately as income, regardless of whether

or not the client has actually paid the bill. A firm could have other sources of income, such as interest income or expense recovery (such as charges to the client's account for photocopies).

3. Expenses, as previously defined, are costs incurred by the business for the purpose of earning income. These include operating costs, such as advertising expenses, dues and licences, interest, motor vehicle expenses, rent, telephone, utilities, and wages.

Net income is calculated by taking the total income of the firm minus total expenses. When income exceeds expenses, this is usually referred to as **profit**. When expenses exceed income (when revenues are lower than expenses), the firm will have a **net loss**, which causes a decrease in equity. If there is net income or profit from operations, the amount is added to the capital account, with a resulting increase in equity. If there is a loss, it will be deducted from the capital account, with a resulting reduction in equity. Remember, the capital account is the investment by the owner in the business.

The expanded accounting equation is stated as follows and is illustrated in Figure 2.4.

Assets = Liabilities + [Capital − Withdrawals + (Income − Expenses)]

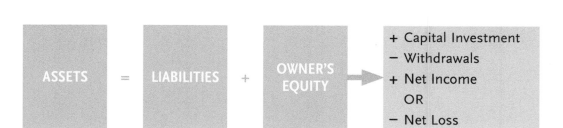

FIGURE 2.4   The expanded accounting equation

Owner's equity typically is increased or decreased depending on the following conditions:

- *Investments made by the owner, such as cash, computer equipment, and office furniture, increase owner's equity* (this is also referred to as capital contribution).
- *Income from the operation of the business increases the owner's equity.* When profits are earned, they can be retained (or reinvested) within the business to increase the owner's investment in the firm.
- *Expenses from the operation of the business will decrease the owner's equity.* When the expenses are greater than revenues, a net loss results and the owner's equity is decreased.
- *Withdrawals by the owner will decrease the owner's equity.* A sole proprietor does not receive a salary from the business. Instead, when the owner writes a cheque to himself for personal use, the amount withdrawn from the bank account results in a reduction of the amount of money in the general bank account as well as a reduction in the equity of the owner. If the proprietor removes an asset other than cash from the firm, the transaction is recorded as a withdrawal and will reduce the owner's equity in the firm.

The first step in analyzing transactions is to identify which accounts are being affected. Figure 2.5 shows how Justin's transactions and the expanded equation work together.

Transaction	ASSETS				=	LIABILITIES			+	OWNER'S EQUITY						
	General Bank Account	Accounts Receivable	Computer Equipment	Office Furniture		Personal Loan	Credit Card Debt	Accounts Payable		J. Case Capital	−	Withdrawals	+	Fees Earned	−	Expenses
1	5,000		900	150	=	4,000	500		+	1,550	−		+		−	
BAL	5,000		900	150	=	4,000	500		+	1,550	−		+		−	
2	−600		600		=				+		−		+		−	
BAL	4,400		1,500	150	=	4,000	500		+	1,550	−		+		−	
3				200	=			200	+		−		+		−	
BAL	4,400		1,500	350	=	4,000	500	200	+	1,550	−		+		−	
4	−1,000				=				+		−	1,000	+		−	
BAL	3,400		1,500	350	=	4,000	500	200	+	1,550	−	1,000	+		−	
5	800				=				+		−		+	800	−	
BAL	4,200		1,500	350	=	4,000	500	200	+	1,550	−	1,000	+	800	−	
6		1,200			=				+		−		+	1,200	−	
BAL	4,200	1,200	1,500	350	=	4,000	500	200	+	1,550	−	1,000	+	2,000	−	
7	−300				=				+		−		+		−	300
END BAL	3,900	1,200	1,500	350	=	4,000	500	200	+	1,550	−	1,000	+	2,000	−	300
	TOTAL ASSETS					TOTAL LIABILITIES			+	TOTAL OWNER'S EQUITY						
	6,950				=	4,700										
	6,950				=	4,700										

CAPITAL: 1,550 − 1,000 = 550
PROFIT: 2,000 − 300 = 1,700
550 + 1,700 = 2,250

6,950

TRANSACTIONS

1	Balances from the opening balance sheet were entered.
2	A shift in assets occurred. Computer equipment costing $600 was purchased and paid for using cash. Because cash was used to pay for the equipment, cash or the General Bank Account balance has been reduced, and there is an addition to the account for computer equipment.
3	Justin purchased $200 worth of office furniture from a furniture store on credit. Justin has not used cash to pay for the item, but he now owes the store $200, which is recorded under Accounts Payable. Justin has increased what he owes to creditors.
4	Justin needed money to pay for personal expenses, so he withdrew $1,000 from the firm's bank account. This withdrawal results in a reduction in the General Bank Account and is shown in Owner's Equity under Withdrawals.
5	Legal fees of $800 were invoiced to a client and the client paid the bill. The transaction provided an inward flow of cash in the General Bank Account and an increase in income as a result of legal fees charged.
6	Legal fees of $1,200 were invoiced to a client and the client has not paid the bill. These fees billed are an asset for the firm called Accounts Receivable and an increase in legal fees.
7	Justin paid one month's rent in the amount of $300. This is an expense (rent expense), which reduces Owner's Equity as well as the General Bank Account balance.

FIGURE 2.5   Demonstration of expanded accounting equation

Classifying Expenses

It can sometimes be difficult to decide whether something purchased is an asset or an expense. For example, Justin may go out and purchase office supplies at a cost of $1,000, including such items as pens, paper, and ink for printers. Should these items be recorded as assets (something of value owned by the business), or should they be recorded as expenses (something that will be used up within the fiscal period)?

There are different ways to handle such an entry. Justin may want to show the supplies as an asset (which Justin has numbered Account 130) and at the end of the fiscal year conduct a physical inventory to determine what supplies remain and record what supplies have been used up. He would record as an expense only the number of supplies used, leaving the remaining balance of total supplies purchased in the asset portion of the balance sheet. If the total amount of supplies purchased is small in relation to the overall inventory value, it will be easier for Justin to simply record the entire purchase as an office supplies expense (numbered as account 535).

POTENTIAL PARALEGAL PITFALLS

- **Potential pitfall:** Mixing business finances with personal finances.
- **Possible fallout:** A CRA audit could reveal that you are claiming personal expenses in your business deductions and as a result may reassess your tax return. You may owe interest and penalties on any balance reassessed by the CRA.
- **Proposed recommendation:** Keep separate personal accounts and business accounts and separate personal credit cards and business credit cards.

CHAPTER SUMMARY

One of the first challenges a paralegal starting a firm might encounter is obtaining financing for the business. This involves preparing a business plan that presents the investment being made and forecasts the anticipated income and expenses. Knowing the language of accounting will help you to communicate your plans and needs to an investor, whether a financial institution or an individual. You want to understand the general principles applied in maintaining records and be able to present a financial plan in a professional manner when asked to do so. Many situations may require you to be conversant with the language and principles that apply to record-keeping.

You have seen the categories of accounts and know why you need to have a chart of accounts. The rules of debit and credit will be explored in detail in the chapters that follow.

KEY TERMS

accounting equation, 24

accounting standards for private enterprises (ASPE), 21

accrual basis of accounting, 21

assets, 22

capital account, 26

cash basis of accounting, 22

chart of accounts, 23

closing balance, 26

current assets, 22

double-entry bookkeeping, 24

expanded accounting equation, 26

expenses, 23

external users, 20

fixed or capital assets, 22

general journal, 22

generally accepted accounting principles (GAAP), 21

government users, 20

income, 23

internal controls, 24

internal users, 20

international financial reporting standards (IFRS), 21

liabilities, 23

net income, 27

net loss, 27

normal balance, 23

opening balance, 26

owner's equity, 23

profit, 27

shareholder's equity, 23

stakeholders, 20

withdrawals, 26

FURTHER READING

CPA Canada Handbook: Accounting (Toronto: Chartered Professional Accountants of Canada, 2017 with annual updates).

REVIEW QUESTIONS

True or False

_____ 1. Cash and capital are equivalent terms that can be used interchangeably. (LO3)

_____ 2. Going concern is one of the principles of accounting. (LO2)

_____ 3. In accrual accounting, cash must be received before the transaction is recognized on the financial statement. (LO2)

_____ 4. For every transaction reported on a financial statement, there are at least two entries. (LO5)

_____ 5. A chart of accounts is a standardized list of accounts that is only created using accounting software. (LO3)

_____ 6. Businesses are concerned only about external stakeholders in their financial reporting. (LO1)

_____ 7. Paying down a bank loan or other forms of credit will decrease equity. (LO5)

_____ 8. Purchasing or selling assets will increase equity. (LO5)

_____ 9. The normal balance of a liability is a debit. (LO3)

_____ 10. Sole proprietors and partners take money out of their business by way of a salary. (LO5)

_____ 11. The equity account for a corporation is typically identified as shareholder's equity. (LO3)

Short Answer

1. What does it mean to understand the financial position of your business (or even your personal finances)? (LO1)

2. Which accounts have an impact on owner's equity? (LO5)

PRACTICE EXERCISES

PRACTICE
EXCEL

Practice Exercise 2.1

Using the definitions explained in this chapter, determine the classification (assets, liabilities, owner's equity, income, and expenses) of each of the following account names. **(LO3, LO5)**

	Account Name	Category
1	Cash	Asset
2	Motor Vehicle	
3	Telephone Expense	
4	Salaries and Wages	
5	Professional Fees Earned	
6	Capital	
7	Computer Equipment	
8	Accounts Receivable	
9	Advertising Expense	
10	Interest Earned	
11	Prepaid Rent	
12	General Bank Account	
13	Office Equipment	
14	Withdrawals	

PRACTICE
EXCEL

Practice Exercise 2.2

Balance the accounting equation on each line by calculating the value of the missing number. **(LO3)**

	Assets	=	Liabilities	+	Owner's Equity
Example:	35,000	=	15,000	+	?
			Answer: 35,000 – 15,000 = 20,000		
1	40,000	=	10,000	+	?
2	80,000	=	?	+	60,000
3	?	=	24,000	+	10,000
4	?	=	5,000	+	10,000
5	20,000	=	?	+	6,000
6	31,000 + ?	=	24,000	+	10,000
7	58,500	=	2,500	+	80,000 – ?
8	1,700 + 5,000	=	?	+	700
9	?	=	10,000	+	30,000
10	20,000 – 5,000	=	5,400 + ?	+	8,000

Practice Exercise 2.3

In the following list of accounts, complete the table to show the category of account: asset, liability, capital, withdrawal, income, or expense. **(LO3, LO5)**

	Account Name	Category
1	Accounting and Bookkeeping Expense	Expense
2	Accounts Payable/General	
3	Auto Expense	
4	Credit Card Debt	
5	Fees Earned	
6	General Bank Account	
7	Insurance—Prof. Liability	
8	Interest Income	
9	Accounts Payable/General	
10	Office Furniture	
11	Owner, Capital	
12	Owner, Drawings	
13	Photocopy Expense	
14	Prepaid Insurance	
15	Prepaid Rent	
16	Salaries	
17	Utilities	
18	Vacation Accrual Payable	
19	General Bank Account	

Practice Exercise 2.4

Using the worksheet provided, complete the expanded accounting equation by recording the following transactions. (LO5)

1	Balances from the opening balance sheet were entered by Ann Litigate. She had invested $8,000 in her firm.
2	Office equipment costing $800 was purchased and paid for using cash.
3	Ann purchased $900 worth of office furniture from a furniture store on credit.
4	Ann paid for personal expenses from the firm's bank account in the amount of $1,500.
5	Legal fees of $1,600 were invoiced to a client and the client paid the bill.
6	Legal fees of $800 were invoiced to a client and the client has not paid the bill.
7	Ann paid one month's salaries expense in the amount of $2,000.

	ASSETS			=	LIABILITIES	+	OWNER'S EQUITY						
Transaction	General Bank Account	Accounts Receivable	Office Furniture and Equipment	=	Accounts Payable	+	A. Litigate Capital	−	Withdrawals	+	Fees Earned	−	Expense
1	8,000						8,000						
BAL	8,000	0	0	=	0	+	8,000	−	0	+	0	−	0
2													
BAL				=		+		−		+		−	
3													
BAL				=		+		−		+		−	
4													
BAL				=		+		−		+		−	
5													
BAL				=		+		−		+		−	
6													
BAL				=		+		−		+		−	
7													
END BAL				=		+		−		+		−	

TOTAL ASSETS	=	TOTAL LIABILITIES	+	TOTAL OWNER'S EQUITY			
	=		+	CAPITAL	+	PROFIT	
				−	+	−	
					+		
	=		+				
	=						

Practice Exercise 2.5

For each of the following transactions, identify the account names and the account type using the chart of accounts printed on the inside cover of this textbook. **(LO5)**

Transaction	Account Name/Type
1. Paralegal contributed $10,000 to the legal services firm from personal funds.	
2. Paralegal took a draw ($1,200) against the legal services firm's equity for personal use.	
3. Paralegal purchased a new all-in-one printer for the office ($350) with cash.	
4. Paralegal paid bookkeeper for bookkeeping services ($1,000) with cash.	
5. Paralegal paid office rent, which included utilities and telephone ($1,500), with cash.	
6. Paralegal billed a client for professional fees and received payment from the client ($1,700).	
7. Paralegal paid Law Society dues ($1,100).	
8. Paralegal paid principal and interest on her bank loan ($500 principal; $100 interest).	

Practice Exercise 2.6

Using the transactions from Practice Exercise 2.5, complete the following accounting equations.

Assume that the opening balances are as follows: Assets: $5,000; Liabilities: $2,500; and Owner's Equity: $2,500 (Capital). List each transaction entry under the appropriate heading of the expanded accounting equation. **(LO5)**

**Ann Litigate Paralegal Services** May 1 – May 31												
TRANSACTION	**ASSETS**			**LIABILITIES**		**OWNER'S EQUITY**						
		=			+	Capital	–	Withdrawals	+	Revenue	–	Expenses
Opening	5,000	=		2,500	+	2,500	–		+		–	
1		=			+		–		+		–	
2		=			+		–		+		–	
3		=			+		–		+		–	
4		=			+		–		+		–	
5		=			+		–		+		–	
6		=			+		–		+		–	
7		=			+		–		+		–	
8		=			+		–		+		–	
Ending Balance		=			+		–		+		–	
PROOF		=										

PUT IT INTO PRACTICE

Prepare Your Personal Balance Sheet

Using the table below, make a list of items you own on the left-hand side and a list of debts you owe to creditors on the right-hand side, then calculate your personal net worth.

Assets		Liabilities		
		Total Liabilities		
		Owner's Equity		
		Capital		
Total Assets		Total Liabilities and Owner's Equity		

3 Keeping Books and Records

Accounting Period   40

The Accounting Cycle   41

Basic Rules of Debit and Credit   43

Business Transaction Source Documents   46

Analyzing the Transaction   47

Recording Transactions Using the Basic Accounting Equation   48

Examples of Transactions   49

The General Journal   59

Recording the Opening Balance Sheet in the Firm's Records   59

Chapter Summary   61

Key Terms   61

Further Reading   61

Review Questions   62

Practice Exercises   63

Put It into Practice   71

LEARNING OUTCOMES

After reading this chapter, you should be able to:

LO1 Understand the concept of a fiscal year.
LO2 Understand the accounting cycle.
LO3 Demonstrate an understanding of debits and credits.
LO4 Complete an analysis of transactions using double-entry bookkeeping.
LO5 Record opening entries in PCLaw®.
LO6 Record transactions in a general journal.

LO1 Accounting Period

Accounting records are prepared, and procedures are performed, over the course of the **accounting period**. The process that begins with analyzing and recording business transactions into journals and ends with the completion of financial statements and a post-closing trial balance is referred to as the **accounting cycle**. The steps in the accounting cycle are described in the next section.

Accounting periods of equal length, called **fiscal periods**, are used to measure the financial progress of a business over time. Periods may be defined as monthly, quarterly, or annual. The accounting or fiscal period refers to the period of time for which an income statement is prepared. The length of each accounting period will vary depending on the type and size of business being conducted. If the results are to be compared from one period to the next, the results must be examined over consistent periods of time. It is not usually helpful to compare the results for a 6-month period with results for a 12-month period. When filing tax returns, the results reported to the CRA must cover a 12-month period. When the period covers 12 months, it is called the **fiscal year**. The fiscal year-end is the date upon which the financial year finishes. The fiscal year-end does not have to be December 31; it can be any day of the year as long as it is consistent from one year to the next.

Selecting a year-end for a business depends on various concerns the owner may have, such as the following:

- Are tax benefits available if the business does not use December 31 (the calendar year) as the year-end?
- What additional records will be required if the business does not use the calendar year?
- Is the business seasonal, and does the owner prefer a fiscal period that corresponds to a quiet time of the year?
- On what date did the firm originally begin business?

Once the fiscal year-end has been selected for tax purposes, the CRA will not allow the selected date to be changed without its consent, as this would create inconsistencies in the financial reports. Having a year-end that does not finish on December 31 complicates the bookkeeping because many expenses—such as LSO dues, remittances of employees' tax deductions, and CPP and Employment Insurance (EI) premiums—must be calculated on a calendar-year basis. T4 slips issued to employees must cover salary over the calendar year. The additional record-keeping required when selecting a year-end other than December 31 is often a deterrent.

LO2 The Accounting Cycle

The accounting cycle is the process of analyzing and recording business transactions and producing financial statements from the information. This cycle takes place over a fiscal period covered by the income statement. A business owner may wish to complete the cycle once every month, every quarter, or once a year. Most businesses report on their financial activity monthly. Many paralegals use a one-year accounting period but may produce interim reports each month.

The steps in the accounting cycle are completed in the following order:

1. After a business transaction occurs, journalize the transaction using a general journal, trust journal, and/or specialized journal.
2. Post the journal entry to the general ledger and/or trust ledger.
3. Prepare the trial balance.
4. Prepare the worksheet.
5. Prepare the adjusted trial balance.
6. Prepare the financial statements.
7. Record adjusting and closing entries.
8. Calculate the **post-closing trial balance**.

Figure 3.1 illustrates the steps of the accounting cycle.

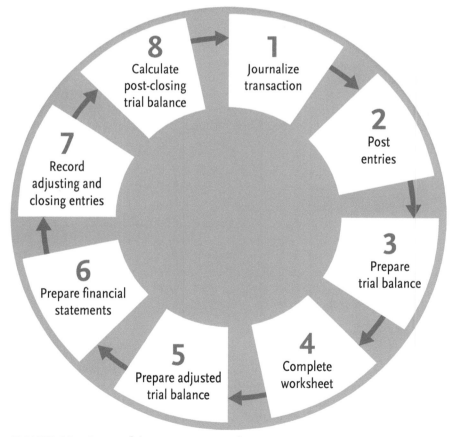

FIGURE 3.1   Steps of the accounting cycle

Note that the post-closing trial balance in step 8 is carried forward as the opening balance for the next period.

Transactions

All financial activities involving the business are transactions. The process starts when the business enters into a financial transaction. The transaction might be for cash (or cheque) or for credit. As an example, the paralegal may purchase a piece of equipment, pay rent, or charge fees to a client. An additional consideration for paralegals is that the transaction may involve the trust account and trust records, instead of only the general bank account.

Journal Entries

As discussed in Chapter 2, the general journal is where journal entries are recorded. The general journal is a chronological list of the transactions that occurred during an accounting period. It is called the "book of original entry" because this is where transactions are first recorded in chronological order. The basic general journal usually has two columns—a debit column and a credit column. The **journal entries** involve a double-entry system in which there is at least one debit entry and one credit entry for every transaction. The basic trust journals, which are also books of original entry, are used to record funds received in the trust account and disbursements made from the trust account.

Posting

Once the entries have been recorded in the general journal, they are summarized using a **general ledger.** The general ledger contains all the company accounts and is used to keep a running total of the balance in each asset, liability, equity, income, and expense account. The firm's books will have one general ledger with a chart for each of the accounts used in the business. Each general journal entry is posted to the account affected by the transaction. The process of recording general journal entries to the general ledger is called posting. **Posting** also will be done from the trust journal to the individual client trust ledgers so that the funds held in the mixed trust account are properly accounted for.

Trial Balance

When the accounting period ends (month-end, quarter-end, or year-end), a list of the ending balances in all the ledger accounts is prepared. This list is called a **trial balance** and it is performed to ensure that the total debits are equal to the total credits. If they are not equal, this indicates that an error occurred in one or more journal entries or in a general journal posting. Errors must be corrected before proceeding to the completion of the financial statements. It is important to note that a balanced trial balance does not necessarily mean that all the transactions were recorded without error.

Worksheet

Sometimes period-end adjustments are needed for certain accounts. For example, a paralegal may have paid motor vehicle insurance premiums and entered the amount as an asset under the account called "prepaid insurance." At the end of the period, part of the premium will have been used up, and the amount used must be moved from the prepaid asset account on the balance sheet to the expense account on the income statement. An adjusting entry would be made to reduce the amount in the asset account (prepaid insurance) and increase the insurance expense amount in the books to show how much insurance was expended.

If **adjustments** need to be made to the balances in any accounts after the trial balance is prepared, a **worksheet** is used to make the changes required. The worksheet is an internal document used to track the changes made to various accounts, usually after the period transactions have been recorded in order to adjust accounts to their correct balances. Once the adjustments for the period are done, an updated trial balance is prepared to ensure that the debits and credits are still equal. This updated trial balance that occurs after the adjustments have been made is called the **adjusted trial balance**.

Adjusting Journal Entries

Any adjustments made on the worksheet must be entered into the general journal and then posted to the general ledger accounts in order to update and bring the entries from the worksheet into the closing balances of the firm.

Financial Statements

The **financial statements**—an income statement, a statement of owner's equity, and a balance sheet—are prepared once the adjusting entries have been entered in the general ledger, and an adjusted trial balance has been prepared.

Closing the Books

The owner will want to start a new accounting cycle each fiscal year, so the revenue and expense accounts in the ledgers (referred to as *temporary accounts*) must be closed. Revenue and expense accounts are temporary because they are closed out each year-end and start the next year at zero. **Closing the books** is the final step of the accounting cycle after adjusting a entries are recorded, financial statements are prepared, and the closing entries are completed. The balance sheet accounts (the *permanent accounts*) are not closed at the end of the cycle because the amounts in those accounts are carried forward from period to period.

LO3 Basic Rules of Debit and Credit

As a rule, the left side of the **T-account** is the debit side. The right side is the credit side. Do not give any other meaning to the words debit and credit. Debit means left; credit means right.

	(T-account)
Debits (Dr.)	= Credits (Cr.)
Left side	= Right side

The double-entry method of accounting requires that at least two entries be made for each transaction: a debit entry in one (or more) account(s) is always offset by an equal credit entry in another account (or more than one account). In order for the books to be balanced, the total value of the debits entered must always equal the total value of credits.

Debits and Credits

Points to keep in mind about the terms *debit* and *credit*:

- Assets are shown on the left side of the accounting equation and normally have a debit balance (**normal debit balance**).
- Liabilities and owner's equity are shown on the right side of the accounting equation and normally have a credit balance (**normal credit balance**).
- Every transaction you record will have at least one debit and one credit. The total value of the debits and credits must be equal when you are finished the entry.
- There may be a transaction, called a **compound entry**, that affects three or more accounts. At the end of the entry, the total value of debits must still equal the total value of credits. For instance, if a $10,000 vehicle is purchased with $4,000 cash and a $6,000 loan, then there would be one debit entry (vehicle account) and two credit entries (one for cash and one for the loan).
- A debit entry might increase the balance in some accounts (asset, withdrawal, and expense accounts), but a debit entry might decrease the balance in other accounts (liability, capital, and revenue accounts).
- The ending account balance is the net amount of the debit entries and credit entries posted to each specific account.
- A credit entry can increase the balance in some accounts (liability, capital, and revenue accounts), and a credit entry can decrease the balance in some accounts (asset, withdrawals, and expense accounts).

Loan Payable (Liability Account)	
Dr.	Cr.
Entry on this side *decreases* balance	Entry on this side *increases* balance

General Bank Account (Asset Account)	
Dr.	Cr.
Entry on this side *increases* balance	Entry on this side *decreases* balance

- What is known as a debit or credit on bank statements is actually the opposite of what debits and credits mean in accounting. Although personal bank statements may show deposits as a credit, a credit in a cash or general bank account in accounting records does not result in an increase in the bank account balance; it actually represents a *decrease* in the account balance. Bank statements are done from the perspective of the bank and what it owes to its customers. When the bank issues an account statement, it shows deposits made as a credit because the deposit is actually a liability for the bank—the bank owes its customer the money they have deposited in their bank account.
- Making an entry on the debit side (left side) or credit side (right side) is simply a system used to increase or decrease the balance in an account—nothing more.
- All asset accounts, such as cash, equipment, or office furniture, normally have a debit balance. Therefore, to increase the balance in an asset account, it is necessary to debit the account. For example, if $1,000 in cash is deposited into the bank account, the deposit will show in the books as a "general bank account" debit.

General Bank Account	
Dr.	Cr.
Increase	Decrease
1,000	

- If a cheque for $50 is written from the general bank account, it is necessary to credit the general bank account by that amount because the balance in the asset (general bank account) is decreasing by $50 (credit), leaving a debit balance of $950.

General Bank Account

Dr.	Cr.
Increase	Decrease
1,000	
	50
Bal. 950	

- Liability accounts (such as loans payable or credit card debt) are shown on the right side of the accounting equation and have a normal credit balance. To increase the balance in a liability account, the account is credited. For example, if a charge of $120 is made to the credit card, it is necessary to credit the credit card debt account because the debt is increasing.

Credit Card Debt

Dr.	Cr.
Decrease	Increase
	120

- If a payment is made on the credit card debt, the amount of the debt decreases, which is a liability, and an entry will need to be made on the debit side. If $100 was paid on the credit card, it would show it as a debit, leaving a balance of $20 owing on the credit card.

Credit Card Debt

Dr.	Cr.
Decrease	Increase
	120
100	
	Bal. 20

- Owner's equity is on the right side of the accounting equation. The capital account, which shows the investment made by the owner in the business, has a normal credit balance. If the owner invests $1,000 into the business, the capital account must be credited to show an increase in the balance.

Justin Case, Capital

Dr.	Cr.
Decrease	Increase
	1,000

- When a business owner takes $800 out of the business for personal use, it is called a withdrawal. The drawings account (which has a normal debit balance) is debited when a withdrawal is made because the owner's capital (which has a normal credit balance) is being decreased.

Justin Case, Withdrawal

Dr.	Cr.
Increase	Decrease
800	

- Revenues are entered as a credit because when income is earned, this ultimately results in an increase in the owner's capital (which has a normal credit balance). Fees earned of $2,000 would be shown on the credit side in the fees earned (revenue) account (which has a normal credit balance).

Fees Earned

Dr.	Cr.
Decrease	Increase
	2,000

- Expenses are entered as a debit because they ultimately reduce the owner's capital. For example, a telephone expense of $180 would be recorded as a debit.

Telephone Expense

Dr.	Cr.
Increase	Decrease
180	

Business Transaction Source Documents

When a business transaction occurs, documented evidence of that transaction must be retained. This may be an invoice sent online or in the mail, a receipt or voucher from a purchase made at a store with cash or credit, or a deposit slip from the bank.

TAX TIP

Receipts

When reporting to the CRA, all receipts must be kept to prove the nature of all business transactions. A charge shown on a credit card or bank statement, or even a cancelled cheque, is not considered a valid receipt for tax purposes. The original invoice from a vendor must be available for the purpose of auditing. The reason is that although the charge shown on a bank statement or credit card indicates that something was purchased at an office supply store, it does not specify what was bought—were the purchases really office supplies for the business, or school supplies for the owner's children? The original receipt from the store explains what the expense was for, not just the fact that money was spent at a particular place of business.

The receipt obtained must be entered into the firm's books. A system for filing and maintaining receipts must be established. Some people like to file bills by order of date. Others prefer to have separate file folders by account. This enables a business owner to look at the file and see all the bills charged to that account. For example, a business owner may wish to have a file folder named Telephone Expense and place all bills related to telephone expenses for the office in that file. If a question arises, the business owner needs to look through only one folder rather than through the bills for all the items the firm may have purchased over a particular period of time. Further, some choose to file their documents by clients and vendors.

If a bill shows a charge for GST or HST, the registration number of the business must be included on the bill. If the registration number is not shown, the tax department may refuse to allow a credit for the tax paid.

LO4 Analyzing the Transaction

Business transactions must be recorded in the firm's books. As previously mentioned, the general journal is the book of original entry. When a general journal entry is made, the transaction must be analyzed to determine which accounts in the firm's chart of accounts are affected. The following five steps will help with the analysis:

- Which accounts are affected by the transaction? Think about what the firm is giving and receiving in the transaction. Look at the chart of accounts and identify which accounts will be used to record the transaction.
- Are the account balances increasing or decreasing?
- Which category does each affected account belong to? Is it an asset, liability, withdrawal, capital, income, or expense account?
- Given the increase or decrease of each account and the rules of debit and credit, which accounts will be debited and which accounts will be credited?
- Record the entry to the general journal or the T-accounts. Is the entry balanced? Are debits and credits equal after the entry is made?

The biggest challenge for people learning double-entry bookkeeping is knowing which account to use and when to debit or credit an account. One simple memory device to help distinguish debits from credits is the acronym **DEAD CLIC** (Figure 3.2).

Side of the account used to record an increase

	Debit	**C**redit	
Accounts with a normal debit balance + = Dr.	**E**xpenses	**L**iabilities	Accounts with a normal credit balance + = Cr.
	Assets	**I**ncome	
	Drawings	**C**apital	
	DEAD	**CLIC**	

FIGURE 3.2   **The acronym DEAD CLIC will help you distinguish debits from credits**

DEAD stands for the categories of accounts that have a normal debit balance, that is, expenses, assets, and drawings are debited to increase their balance. To decrease the balance in any of these accounts, the account will need to be credited.

CLIC stands for the categories of accounts that have a normal credit balance, that is, liabilities, income, and capital. To increase the balance in any of these accounts, the account must be credited; to decrease the balance, the account will need to be debited.

The first step in using DEAD CLIC is to learn to recognize the category of account that is being dealt with.

In a double-entry bookkeeping system, two or more accounts will be affected by any transaction. Remember that the total debits and credits must be equal after each entry is made in the general journal.

Recording Transactions Using the Basic Accounting Equation

Let's go back to the original Justin Case opening balance sheet from Chapter 2, which is shown again here in Figure 3.3.

Justin Case, Paralegal Opening Balance Sheet Oct. 1, 20**			
Assets		**Liabilities**	
General Bank Account (cash)	$5,000	Personal Loan	$4,000
Computer Equipment	900	Credit Card Debt	500
Office Furniture	150	Total Liabilities	$4,500
		Owner's Equity	
		Justin Case, Capital	1,550
Total Assets	$6,050	Total Liabilities and Owner's Equity	$6,050

FIGURE 3.3   Opening balance sheet

The T-accounts in Figure 3.4 illustrate how posting the opening entries affects the individual ledger accounts. The total debits equal the total credits once all posting is completed. When making the entries in the general journal, there are at least two entries for each transaction—an entry on the left side, **debit (Dr.)**, and an entry on the right side, **credit (Cr.)**. The total debits are equal to the total credits.

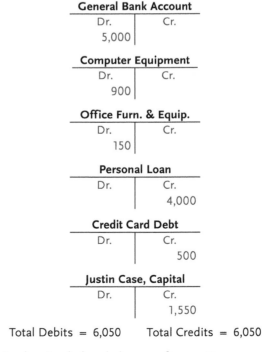

FIGURE 3.4   T-accounts showing ledger balances after posting

Other Types of Entries

Sometimes you may run into an entry that involves more than two accounts or a shift in assets.

Compound Entries

As previously mentioned, a compound entry requires more than one debit or more than one credit. For example, if office furniture is purchased for $2,000, and $500 is paid by cheque and $1,500 is purchased on credit, there will be three lines in the journal entry (see Figure 3.5).

	Debit	Credit
Office Furniture	2,000	
General Bank Account		500
Accounts Payable/General Liabilities		1,500
To record purchase of office furniture		

FIGURE 3.5   **Recording a compound entry**

Shift in Assets

A shift in assets occurs when two asset accounts are affected by the same transaction. For example, suppose computer equipment that costs $1,000 is purchased, and it is paid for with cash or cheque. There will be an increase in the computer equipment account, and the general bank account will decrease. The total value of assets has not changed; however, the value of the computer equipment account has increased and the value of the general bank account has decreased, reflecting a shift in assets. This entry would be shown by debiting the computer equipment account and crediting the general bank account (see Figure 3.6).

	Debit	Credit
Computer Equipment	1,000	
General Bank Account		1,000
To record purchase of computer equipment		

FIGURE 3.6   **Recording a shift in assets**

Examples of Transactions

The following examples illustrate the application of debits and credits in double-entry bookkeeping and recording transactions in a general journal.

EXAMPLE 1

On October 5, Justin Case wrote a cheque for $300 to Bell Canada to pay the telephone bill for his office.

Analysis of Transaction		Result
Step 1:	Which accounts are affected by the transaction?	• Telephone Expense is used to record telephone bills received. • General Bank Account is used to record payment.
Step 2:	Are the account balances increasing or decreasing?	• Telephone Expense will increase. • General Bank Account will decrease.
Step 3:	Which category does each affected account belong to?	• Telephone Expense is an expense account. • General Bank Account is an asset account.
Step 4:	Which accounts will be debited and which accounts will be credited?	• Telephone Expense will be debited $300. • General Bank Account will be credited $300.
Step 5:	Record the entry to the general journal or the T-accounts. Is the entry balanced?	• Yes, there is a debit of $300 and a credit of $300.

General Journal					GJ2
Date 20**		Description	PR	Debit	Credit
Oct.	5	Telephone Expense		300	
		General Bank Account (Cash)			300
		Paid telephone expense for Oct.			

EXAMPLE 2

Compound entry: On October 5, Justin Case purchased office furniture from IKEA for $2,000. He paid $500 by cheque and $1,500 was put on his credit card. This compound entry will involve three different accounts.

Analysis of Transaction		Result
Step 1:	Which accounts are affected by the transaction?	• Office Furniture and Equipment Fixtures is the account used for furniture received. • General Bank Account is used to record payment for the furniture. • Credit Card Debt is used to record the liability incurred on the card.
Step 2:	Are the account balances increasing or decreasing?	• Office Furniture and Equipment will increase. • General Bank Account will decrease. • Credit Card Debt will increase.
Step 3:	Which category does each affected account belong to?	• Office Furniture and Equipment is an asset account. • General Bank Account is an asset account. • Credit Card Debt is a liability account.
Step 4:	Which accounts will be debited and which accounts will be credited?	• Office Furniture and Equipment will be debited $2,000. • General Bank Account will be credited $500. • Credit Card Debt will be credited $1,500.
Step 5:	Record the entry to the general journal or the T-accounts. Is the entry balanced?	• Yes, there is a debit of $2,000 and a credit of $500 plus $1,500.

General Journal					GJ2
Date 20**		Description	PR	Debit	Credit
Oct.	5	Telephone Expense		300	
		General Bank Account (Cash)			300
		Paid telephone expense for Oct.			
	5	Office Furniture and Equipment		2,000	
		General Bank Account (Cash)			500
		Credit Card Debt			1,500
		To record furniture purchased from IKEA			

EXAMPLE 3

On October 8, Justin Case received $500 by way of a scholarship for having obtained the highest marks in his class. Justin wishes to invest this amount in his firm.

Analysis of Transaction		Result
Step 1:	Which accounts are affected by the transaction?	• General Bank Account is used to record cash received. • Justin Case, Capital is used to record an increase in investment by the owner.
Step 2:	Are the account balances increasing or decreasing?	• General Bank Account will increase. • Justin Case, Capital will increase.
Step 3:	Which category does each affected account belong to?	• General Bank Account is an asset. • Justin Case, Capital is an owner's equity account.
Step 4:	Which accounts will be debited and which accounts will be credited?	• General Bank Account will be debited $500. • Justin Case, Capital will be credited $500.
Step 5:	Record the entry to the general journal or the T-accounts. Is the entry balanced?	• Yes, there is a debit of $500 and a credit of $500.

General Journal					GJ2
Date 20**		Description	PR	Debit	Credit
- - - - - - - -	- - - - - - - -	- -	- - - -	- - - -	- - -¹
Oct.	5	Office Furniture and Equipment		2,000	
		General Bank Account (Cash)			500
		Credit Card Debt			1,500
		To record furniture purchased from IKEA			
	8	General Bank Account		500	
		Justin Case, Capital			500
		To record investment of scholarship			

---

1   The broken lines here and in the tables that follow indicate that the page has been split, so that the whole general journal need not be shown each time.

EXAMPLE 4

On October 10, Justin opened an account with a legal stationer, Legal Supplies Inc., and purchased office supplies from them worth $580. Terms for payment on account are net 30 days, after which interest will be charged.

Analysis of Transaction		Result
Step 1:	Which accounts are affected by the transaction?	• Office Supplies/General Expense is used because the supplies will be used up within the year. • Accounts Payable/General Liabilities is used to record the promise to pay Legal Supplies Inc. for the purchase on credit.
Step 2:	Are the account balances increasing or decreasing?	• Office Supplies/General Expense will increase. • Accounts Payable/General Liabilities will increase.
Step 3:	Which category does each affected account belong to?	• Office Supplies/General Expense is an expense account. • Accounts Payable/General Liabilities is a liability account.
Step 4:	Which accounts will be debited and which accounts will be credited?	• Office Supplies/General Expense will be debited $580. • Accounts Payable/General Liabilities will be credited $580.
Step 5:	Record the entry to the general journal or the T-accounts. Is the entry balanced?	• Yes, there is a debit of $580 and a credit of $580.

General Journal					GJ2
Date 20**		Description	PR	Debit	Credit
- - - -	- - -	- -	- - - -	- - - -	- - - -
Oct.	8	General Bank Account		500	
		Justin Case, Capital			500
		To record investment of scholarship			
	10	Office Supplies/General Expense		580	
		Accounts Payable/General Liabilities			580
		To record purchase from Legal Supplies Inc.			

EXAMPLE 5

Shift in assets: On October 15, Justin purchased a second-hand filing cabinet at Office Equipment Inc., a used office equipment store. He paid $100 by cheque.

Analysis of Transaction		Result
Step 1:	Which accounts are affected by the transaction?	• Office Furniture and Equipment is used for the item received. • General Bank Account is used for the item given.
Step 2:	Are the account balances increasing or decreasing?	• Office Furniture and Equipment will increase. • General Bank Account will decrease.
Step 3:	Which category does each affected account belong to?	• Office Furniture and Equipment is an asset account. • General Bank Account is also an asset account.
Step 4:	Which accounts will be debited and which accounts will be credited?	• Office Furniture and Equipment will be debited $100. • General Bank Account will be credited $100.
Step 5:	Record the entry to the general journal or the T-accounts. Is the entry balanced?	• Yes, there is a debit of $100 and a credit of $100.

General Journal					GJ2
Date 20**		Description	PR	Debit	Credit
- - - - -		- - - - - - - - - - - - - - - - -	- - -	- - - -	- - - -
Oct.	10	Office Supplies/General Expense		580	
		Accounts Payable/General Liabilities			580
		To record purchase from Legal Supplies Inc.			
	15	Office Furniture and Equipment		100	
		General Bank Account			100
		Purchased filing cabinet from Office Equipment Inc.			

EXAMPLE 6

Payment for services rendered: On October 20, Justin gave a bill to his first client, Judith Sabourin, in the amount of $3,000, and she paid him with a cheque.

Analysis of Transaction		Result
Step 1:	Which accounts are affected by the transaction?	• General Bank Account is used to record the payment received. • Fees Earned is used to record the bill given to the client for the services rendered.
Step 2:	Are the account balances increasing or decreasing?	• General Bank Account will increase. • Fees Earned will increase.
Step 3:	Which category does each affected account belong to?	• General Bank Account is an asset account. • Fees Earned is an income account.
Step 4:	Which accounts will be debited and which accounts will be credited?	• General Bank Account will be debited $3,000. • Fees Earned will be credited $3,000.
Step 5:	Record the entry to the general journal or the T-accounts. Is the entry balanced?	• Yes, there is a debit of $3,000 and a credit of $3,000.

General Journal					GJ2
Date 20**		Description	PR	Debit	Credit
- - - - - - -	- - - -	- -	- - - -	- - - -	- - - - -
Oct.	15	Office Furniture and Equipment		100	
		General Bank Account			100
		Purchased filing cabinet from Office Equipment Inc.			
	20	General Bank Account		3,000	
		Fees Earned			3,000
		To record fees billed to Sabourin and paid			

EXAMPLE 7

Expenses: On October 30, Justin Case paid rent of $500 for one month. Use the same process to record this expense as was used in example 1 to record an expense.

Analysis of Transaction		Result
Step 1:	What accounts are affected by the transaction?	• Rent Expense is used to record rent charged. • General Bank Account is used to record payment given.
Step 2:	Are the accounts increasing or decreasing?	• Rent Expense will increase. • General Bank Account will decrease.
Step 3:	What category does each affected account belong to?	• Rent Expense is an expense account. • General Bank Account is an asset account.
Step 4:	Which account will be debited and which account will be credited?	• Rent Expense will be debited $500. • General Bank Account will be credited $500.
Step 5:	Record the entry to the general journal or T-accounts. Is the entry balanced?	• Yes, there is a debit of $500 and a credit of $500.

General Journal					GJ2
Date 20**		Description	PR	Debit	Credit
Oct.	20	General Bank Account		3,000	
		Fees Earned			3,000
		To record fees billed to Sabourin and paid			
	30	Rent Expense		500	
		General Bank Account			500
		To record rent paid for one month			

Figure 3.7 shows the general journal after all October transactions (Examples 1 through 7) have been entered and totalled.

General Journal				GJ2
Date 20**	Description	PR	Debit	Credit
Oct. 5	Telephone Expense		300	
	General Bank Account (Cash)			300
	Paid telephone expense for Oct.			
5	Office Furniture and Equipment		2,000	
	General Bank Account (Cash)			500
	Credit Card Debt			1,500
	To record furniture purchased from IKEA			
8	General Bank Account		500	
	Justin Case, Capital			500
	To record investment of scholarship			
10	Office Supplies/General Expense		580	
	Accounts Payable/General Liabilities			580
	To record purchase from Legal Supplies Inc.			
15	Office Furniture and Equipment		100	
	General Bank Account			100
	Purchased filing cabinet from Office Equipment Inc.			
20	General Bank Account		3,000	
	Fees Earned			3,000
	To record fees billed to Sabourin and paid			
30	Rent Expense		500	
	General Bank Account			500
	To record rent paid for one month			
	Totals		6,980	6,980

FIGURE 3.7   General journal after all October transactions have been entered and totalled

LO5 Recording Opening Entries in PCLaw®

To get started, Justin Case must enter the account opening balances in the accounting system to create an opening balance sheet. He has added any missing accounts using the set-up menu for the software. He has also recorded the amounts for his investment in the firm in order to calculate his equity (or investment) in the firm. Figure 3.8 shows the general ledger opening account balances as they appear in PCLaw®.

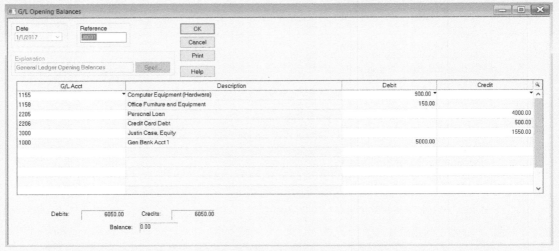

FIGURE 3.8   General ledger opening balances for Justin Case, shown in PCLaw®

The amount to be entered on the line for Justin Case, Equity was shown at the bottom of the screen in the Description column. Once the equity amount of $1,550 is entered, the Debits and Credits boxes at bottom of the screen show debits of $6,050 and credits of $6,050 and the Balance box shows a zero balance, indicating that the debits and credits are balanced. The system does not allow you to exit this screen if the total debits and total credits are not equal so that the balance is zero.

Once the opening balances have been entered, Justin is able to print an opening balance sheet (Figure 3.9).

FIGURE 3.9   Opening balance sheet for Justin Case, Paralegal, shown in PCLaw®

LO6 The General Journal

As each transaction in Examples 1 through 7 was analyzed, it was recorded on page 2 (GJ2) in the general journal. All the information regarding each transaction is captured in this journal—the date the transaction occurred, the names of the accounts affected, the amounts debited and credited, and an explanation of what the entry was for.

There are a number of conventions regarding journal entries that should be kept in mind:

- Enter the year on the first line at the top left of the first column.
- Enter the month on the first line of the journal entry. It is not necessary to enter the month again until a new page is started or the month changes.
- Enter the date of the transaction in the second column on the first line of each entry. Transactions are entered in chronological order (by order of date).
- Enter the name of the account to be debited on the first line of the entry. Note that debits are always entered first. Use the name of the account as it is shown on the chart of accounts being used by the firm. The description of the debit entry should be aligned at the left margin. Enter the amount to be debited in the debit column on the same line. Dollar signs are not used in journals and ledgers.
- Enter the name of the account to be credited on the next line of the entry, below the debit line(s). Use the name of the account as it is shown on the chart of accounts being used by the firm. The description of the credit entry should be indented by about three spaces (or 1 cm). This provides a visual clue that the line is a credit entry. Enter the credit amount in the credit column.
- Enter a brief explanation of what the entry is for. This entry is sometimes indented to distinguish it from the credit entries. When providing the explanation for the transaction, indicate the name of who was paid or what month the bill was for.
- Leave one blank line between each new entry.

Post Reference Column

The post reference (PR) column in the general journal is left blank when a transaction is initially recorded. Individual account numbers will be entered into the PR column when the entry is posted to the general ledger accounts.

Recording the Opening Balance Sheet in the Firm's Records

The numbers from the opening balance sheet in Figure 3.3 are recorded in the firm's general journal when the firm's books are first set up (see Figure 3.10). These entries are then posted to the firm's general ledger accounts as opening entries.

Justin Case, Paralegal General Journal					GJ1
Date 20**		Description	PR	Debit	Credit
Oct.	1	General Bank Account	100	5,000	
		Computer Equipment	155	900	
		Office Furniture and Equipment	158	150	
		Personal Loan	205		4,000
		Credit Card Debt	210		500
		Justin Case, Capital	300		1,550
		To record opening balance sheet			

FIGURE 3.10   Opening entries

The balances from the opening balance sheet are recorded in the general journal. The heading indicates that the page number is 1 (GJ1), which is the first page of the general journal. In addition:

1. The month and year are placed in the first column for the first entry. The month does not repeat for entries that follow because the date did not change.
2. The descriptions of the debit entries (in the Description column) are aligned at the left margin and the descriptions of the credit entries are indented by about three spaces (or 1 cm).
3. The PR column shows the general ledger account to which the amount was posted. The account number is entered only after the amount has been recorded in the firm's general ledger.
4. "To record opening balance sheet" is the description of the general journal entries above.

POTENTIAL PARALEGAL PITFALLS

- **Potential pitfall:** Not safeguarding books and records.
- **Possible fallout:** If you lose your financial information, be it paper or electronic, you will be unable to properly report to the CRA, the LSO, or the LFO. You may face fines or penalties for failing to report on time. You would waste valuable billing time spent recreating your financial information.
- **Proposed recommendation:** Store duplicate copies of paper documents offsite. If using an electronic bookkeeping system, make sure you backup your data regularly and store copies of electronic records offsite. Update computers and software when needed.

CHAPTER SUMMARY

The accounting cycle has been briefly described in this chapter. You have learned about the practical factors to consider in selecting a fiscal year. The concepts of debit and credit have been explained, and you should understand how to analyze transactions. You should be starting to understand the accounting equation and the rules of debit and credit.

Analyzing business transactions and entering them into a journal are only the first two steps in the accounting cycle, but getting them right at this stage will make completion of the other steps in the cycle much easier. The accuracy of entries in the general journal and other journals is the key to smooth sailing for completion of the other steps.

KEY TERMS

accounting cycle, 40

accounting period, 40

adjusted trial balance, 43

adjustments, 43

closing the books, 43

compound entry, 44

credit (Cr.), 48

DEAD CLIC, 47

debit (Dr.), 48

financial statements, 43

fiscal periods, 40

fiscal year, 40

general ledger, 42

journal entries, 42

normal credit balance, 44

normal debit balance, 44

post-closing trial balance, 41

Posting, 42

T-accounts, 43

trial balance, 42

worksheet, 43

FURTHER READING

Law Society of Ontario, *The Bookkeeping Guide for Paralegals* (Toronto: LSO, December 2015), online: <https://lawsocietyontario.azureedge.net/media/lso/media/legacy/pdf/p/paralegal_bookkeeping_guide_final-s.pdf>.

REVIEW QUESTIONS

True or False

_____ 1. Debit entries always cause an increase in an account. (LO3)

_____ 2. Adjustments made on a worksheet should be transferred directly to the appropriate financial statement. (LO2)

_____ 3. Credit entries are found on the right side of the accounting equation or T-account. (LO3)

_____ 4. The accounting period is established by the tax regulator (for example, the CRA). (LO1)

_____ 5. Accounting periods or fiscal periods may be calculated monthly, quarterly, or annually. (LO1)

_____ 6. The normal balance for expense accounts is a debit entry. (LO3)

_____ 7. The normal balance for asset accounts is a credit entry. (LO3)

_____ 8. Each transaction must have a minimum of one debit record entry and one credit record entry. (LO3)

Short Answer

1. What are the pros and the cons of electing a December 31 fiscal year-end? (LO1)

2. What does it mean to _close the books_? (LO2)

PRACTICE EXERCISES

Practice Exercise 3.1

In the following list of accounts, complete the table as follows:

a. Indicate the category of account: asset, liability, capital, withdrawal, income, or expense. **(LO3)**

b. Indicate the normal balance for that category of account. **(LO3)**

c. Indicate whether the balance in the account increases or decreases when an entry is made on the side indicated. **(LO4)**

	Account Name	Category	Normal Balance	Side	Increases/ Decreases
1	Accounting and Bookkeeping Expense	Expense	Debit	Dr.	Increases
2	Accounts Payable/General			Dr.	
3	Auto Expense			Cr.	
4	Credit Card Debt			Cr.	
5	Fees Earned			Cr.	
6	General Bank Account			Dr.	
7	Insurance—Prof. Liability			Dr.	
8	Interest Income			Cr.	
9	Office Furniture			Dr.	
10	Owner, Capital			Cr.	
11	Owner, Drawings			Cr.	
12	Photocopy Expense			Dr.	
13	Prepaid Insurance			Dr.	
14	Prepaid Rent			Cr.	
15	Salaries			Dr.	
16	Utilities			Cr.	
17	Vacation Accrual Payable			Cr.	
18	General Bank Account			Cr.	

Practice Exercise 3.2

Complete the T-account chart based on the opening balances provided for each account and the transactions listed. Calculate the ending balance for each account. Opening balances are shown in green. (LO3)

1	Withdrew $5,000 from legal practice for personal use.
2	Billed and received payment for legal services rendered, $2,300 (Client A).
3	Received payment for legal services rendered, $1,800 (Client B). This client was billed previously and an account receivable for the amount of the account had been recorded at that time.
4	Paid supplier for legal texts, $400.
5	Paid process server for filing court documents, $130.
6	Paid for Internet and business email services, $105.
7	Obtained business line of credit, $15,000.
8	Paid interest on bank loan, $85.

General Bank Account

Dr.	Cr.
8,000	

Accounts Receivable

Dr.	Cr.
3,000	

Liabilities

Dr.	Cr.
	2,000

Owner's Equity

Dr.	Cr.
	9,000

Professional Fees Earned

Dr.	Cr.

Expenses

Dr.	Cr.

Practice Exercise 3.3

Using the examples in the box below as a guide, show the increase and decrease that occurs for each of the transactions in the following T-accounts. Identify and insert the name of the account affected in each transaction and place the amount on the debit or credit side depending on whether the account is increasing or decreasing. **(LO3)**

Example of T-account form:

> Accounting Equation: Assets (left) = Liabilities + Owner's Equity (right)

Example balance sheet:

Assets (100)	
Debit	Credit
(+) Increase	(−) Decrease

Liabilities (200)	
Debit	Credit
(−) Decrease	(+) Increase

Owner's Equity (300)	
Debit	Credit
(−) Decrease	(+) Increase

Owner, Drawings (350)	
Debit	Credit
(+) Increase	(−) Decrease

Example income statement:

Income (400)	
Debit	Credit
(−) Decrease	(+) Increase

Expenses (500)	
Debit	Credit
(+) Increase	(−) Decrease

Transactions

a. A paralegal invests capital ($10,000) in a legal services firm.

Dr.	Cr.

Dr.	Cr.

b. A paralegal bills a client for fees ($8,000) on account.

Dr.	Cr.

Dr.	Cr.

c. A paralegal receives a cheque as payment from a client ($5,000) on an outstanding account for legal services.

Dr.	Cr.

Dr.	Cr.

d. A paralegal pays an invoice for professional liability insurance with cash ($1,100).

Dr.	Cr.

Dr.	Cr.

Practice Exercise 3.4

Using the examples in the box below as a guide, analyze each transaction that follows and record the appropriate entries in general journal format. (LO3, LO4)

Example: On October 1, Judy Roth wrote a cheque for $300 to Minitel in payment of the phone bill.

Which two accounts are affected?	
General Bank Account	Telephone Expense

To which category do the affected accounts belong?	
Assets	Expenses

Is the affected account balance increasing or decreasing?	
Decreasing	Increasing

Will the account be debited or credited?	
Credit	Debit

What amount will be debited or credited to each account?	
300	300

Record the journal entry for this transaction:

Date 20**		Description	Dr.	Cr.
Oct.	1	Telephone Expense	300	
		General Bank Account		300
		Payment of September telephone bill		

Transactions

a. On October 1, Judy Roth invested $2,000 in her firm.

b. On October 1, Judy Roth purchased computer equipment on account (that is, on credit) for $800.

c. On October 5, Judy Roth invoiced a client for professional fees of $2,500.

d. On October 10, Judy Roth received partial payment of $1,500 from a client for the invoice sent in transaction (c), above.

e. On October 15, Judy Roth paid $600 cash for office furniture.

Use a general journal format to illustrate the transactions in Practice Exercises 3.5 through 3.10.

Practice Exercise 3.5

Paying Office Expenses (LO3, LO4, LO6)

a. May 1: Ann Litigate wrote a general cheque #25 for $200 to pay her telephone bill.

b. May 1: Ann Litigate wrote a general cheque #26 for $25 to pay Staples for office supplies expense.

Practice Exercise 3.6

Compound Entries (LO3, LO4, LO6)

a. May 1: Ann Litigate purchased a computer for $1,000 from Computers R Us. She paid for the computer using a credit card and a general cheque. The cheque (#27) was written for $300 and she put $700 on the credit card.

b. May 1: Ann Litigate paid three months' rent with a general cheque #28 in the amount of $3,000 ($1,000 per month). Of that amount, $1,000 was rent expense for the current month and $2,000 was prepaid rent for the next two months' rent.

Practice Exercise 3.7

Recording and Paying Accounts Payable (LO3, LO4, LO6)

a. May 15: Ann Litigate purchased a photocopier on account (on credit) from Sharpie Copiers. The cost of the copier is $5,000 and payments are to be made at the rate of $300 per month until the amount is paid in full. Her first payment is due on June 15.

b. June 15: Ann Litigate made a payment to Sharpie Copiers against the amount owed to them for the copier in the amount of $300 (cheque #29).

Practice Exercise 3.8

Recording a Shift in Assets (LO3, LO4, LO6)

a. May 15: Ann Litigate purchased a fax machine from FaxMe and paid $150 with a general cheque #30.

Practice Exercise 3.9

Recording Invoices Sent to a Client and Recording Payment on Account by a Client (LO3, LO4, LO6)

a. May 1: Ann Litigate prepared invoice #10 for fees earned and mailed it to her client Barbara Short for $1,500.

b. May 30: Barbara Short sent a cheque for $1,000 to the firm in partial payment of invoice #10.

Practice Exercise 3.10

Recording Investment by Owner and Withdrawal by Owner (LO3, LO4, LO6)

a.   May 1: Ann Litigate deposited $10,000 of her personal funds as an investment in her firm.

b.   May 15: Ann Litigate withdrew $800 from the firm for her own personal living expenses (cheque #31).

Practice Exercise 3.11

Ann Litigate opened her paralegal service practice, Ann Litigate Paralegal Services, in January 20**. For each of the following transactions, analyze the transaction and prepare the appropriate general journal entry. (LO3, LO4, LO6)

January 1–31, 20**:

1   Made initial capital investment, $10,000

1   Paid professional liability insurance expense in full for the next 12 months with cash, $1,100

1   Law Society membership dues paid for one month with cash, $125

2   Paid monthly business insurance with cash, $50

3   Purchased office furniture with cash, $500

4   Paid for computer software by credit card, $250

5   Paid for cellphone bill by credit card, $75

5   Paid for telephone and Internet service by credit card, $145

10 Paid for court filing fee by credit card (for client R. Scott), $200

15 Invoiced client (L. Bailey, invoice #101) for initial consultation, $175

15 Paid biweekly salary for secretary with cash, $1,000

18 Paid installment payment for leased photocopier (equipment) with cash, $240

23 Invoiced client (R. Smythe, invoice #102) for provincial offences file, $300

25 Paid process server for service of court documents and court filing by credit card for client (R. Scott), $108

26 Purchased legal accounting publication, *Law Practice, Billing & Accounting*, by credit card, $100

27 Retained bookkeeper based on a one-year contract and paid in advance with cash, $2,000

30 Withdrew cash from the business for personal use, $800

30 Paid biweekly salary for secretary with cash, $1,000

30 Paid bank account charges with cash (direct bank payment), $35

Ann Litigate Paralegal Services General Journal				GJ1
Date 20**	Description	PR	Debit	Credit

Practice Exercise 3.12

a. Complete the T-accounts based on the transactions in Practice Exercise 3.11 and provide the balance for each balance sheet account. *Note: Each account starts with $0 opening balance for the purpose of this exercise.* (LO3, LO4)

T-Accounts (Assets)

General Bank Account (100)

Dr. (+)	Cr. (−)
0	
OPENING BALANCE	

Computer Software (160)

Dr. (+)	Cr. (−)
0	
OPENING BALANCE	

Prepaid Insurance (125)

Dr. (+)	Cr. (−)
0	
OPENING BALANCE	

T-Accounts (Liabilities)

Credit Card Debt (210)

Dr. (−)	Cr. (+)
	0
	OPENING BALANCE

Prepaid Expense (135)

Dr. (+)	Cr. (−)
0	
OPENING BALANCE	

T-Accounts (Owner's Equity)

Owner, Capital (300)

Dr. (−)	Cr. (+)
	0
	OPENING BALANCE

Accounts Receivable (120)

Dr. (+)	Cr. (−)
0	
OPENING BALANCE	

Owner, Drawings (301)

Dr. (+)	Cr. (−)
0	
OPENING BALANCE	

Office Furniture and Equipment (159)

Dr. (+)	Cr. (−)
0	
OPENING BALANCE	

b. Complete the T-accounts based on the transactions in Practice Exercise 3.11 and add up the totals for each income and expense account; then, as a final step, total all the income and expense accounts. (LO3, LO4)

T-Accounts (Income)

Fees Earned (400)

Dr. (−)	Cr. (+)

T-Accounts (Expenses)

Salaries Expense (511)

Dr. (+)	Cr. (−)

General Disbursement Expense (525)

Dr. (+)	Cr. (−)

Telephone (and Internet Service) Expense (565)

Dr. (+)	Cr. (−)

Library and Subscriptions (530)

Dr. (+)	Cr. (−)

Membership/Professional Dues (534)

Dr. (+)	Cr. (−)

Insurance/Other (528)

Dr. (+)	Cr. (−)

Equipment Lease (524)

Dr. (+)	Cr. (−)

Bank Charges (507)

Dr. (+)	Cr. (−)

Total Income and Expenses

TOTAL INCOME: $ _____   TOTAL EXPENSES: $ _____

PUT IT INTO PRACTICE

Case Example: Analysis of Transactions

Ann Litigate is updating her bookkeeping records in preparation for the monthly meeting with her accountant. She has the following transactions to enter in the general journal, but she is not sure how to analyze the transactions in order to complete the entries. Use the chart of accounts on the inside front cover of this textbook and provide your analysis of the transactions listed below:

1. Ann invoiced her client on January 1 ($3,000), but the account is now more than 40 days past due. What is the entry? What options are available to Ann?
2. Ann earned $1,200 for legal services rendered on another client file. She received a partial payment ($700) by cheque, but there is an outstanding balance of $500. What is the entry?

4 Posting and Trial Balance

General Ledger 74

Posting. 75

Preparing the Trial Balance 80

Chapter Summary 84

Key Terms 84

Further Reading. 84

Review Questions 85

Practice Exercises 85

Put It into Practice. 97

After reading this chapter, you should be able to:

LO1 Post transactions from the general journal to the general ledger.

LO2 Prepare a trial balance.

In Chapter 3, we recorded the opening balance in a general journal, and we recorded transactions for the month of October in the general journal. The next step in the accounting cycle is to post these entries to a general ledger.

General Ledger

The general ledger provides a summary of the information contained in the general journal. The information from the general journal is summarized by posting or transferring the information to the accounts in the general ledger. Without a summary, the firm cannot know what its bank balance is or how much money has been spent to date in any particular account. The summary is also required for preparation of financial statements.

The general ledger contains a chart or table for each of the accounts listed on the company's chart of accounts, along with the account number. The example in Figure 4.1 shows the format for a simple general ledger. The name of the account is General Bank Account; the account number is 100. The **post reference (PR)** column is used to indicate the page number of the general journal where the original transaction was recorded. This makes it easy to cross-reference and identify journal entries.

The columns in the ledger table include a column for the year and date, an explanation, the post reference, a column for debits, a column for credits, and a column for the ending balance. The column to the left of the balance column is headed "Dr./Cr." This column is used to indicate whether the running balance is a debit balance or a credit balance. It does not refer to the entry made on that line, but to the running balance of the account. The running total will need to be calculated after making each entry in the general ledger accounts.

A general bank account is an asset and usually has a "Dr." balance, unless the account is overdrawn (or "in the red"). If the balance in the bank is negative, indicate "Cr." in the Dr./Cr. column. The ledger accounts are grouped by category in the same order as they appear in the chart of accounts: assets, liabilities, owner's equity, income, and expenses.

General Bank Account						Account No. 100	
Date 20**		Explanation	PR	Debit	Credit	Dr./Cr.	Balance

FIGURE 4.1   Sample general ledger account

LO1 Posting

Each entry in the general journal (see Figure 4.2) must be copied to the individual general ledger accounts. Each debit and credit entry must be posted in the same order as it appears in the general journal. *Posting* is recording the debits and credits for each transaction from the general journal into the general ledger.

EXAMPLE

Justin Case, Paralegal General Journal					GJ1
Date 20**		Description	PR	Debit	Credit
Oct.	1	General Bank Account	6100	5,000	
		Computer Equipment (Hardware)	6155	900	
		Office Furniture and Equipment	6158	150	
		Personal Loan	6205		4,000
		Credit Card Debt	6210		500
		Justin Case, Capital	6300		1,550
		To record account balances from opening balance sheet			
		Totals		6,050	6,050

FIGURE 4.2   General journal entry to record opening account balances

To post the general journal entry dated October 1 (Figure 4.2) to the general ledger, the following steps should be taken (the numbered steps are shown in superscript in Figure 4.2 and in the following posting entries):

STEP 1

In the general ledger, find the account called General Bank Account (Figure 4.3). Enter the amount of $5,000 in the debit column. Because the $5,000 is debited in the general journal, it must be shown as a debit in the general ledger.

STEP 2

Enter "GJ1" in the PR column of the ledger. This tells anyone looking at the books that the debit came from page 1 of the general journal.

STEP 3

Enter the transaction date in the date column of the ledger as shown in the general journal.

STEP 4

Calculate the running balance.

STEP 5

Indicate whether the balance is a debit or a credit balance in the Dr./Cr. column.

STEP 6

Put the number of the account to which the entry was posted in the "PR" column of the general journal (Figure 4.2). Post referencing indicates which transactions have or have not been posted from the general journal to the general ledger, and also indicates the account to which the entry has been posted.

Repeat steps 1 to 6 to post the second line of the general journal entry (the credit side) to the Computer Equipment (Hardware) account in the general ledger (Figure 4.3).

The process provides a trail to show the ledger account to which an entry in the general journal was posted, and also shows where the number in the ledger came from. This process continues until each transaction is entered in the correct general ledger and the amounts in the general ledger are totalled to summarize the transactions.

An explanation is usually provided for opening entries, adjustments, or closing entries. Note that otherwise, no explanation is required in the general ledger. This is because the explanation is in the general journal. If anyone needs to know what the $1,000 posted on October 1 was for, he or she can refer back to page 1 of the general journal (GJ1), where the explanation is found. However, an explanation may be added if the bookkeeper wishes to provide extra details about an entry.

Once all the journal entries for the opening account balances have been posted, the general ledger accounts for Justin Case's firm will appear as in Figure 4.3.

General Ledgers — Justin Case							

General Bank Account						Acct. No. [6]100	
Date 20**		Explanation	PR	Debit	Credit	Dr./Cr.	Balance
[3]Oct.	1	Opening Entry	[2]GJ1	[1]5,000		[5]Dr.	[4]5,000

Computer Equipment (Hardware)						Acct. No. [6]155	
Date 20**		Explanation	PR	Debit	Credit	Dr./Cr.	Balance
[3]Oct.	1	Opening Entry	[2]GJ1	[1]900		[5]Dr.	[4]900

Office Furniture and Equipment						Acct. No. [6]158	
Date 20**		Explanation	PR	Debit	Credit	Dr./Cr.	Balance
[3]Oct.	1	Opening Entry	[2]GJ1	[1]150		[5]Dr.	[4]150

Personal Loan						Acct. No. [6]205	
Date 20**		Explanation	PR	Debit	Credit	Dr./Cr.	Balance
[3]Oct.	1	Opening Entry	[2]GJ1		[1]4,000	[5]Cr.	[4]4,000

Credit Card Debt						Acct. No. [6]210	
Date 20**		Explanation	PR	Debit	Credit	Dr./Cr.	Balance
[3]Oct.	1	Opening Entry	[2]GJ1		[1]500	[5]Cr.	[4]500

Justin Case, Capital						Acct. No. [6]300	
Date 20**		Explanation	PR	Debit	Credit	Dr./Cr.	Balance
[3]Oct.	1		[2]GJ1		[1]1,550	[5]Cr.	[4]1,550

FIGURE 4.3   Posting opening entries to the general ledger accounts

Assume that the journal entries for the rest of October extend to the next page in the general journal (GJ2). Once all the journal entries for the remainder of October have been posted, the general journal for Justin Case's firm will appear as in Figure 4.4.

Justin Case, General Journal					GJ1
Date 20**		Description	PR	Debit	Credit
Oct.	1	Opening Entries			
		General Bank Account	100	1,000	
		Justin Case, Capital	300		1,000
		To record funds invested by owner			
	1	General Bank Account	100	4,000	
		Personal Loan	205		4,000
		To record loan from father, James Case			
	1	Computer Equipment, Hardware	155	900	
		Justin Case, Capital	300		900
		To record computer equipment invested by owner at fair market value			
	1	Office Furniture and Equipment	158	150	
		Justin Case, Capital	300		150
		To record office furniture invested by owner at fair market value			
		Totals		6,050	6,050

Justin Case, General Journal					GJ2
Date 20**		*Description*	PR	Debit	Credit
Oct.	5	Telephone Expense	565	300	
		General Bank Account (Cash)	100		300
		To record telephone expense for Oct.			
	5	Office Furniture and Equipment	158	2,000	
		General Bank Account (Cash)	100		500
		Credit Card Debt	210		1,500
		To record furniture purchased from IKEA			
	8	General Bank Account	100	500	
		Justin Case, Capital	300		500
		To record investment of scholarship			
	10	Office Supplies/General Expense	535	580	
		Accounts Payable/General Liabilities	200		580
		To record purchase from Legal Supplies Inc.			
	15	Office Furniture and Equipment	158	100	
		General Bank Account	100		100
		Purchased filing cabinet from Office Equipment Inc.			
	20	General Bank Account	100	3,000	
		Fees Earned	400		3,000
		To record fees billed to Sabourin and paid			
	30	Rent Expense	538	500	
		General Bank Account	100		500
		To record rent paid for one month			
		Totals		6,980	6,980

FIGURE 4.4   General journal entries for October transactions

After Justin Case has posted all the entries made to date on pages GJ1 and GJ2, the general ledger will have the balances shown in Figure 4.5. Note that the accounts that do not have any entries are omitted at this time. The general ledger accounts will be added as required as we complete the posting.

General Ledgers — Justin Case							

General Bank Account						**Acct. No. 100**	
Date 20**		Explanation	PR	Debit	Credit	Dr./Cr.	Balance
Oct.	1		GJ1	5,000		Dr.	5,000
	5		GJ2		300	Dr.	4,700
	5		GJ2		500	Dr.	4,200
	8		GJ2	500		Dr.	4,700
	15		GJ2		100	Dr.	4,600
	20		GJ2	3,000		Dr.	7,600
	30		GJ2		500	Dr.	7,100

Computer Equipment (Hardware)						**Acct. No. 155**	
Date 20**		Explanation	PR	Debit	Credit	Dr./Cr.	Balance
Oct.	1	Opening Balance	GJ1	900		Dr.	900

Office Furniture and Equipment						**Acct. No. 158**	
Date 20**		Explanation	PR	Debit	Credit	Dr./Cr.	Balance
Oct.	1	Opening Balance	GJ1	150		Dr.	150
	5		GJ2	2,000		Dr.	2,150
	15		GJ2	100		Dr.	2,250

Accounts Payable/General Liabilities						**Acct. No. 200**	
Date 20**		Explanation	PR	Debit	Credit	Dr./Cr.	Balance
Oct.	10	Legal Supplies Inc.	GJ2		580	Cr.	580

Personal Loan						**Acct. No. 205**	
Date 20**		Explanation	PR	Debit	Credit	Dr./Cr.	Balance
Oct.	1	Opening Balance—James Case	GJ1		4,000	Cr.	4,000

Credit Card Debt						**Acct. No. 210**	
Date 20**		Explanation	PR	Debit	Credit	Dr./Cr.	Balance
Oct.	1	Opening Balance	GJ1		500	Cr.	500
	5		GJ2		1,500	Cr.	2,000

Justin Case, Capital | | | | | | | **Acct. No. 300**

Date 20**		Explanation	PR	Debit	Credit	Dr./Cr.	Balance
Oct.	1	Opening Balance	GJ1		1,550	Cr.	1,550
	8		GJ2		500	Cr.	2,050

Fees Earned | | | | | | | **Acct. No. 400**

Date 20**		Explanation	PR	Debit	Credit	Dr./Cr.	Balance
Oct.	20		GJ2		3,000	Cr.	3,000

Office Supplies/General Expense | | | | | | | **Acct. No. 535**

Date 20**		Explanation	PR	Debit	Credit	Dr./Cr.	Balance
Oct.	10		GJ2	580		Dr.	580

Rent Expense | | | | | | | **Acct. No. 538**

Date 20**		Explanation	PR	Debit	Credit	Dr./Cr.	Balance
Oct.	30		GJ2	500		Dr.	500

Telephone Expense | | | | | | | **Acct. No. 565**

Date 20**		Explanation	PR	Debit	Credit	Dr./Cr.	Balance
Oct.	5		GJ2	300		Dr.	300

FIGURE 4.5   General ledger accounts after October posting completed

LO2 Preparing the Trial Balance

A trial balance lists all the accounts in the general ledger with the debit or credit balance shown for each account (see Figure 4.6). The trial balance is not a financial statement, but the information in it is used to prepare financial statements. List the accounts in the trial balance in the same order as they appear in the general ledger. The ending balance from each of the ledger accounts must be entered in the appropriate debit or credit column. At the end, the total is calculated for each column, and the total debits must equal the total credits. Draw a single line above the totals and a double line below the totals.

The heading of the trial balance contains three lines: who, what, and when. The first line identifies the firm (who), the second line names the statement (what), and the third line shows the date of the statement or the period it covers (when).

The trial balance is important because it proves that the entries were properly balanced in the general journal, that they were properly posted to the general ledger, and that the balances in the general ledger were correctly calculated.

#	Account	Debit	Credit
	**Justin Case, Paralegal** **Trial Balance** **October 31, 20****		
100	General Bank Account	$7,100	
155	Computer Equipment (Hardware)	900	
158	Office Furniture and Equipment	2,250	
200	Accounts Payable/General Liabilities		$580
205	Personal Loan		4,000
210	Credit Card Debt		1,500
300	Justin Case, Capital		2,550
400	Fees Earned		3,000
535	Office Supplies/General Expense	580	
538	Rent Expense	500	
565	Telephone Expense	300	
		$11,630	$11,630

FIGURE 4.6   Trial balance

If the totals in the trial balance are not equal, it is likely that one or more errors were made. These must be found before proceeding further.

Finding Errors in the Trial Balance

To find any errors, follow these steps and work backwards from the last step that was completed:

1. *Calculation error:* Check the calculation of the totals in the trial balance. Subtract total debits from total credits to see what the difference is, then notice if that amount is recognizable from a journal entry or general ledger that may have been incorrectly posted or accidentally omitted.
2. *Copying error:* Check to ensure that the amounts in the general ledger were copied correctly to the trial balance.
3. *Calculation error:* Check the arithmetic to ensure that an error was not made in calculating one or more balances in the ledger accounts.
4. *Wrong column:* Check to see if a credit amount was entered into the debit column in the ledger account while posting from the general journal.
5. *Wrong column:* Check to see if a debit amount was entered into the credit column in the ledger account while posting from the general journal.

Some errors can still exist even if the debit and credit totals in the trial balance are equal:

- Amounts posted to the wrong ledger account.
- Leaving out an entire transaction when posting from the general journal to the general ledgers.
- Compensating errors (an error on the debit side that offsets an error of equal value on the credit side).

Common Mistakes

Trying to find mistakes in the trial balance can be frustrating, so here are a few tricks:

1. There is probably a *mathematical error* if the difference between the total debits and credits is off by 10, 100, 1,000, and so on.

2. There is probably an *omission error* if the difference is equal to the balance in one of the general ledger accounts. The amount may accidentally have been omitted. It is also possible that the number was not posted from the general journal.

3. There is probably a *posting error* if you can divide the difference in debits and credits by two. Check to see if a debit was entered on the credit side by mistake, or vice versa, in the ledger or in the trial balance. For example, a difference of $60 divided by two is $30. This means that $30 was debited to an account instead of correctly entering the amount as a credit, or vice versa.

4. There is probably a *transposition error* if the difference is divisible by nine. A **transposition** is the accidental reversal of digits—for example, entering $91 instead of $19 or $5,520 instead of $5,250. When the numbers are subtracted from each other and the difference is divided by nine, the result will be an even number. For example, $5,520 – $5,250 is $270. When $270 is divided by nine, the result is an even $30, which indicates a possible transposition error.

5. There is possibly a *slide error*. A **slide** is an error resulting from incorrect placement of the decimal point in writing numbers. For example, $5,250 may have been entered as $52.50.

6. There may be a *copying error*. Compare the balances in the trial balance with the ledger accounts to check for copying errors.

7. There may be a *calculation error*. Recalculate the balances in each ledger account.

8. There may be a *posting error*. Trace all postings from the journal to the ledger.

If the error cannot be found after having completed all these steps, take a break. Next time you look at the numbers with fresh eyes, the error will probably jump out at you.

POTENTIAL PARALEGAL PITFALLS

- **Potential pitfall:** Confusing the general ledger charts columns. Each account has a separate general ledger to track the running total. The columns highlighted in **blue** below (the "Debit" and "Credit" columns) are like a mini T-account. This is where the debit or credit from that particular journal entry is recorded. The **yellow** columns on the right (the "Dr./Cr." and "Balance" columns) are the running total of that account, to be kept up to date after each transaction line is posted. The Dr./Cr. column indicates the sign of the ending account balance. For instance, if the General Bank has a balance of $12,500 and $2,000 is spent, then the $2,000 is credited in the **blue** column. The **yellow** column shows that the ending balance in General Bank is $10,500 and the Dr. associated with the ending balance represents positive cash remaining. If the column indicated Cr., then that would mean there is a negative cash balance.

General Bank Account						Acct. No. 100	
Date 20**		Explanation	PR	Debit	Credit	Dr./Cr.	Balance
Mar	1	Opening balance		12,500		Dr.	12,500
	3				2,000	Dr.	10,500

- **Possible fallout:** Incorrect ending balances in the general ledger leads to an imbalanced trial balance and incorrect financial statements.
- **Proposed recommendation:** Be sure to understand the two right-hand columns on the general ledger and double check the balances for whether or not the ending balance makes sense.

Trial Balance

Once opening balances and transactions for the month of October are entered in PCLaw®, the trial balance is produced using the GL Statements function, as shown in Figure 4.7.

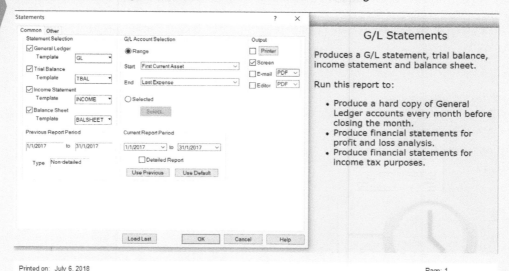

G/L Statements

Produces a G/L statement, trial balance, income statement and balance sheet.

Run this report to:

- Produce a hard copy of General Ledger accounts every month before closing the month.
- Produce financial statements for profit and loss analysis.
- Produce financial statements for income tax purposes.

Printed on: July 6, 2018   Page: 1

Justin Case, Paralegal
Trial Balance
For Period Ending: October 31, 2017

Nickname	Account Name	Debits	Credits
1000	Gen Bank Acct 1	7,100.00	
1155	Computer Equipment (Hardware)	900.00	
1158	Office Furniture and Equipment	2,250.00	
2000	General Liabilities		580.00
2205	Personal Loan		4,000.00
2206	Credit Card Debt		2,000.00
3000	Justin Case, Equity		2,050.00
4000.jc	Fees-Justin Case		3,000.00
5350	Office/Gen. Expense	580.00	
5380	Rent	500.00	
5540	Telephone Expense	300.00	
	Totals	**$11,630.00**	**$11,630.00**
	Overall balance		**$0.00**

FIGURE 4.7   In PCLaw®, the trial balance is produced using the GL Statements function

CHAPTER SUMMARY

The accounting cycle starts with an analysis of transactions, which are then recorded in a general journal. Once the entries have been added to the journal, they must be summarized; this is accomplished by posting the entries to general ledger accounts and calculating the balance for each general ledger account. The balances in the general ledger are then entered in a trial balance to ensure that the debits are equal to the credits.

KEY TERMS

post reference (PR), 74
slide, 82

transposition, 82

FURTHER READING

Law Society of Ontario, *The Bookkeeping Guide for Paralegals* (Toronto: LSO, February 2014), online: <https://lawsocietyontario.azureedge.net/media/lso/media/legacy/pdf/p/paralegal_bookkeeping_guide_final-s.pdf>. (See especially item 7, Clients' General Ledger.)

In re Nortel Networks Corp Securities Litigation, Master File No 04 Civ 2115 (LAP) (10 September 2004 and 16 September 2005).

Nortel Networks Corporation (Re), 55 CBR (5th) 229, 2009 CanLII 39492 (Ont Sup Ct J).

Ontario Public Service Employees Union Pension Trust Fund v Clark, 77 OR (3rd) 38, 2005 CanLII 51027 (Ont Sup Ct J).

Re Nortel Networks Corporation (2006), 29 OSC Bull 8608.

REVIEW QUESTIONS

Short Answer

1. What does it mean to "post" to the general ledger? (LO1)

2. When receiving a payment in cash, does this increase or decrease the general bank account? How do you record an increase in this account? How do you record a decrease? (LO1)

3. How do you characterize or recognize a payment to the owner of the law firm (for example, Justin Case) for his services? (LO2)

4. What is meant by the opening balance on the ledger? What is meant by the closing balance on the ledger? (LO1)

5. What information gets recorded on the trial balance? (LO2)

6. How do you find and correct errors on the trial balance? (LO2)

7. What are the steps involved in entering transactions in the general journal? (LO1)

(Note: Journal entries are written in chronological order, not according to category; debits are always written first in the account list when writing journal entries; no balancing or tallying is done.)

PRACTICE EXERCISES

Worksheets containing the forms you need to complete the practice exercises are provided separately in the working papers for this chapter.

Practice Exercise 4.1

Using the worksheets provided:

a. Prepare general journal entries for the following transactions for June Lang that occurred during September 20**. (LO1)

b. Post your entries to the general ledgers. (LO1)

The accounts for June Lang's firm are the following:

100	General Bank Account	200	Accounts Payable/General Liabilities
120	Accounts Receivable	300	June Lang, Capital
130	Office Supplies	350	June Lang, Drawings
140	Motor Vehicle	400	Fees Earned
158	Office Furniture and Equipment	538	Rent Expense

Transactions:

Sep.	3	June Lang invested $20,000 cash and office equipment worth $2,000 in her business
	6	Purchased a motor vehicle on account for $15,000. She paid $1,000 by cheque and the balance on credit
	13	Bought office supplies for $1,000
	15	Withdrew $500 from the business for personal use
	20	Invoiced Fred Popper $2,000 for services rendered. Account remains outstanding
	30	Paid rent expense to Minto Developments, $650

Worksheets:

June Lang, General Journal					GJ4
Date 20**	Description	PR	Debit	Credit	

General Ledgers — June Lang

General Bank Account						Account No. 100
Date 20**	Explanation	PR	Debit	Credit	Dr./Cr.	Balance

Accounts Receivable — Account No. 120

Date 20**		Explanation	PR	Debit	Credit	Dr./Cr.	Balance

Office Supplies — Account No. 130

Date 20**		Explanation	PR	Debit	Credit	Dr./Cr.	Balance

Motor Vehicle — Account No. 140

Date 20**		Explanation	PR	Debit	Credit	Dr./Cr.	Balance

Office Furniture and Equipment — Account No. 158

Date 20**		Explanation	PR	Debit	Credit	Dr./Cr.	Balance

Accounts Payable/General Liabilities — Account No. 200

Date 20**		Explanation	PR	Debit	Credit	Dr./Cr.	Balance

June Lang, Capital — Account No. 300

Date 20**		Explanation	PR	Debit	Credit	Dr./Cr.	Balance

June Lang, Capital Account No. 300

Date 20**	Explanation	PR	Debit	Credit	Dr./Cr.	Balance

June Lang, Drawings Account No. 350

Date 20**	Explanation	PR	Debit	Credit	Dr./Cr.	Balance

Fees Earned Account No. 400

Date 20**	Explanation	PR	Debit	Credit	Dr./Cr.	Balance

Rent Expense Account No. 538

Date 20**	Explanation	PR	Debit	Credit	Dr./Cr.	Balance

Practice Exercise 4.2

PRACTICE EXCEL

Using the worksheets provided, post the general journal entries for the following transactions for Frank Piper that occurred during June 20** to the general ledgers. (LO1)

The partial ledger of Frank Piper uses the following accounts:

100	General Bank Account (Cash)	200	Accounts Payable/General Liabilities
158	Office Furniture and Equipment	300	Frank Piper, Capital

Frank Piper, Paralegal General Journal					GJ5
Date 20**		Description	PR	Debit	Credit
		Opening Entries			
June	1	General Bank Account (Cash)		10,000	
		Frank Piper, Capital			10,000
		To record funds invested by owner			
	1	Office Furniture and Equipment		1,000	
		Accounts Payable/General Liabilities			1,000
		Purchased photocopier from Sharp			

General Ledgers — Frank Piper

General Bank Account (Cash)					Account No. 100	
Date 20**	Explanation	PR	Debit	Credit	Dr./Cr.	Balance

Office Furniture and Equipment					Account No. 158	
Date 20**	Explanation	PR	Debit	Credit	Dr./Cr.	Balance

Accounts Payable/General Liabilities					Account No. 200	
Date 20**	Explanation	PR	Debit	Credit	Dr./Cr.	Balance

Frank Piper, Capital						Account No. 300	
Date 20**		Explanation	PR	Debit	Credit	Dr./Cr.	Balance

Practice Exercise 4.3

PRACTICE EXCEL

a. Answer the following questions:

    i. Calculate the running balance for the following general ledger account. Indicate whether the balance column has a debit or credit balance. **(LO1)**

    ii. Was the account overdrawn at any point? **(LO1)**

    iii. What does the post reference refer to? **(LO1)**

General Bank Account						Account No. 100	
Date 20**		Explanation	PR	Debit	Credit	Dr./Cr.	Balance
Oct.	1		GJ1	1,000			
	1		GJ1	700			
	5		GJ2		2,000		
	5		GJ2	100			
	6		GJ2	400			
	8		GJ2		100		

b. Calculate the running balance for the following general ledger account. Indicate whether the balance column has a debit or credit balance.

Rent Expense						Account No. 538	
Date 20**		Explanation	PR	Debit	Credit	Dr./Cr.	Balance
Oct.	1		GJ2	1,000			
Nov.	1		GJ2	1,000			
	5		GJ2		30		
Dec.	1		GJ2	900			

c. Calculate the running balance for the following general ledger account. Indicate whether the balance column has a debit or credit balance.

Accounts Payable/General Liabilities						Account No. 200	
Date 20**		Explanation	PR	Debit	Credit	Dr./Cr.	Balance
Oct.	1		GJ2		5,000		
Nov.	1		GJ2	300			
	5		GJ2		200		
Dec.	1		GJ2	1,000			
	15		GJ2	800			

Practice Exercise 4.4

Comprehensive Problem

The following are transactions for Ann Litigate Paralegal Services that occurred in the month of May:

#	Date 20**	Transaction	Amount
1	May 1	Ann received a cheque from her client, Alan Smith, for legal services provided in a criminal law matter	4,000
2	May 1	Ann took a draw against the firm's equity for her personal use	1,500
3	May 1	Ann paid one month's office rent	1,200
4	May 5	Ann paid for filing fees to the Landlord and Tenant Board on behalf of her client, Ellen Page, with her business credit card	145
5	May 10	Ann paid her telephone and Internet bill	120
6	May 11	Ann purchased accounting software to help manage her bookkeeping	600
7	May 15	Ann paid salary to her assistant	1,000
8	May 15	Ann paid interest expense on her bank line of credit account	90
9	May 18	Ann purchased office supplies on account (on credit with Legal Stationers Inc.) to replenish her office supplies	250
10	May 25	Ann purchased new office furniture (filing cabinet)	600
11	May 30	Ann paid bank fees and charges for the month of May	30
12	May 30	Ann paid her credit card bill	100
13	May 30	Ann paid for one month of dues to the Law Society	267

Using the chart of accounts found on the inside front cover of this textbook and the worksheets provided:

a. Prepare general journal entries for the transactions.

b. Post (transfer) the general journal entries to the general ledger accounts. (LO1)

c. Prepare a trial balance. (LO2)

The following balances have already been recorded for you in the general ledger for the end of April as the opening balance on May 1:

	Ann Litigate, Paralegal Trial Balance April 30, 20**		
#	Account	Debit	Credit
100	General Bank Account	$3,000	
120	Accounts Receivable	635	
130	Office Supplies	800	
158	Office Furniture and Equipment	5,000	
160	Intangible Assets (Computer Software)	1,865	
200	Accounts Payable/General Liabilities		$800
210	Credit Card Debt		1,500
250	Bank Line of Credit		5,000
300	Ann Litigate, Capital		5,500
350	Ann Litigate, Drawings	1,500	
		$12,800	$12,800

Worksheet a:

Ann Litigate, General Journal					GJ4
Date 20**	Description	PR	Debit	Credit	

Worksheet b:

General Ledgers — Ann Litigate

General Bank Account   Account No. 100

Date 20**		Explanation	PR	Debit	Credit	Dr./Cr.	Balance
May	1	Opening balance	✓	3,000		Dr.	3,000

Accounts Receivable   Account No. 120

Date 20**		Explanation	PR	Debit	Credit	Dr./Cr.	Balance
May	1	Opening balance	✓	635		Dr.	635

Office Supplies   Account No. 130

Date 20**		Explanation	PR	Debit	Credit	Dr./Cr.	Balance
May	1	Opening balance	✓	800		Dr.	800

Office Furniture and Equipment   Account No. 158

Date 20**		Explanation	PR	Debit	Credit	Dr./Cr.	Balance
May	1	Opening balance	✓	5,000		Dr.	5,000

Intangible Assets (Computer Software)   Account No. 160

Date 20**		Explanation	PR	Debit	Credit	Dr./Cr.	Balance
May	1	Opening balance	✓	1,865		Dr.	1,865

Accounts Payable/General Liabilities   Account No. 200

Date 20**		Explanation	PR	Debit	Credit	Dr./Cr.	Balance
May	1	Opening balance	✓		800	Cr.	800

Credit Card Debt   Account No. 210

Date 20**		Explanation	PR	Debit	Credit	Dr./Cr.	Balance
May	1	Opening balance	✓		1,500	Cr.	1,500

Bank Line of Credit   Account No. 250

Date 20**		Explanation	PR	Debit	Credit	Dr./Cr.	Balance
May	1	Opening balance	✓		5,000	Cr.	5,000

Ann Litigate, Capital   Account No. 300

Date 20**		Explanation	PR	Debit	Credit	Dr./Cr.	Balance
May	1	Opening balance	✓		5,500	Cr.	5,500

Ann Litigate, Drawings   Account No. 350

Date 20**		Explanation	PR	Debit	Credit	Dr./Cr.	Balance
May	1	Opening balance	GJ4	1,500		Dr.	1,500

Fees Earned   Account No. 400

Date 20**		Explanation	PR	Debit	Credit	Dr./Cr.	Balance

Bank Charges and Credit Card Expense						Account No. 507	
Date 20**	Explanation	PR	Debit	Credit	Dr./Cr.	Balance	

Salaries Expense						Account No. 511	
Date 20**	Explanation	PR	Debit	Credit	Dr./Cr.	Balance	

General Disbursement Expense						Account No. 525	
Date 20**	Explanation	PR	Debit	Credit	Dr./Cr.	Balance	

Interest Expense						Account No. 529	
Date 20**	Explanation	PR	Debit	Credit	Dr./Cr.	Balance	

Membership/Professional Dues						Account No. 534	
Date 20**	Explanation	PR	Debit	Credit	Dr./Cr.	Balance	

Rent Expense						Account No. 538	
Date 20**	Explanation	PR	Debit	Credit	Dr./Cr.	Balance	

Telephone Expense						Account No. 565	
Date 20**		Explanation	PR	Debit	Credit	Dr./Cr.	Balance

Worksheet c:

	Ann Litigate, Paralegal Trial Balance May 31, 20**		
#	Account	Debit	Credit
	Total		

PUT IT INTO PRACTICE

Case Example: Accounting Standards

Nortel Networks

The *Nortel Networks* case is an infamous and well-documented example of the lack of oversight and compliance with accounting standards in the corporate context.

Since as early as 2001, various class-action proceedings and other lawsuits were commenced against Nortel Networks Corporation, a telecommunications company, and its directors and officers for discrepancies in the company's financial reporting. The affected stakeholders were internal, external, and international in nature. For example, the government securities regulators in Canada and the United States brought charges against the company; current and former employees joined in a class action to protect themselves from losses on their pension plans as well as employment interruptions as a result of Nortel's financial losses; and shareholders and investors were defrauded and misinformed about the company's financial health. In 2009, Nortel filed for bankruptcy protection under the *Companies' Creditors Arrangement Act* (CCAA) in Ontario. Appeals and motions against the company are still before the courts, and the fallout from Nortel's decisions since 2000 continues.

Some of the charges laid against the company include these from the class-action suit[1] brought by David Lucescu, individually, and on behalf of other shareholders against Nortel:

- Statements made by the company about its financial position were materially false and misleading (para 28).
- The financial results made by the company were materially overstated (para 28).
- "The [defendants] lacked a reasonable basis for their positive statements about the Company, its business, operations, earning and prospects" (para 28).
- The defendants "materially misled the investing public, thereby inflating the price of Nortel common stock, by publicly issuing false and misleading statements and omitting to disclose material facts necessary to make Defendant's statements, as set forth herein, not false and misleading. Said statements and omissions were materially false and misleading in that they failed to disclose material adverse information and misrepresented the truth about the Company, its business and operations, as alleged herein" (para 36).

See the Further Reading section for this case and related cases.

Use the table below to identify and discuss the accounting standards and generally accepted accounting principles that Nortel violated based on the charges identified in the class action against Nortel Networks.

---

1   See <http://securities.stanford.edu/filings-documents/1043/NTL09_01/2009518_f01c_0904691.pdf>.

	Action taken by/charge laid against Nortel	Accounting principle/standard violated
1.	The company made materially false and misleading statements about its financial position	• Reliability • Going concern • Relevance principle
2.	The financial results were materially overstated	
3.	There was no reasonable basis for the company's positive outlook	
4.	The company materially misled the investing public	
5.	The company's stock value was overinflated	
6.	The company failed to disclose adverse material facts	
7.	The company misrepresented the truth about the company, its business, and its operations	

Case Example: Accounting Application

1. When Ann Litigate calculates her company's trial balance, she recognizes that there was an error in the recording of a retainer received from Sam Fisher. The trial balance is understated and out by $200. How can Ann check and correct this error?

2. On April 5, a new client, Sheila McKay, advised that she would like to retain Ann to commence a small claims proceeding against her neighbour, who borrowed $10,000 but has failed to pay her back as agreed and as evidenced by a promissory note. Ann prepared the claim for Sheila and served and filed the plaintiff's claim form at the Small Claims Court (Superior Court of Justice). On June 1, 20**, Ann invoiced Sheila for the services rendered from April 5 to May 30, 20** (invoice #101) as well as for the related disbursements. The total fee charged was equal to $1,500; the total disbursements (paid by and reimbursable to Ann) were equal to $200, which included the filing fee, the process server costs, and miscellaneous photocopy/printing costs. Harmonized sales tax (HST; 13 percent) is chargeable on both fees and disbursements. Calculate the total amount of the invoice that would be sent to the client including fees, disbursements, and HST.

5 Preparing Financial Statements

Preparing the Income Statement 100

Preparing the Statement of Owner's Equity. 105

Preparing the Balance Sheet 106

Chapter Summary 110

Key Terms 110

Further Reading. 110

Review Questions 111

Practice Exercises 111

LEARNING OUTCOMES

After reading this chapter, you should be able to:

LO1 Prepare and interpret the income statement.

LO2 Prepare and interpret the statement of owner's equity.

LO3 Prepare and interpret the balance sheet.

LO4 Use PCLaw® to prepare the trial balance and financial statements.

In Chapter 4, we posted journal entries to a general ledger and prepared the trial balance. The next step in the accounting cycle is to prepare the financial statements.

The trial balance (see Figure 5.1) is used to prepare *financial statements*—first the income statement, then the statement of owner's equity, and finally the balance sheet.

It is important to prepare the financial statements in the correct order. The net income or loss from the income statement is used to calculate the statement of owner's equity. Once you know the balance of the owner's equity, you are able to record that information on the balance sheet, so it is imperative that the statements be completed in that order. All the information required for each of the statements is found in the trial balance.

The financial statements do not have debit or credit columns. The left column in the income statement (Figure 5.2) and in the statement of owner's equity (Figure 5.3) is used to calculate subtotals, which are then placed in the column to the right. The balance sheet (Figure 5.4) is displayed with assets on the left-hand side and liabilities and owner's equity on the right-hand side. Additional columns can be placed on either side to add up asset or liability subtotals, if necessary.

LO1 Preparing the Income Statement

The first statement prepared is the **income statement**, which shows the revenues and expenses for a particular accounting period and is sometimes called the *profit and loss statement*. The heading includes the name of the business (who), the name of the statement (what), and the period covered by the report (when).

The income statement must be prepared at the end of each fiscal year, but is usually prepared more frequently, typically each month, to inform the owner of the profit or loss for the period. This information is often required by the firm's bank and investors.

Income statements show the income earned less expenses incurred over a period of time to determine whether the firm has made a profit or a loss. If the firm's total income is higher than the total expenses, the firm has made a profit. If the firm's expenses are higher than total income, the firm has suffered a loss. The profit or loss for the period affects the owner's capital account because losses are deducted from the capital account and profits are added to the capital account. The amount of profit or loss calculated on the income statement is needed in order to prepare the second statement—the statement of owner's equity.

The simple form of the income statement is sufficient for the purposes of a paralegal firm. It will show the revenues earned less the expenses incurred for the period to arrive at a net profit or net loss.

\#	Account	Debit	Credit
\multicolumn{4}{c}{**Justin Case, Paralegal**}
100	General Bank Account	$7,100	
155	Computer Equipment (Hardware)	900	
158	Office Furniture and Equipment	2,250	
200	Accounts Payable/General Liabilities		$580
205	Personal Loan		4,000
210	Credit Card Debt		2,000
300	Justin Case, Capital		2,050
301	Justin Case, Drawings		0
400	Fees Earned		3,000
535	Office Supplies/General Expense	580	
538	Rent Expense	500	
565	Telephone Expense	300	
		$11,630	$11,630

Justin Case, Paralegal
Trial Balance
October 31, 20**

Balance Sheet Accounts

Statement of Owner's Equity Accounts

Income Statement Accounts

FIGURE 5.1   Trial balance showing balance sheet, statement of owner's equity, and income statement accounts

Steps in Preparing the Income Statement

When preparing the income statement, keep the following points in mind:

1. The heading section has three lines: the name of the firm (who), the name of the statement (what), and the period covered by the statement (when).
2. Although the statement format has two columns for amounts, they are not debit and credit columns. The inside column is used to list the balance for each individual account and for subtotalling, and the outside column is used for the totals of each account category, revenues, and expenses.
3. The account balances needed to complete the income statement are found on the trial balance.
4. The statement has four main parts:
    a. *Heading:* The heading includes the *who*, the *what*, and the *when*. Place the name of the firm, the name of the statement, and the period covered by the statement in the heading. Income statements report on the income earned over a period of time, whether a month, a quarter, or a year. The heading should have a statement that reads "For the Period Ended _____."

b. *Income:* List each source of income below the heading "Income" (or "Revenue") in the body of the statement. If there is only one source of income, place the amount in the outside column. If there is more than one source of income, list the account names, indented under the "Income" heading. Then place the amounts in the inside column. Draw a subtotal line under the last number entered and place the total income amount in the outside column.

c. *Expenses:* List each expense account that has a balance and enter the amount in the inside column. Place a subtotal line under the last number and enter the total in the outside column on the "Total Expenses" line at the end of the list.

d. *Net income* or *net loss:* Take the difference between the total income and the total expenses to calculate the net income or net loss. Negative values are recorded in parentheses to indicate a net loss.

Figure 5.2 illustrates these points.

The information contained in the income statement is not only useful to the owner of the firm but will also be of interest to the firm's banker if there is an outstanding line of credit. It is also used by the CRA for income tax purposes. In a sole proprietorship, the net income shown on the income statement represents the taxable income of the owner. Remember that drawings (withdrawals) are what the owner took out of the business for personal use. Income tax will be payable on the net income for the firm if it is a sole proprietorship.

Justin Case, Paralegal **Income Statement** **for the period ended October 31, 20****		
Revenue		
Fees Earned		$3,000
Expenses		
Office Supplies/General Expense	$580	
Rent Expense	500	
Telephone Expense	300	
Total Expenses		1,380
Net Income		$1,620

FIGURE 5.2   Income statement

Interpreting Information from the Income Statement

The income statement will help to provide answers to the following questions.

With regard to income:

1. Is the income earned during the period reasonable considering the amount of time and effort spent?

2. Should a review of billing practices be done to see if work completed is being billed effectively?
3. Does the owner need to work harder to increase the amount of income being earned?
4. Is the income earned during the period enough to cover the expenses incurred over the same period? If not, what needs to be done to improve the situation?

With regard to expenses:

1. Review each of the expenses listed to determine whether the amount being spent on each account is reasonable.
2. Can the firm afford to increase salaries expense? Would bringing in extra help assist in increasing revenues?
3. Does the firm need to cut back to reduce expenses (especially if expenses are higher than income)? If so, where can the firm cut back?

Reporting Income and Expenses

The CRA's website has detailed and extensive information for businesses outlining what is to be declared as income and how expenses can be claimed. The following headings emphasize some (but not necessarily all) of the tax considerations business owners should be aware of as a licensee when preparing records for tax purposes. Income tax interpretation bulletins published by the CRA provide detailed guidelines for interpretation of various sections of the *Income Tax Act* and should be consulted when in doubt.

Accounting for Earnings (Income)

Generally, business income must be reported using the accrual method of accounting. Under the accrual method, income must be reported in the fiscal period it was earned, regardless of when payment is received. Similarly, allowable expenses are deducted in the fiscal period in which they are incurred, whether or not they are paid for in that period. *Incur* means the firm has used up or benefitted from the expense.

Other Income

The total income received from other sources, such as a recovery of an amount previously written off as a bad debt in a previous year, must also be reported, as well as interest income received for late payment of invoices or on business investments.

Barter Transactions

A **barter transaction** takes place when any two persons agree to an exchange of goods or services and carry out that exchange without using money. If anyone in the firm is involved in a barter transaction, the goods or services that were received could be considered proceeds from a business operation. For example, if a paralegal gives free legal services to the mechanic who fixes his car, this would be considered a barter transaction, and the paralegal would be required to include the value of the goods or services he provided to the mechanic in his income. Barter transactions may also have GST/HST implications.

Accounting for Business Expenses

A business expense is a cost incurred for the sole purpose of earning business income. Business expense claims must be documented with a purchase invoice, an agreement of purchase and sale, a receipt, or some other voucher that supports the expenditure. If cash is used to pay for any business expenses, be sure to get receipts or other evidence. Receipts should include the vendor's name and the date as well as GST/HST information, which includes the percentage rate and the dollar amount of GST/HST charged as well as the vendor's GST/HST registration number.

As a sole proprietor or partner in a partnership, when recording expenses, only enter the business part of the expense. This means that the following are not included as part of the expenses:

- salary or wages (including drawings) paid to self or partner(s);
- cost of goods or services that the business owner, the business owner's family, or the business owner's partners and their families used (including such items as food, home maintenance, or business properties);
- interest and penalties paid on income tax;
- life insurance premiums;
- the part of any expenses that can be attributed to non-business use of business property; and
- most fines and penalties imposed after March 22, 2004 under the law of Canada or a province or a foreign country (this includes parking tickets).

Business-Use-of-Home Expenses

Expenses for the business use of a work space in the business owner's home can be deducted as long as *one* of these conditions is met:

- it is the business owner's principal place of business, OR
- the space is used to only earn business income and is used as a place to meet clients or customers on a regular and ongoing basis.

Maintenance costs, such as heating, home insurance, electricity, and cleaning materials, can also be deducted, as can a part of the business owner's property taxes, mortgage interest, and capital cost allowance. To calculate what percentage of these expenses can be deducted, use a reasonable basis, such as the area of the workspace divided by the total area of your home.

- **Potential pitfall:** When reviewing corporate financial statements, it may be easy to look at a low net income amount and think that the company has not performed well. However, when owners pay themselves a salary, as they do in a corporation, they could be still paying themselves very well personally, despite the low company net income.
- **Possible fallout:** If you do not understand financial statements, you may misinterpret or misjudge a corporation based on an uninformed or quick review.
- **Proposed recommendation:** When reading financial statements, consider all accounts and ask questions of the corporation. Clients can provide answers to any analysis questions you may have in order to better understand the financial position of a corporation.

LO2 Preparing the Statement of Owner's Equity

The second statement prepared is the **statement of owner's equity**. The heading includes the name of the business (who), the name of the statement (what), and the period covered by the report (when).

The goal of this statement is to calculate owner's equity in the firm after taking into account any profits or losses of the firm (essentially reinvestments in the business) less money withdrawn by the owner (which decreases the amount of equity the owner has maintained in the business). The calculation determines how the owner's investment in the firm has been affected by the operations of the business. The amount calculated for owner's equity at the end of the period will be carried over to the balance sheet. In Figure 5.3, it can be seen that at the end of October, Justin Case's equity in the firm went up to $3,670 ($2,050 opening balance + $1,620 net income) because of the profit from operations during the month of October. The amount of the profit ($1,620 to reinvest in the company) was added to the capital at the beginning of the period ($2,050) to calculate the balance in the capital account or owner's equity at the end of the period. If Justin had withdrawn funds from the firm, the amount withdrawn would have been deducted from capital, resulting in a decrease in the owner's equity.

The steps for preparing the statement of owner's equity are as follows:

1. The heading section has three lines: the name of the firm (who), the name of the statement (what), and the period covered by the statement (when).
2. The statement format for preparing the statement of owner's equity also uses columns for calculations. The columns do not designate debit and credit entries.
3. The amounts are taken from the trial balance.
4. First, enter the owner's capital at the beginning of the period as shown on the trial balance. Place this amount in the outside column.
5. The next line is the net income or net loss for the period. Take the amount shown on the income statement that was just prepared and place that amount in the inside column.
6. On the next line, record total withdrawals that were made by the owner during the period. This amount needs to be deducted from the net income. If there was a net loss, the net loss and the amount of withdrawals will be added together, which results in a greater deduction from capital.
7. On the next line, indicate whether there was an increase or a decrease in the capital account.
   a. In the case of a net profit: calculate net income less withdrawals. If the figure is positive, there has been an increase in the capital account. If the figure is negative, there has been a decrease in capital.
   b. In the case of a net loss: add together the net loss and the withdrawals taken during the period. The total is the decrease in capital that occurred over the period.
   c. Enter the amount of the increase or decrease in capital and extend the calculation to the outside column.
8. Total the outside column to arrive at the capital at the end of the period. In the case of a decrease in capital, subtract the decrease from the first line (owner's capital at the beginning of the period). In the case of an increase in capital, add the increase to the first line (owner's capital at the beginning of the period). This total amount will be used in completing the owner's equity portion of the balance sheet.

Figure 5.3 illustrates these points.

Justin Case, Paralegal Statement of Owner's Equity for the Period Ended October 31, 20**		
Justin Case, Capital, Oct. 1, 20**		$2,050
Add: Capital Investment in October		0
Total Capital, October 31, 20**		$2,050
Net Income for Oct. 20**	$1,620	
Less: Withdrawals for Oct.	0	
Increase in Capital		1,620
Justin Case, Capital Oct. 31, 20**		$3,670

FIGURE 5.3   Statement of owner's equity

Interpreting Information on the Statement of Owner's Equity

The statement of owner's equity at the end of a period helps to provide answers to the following questions:

1. Has the owner's investment in the firm increased or decreased? In other words, is the investment in the firm worth more or less than at the beginning of the period?
2. How much could the owner justify asking for the firm if he or she decided to sell it?
3. How much should the owner ask a partner to invest in the firm if the owner wanted to take one on? If a partner were to receive a 50 percent interest in the firm, it would be wise to ask that he or she invest 50 percent of the amount of capital at the end of the period.

LO3 Preparing the Balance Sheet

The third statement prepared is the balance sheet. The **balance sheet** is a snapshot of the financial position of the firm on a particular date, typically the end of the financial period being reported. The heading includes the name of the business (who), the name of the statement (what), and the date of the report (when).

This statement format can be laid out in different ways. The balance sheet is often laid out in the shape of a T-account, with the assets on the left and the liabilities and owner's equity on the right (see, for example, Figure 2.3 in Chapter 2). This is the format that will be used for the purposes of this chapter.

Accounting software tends to lay out the balance sheet by placing the assets at the top of the page and the liabilities and owner's equity below. When the balance sheet is laid out this way, the last three columns are usually used for calculations—two for calculating subtotals and the last one for calculating the final totals.

The balance sheet provides important information about the financial position of the firm. In other words, the balance sheet shows what the company owns (assets), what it owes (liabilities), and the owner's investment and reinvestment in the business year after year (owner's equity). For example, Figure 5.4 shows that Justin has enough cash in the bank to meet his current liabilities. The company has $7,100 in the General Bank Account and only $580 owing to creditors in the current period. It can also be seen that Justin's investment in the firm has increased since he started the business on October 1, because his owner's equity has gone up. The amount of debt can also be compared to the amount of equity in a company, as the balance sheet shows everything that a company owns (assets) and that it got either from borrowing (liabilities) or investing its own money (owner's equity).

Follow these steps to prepare the balance sheet:

1. The heading section has three lines: who (the name of the firm), what (the name of the statement), and when (the date of the statement). A balance sheet gives a snapshot of the firm at a particular date, so the date at the top does not refer to a period as in the income statement and statement of owner's equity. Rather, it shows the date for which the statement is being prepared.
2. The amounts that will be entered on the balance sheet are found in the trial balance.
3. Place the title "Assets" above the first column. Place the value of each asset in the third column. Total the value of the assets, and then enter the total assets at the bottom.
4. Note that the first number in the column has a dollar sign, and then the grand totals. Follow this convention.
5. Place a dollar sign in front of the total assets and a double underline under the total.
6. Complete the liabilities section by listing the liabilities as shown on the trial balance. They should be totalled and the sum placed in the outside column.
7. Enter the amount of the capital that was calculated on the statement of owner's equity in the owner's equity section.
8. Add the total liabilities and owner's equity together. This number should be equal to the total assets shown above.
9. The balance sheet has now been completed. Place a dollar sign and double underline under the total for liabilities and owner's equity.

Justin Case, Paralegal Balance Sheet October 31, 20**				
Assets			Liabilities	
General Bank Account	$ 7,100		Accounts Payable/General Liabilities	$580
Computer Equipment (Hardware)	900		Personal Loan	4,000
Office Furniture and Equipment	2,250		Credit Card Debt	2,000
			Total Liabilities	$ 6,580
			Owner's Equity	
			Justin Case, Capital	3,670
Total Assets	$10,250		Total Liabilities and Owner's Equity	$10,250

FIGURE 5.4   Balance sheet

Interpreting Information from the Balance Sheet

The balance sheet will help to provide answers to the following questions:

1. Does the firm have sufficient resources to meet its liabilities?
2. Does the firm need to seek additional investment to meet its expenses or to expand?
3. How much are the outstanding accounts receivable? Should steps be taken to have accounts paid more quickly so that they do not become bad debts? In that regard, does the firm need to consider increasing the amounts charged for retainers from clients so that accounts are paid in a timely manner?
4. Does the firm have excess cash that should be invested in short-term or long-term investments to gain interest income?
5. Are the debts excessive in relation to the owner's investment? If so, is the firm at risk of going bankrupt?

Financial Statements

Once opening balances and transactions for the month of October are entered in PCLaw®, the General Ledger and Financial Statements are created using the GL Statements function. A statement selection is made, the Current Report Period is selected, and the system automatically creates the statements. The trial balance was produced in Chapter 4. The Income Statement and Balance Sheet are shown below.

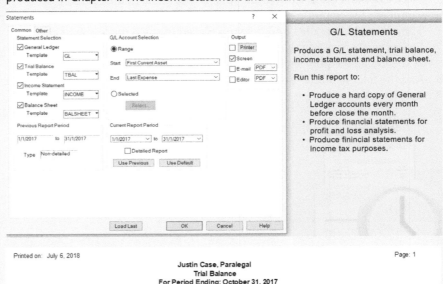

G/L Statements

Produces a G/L statement, trial balance, income statement and balance sheet.

Run this report to:

- Produce a hard copy of General Ledger accounts every month before close the month.
- Produce financial statements for profit and loss analysis.
- Produce finincial statements for income tax purposes.

Printed on: July 6, 2018 — Page: 1

Justin Case, Paralegal
Trial Balance
For Period Ending: October 31, 2017

Nickname	Account Name	Debits	Credits
1000	Gen Bank Acct 1	7,100.00	
1155	Computer Equipment (Hardware)	900.00	
1158	Office Furniture and Equipment	2,250.00	
2000	General Liabilities		580.00
2205	Personal Loan		4,000.00
2206	Credit Card Debt		2,000.00
3000	Justin Case, Equity		2,050.00
4000.jc	Fees-Justin Case		3,000.00
5350	Office/Gen. Expense	580.00	
5380	Rent	500.00	
5540	Telephone Expense	300.00	
	Totals	**$11,630.00**	**$11,630.00**
	Overall balance		**$0.00**

The income statement shows the income for the current period as well as for the year to date.

Page: 1

Justin Case, Paralegal
Income Statement
For the Period Ending October 31, 2017

	Current Period		Year To Date	
REVENUE	Amount	%	Amount	%
Fees–Justin Case	3,000.00	100.00%	3,000.00	100.00%
Total Revenue	**$3,000.00**	**100%**	**$3,000.00**	**100%**
EXPENSES				
Office/Gen. Expense	580.00	42.03%	580.00	42.03%
Rent	500.00	36.23%	500.00	36.23%
Telephone Expense	300.00	21.74%	300.00	21.74%
Total Expenses	**$1,380.00**	**100%**	**$1,380.00**	**100%**
Net Income	**$1,620.00**		**$1,620.00**	

In PCLaw®, there is no statement of owner's equity. The system automatically calculates the equity and adds the profit (or subtracts the loss) for the period to arrive at the owner's equity in the balance sheet.

Printed on: July 6, 2018

Page: 1

Justin Case, Paralegal
Balance Sheet
As at: October 31, 2017

ASSETS			
Current Assets			
Gen Bank Acct 1	7,100.00		
Total Current Assets		$7,100.00	
Fixed Assets			
Computer Equipment (Hardware)	900.00		
Office Furniture and Equipment	2,250.00		
Total Fixed Assets		$3,150.00	
Total Assets			$10,250.00
LIABILITIES			
Short Term Liabilities			
General Liabilities	580.00		
Personal Loan	4,000.00		
Credit Card Debt	2,000.00		
Total Short Term Liabilities		$6,580.00	
Long Term Liabilities			
Total Long Term Liabilities		$0.00	
Total Liabilities			$6,580.00
EQUITY			
Justin Case, Equity	2,050.00		
Income for Alloc	1,620.00		
Total Equity			$3,670.00
Total Liabilities & Equity			$10,250.00

CHAPTER SUMMARY

In Chapter 4, the trial balance was prepared after posting the journal entries to the general ledgers. Once the trial balance is completed, financial statements—income statement, statement of owner's equity, and balance sheet—can be prepared for review and analysis of the company's financial performance.

KEY TERMS

balance sheet, 106

barter transaction, 103

income statement, 100

statement of owner's equity, 105

FURTHER READING

Canada Revenue Agency (CRA), Checklist for New Small Businesses, online: <https://www.canada.ca/en/revenue-agency/services/tax/businesses/small-businesses-self-employed-income/checklist-small-businesses.html>.

Canada Revenue Agency (CRA), Reporting Business Income and Expenses (video series). See especially "Segment 2: Record Keeping," online: <https://www.canada.ca/en/revenue-agency/news/cra-multimedia-library/businesses-video-gallery/transcript-reporting-business-income-expenses-segment-2-record-keeping.html>.

Law Society of Ontario, *The Bookkeeping Guide for Paralegals* (Toronto: LSO, December 2015), online: <https://lawsocietyontario.azureedge.net/media/lso/media/legacy/pdf/p/paralegal_bookkeeping_guide_final-s.pdf>. (See especially item 7: Clients' General Ledger.)

System for Electronic Document Analysis and Retrieval (SEDAR), online: <https://www.sedar.com/>. SEDAR is the official site that provides access to most public securities documents and information filed by public companies and investment funds with the 13 provincial and territorial securities regulatory authorities (Canadian Securities Administrators).

REVIEW QUESTIONS

Short Answer

Give a full answer for each question:

1. What information gets recorded on the income statement? (LO1)

2. What information gets recorded on the statement of owner's equity? (LO2)

3. What information gets recorded on the balance sheet? (LO3)

4. What is a financial statement, and how do you prepare one? (LO1, LO2, LO3)

5. Briefly describe the information that the following financial statements can provide to a business owner and interested third parties or stakeholders: (LO1, LO2, LO3)

   a. income statement

   b. statement of owner's equity

   c. balance sheet

6. Review, analyze, and discuss one of Air Canada's completed financial statements. To find a statement, go to <http://sedar.com/DisplayProfile.do?lang=EN&issuerType=03&issuerNo=00001324>. Click on "View" to display the company's public records, and then select the most recent audited financial statement from the list (for example, February 16, 2018). (LO1, LO2, LO3)

PRACTICE EXERCISES

Worksheets containing the forms you need to complete the practice exercises are provided separately in the working papers for this chapter.

Practice Exercise 5.1

Comprehensive Problem

Using the trial balance below:

   a. Prepare the income statement. (LO1)

   b. Prepare the statement of owner's equity. (LO2)

   c. Prepare the balance sheet. (LO3)

The following balances have already been recorded at May 31.

	Ann Litigate, Paralegal **Trial Balance** **May 31, 20****		
#	*Account*	*Debit*	*Credit*
100	General Bank Account	$1,493	
120	Accounts Receivable	635	
130	Office Supplies	1,050	
158	Office Furniture and Equipment	5,600	
160	Intangible Assets (Computer Software)	2,465	
200	Accounts Payable/General Liabilities		$1,050
210	Credit Card Debt		1,545
250	Bank Line of Credit		5,000
300	Ann Litigate, Capital		5,500
350	Ann Litigate, Drawings	3,000	
400	Fees Earned		4,000
507	Bank Charges and Credit Card Expense	30	
511	Salaries Expense	1,000	
525	General Disbursement Expense	145	
529	Interest Expense	90	
534	Membership/Professional Dues	267	
538	Rent Expense	1,200	
565	Telephone Expense	120	
	Total	$17,095	$17,095

Worksheet a:

Ann Litigate, Paralegal **Income Statement** **for the period ended May 31, 20****		
Revenue		
Expenses		

Net Profit		

Worksheet b:

Ann Litigate, Paralegal Statement of Owner's Equity for the period ended May 31, 20**		

Worksheet c:

Ann Litigate, Paralegal Balance Sheet May 31, 20**			
Assets		Liabilities	
		Owner's Equity	
Total Assets		Total Liabilities and Owner's Equity	

Practice Exercise 5.2
Comprehensive Problem

Using the worksheets provided, prepare the financial statements for ABC Legal Services based on the trial balance shown below. Assume that the adjustments have been entered in the journal and have been entered and posted to the account ledgers. (LO1, LO2, LO3)

ABC Legal Services Adjusted Trial Balance December 31, 20**		
Account Titles	*Dr.*	*Cr.*
General Bank Account	$15,000	
Trust Bank Account	35,000	
Accounts Receivable	20,250	
Prepaid Insurance	700	
Prepaid Expense (Rent)	700	
Office Supplies	150	
Computer Equipment (Hardware)	4,750	
Accounts Payable/General Liabilities		$2,025
Personal Loan		6,000
Credit Card Debt		4,500
Trust Funds Owed		35,000
ABC, Capital		17,165
ABC, Drawings	5,000	
Fees Earned		23,000
Expense Recovery		750
Salaries Expense	1,700	
Insurance—Professional Liability	2,500	
Membership/Professional Dues	200	
Office Supplies/General Expense	500	
Rent Expense	1,800	
Telephone Expense	190	
Total	$88,440	$88,440

ABC Legal Services Income Statement for the Period Ended December 31, 20**		
Income		
Total Income		
Expenses		
Total Expenses		
Net Income		

ABC Legal Services Statement of Owner's Equity for the Period Ended December 31, 20**		
ABC, Capital, December 31, 20**		
ABC Legal Services, Capital, December 31, 20**		

ABC Legal Services Balance Sheet December 31, 20**			
Assets			
Current Assets			
Total Current Assets			
Fixed Assets			
Total Fixed Assets			
Total Assets			
Liabilities and Owner's Equity			
Liabilities			
Total Liabilities			
Owner's Equity			
Total Liabilities and Owner's Equity			

6

Special Journals

Why Use Special Journals? 118

Client Billing. 118

Billing Out Time on a Client File. 119

Disbursements 120

Expense Recovery 120

Client Trust Ledger 120

Fees Book 123

Recording Payment of an Invoice 124

Accounts Receivable Journal. 124

Other Specialized Journals 125

Recording Transactions in Specialized Journals 125

Posting from Special Journals. 131

Analysis of Each Transaction in November 131

Completed Journal and Ledgers to November 30 134

Chapter Summary 140

Key Terms 140

Further Reading. 140

Review Questions 141

Practice Exercises 141

Put It into Practice. 156

After reading this chapter, you should be able to:

LEARNING OUTCOMES

LO1 Use special journals.
LO2 Record fees billed in the fees book or accounts receivable journal.
LO3 Record receipts in the general receipts journal.
LO4 Record disbursements in the general disbursements journal.
LO5 Post from the special journals to the appropriate general ledger and client general ledger.

LO1 A general journal is too inefficient to be useful for recording all transactions in a legal practice. Using specialized journals to record certain transactions is preferable and simplifies the bookkeeping process. The **special journals** that are most useful in a small firm are:

- a fees book (also called a **fees journal**),
- a general receipts journal, and
- a general disbursements journal.

Paralegals need to understand how these special journals work and their relationship to the accounts in the general ledgers.

The special journals discussed in this chapter are in addition to the specialized *trust bank journal* (sometimes called the *trust receipts and disbursements journal*), which will be discussed in Chapter 7.

Special journals are set up to efficiently record transactions and eliminate the need to post every single entry made in the general journal and general ledgers. As you work through this chapter, you will appreciate that learning to use special journals can be challenging but worthwhile. The manual approach demonstrated in this chapter illustrates how information moves through a computerized system. Understanding the special journals produced in this chapter will help you interpret journals and reports prepared using an electronic system. The task of creating entries manually is simplified when special journals are used.

Why Use Special Journals?

- A specialized or combination journal saves time and effort by reducing unnecessary writing.
- Special or combination journals are more efficient and capture specific information.
- Posting to ledger accounts from specialized journals is simpler and more efficient, because not every entry must be posted individually. For example, instead of posting each deposit or cheque made individually to the general bank account ledger sheet, totals are posted at the end of a period.

LO2 Client Billing

An invoice must be prepared and sent to the client before payment on account can be received. The following information is required to prepare an invoice:

- the amount billed for hours (or partial hours) spent on a file;
- disbursements paid out of the firm's general bank account on behalf of the client;

- recovery of expenses incurred in the office that should be charged to the client, such as the cost of photocopies, faxes, and postage; and
- a client trust ledger statement showing the amounts on the file received in trust and paid out from the trust account. (The client trust ledger will be covered in Chapter 7.)

Clients should be billed on a regular basis to keep them informed of the cost of the legal services being provided. This practice avoids disagreements that can arise if matters are not billed promptly, because clients can be surprised by the cost of services rendered.

Billing Out Time on a Client File

Many firms use accounting software to track the amount of time spent on a file and bill the client at an hourly rate that will have been discussed at the time a retainer agreement was entered into. Firms may also bill out files using a flat rate if the parties have agreed on the amount that will be charged for a specific file. More information on recording and billing time is covered in Chapter 12, which deals with computerized time and money management.

Docketing Time and Preparing Invoices

Time spent performing work on a file is recorded using time dockets. Work may be non-billable or billable. **Non-billable work** is work performed by the licensee that will not be charged to the client. This could include, for example, a free consultation or secretarial duties. **Billable work**—work that is charged to the client—typically includes meeting with clients, telephone calls, preparation of legal documents, legal research, and court time.

Lawyers and paralegals generally bill for all time spent on a client file, including work done by associates, law clerks, and legal assistants. Work performed by a secretary is not charged to clients because it is considered part of the overhead incurred in running an office.

A variety of docketing methods are available to track the time spent on a file. Law firms generally express billable time in six-minute (one tenth of an hour) intervals. A minutes-to-decimal conversion chart, as shown in Figure 6.1, is helpful in making this conversion.

Minutes	Decimal Conversion Factor
1-6	0.1
7-12	0.2
13-18	0.3
19-24	0.4
25-30	0.5
31-36	0.6
37-42	0.7
43-48	0.8
49-54	0.9
55-60	1.0

FIGURE 6.1   Minutes-to-decimals conversion chart

EXAMPLE

If Justin Case worked on a file for 53 minutes at an hourly rate of $100, the amount to bill would be calculated as follows:

STEP 1

As can be seen in Figure 6.1, 53 minutes falls within the range of 49-54 in the "Minutes" column, for which the corresponding decimal conversion factor is 0.9. Justin's hourly rate of $80/hour is multiplied by the conversion factor of 0.9 to obtain the converted hourly rate of $72 ($80 × 0.9 = $72).

Alternatively, if a conversion chart isn't handy, a conversion rate can be determined by dividing 53 minutes by 60 minutes (per hour) to obtain the conversion rate of 0.88 (53/60 = 0.88), which can then be rounded up to 0.9.

STEP 2

In a docket sheet usually kept in the file, a short explanation of the work that was done (and any additional description needed) is recorded.

STEP 3

Once all the time docket entries are completed, the information will be used to produce the invoice to the client.

Disbursements

Expenses incurred on behalf of clients, such as charges for deliveries, service of documents, and any other charges paid by the firm from the general bank account, can be recovered from the client. These expenses also need to be journalized and posted to the client's general ledger account.

Expense Recovery

The firm will want to account for **expense recovery**—disbursements incurred in the office that are to be charged to the client.

The LSO has generally taken the position that firms should not profit from disbursements charged to clients.[1] Legitimate expenses that can be passed on to clients include the cost of photocopies, faxes, long-distance phone calls, postage, and sometimes special office supplies needed for court. The amounts passed on to clients must be fair, reasonable, and disclosed to the client in a timely manner. All items that will be charged as disbursements must be discussed with the client, and the amount charged should be shown on the statement of account sent to the client.

Client Trust Ledger

Any amounts paid out of the trust bank account are not included on the invoice but rather are shown on the statement of trust funds sent to the client. The trust statement included with the invoice lists all amounts received from the client and deposited into the trust account, as well as amounts paid from the trust account on the client's behalf. (Trust statements will be discussed in more detail in Chapter 7.)

Figure 6.2 shows a sample invoice for Justin Case's firm.

---

1 Law Society of Ontario, "Managing Money: Fees and Disbursements," online: <https://lso.ca/paralegals/practice-supports-and-resources/topics/managing-money/fees-and-disbursements>.

Justin Case, Paralegal
135 Main Street, Yourtown, Ontario K3P 1G9

Telephone: 905-992-8555   Facsimile: 905-992-8556

File #2   **Invoice #4**

November 22, 20**

Robert Simpson
10 The Driveway
Yourtown, ON
K9G 1V8

Re: *Carpenter*

DATE	DESCRIPTION	HOURS	AMOUNT	WORK DONE BY
Oct. 5	Meeting with client to receive instructions	0.5	50.00	JC
15	Legal research	1.0	100.00	JC
30	Document preparation	1.0	100.00	JC
	Totals		250.00	
	Total HST on Fees		32.50	

DISBURSEMENTS

	Paid, Quick Courier	20.00		
	HST on Disbursements	2.60	22.60	
	Total Fees and Disbursements		305.10	
	AMOUNT DUE		305.10	

This is my account.

Justin Case
Justin Case

HST 12345 6789 RT0001

TRUST STATEMENT		Disbursements	Receipts
Oct. 8	Received from Robert Simpson, retainer		500.00
27	Paid, Canada Post for registered mail	12.00	
30	Total Trust	12.00	500.00
	Trust Balance		488.00

FIGURE 6.2   Sample invoice with trust statement

Creating Time Entries Using a Time Sheet

A matter (a new file) should be opened in the legal software being used as soon as a client retains the firm's services in order to generate a file for that particular matter and client number for that client. Time worked on the file will be recorded using the time sheet feature (see Figure 6.3). In this example, time was entered for the client, Robert Simpson, for the period October 5 to October 30. The task shows "BW," which stands for *billable work*. The file was set up to bill work at the rate of $100/hour, and the system automatically calculated the amount for each entry. The explanation code is a shortcut used to describe the work done, so "mwc" stands for *meeting with client*. Once the code was added, a description of the purpose for the meeting was added in the adjacent column. The information in the time sheet will be used to create the client's bill, so it is important that what is written on the time sheet is grammatically correct.

A file number is also necessary to track any payments made on behalf of the client that need to be charged to the client. In the given example, a disbursement for courier charges was recorded and billed to the client.

Date	Matter	Client Name	Lwyr	Task	Hours	Rate	Amount	Expl. Code	
5/10/2017	2	Simpson, Robert	jc	BW	0.50	100.00	50.00	mwc	Meeting with client to receive instructions
15/10/2017	2	Simpson, Robert	jc	BW	1.00	100.00	100.00	lr	Legal Research
30/10/2017 ▼	2	▼ Simpson, Robert	jc	▼ BW ▼	1.00 ▼	0.00 ▼	100.00 ▼	▼	Document Preparation

FIGURE 6.3   PCLaw® client time sheet

As client time sheet entries are made (see Figure 6.4a), the time spent is totalled, and the amount owing is calculated and displayed as a time entries summary in the time sheet (see Figure 6.4b). The system also shows any disbursements paid by the firm on the client's behalf. Non-billable work is often shown on the bill so that the client can appreciate time spent on the file for which they are not being charged. For example, if the licensee has provided a free half-hour consultation, the time spent could be shown on the bill at no charge.

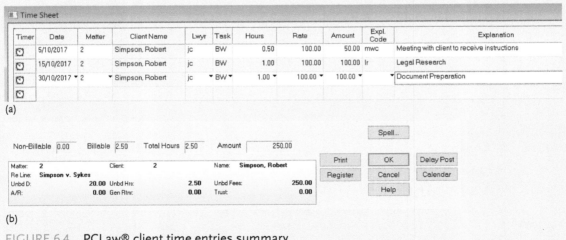

(a)

(b)

FIGURE 6.4   PCLaw® client time entries summary

Fees Book

Part V, section 18(7) of the LSO's by-law 9 requires licensees to maintain a **fees book**—a chronological file of copies of billings, showing all fees charged and other billings made to clients. This can be done by recording the information in the fees book or by keeping a copy of each invoice in chronological order in a file or binder with tab dividers for each month.

The information in the fees book would be completed as shown in Figure 6.5 and described below, assuming Justin Case has registered with the CRA for collecting and paying HST going forward.

			Justin Case, Paralegal Fees Book					FB1
Date 20**		Inv. #	Client/Re	File No.	Fees Billed Cr.	Disbursements Billed Cr.	HST Billed Cr.	Total Billed AR Dr.
Nov.	1	2	Howes, Cliff re Small Claims Court	1	800.00		104.00	904.00
	10	3	Jones, Frank re *Highway Traffic Act*	2	400.00		52.00	452.00
	22	4	Zimmer, Ruth re Carpenter	4	250.00	20.00	35.10	305.10
			Totals		1,450.00	20.00	191.10	1,661.10
					(400)	✓	(240)	(120)

FIGURE 6.5   Fees book for November 20** (after posting)

Date: Record the date of the invoice.

Inv. #: Record the invoice number. Invoices are usually numbered consecutively.

Client/Re: Write the name of the client and the name of the file. Remember that some clients may have more than one file in the office, so it is important to indicate the file to which the invoice applies.

File No.: Once the amount from the Fees Billed Cr. column is posted to the general client ledger, enter the client file number in the File No. column.

Fees Billed Cr.: Enter the total amount (before tax) of fees for services rendered in this column. The amount billed for fees should be posted to the client's general ledger as soon as the bill is recorded.

Disbursements Billed Cr.: Enter the amount billed for disbursements out of the general bank account in this column. Note that this number is obtained from the client general ledger sheet for the particular client when the bill is prepared. This amount will not need to be posted to the client general ledger because the total disbursements were posted when the entries were made in the general disbursements journal (discussed later in the chapter). Note that any amounts paid out of the trust account do not appear on the invoice. The client is not billed since the amount was paid with their own trust money and the amounts paid out of trust are shown on a trust statement, which is attached to the invoice (see Figure 6.2).

HST Billed Cr.: The amount billed for HST on fees and disbursements as shown on the invoice to the client must be entered in this column.

Total Billed AR (accounts receivable) Dr.: Enter the total amount billed to the client (including HST) in this column. Once an invoice is sent out, the total amount of the invoice is an account receivable (which is an asset on the balance sheet). The total amount billed is entered in this column and is the sum of the three previous columns: fees, disbursements, and HST.

Posting from the Fees Book

Some notes about posting from the fees book:

1. The individual amounts in the Fees Billed Cr. column are posted to each client's Accounts Receivable ledger account on a daily basis. The amount of HST billed would also be posted daily to the individual client's general ledger account. Posting to the client ledgers every day keeps each client's balance up to date at all times.

2. The total of the Fees Billed Cr. column is posted as a credit to the Fees Earned account (400) in the general ledger. Once the total is posted, show the account number below the total in parentheses to show that the total was posted (see Figure 6.5).

3. Disbursements billed are not posted to the client's general ledger, because the entry was posted when the disbursement was paid out of the general bank account when the expense was incurred. For example, in Figure 6.5, the amount of $20 paid by the firm on the Zimmer file was recorded in the client's general ledger at the time the payment was made on the client's behalf. This is indicated by placing a checkmark below the total.

4. The total of the HST Billed Cr. column will be posted to the HST/GST Payable account (240) as a credit. HST billed by the firm is remitted to the CRA minus any HST paid for the period. Once the total is posted, show the account number below the total to show that the total was posted.

5. The total of the Total Billed AR Dr. column is posted to a control account in the general ledger called Accounts Receivable (120). Once the total is posted, show the account number below the total to show that it was posted. (Note that the individual amounts in this column are not posted daily as in step 1.)

Once the entries have been posted, the fees book would appear as shown in Figure 6.5.

Recording Payment of an Invoice

Invoices sent to clients and payments received for those invoices will need to be tracked. The following steps help track client invoices:

1. An invoice is sent to the client.
2. The amount billed is entered in the fees book.
3. The client pays the bill to the firm *or* the firm writes a cheque from the trust account from funds held on behalf of the client in trust.
4. The client's payment of the accounts receivable is deposited into the general bank account and the deposit is recorded in the general receipts journal.
5. The entry from the general receipts journal is posted to the client's general ledger account to show that payment has been received.

Accounts Receivable Journal

It is recommended that firms maintain an accounts receivable journal in which amounts billed to and paid by clients are tracked. Typically, accounts receivable journals will provide details of amounts billed to clients and amounts collected. They may be organized by client or by lawyer/paralegal, showing dates and amounts billed and amounts paid. The amounts receivable may be shown by amounts outstanding for less than 30 days, for 31-60 days, for 61-90 days, and so forth. Tracking accounts receivable in this manner helps to ensure accounts are paid in a timely fashion and that delinquent accounts are easily identified. Most legal accounting software can produce an accounts receivable journal on demand. If an accounts receivable journal is not used, a column can be added to the client general ledger to track accounts receivable and be used to summarize the accounts receivable by way of a list, as shown in Figure 6.14 later in this chapter.

POTENTIAL PARALEGAL PITFALLS

- **Potential pitfall:** Not setting aside time to bill clients.
- **Possible fallout:** Companies need money coming in from revenue in order to pay their liabilities and expenses as they come due. If you do not keep up to date with client billing, then revenue will not be collected quickly enough to best manage cash flow.
- **Proposed recommendation:** Set aside a regular time to bill clients and follow up on uncollected client bills. This may be daily, weekly, biweekly, and monthly. Set a calendar reminder so you don't forget.

Other Specialized Journals

In addition to the fees book and the accounts receivable journal, there are two specialized journals known as the *general receipts journal* and the *general disbursements journal.* Many of the general journal entries that were recorded in Chapter 3 can be recorded in these specialized journals instead. In Chapter 7, the use of the trust bank journal and two more specialized journals known as the *trust receipts journal* and the *trust disbursements journal* will be demonstrated. The trust bank journal is a general journal that can be used in place of the specialized trust (receipts and disbursements) journals.

The general journal, used as a book of original entry in Chapter 2, must still be used for some situations, such as when a transaction is of a type for which there is no specialized journal, or when recording adjusting and closing entries. For example, for the purposes of this course, we have not created a specialized purchases journal for recording accounts payable. Accounts payable could be recorded using the general journal, or a specialized journal could be created for the purpose of recording accounts payable if there is sufficient need.

Recording Transactions in Specialized Journals

Figure 6.6 lists the transactions made by Justin Case in November, a brief description of the journal that must be used to record the transaction, and to which ledger the transaction will be posted. The completed journals and ledgers used for posting are included at the end of the chapter (Figures 6.10-6.14). Trust transactions are not shown here because they will be covered in Chapter 7.

Date 20**		Transaction	Journal Used	Post to Ledger
Nov.	1	Invoice #2 was sent to Cliff Howes re Small Claims Court for $800 plus HST of $104.	Fees book	Client's general ledger
	1	Rent was paid to Lucky Landlord in the amount of $300 plus $39 HST, general cheque #4.	General disbursements journal	General ledger
	3	A new client file was opened for *Ruth Zimmer v. Bud Carpenter* re work improperly done on her property. She is claiming damages in the amount of $24,000 for repairs that had to be made. Open a file for Ruth Zimmer (file #4). No retainer was received.	N/A. This does not require a journal entry because no financial transaction occurred	Client's general and trust ledger sheets must be opened for client in order to record future transactions
	4	Justin paid $268.75 plus $34.94 HST for a total of $303.69 to cover Law Society of Ontario membership dues for October, November, and December—general cheque #5.	General disbursements journal	General ledger
	5	Justin wrote a cheque to himself for $800 for personal expenses. General cheque #6.	General disbursements journal	General ledger
	6	A letter was sent to Bud Carpenter on the Zimmer file setting out the claim. The letter was sent by Quick Courier at a cost of $20 plus $2.60 for HST for a total of $22.60. The amount was paid by general cheque #7.	General disbursements journal	Client's general ledger (excluded HST amount)
	10	Fees were billed to Frank Jones re *Highway Traffic Act* for $400 plus $52 HST (invoice #3). There were no disbursements.	Fees book	Client's general ledger
	10	Partial payment on account was received from Cliff Howes for $700 (trust cheque #4).	General receipts journal	Client's general ledger
	15	Justin paid the telephone bill in the amount of $80, plus $10.40 for HST, general cheque #8, general bank account.	General disbursements journal	General ledger
	20	Justin received the amount of $300 from Frank Jones to be applied to invoice #3.	General receipts journal	Client's general ledger
	21	Justin sold the printer he had invested in the firm to Jane Crozier. He received $50 for the printer.	General journal	General ledger
	22	Justin sent an interim bill to Ruth Zimmer in the amount of $250 for fees and for disbursements of $20 plus HST of $35.10 for a total of $305.10 (invoice #4). The bill was paid immediately in cash when it was handed to Ruth.	Fees book and general receipts journal	Client's general ledger
	30	Justin received a bill from the Law Society for $1,075 plus HST of $139.75 for a total of $1,214.75. The first payment on account is not due until April 14 next year. He wishes to enter this as an account payable.	General journal, because we do not have an accounts payable journal	General ledger

FIGURE 6.6   Transactions made by Justin Case, November 20**

LO3 General Receipts Journal

The **general receipts journal** is used to record money received by the firm and deposited in the general bank account. Pursuant to the LSO by-laws, licensees are required to maintain a book of original entry showing all money received[2] by the firm and must record:

- the date on which money is received,
- the method by which money is received,
- the amount of money received, and
- the person from whom money is received.

The types of entries that are entered in the general receipts journal are:

- money received from a client for payment on account,
- money transferred from the trust bank account to the general bank account for payment of an invoice sent to the client, and
- money transferred from the trust bank account to the general bank account to cover payment of disbursements properly made by the firm. This can be done even if the amount has not yet been billed to the client.

The headings used in a general receipts journal designed to suit the requirements of a paralegal firm are illustrated in Figure 6.7. Additional columns could be added at the discretion of the bookkeeper to capture specific information. The journal in Figure 6.7 contains the information required by the LSO.

| | Justin Case, Paralegal
General Receipts Journal | GRJ1 |

Date 20**		Name of Account	Particulars/ Method of Payment	File No.	General Bank Dr.	Accounts Receivable Cr.
Nov.	10	Howes, Cliff re Small Claims Court	Transfer from trust chq. #4, inv. #2	1	700.00	700.00
	15	Jones, Frank re Highway Traffic Act	Transfer from trust chq. #5, inv. #3	2	300.00	300.00
	22	Zimmer, Ruth re Carpenter	Payment on inv. #4, cash	4	305.10	305.10
	30		Totals		1,305.10	1,305.10
					(100)	(120)
			Proof		Dr.	Cr.
					1,305.10	
						1,305.10
					1,305.10	1,305.10

FIGURE 6.7   General receipts journal for November 20** (after posting)

Date: The date column is used to record the date the money is received.

Name of Account: The name of the client and the name of the matter for which payment is being made is shown in this column. It is important to record sufficient information so that it is clear to which client ledger account the amount needs to be posted.

2   By-law 9, part V, s 18(5).

Particulars/Method of Payment: An explanation providing details regarding the transaction is placed here. These details should include the invoice number to which the payment is to be applied, if applicable. The LSO also requires that the method of payment be shown—for example, whether payment is made by cheque, cash, debit, money order, or other means. The client file number is entered in this column when posting is done to the client ledger.

General Bank Dr.: The total amount received and being deposited in the general bank account is recorded in this column.

Accounts Receivable Cr.: When payment is received from a client on an outstanding invoice, the amount paid on the account for fees and disbursements is recorded in the accounts receivable column. Entries recorded in this column should be posted immediately to the client's general ledger account so that client accounts are kept up to date.

All receipts deposited into the general bank account are recorded in the general receipts journal. The total of the General Bank Dr. column is posted to the general bank account as a debit at the end of the period because debits increase assets and receipts increase cash in the bank. The individual amounts will be posted to the individual ledgers, either in the general ledger or in the client general ledger, wherever appropriate.

You may wonder what happened to debits and credits and the double-entry system of bookkeeping. Even though special journals are being used, the entries will be posted to two places. The sum of the General Bank Dr. column is posted as a debit to the general bank account ledger sheet in the general ledger. The individual amounts in the Accounts Receivable Cr. column are posted as a credit to the client general ledger accounts.

Each line recorded in the general receipts journal must be a balanced entry. The General Bank Dr. amount must be equal to the Accounts Receivable Cr. amount.

After all the entries for the month are recorded, the columns are totalled, and the balance is proven by comparing the credit total to the debit total. Figure 6.7 shows that the journal debits and credits balance. Although bookkeepers do not usually show the proof at the bottom of the journal sheet, students are encouraged to show the proof on every journal.

Posting from the General Receipts Journal

Entries in the general receipts journal must be posted to the appropriate ledgers, where information is summarized.

1. *General Bank Dr.*: Individual lines do not need to be posted. The total of this column is debited to the general ledger in the account called General Bank Account (100). The advantage of using the general receipts journal is that the need to post each individual transaction to the general bank account is avoided.
2. *Accounts Receivable Cr.*: The individual amounts listed in this column must be posted as a debit to each client account affected by the transaction. The amount is entered in the Payments from Client column in the client's general ledger. The client file number is placed in the PR column in the journal to indicate that the individual amounts were posted to each client's general ledger. At the end of the month, a list of the accounts receivable is prepared showing the amount owed by each client on that date.

The column total is credited to the Accounts Receivable account (120) in the general ledger. It is a good practice to prepare a list of accounts receivable each period by listing the client files and the balance owed as shown in the client's general ledger at the end of the month.

LO4 General Disbursements Journal

Payments made out of the general bank account can be recorded in the **general disbursements journal**. A general disbursements journal designed to suit the requirements of a paralegal firm is illustrated in Figure 6.8. Additional columns may be added at the discretion of the bookkeeper if specific information needs to be captured.

Pursuant to the LSO by-laws, licensees are required to maintain a book of original entry showing all money paid out[3] by the firm and must record:

- the date on which money is disbursed;
- the method by which money is paid, including the identifier of any document used to pay money (such as a cheque number, debit transaction number, etc.);
- the amount of money disbursed; and
- the person to whom money is paid.

The information in the general disbursements journal would be completed as shown in Figure 6.8.

Justin Case, Paralegal **General Disbursements Journal**							**GDJ1**
Date 20**	Method/ Ref. #	Paid To/Particulars Client/Re	File No./ PR	General Ledger Acct. Dr.	Client's General Ledger Dr.	HST Paid Dr.	General Bank Acct. Cr.
Nov. 1	chq. #4	Lucky Landlord, Rent Exp.	538	300.00		39.00	339.00
4	chq. #5	LSO re Dues Oct. – Dec.	534	268.75		34.94	303.69
5	chq. #6	J. Case, Drawings	350	800.00			800.00
6	chq. #7	Quick Courier, Zimmer re Courier Exp.	4		20.00	2.60	22.60
15	chq. #8	Unitel re Telephone Exp.	565	80.00		10.40	90.40
30		Totals		1,448.75	20.00	86.94	1,555.69
						(240)	(100)
		Proof		Dr.	Cr.		
				1,448.75	1,555.69		
				20.00			
				86.94			
				1,555.69	1,555.69		

FIGURE 6.8 General disbursements journal for November 20** (after posting)

Date: The date column is used to record the date the transaction occurs.

Method/Ref. #: Indicate how the payment was made by showing the cheque number, the debit reference, or other relevant information.

Paid To/Particulars: Record the name of the payee (person or company paid) and what the payment was for (for example, telephone expense, salaries, filing court documents). If a

---

3 By-law 9, part V, s 18(6).

disbursement made on behalf of a client is being recorded, record the name of the payee, the file name, and the reason the funds were paid (for example, Quick Courier, Zimmer re Courier Exp.). You may use more than one line to make the entry.

General Ledger Acct. Dr.: Record the amount to be debited to the general ledger account for the expense incurred. For example, in Figure 6.8, $90.40 was paid to Unitel for telephone expense (the phone cost $80, plus $10.40 HST), so $80 was recorded in this column. This amount should be posted to the general ledger account called Telephone Expense (565); the $10.40 amount paid for HST will be put in the HST Paid Dr. column, and the column total will be posted in the general ledger.

Client's General Ledger Dr.: When the firm pays expenses on behalf of a client from the general bank account, the amount paid will be entered in this column and it will be posted to the client's general ledger sheet. The amount paid out for the client's file will be charged to the client at the time of billing.

HST Paid Dr.: The amount of HST paid on the transaction should be entered in this column. Once the firm starts to remit HST, the amount collected and the amounts paid out will be deducted from one another, and any payment owing will have to be remitted to the CRA. HST will be dealt with more thoroughly in Chapter 11.

General Bank Acct. Cr.: Enter the total amount of the cheque written in this column.

Posting from the General Disbursements Journal

Entries in the general disbursements journal must be posted to the appropriate ledgers, where information is summarized.

1. *General Ledger Acct. Dr.*: The amounts in this column must be posted to the individual accounts affected. The number in the preceding PR column indicates the account to which the entry was posted.
2. *Client's General Ledger Dr.*: This amount paid out on behalf of a client is recorded in the client's general ledger account. The number in the PR column corresponds to the client file number in the client's general ledger.
3. *HST Paid Dr.*: The total amount is posted to the HST/GST Payable account (this is a liability account [240], but note that the entry is a debit, which means it is a decrease in the liability for HST). The HST/GST Payable account number (240) is entered at the bottom of the column to show that the amount was posted.
4. *General Bank Acct. Cr.*: The total for this column is posted to the general bank account in the general ledger and the General Bank Account number (100) is entered at the bottom of the column to show that the amount was posted.

General Journal Entries

When a particular transaction does not fit into one of the special journals used by the firm, the entry can be made using the general journal. Each line is then posted to the appropriate ledger account. Figure 6.10 at the end of this chapter shows examples of such general journal entries.

LO5 Posting from Special Journals

Chapters 2 and 3 detailed how a general journal is used to record transactions for a business and how the transactions are then posted to the general ledger. There are several different types of ledgers that will be encountered when working in a legal practice:

- *General ledger*: This ledger records receipts and disbursements for the firm that are used for the purposes of preparing the financial statements—the income statement, statement of owner's equity, and balance sheet. The general ledger will have a ledger sheet for each of the accounts listed in the chart of accounts. The entries made in the general journal are posted to the general ledger.
- *Client's general ledger*: This ledger contains a separate sheet for each client file. All the payments received from a client for payment on invoices, payments made from the firm's general bank account on behalf of a client, and expense recovery items, such as charges for photocopies and faxes charged to a client, are recorded in the client's general ledger. A running total of the balance is calculated.
- *Client's trust ledger*: This ledger contains a separate sheet for each client file. All the receipts and payments from the trust bank account related to a client file will have to be posted to the client's trust ledger. It is important to keep a running total of the balance in the client's trust ledger account so that the balance held for each client is always up to date. The entries made in the trust bank journal are posted to the individual client trust ledger sheet for each client. The total receipts and payments from the trust bank journal are posted to the account in the general ledger. Because the trust bank journal and trust ledgers will be covered in Chapter 7, they have not been included in this chapter.
- *Combined client's general and trust ledger*: It is sometimes convenient to combine the client's general ledger sheets and the client's trust ledger sheets for each file on one page. In that way, only one ledger sheet needs to be looked at to view the status of a client's account. The information found in a ledger that combines both the client general ledger and client trust ledger transactions will include the following items:
  - all transactions that were posted from the trust bank journal showing all receipts and payments made in trust on behalf of a client;
  - all transactions that were posted from the general journal to the client ledger accounts for individual clients;
  - all invoices recorded in the fees book that have been billed to the client; and
  - all payments received from a client and the balance owing on the account, if any.

Analysis of Each Transaction in November

Figure 6.9 shows an analysis of all the transactions referred to above. The completed journal and ledgers are shown at the end of this chapter (Figures 6.10-6.14).

Nov. 1—Invoice #2 was sent to Cliff Howes re Small Claims Court for $800 plus HST of $104.		
1.	Which journal is to be used?	• The amount of fees charged on an invoice must be recorded in the fees book in the column Fees Billed Cr.
2.	How will this entry be posted?	• The amounts $800 and $104 are entered in the client's general ledger for Cliff Howes under the appropriate columns for fees and HST.
Nov. 1—Rent was paid to Lucky Landlord in the amount of $300 plus $39 HST, general cheque #4.		
3.	Which journal is to be used?	• This is a disbursement out of the general bank account, so the total amount of the entry must be placed in the general disbursements journal under the General Bank Acct. Cr. column. • Record the amount for rent ($300) in the General Ledger Acct. Dr. column. • Record the amount of HST in the HST Paid Dr. column.
4.	How will this entry be posted?	• Post the amount of $300 for rent expense to the general ledger account. • Do not post the individual amounts for the other two columns because the totals will be posted at the end of the month.
Nov. 3—A new client file was opened for *Ruth Zimmer v. Bud Carpenter* re work improperly done on her property. She is claiming damages in the amount of $24,000 for repairs that had to be made. Open a file for Ruth Zimmer (file #4). No retainer was received.		
5.	Which journal is to be used?	• N/A. Opening of a file does not require a journal entry.
6.	How will this entry be posted?	• You will need to open a client ledger sheet for Zimmer in the client's general and trust ledgers for the purpose of making entries in the future.
Nov. 4—Justin Case paid $268.75 plus $34.94 HST for a total of $303.69 to cover LSO membership dues for October, November, and December—general cheque #5.		
7.	Which journal is to be used?	• This is a payment out of the general bank account, so record the transaction in the general disbursements journal: – General Ledger Acct. Dr. column: $268.75 – HST Paid column: $34.94 – General Bank Acct. Cr. column: $303.69
8.	How will this entry be posted?	• Post the expense of $268.75 for Law Society membership dues to the general ledger account called Membership/Professional Dues.
Nov. 5—Justin wrote a cheque to himself for $800 for personal expenses—general cheque #6.		
9.	Which journal is to be used?	• This is a payment out of the general bank account, so record the transaction in the general disbursements journal: – General Ledger Acct. Dr. column: $800 – General Bank Acct. Cr. column: $800
10.	How will this entry be posted?	• Post the withdrawal of $800 to the general ledger account called Justin Case, Drawings.
Nov. 6—A letter was sent to Bud Carpenter on the Zimmer file setting out the claim. The letter was sent by Quick Courier at a cost of $20 plus $2.60 for HST for a total of $22.60. The amount was paid by general cheque #7.		
11.	Which journal is to be used?	• This is a disbursement out of the general bank account, so the total amount of the entry should be placed in the general disbursements journal under the General Bank Acct. Cr. column. • Also enter the amount of $20 in the Client's General Ledger Dr. column of the general disbursements journal.
12.	How will this entry be posted?	• Post the amount from the Client's General Ledger Dr. column to the ledger sheet for Zimmer. Do not post the amount of $2.60 for HST because this will be included in the total posted to the general ledger at the end of the month.
Nov. 10—Fees were billed to Frank Jones re *Highway Traffic Act* for $400 plus HST of $52 (invoice #3).		
13.	Which journal is to be used?	• The $400 amount of fees charged is to be recorded in the fees book in the column Fees Billed Cr.
14.	How will this entry be posted?	• The amount of $400 is posted to the client's general ledger for Frank Jones under the column Fees. HST will be posted at the end of the month to the general ledger account.

Nov. 10—Partial payment on account was received by transferring funds from the trust account for Cliff Howes. There was $700 in the Cliff Howes trust account, so Justin wrote cheque #4 from trust for $700, then deposited the cheque in his general bank account. Record the receipt of payment in this transaction. (Trust entries not included here.)		
15.	Which journal is to be used?	• The deposit of $700 in the firm's general bank account is recorded in the general receipts journal in the General Bank Dr. column and also in the Accounts Receivable Cr. column.
16.	How will the entry be posted?	• The amount received from the client will be posted to the client's general ledger to show that the client paid $700 on account.
Nov. 15—Justin paid the telephone bill in the amount of $80, plus $10.40 for HST, general cheque #8, general bank account.		
17.	Which journal is to be used?	• Record the amount of $90.40 for telephone expense to the general disbursements journal in the column General Bank Acct. Cr. • Enter the amount of $80 in the General Ledger Acct. Dr. column and the $10.40 in the HST Paid Dr. column.
18.	How will this entry be posted?	• Post the amount of $80 to the general ledger on the sheet for telephone expense.
Nov. 20—Justin transferred the amount of $300 held in trust for Frank Jones by writing cheque #5 on the trust account. He then deposited the cheque in the general bank account and applied payment to invoice #3. Record receipt of the payment of $300 in the general bank account.		
19.	Which journal is to be used?	• The deposit of $300 in the firm's general bank account is recorded in the general receipts journal in the General Bank Dr. column and also in the Accounts Receivable Cr. column.
20.	How will this entry be posted?	• The amount received from the client will be posted to the client's general ledger to show that the client paid $300 on account.
Nov. 21—Justin sold the printer he had invested in the firm to Jane Crozier. He received $50 for the printer.		
21.	Which journal is to be used?	• Record the receipt from the sale of the printer as a debit in the general journal. • Record the decrease in the asset computer equipment on the next line in the general journal.
22.	How will this entry be posted?	• Post the entries to the general ledger as a debit to the General Bank Account and as a credit to the Computer Equipment account.
Nov. 22—Justin presented an interim bill to Ruth Zimmer in the amount of $250 for fees and for disbursements of $20 plus HST of $35.10 for a total of $305.10 (invoice #4). Ruth Zimmer immediately paid the bill in cash when the bill was presented to her.		
23.	Which journal is to be used?	• Record the fees billed in the fees book under the Fees Billed Cr. column. • Record the $20 billed under the Disbursements Billed column and the HST under the HST Billed column. • Show the total amount of the bill ($305.10) in the Total Billed AR Dr. column.
24.	How will this entry be posted?	• Post the amount billed ($250) to the client's general ledger for Ruth Zimmer and post the HST of $35.10. You do not need to post the amount of $20 because it was already entered on November 6.
25.	Which journal is to be used?	• You have received payment in cash from Ruth Zimmer. Record the amount received in the general receipts journal under the General Bank Dr. column and also under the Accounts Receivable Cr. column.
26.	How will this entry be posted?	• Post the amount of $305.10 received to the client's general ledger for Zimmer to show that she has paid the fee.
Nov. 30—Justin received a bill from Trimemco for professional liability insurance, in the amount of $1,075 plus HST of $139.75 for a total of $1,214.75. The first payment on account is not due until April 14 next year.		
27.	Which journal is to be used?	• This entry should be made using the general journal. It is a compound entry. • Record the professional liability insurance expense of $1,075 as an expense (debit) on the first line: Insurance, Professional Liability. • Record the HST of $139.75 as a debit on the second line and record the account payable of $1,214.75 as a credit on the third line. Enter the explanation on the fourth line.
28.	How will the entry be posted?	• Post each entry to the accounts in the general ledger.

FIGURE 6.9   Analysis of all transactions for Justin Case, November 20**

Completed Journal and Ledgers to November 30

		Justin Case, Paralegal General Journal			GJ3
Date 20**		Description	PR	Debit	Credit
Nov.	21	General Bank Account	100	50.00	
		Computer Equipment	155		50.00
		To record funds received on sale of printer			
	30	Membership/Professional Dues	534	1,075.00	
		HST/GST Payable	240	139.75	
		Accounts Payable	200		1,214.75
		To record professional dues payable			
		Totals		1,264.75	1,264.75

FIGURE 6.10   Justin Case, general journal entries for November 20**

		Justin Case, Paralegal General Ledgers					
General Bank Account						**Account No. 100**	
Date 20**		Explanation	PR	Debit	Credit	Dr./Cr.	Balance
Oct.	1		GJ1	1,000.00		Dr.	1,000.00
	1		GJ1	4,000.00		Dr.	5,000.00
	5		GJ2		300.00	Dr.	4,700.00
	5		GJ2		2,000.00	Dr.	2,700.00
	6		GJ2	500.00		Dr.	3,200.00
	15		GJ2		100.00	Dr.	3,100.00
	20		GJ2	3,000.00		Dr.	6,100.00
	30		GJ2		500.00	Dr.	5,600.00
Nov.	21	Sale of Printer to Crozier	GJ3	50.00		Dr.	5,650.00
	30	Totals from General Receipts Journal	GRJ1	1,305.10		Dr.	6,955.10
	30	Totals from General Disb. Journal	GDJ1		1,555.69	Dr.	5,399.41

Trust Bank Account — Account No. 115

Date 20**		Explanation	PR	Debit	Credit	Dr./Cr.	Balance
Oct.	30	Trust Totals for October	TJ1	4,100.00	2,820.00	Dr.	1,280.00
Nov.	30	Trust Totals for November	TJ2		1,000.00	Dr.	280.00

Accounts Receivable — Account No. 120

Date 20**		Explanation	PR	Debit	Credit	Dr./Cr.	Balance
Nov.	30	Total AR—November	FB1	1,661.10		Dr.	1,661.10
Nov.	30	Totals for November	GRJ1		1,305.10	Dr.	356.00

Computer Equipment (Hardware) — Account No. 155

Date 20**		Explanation	PR	Debit	Credit	Dr./Cr.	Balance
Oct.	1		GJ1	900.00		Dr.	900.00
Nov.	21	Sale of Printer to Crozier	GJ3		50.00	Dr.	850.00

Office Furniture and Equipment — Account No. 158

Date 20**		Explanation	PR	Debit	Credit	Dr./Cr.	Balance
Oct.	1		GJ1	150.00		Dr.	150.00
	5		GJ2	2,000.00		Dr.	2,150.00
	15		GJ2	100.00		Dr.	2,250.00

Accounts Payable/General Liabilities — Account No. 200

Date 20**		Explanation	PR	Debit	Credit	Dr./Cr.	Balance
Oct.	10	Legal Supplies Inc.	GJ2		580.00	Cr.	580.00
Nov.	30	Law Society Dues	GJ3		1,214.75	Cr.	1,794.75

Personal Loan — Account No. 205

Date 20**		Explanation	PR	Debit	Credit	Dr./Cr.	Balance
Oct.	1	J. Case	GJ1		4,000.00	Cr.	4,000.00

Trust Funds Owed						Account No. 215	
Date 20**		Explanation	PR	Debit	Credit	Dr./Cr.	Balance
Oct.	31	Trust Funds Owed to Clients	TJ1	4,100.00	2,820.00	Cr.	1,280.00
Nov.	30	Trust Funds Owed November 30	TJ2		1,000.00	Cr.	280.00

HST/GST Payable						Account No. 240	
Date 20**		Explanation	PR	Debit	Credit	Dr./Cr.	Balance
Nov.	31	Total Billed to Clients	FB1		191.10	Cr.	191.10
Nov.	30	Total Disbursed for November	GDJ1	86.94		Cr.	104.16
	30	HST on Professional Dues	GJ3	139.75		Dr.	35.59

Justin Case, Capital						Account No. 300	
Date 20**		Explanation	PR	Debit	Credit	Dr./Cr.	Balance
Oct.	1		GJ1		1,000.00	Cr.	1,000.00
	1		GJ1		900.00	Cr.	1,900.00
	1		GJ1		150.00	Cr.	2,050.00
	5		GJ2		500.00	Cr.	2,550.00

Justin Case, Drawings						Account No. 350	
Date 20**		Explanation	PR	Debit	Credit	Dr./Cr.	Balance
Nov.	5	Withdrawal of funds for personal expenses	GDJ1	800.00		Dr.	800.00

Fees Earned						Account No. 400	
Date 20**		Explanation	PR	Debit	Credit	Dr./Cr.	Balance
Oct.	20		GJ2		3,000.00	Cr.	3,000.00
Nov.	30	Total Fees Billed—November	FB1		1,450.00	Cr.	4,450.00

Insurance, Professional Liability						Account No. 527	
Date 20**		Explanation	PR	Debit	Credit	Dr./Cr.	Balance
Nov.	30	Insurance premium due April next year	G13	1,075.00		Dr.	1,075.00

Membership/Professional Dues — Account No. 534

Date 20**		Explanation	PR	Debit	Credit	Dr./Cr.	Balance
Nov.	4	Law Society Dues	GDJ1	268.75		Dr.	268.75

Office Supplies/General Expense — Account No. 535

Date 20**		Explanation	PR	Debit	Credit	Dr./Cr.	Balance
Oct.	10		GJ2	580.00		Dr.	580.00

Rent Expense — Account No. 538

Date 20**		Explanation	PR	Debit	Credit	Dr./Cr.	Balance
Oct.	30		GJ2	500.00		Dr.	500.00
Nov.	1		GDJ1	300.00		Dr.	800.00

Telephone Expense — Account No. 565

Date 20**		Explanation	PR	Debit	Credit	Dr./Cr.	Balance
Oct.	5		GJ2	300.00		Dr.	300.00
Nov.	15	Unitel	GDJ1	80.00		Dr.	380.00

FIGURE 6.11   Justin Case, general ledgers as of November 20**

Justin Case, Paralegal
Client General Ledger

Account: HOWES, Cliff re Small Claims Court						File No. 001	
			Client General Ledger				
Date 20**		Received From/Paid To Explanation	Disbursements Expenses Paid	HST	Fees	Payments from Client	Balance Owed
Nov.	1	Invoice #2		104.00	800.00		904.00
	10	Transfer from Trust				700.00	204.00

Account: JONES, Frank re *Highway Traffic Act*						File No. 002
		Client General Ledger				
Date 20**		Received From/Paid To Explanation	Disbursements Expenses Paid	HST	Fees	Payments from Client	Balance Owed
Nov.	10	Fees Billed, invoice #3		52.00	400.00		452.00
	20	Justin Case, Payment on invoice #3				300.00	152.00

Account: ZIMMER, Ruth re *Ruth Zimmer v. Bud Carpenter*						File No. 004
		Client General Ledger				
Date 20**		Received From/Paid To Explanation	Disbursements Expenses Paid	HST	Fees	Payments from Client	Balance Owed
Nov.	6	Quick Courier					20.00
	22	Fees Billed, invoice #4		35.10	250.00		305.10
	22	Zimmer, on Account				305.10	0.00

FIGURE 6.12   Justin Case, client general ledger for November 20**

Supporting Documents

TAX TIP

The CRA requires business owners to keep organized accounting and financial documents that summarize the information from the supporting documents. Examples of such documents include ledgers, journals, financial statements, statements of accounts, income tax returns, and GST/HST tax credit returns.

Documents business owners must keep to support transactions identified in the records include invoices for fees, purchase receipts, vouchers, contracts (such as a lease), bank deposit slips, cancelled cheques, credit card receipts, logbooks, emails, and correspondence supporting transactions.

These records can be kept in English or French.

#	Account	Debit	Credit
	Justin Case, Paralegal **Trial Balance** **November 30, 20****		
100	General Bank Account	$5,399.41	
120	Accounts Receivable	356.00	
155	Computer Equipment (Hardware)	850.00	
158	Office Furniture and Equipment	2,250.00	
200	Accounts Payable		$1,794.75
205	Personal Loan		4,000.00
240	HST/GST Payable	35.59	
300	Justin Case, Capital		2,550.00
350	Justin Case, Drawings	800.00	
400	Fees Earned		4,450.00
527	Insurance, Professional Liability	1,075.00	
534	Membership/Professional Dues	268.75	
535	Office Supplies/General Expense	580.00	
538	Rent Expense	800.00	
565	Telephone Expense	380.00	
		$12,794.75	$12,794.75

FIGURE 6.13   Justin Case, trial balance, November 30, 20**

File No.	Name of Client/Re	Balance Owed
	Justin Case, Paralegal **List of Accounts Receivable** **November 30, 20****	
1	HOWES, Cliff re Small Claims Court	$204.00
2	JONES, Frank re *Highway Traffic Act*	152.00
	Total Owed by Clients	$356.00

FIGURE 6.14   Justin Case, list of accounts receivable

CHAPTER SUMMARY

Learning how to use special journals can seem complicated, but ultimately, they simplify your record-keeping. Special journals do this by grouping certain transactions in one column so that you do not need to post as many entries. This saves time and avoids errors. Keeping the client general ledger and the client trust ledger on the same page will help you to see the flow of transactions between the two ledgers.

Technology is a useful tool for using special journals because the software usually records and posts the information automatically to the correct place. The manual approach used in this chapter helps you to understand how the information flows through a computerized system. If you do not understand how the information is processed manually, you will have difficulty understanding the information created by a computerized system. Further, some paralegals may not be able to afford specialized computer bookkeeping software when they start out—so it is good to know how books must be set up and maintained.

KEY TERMS

billable work, 119

expense recovery, 120

fees book, 123

fees journal, 118

general disbursements journal, 129

general receipts journal, 127

Non-billable work, 119

special journals, 118

FURTHER READING

Canvas Network, Intro to Accounting, "Study: Subsidiary Ledgers and Special Journals," online: <https://learn.canvas.net/courses/37/pages/study-subsidiary-ledgers-and-special-journals>. For additional information, scroll down the page to Additional Resources and select "Special Journals and Subsidiary Ledgers," which links to a video on an external site.

Lawyers' Professional Indemnity Company, *Managing the Finances of Your Practice*, online: <http://www.practicepro.ca/practice/pdf/Managing_Finances_booklet.pdf>. Download a PDF of the booklet to see the sections related to established practices (for example, fee agreements, docketing, and billing).

LexisNexis Canada, PCLaw® billing and accounting software FAQ, online: <http://law.lexisnexis.com/literature/back_office_faqs.pdf>. See the sections related to billing, client disbursements, and time entries.

REVIEW QUESTIONS

True or False

_____ 1. A fees book includes only information about legal fees charged to clients. **(LO2)**

_____ 2. An accounts receivable journal is an example of a special journal. **(LO2)**

_____ 3. The general disbursements journal is used only for disbursements made on behalf of clients, which are recoverable by the paralegal. **(LO4)**

_____ 4. Every receipt shown on the general receipts journal will have a corresponding entry on the general disbursements journal for the same accounting period. **(LO3)**

_____ 5. An invoice should be created each and every time fees and disbursements are billed to a client. **(LO2)**

_____ 6. Entries from a special journal do not need to be posted to the general ledger. **(LO5)**

_____ 7. The Accounts Receivable account found on the general ledger can be further subdivided by clients. **(LO3)**

_____ 8. The general journal replaces the need for special journals. **(LO1)**

Short Answer

1. Which of the following entries would be recorded in the general receipts journal? **(LO3)**

   a. The firm was paid $300 as a retainer by a client.

   b. The firm received a credit of $50 from the landlord for rent.

   c. The firm paid photocopies expense to be recovered from a client.

   d. The firm wrote a cheque to itself from the trust account to pay for an invoice sent to the client.

   e. The firm paid money out of trust to cover filing fees of $150 paid the previous week from the firm's general bank account and deposited the amount in its general bank account.

2. What is the purpose of the general disbursements journal? **(LO4)**

3. What is the benefit of maintaining a fees book? **(LO2)**

4. Which columns in the fees book are posted as a total, and to which account are they posted? **(LO2)**

5. Which individual items in the fees book get posted to the client's general ledger? **(LO2)**

PRACTICE EXERCISES

Practice Exercise 6.1

The following invoices were sent to clients by Justin Case. Record the invoice information in the fees book for the firm. Calculate and enter the HST (13%) for each invoice and the total amount of the bill. **(LO2)**

a. April 1: Sent invoice #102 to L. Forte (File No. 102); fees billed, $800, and disbursements were $120.

b. April 10: Sent invoice #103 to D. W. Coleman (File No. 89); fees billed, $500, and disbursements were $250.

c. April 20: Sent invoice #104 to Ruth Zimmer (File No. 40); fees billed, $250, and disbursements were $20.

d. April 30: Sent invoice #105 to First Time Janitorial (File No. 103); fees billed, $299.99, and disbursements were $14.59.

								FB1
Date 20**	Inv. #	Client/Re	File No.	Fees Billed Cr.	Disbursements Billed Cr.	HST Billed Cr.	Total Billed Cr.	

Justin Case, Paralegal — Fees Book

Practice Exercise 6.2

Using the Fees Journal you completed in Practice Exercise 6.1, post the entries from the Fees Journal to the Client General Ledgers provided below. Note that the disbursements were previously posted from the Disbursements journal so they do not have to be reentered. (LO2)

Justin Case, Paralegal — Client General Ledgers

Account: Ruth Zimmer — File No. 40

Date 20**	Received From/Paid To Explanation	PR	Disbursements Expenses Paid	HST	Fees	Payments from Client	Balance Owed

Account: D. W. Coleman | | | | | | | **File No. 89**

Date 20**	Received From/Paid To Explanation	PR	Disbursements Expenses Paid	HST	Fees	Payments from Client	Balance Owed

Account: L. Forte | | | | | | | **File No. 102**

Date 20**	Received From/Paid To Explanation	PR	Disbursements Expenses Paid	HST	Fees	Payments from Client	Balance Owed

Account: First Time Janitorial | | | | | | | **File No. 103**

Date 20**	Received From/Paid To Explanation	PR	Disbursements Expenses Paid	HST	Fees	Payments from Client	Balance Owed

Practice Exercise 6.3

Prepare the appropriate special journals and client general ledgers based on the following transactions for Ann Litigate in the operation of her paralegal practice during the month of July. Record the amount paid for HST where appropriate. (LO5)

Cheque stubs show the following cheques were written on the Ann Litigate General Bank Account for expenses paid by the firm. Record the entries in the General Disbursements Journal.

1. July 1: Paid rent expense (invoice #1001 payable to Magnum Office Managers), $1,200 plus HST of $156 for a total amount of $1,356, cheque #217, A. Litigate.

2. July 7: Paid courier invoice account (invoice #A0-111 from Fast Courier), $30 plus HST of $3.90 for a total of $33.90, cheque #218.

3. July 7: Paid courier invoice account (invoice #A-112) $60 plus HST of $7.80 recoverable from client, L. Forte, cheque #219.

4. July 9: Paid court filing fees, $240 to the Minister of Finance ($120 recoverable from client L. Bailey; $120 recoverable from R. Smythe) (no HST payable on court fees), cheque #220.

5. July 15: Paid professional liability insurance (payable to ABC Insurance), in the total amount of $167, cheque #221. Insurance has 8 percent tax only.

6. July 30: Paid salary to assistant, $2,000, cheque #222.

The following invoices were billed to clients during the month of July. Record the invoices in the Fees Book for Ann Litigate's legal firm. Refer to the section above on the General Disbursements Journal where necessary.

1. July 9: Billed L. Forte for legal services (invoice #400), $500 (plus HST) plus disbursements previously recorded (courier charge) for a total of $632.80.

2. July 15: Billed L. Bailey for legal services (invoice #401), $1,000 plus HST, plus disbursement of $120 for court filing fees (no HST payable on court fees) for a total of $1,250.

3. July 31: Billed client (R. Smythe) on invoice #402, for disbursements only of $120 (no HST payable) for a total of $120.

Ann Litigate's firm received payment on the following invoices during the month of July. Record the receipts in the General Receipts Journal for the firm.

1. July 23: Received payment by cheque from L. Forte for invoice #400 (L. Forte), in the amount of $632.80.

2. July 30: Received partial payment of invoice #401 (L. Bailey), $750.

Ann Litigate made an investment in her firm. This transaction needs to be recorded in the General Journal for the firm.

1. July 31: Capital investment (from Ann to the firm), $8,000, cheque #24, A. Litigate (from her personal account).

Ann Litigate, Paralegal General Disbursements Journal							GDJ1
Date 20**	Method/ Ref. #	Paid To/Particulars Client/Re	PR /File	General Ledger Acct. Dr.	Client's General Ledger Dr.	HST Paid Dr.	General Bank Account Cr.

Ann Litigate, Paralegal Fees Book							FB1
Date 20**	Inv. #	Client/Re	Ref.	Fees Billed	Disbursements Billed	HST Billed Cr.	Total Billed AR Dr.

Ann Litigate, Paralegal General Receipts Journal						GRJ1
Date 20**	Name of Account	Particulars/ Method of Payment	PR	General Bank Dr.	Accounts Receivable Cr.	

Ann Litigate, Paralegal General Journal					GJ3
Date 20**	Description		PR	Debit	Credit

Practice Exercise 6.4

Once you have completed the entries in the special journals set out in Practice 6.3, post the following entries: (LO5)

1. Post the General Journal Entries to the Individual General Ledger Accounts.

2. Post the entries from the General Disbursements Journal as follows:

    a. Post the entries in the General Ledger Account Dr. to each individual ledger account in the General Ledger or the Client General Ledger. Complete the PR column indicating the account to which the amounts were posted.

    b. Post the totals for the HST Paid and General Bank account to the General Ledger Accounts. Show the post reference of the account posted to in brackets below the column.

3. Post the entries from the Fees Book to the Client General Ledgers and to the General Ledger Accounts. The reference column should show the client account or file number to which the fees were posted.

    a. The disbursements billed column does not need to be posted, as these were posted previously.

    b. Post the totals of the HST Billed column and the Total Billed Accounts Receivable column to the respective General Ledger Accounts. Enter the account number to which the totals were posted in brackets below the total posted.

4. Post the entries from the General Receipts Journal to the Client General Ledgers and the General Ledger.

    a. Post the individual receipted amounts to the Client's General Ledger and indicate the account number in the post reference column.

    b. Post the totals of the General Bank Dr. and Accounts Receivable Cr. Accounts to the General Ledger and show the account number to which the amounts were posted in brackets below the totals.

5. Complete the totals in the General Ledgers and the General Client Ledger once all posting has been completed.

6. Prepare the trial balance.

> **HINT**
>
> Also prepare a list of the total accounts receivable owed to Ann for the month. The total should be equal to the total of the Accounts Receivable Account in the General Ledger.

Ann Litigate, Paralegal
Client General Ledgers

Account: FORTE, L.   **File No. 04**

Date 20**		Received From/Paid To Explanation PR	Disbursements Expenses Paid	HST	Fees	Payments from Client	Balance Owed

Account: BAILEY, L.   **File No. 05**

Date 20**		Received From/Paid To Explanation PR	Disbursements Expenses Paid	HST	Fees	Payments from Client	Balance Owed

Account: SMYTHE, R.   **File No. 06**

Date 20**		Received From/Paid To Explanation PR	Disbursements Expenses Paid	HST	Fees	Payments from Client	Balance Owed

Ann Litigate, Paralegal
General Ledgers as of July 31, 20**

General Bank Account   **Account No. 100**

Date 20**		Explanation	PR	Debit	Credit	Dr./ Cr.	Balance

Accounts Receivable — Account No. 120

Date 20**		Explanation	PR	Debit	Credit	Dr./Cr.	Balance

Office Furniture and Equipment — Account No. 158

Date 20**		Explanation	PR	Debit	Credit	Dr./Cr.	Balance

Accounts Payable/General Liabilities — Account No. 200

Date 20**		Explanation	PR	Debit	Credit	Dr./Cr.	Balance

HST Payable — Account No. 240

Date 20**		Explanation	PR	Debit	Credit	Dr./Cr.	Balance

Ann Litigate, Capital — Account No. 300

Date 20**		Explanation	PR	Debit	Credit	Dr./Cr.	Balance

Ann Litigate, Drawings — Account No. 350

Date 20**		Explanation	PR	Debit	Credit	Dr./Cr.	Balance

Fees Earned

Account No.
400

Date 20**		Explanation	PR	Debit	Credit	Dr./Cr.	Balance

Salaries Expense

Account No.
511

Date 20**		Explanation	PR	Debit	Credit	Dr./Cr.	Balance

Insurance—Professional Liability

Account No.
527

Date 20**		Explanation	PR	Debit	Credit	Dr./Cr.	Balance

Office Supplies/General Expense

Account No.
535

Date 20**		Explanation	PR	Debit	Credit	Dr./Cr.	Balance

Rent Expense

Account No.
538

Date 20**		Explanation	PR	Debit	Credit	Dr./Cr.	Balance

Delivery Expense

Account No.
550

Date 20**		Explanation	PR	Debit	Credit	Dr./Cr.	Balance

#	Account	Debit	Credit
	Ann Litigate, Paralegal **Trial Balance** **July 31, 20****		

PRACTICE EXCEL ## Practice Exercise 6.5

Complete the invoices provided based on the following time docket entries prepared by Ann Litigate. (LO2)

> **HINT**
> To calculate billable time, divide the number of minutes billed by 60 (minutes) and round up to the nearest 0.10.

	Time Docket Entries **A. Johnston—Matter No. 01 (Small Claims Matter—_Johnston v. Delaney_)**				
Date 20**	Description	Start Time	End Time	Total Time	
June 18	Initial consultation with client to discuss options for small claim matter	10:30 a.m.	11:00 a.m.	0.50 hours (30 min/60 min)	
June 20	Conduct research on issues related to trespass	3:00 p.m.	4:15 p.m.	1.30 hours (75 min/60 min)	
June 22	Prepare initial draft of statement of claim and email to client for review	11:20 a.m.	12:50 p.m.	1.50 hours (90 min/60 min)	
June 28	Follow-up meeting with client to discuss draft statement of claim for the purpose of finalizing same statement of claim based on client comments	10:00 a.m.	10:45 a.m.	0.80 hours (45 min/60 min)	

Time Docket Entries J. Palmer—Matter No. 06 (Provincial Offences Matter)				
Date 20**	Description	Start Time	End Time	Total Time
May 15	Phone call and initial consultation with J. Palmer	1:55 p.m.	2:15 p.m.	0.40 hours (20 min/60 min)
May 20	Meeting with client to discuss upcoming court date	5:30 p.m.	6:00 p.m.	0.50 hours (30 min/60 min)
June 5	Review disclosure and conduct research (section 130, *Highway Traffic Act*) in preparation for upcoming court date	10:15 a.m.	11:00 a.m.	0.80 hours (45 min/60 min)
June 12	Attend at Provincial Offences Court and negotiate a settlement with the Crown	9:00 a.m.	10:15 a.m.	1.30 hours (75 min/60 min)

Invoice for A. Johnston

ANN LITIGATE PARALEGAL SERVICES
11 Any Street, Ottawa, Ontario K1A 0B0

INVOICE #1015

June 30, 20**

Mr. Anthony Johnston
123 Avenue Road
Ottawa, Ontario K1A 0C0

FOR SERVICES RENDERED RE SMALL CLAIMS MATTER:

Date	Hours Billed	Description	Billable Rate (/h)	Amount Billed
		FEES:	Subtotal	
			HST (13%)	

DISBURSEMENTS

	Quantity	Description	Unit Price	Amount
	45 pages	Photocopies	0.25/page	
	15 pages	Fax transmissions	1.00/page	
		DISBURSEMENTS:	Subtotal	
			HST (13%)	

TOTAL (FEES, DISBURSEMENTS, AND HST)

	Total	
TOTAL BALANCE OWING		

Invoice for J. Palmer

ANN LITIGATE PARALEGAL SERVICES			INVOICE #1016
11 Any Street, Ottawa, Ontario K1A 0B0			

June 30, 20**

Ms. Janet Palmer
567 Jane Street
Ottawa, Ontario K1A 0C1

FOR SERVICES RENDERED RE HIGHWAY TRAFFIC ACT MATTER:

Date	Hours Billed	Description	Billable Rate (/h)	Amount Billed
		FEES:	Subtotal	
	DISCOUNT, FLAT RATE SERVICE ($450.00):		Subtotal	
			HST (13%)	

DISBURSEMENTS

Quantity	Description	Unit Price	Amount
25 pages	Photocopies	0.25/page	
35 km	Travel to/from Provincial Offences Court	0.40/km	
	DISBURSEMENTS:	Subtotal	
		HST (13%)	

TOTAL (FEES, DISBURSEMENTS, AND HST)

	Total	
	TOTAL BALANCE OWING	

Practice Exercise 6.6

You are a new paralegal with a general bank account balance of $10,000. You have not yet set up a trust account.

The following events take place in your first month of business, November 2014:

1. You are retained by Sarah Smith to commence an action in a Small Claims Court matter. You do not ask her for a money retainer. On November 4, you issue the plaintiff's claim. You pay the fee of $80 with cheque #100. Client matter #1010.

2. You pay for office rent to Laurence Plaza in the amount of $500 (plus HST) with cheque #101 on November 5.

3. The defendant fails to file a defence within the required time. On November 8, you arrange for the clerk to note the defendant in default and enter default judgment. You pay the fee of $40 with cheque #102.

4. You pay for office repairs to Repairs'R'Us in the amount of $120 (plus HST) with cheque #103 on November 13.

5. Your total fees to Sarah Smith are $750 (plus HST). Your final invoice is #1, dated November 14. Include disbursements.

6. You pay yourself $1,000 on November 15 with cheque #104.

7. You receive Sarah Smith's personal cheque for $967.50 on November 20. The cheque is #245. You deposit to the bank on November 20.

Record the transactions in the appropriate form(s) provided. (LO1, LO2, LO3, LO4)

Bank of Hamilton			Credit Account of:
Date:			Mohawk Paralegal
Transit:	98765		**General Account**
Account number:	2345678991		
Cheques and Credit Card Vouchers		Details	Cash
		× $5	
		× $10	
		× $20	
		× $50	
		× $100	
		Cdn Cash Total	
Total		**Credit Card Vouchers and Cheques Forwarded**	

Mohawk Paralegal General Receipts Journal			
Date	Funds received from	Amount	Method of payment

Mohawk Paralegal
General Disbursements Journal

Date	Method of payment/Reference number	Paid to	Particulars	HST paid	Amount

Mohawk Paralegal
Client General Ledgers

Account: Re:
Client matter no.:

Date	Particulars	Expenses paid	HST on expenses	Fees	HST on Fees	Payment from client	Balance owing

Account: Re:
Client matter no.:

Date	Particulars	Expenses paid	HST on expenses	Fees	HST on Fees	Payment from client	Balance owing

Account: Re: Client matter no.:							
Date	Particulars	Expenses paid	HST on expenses	Fees	HST on Fees	Payment from client	Balance owing

Mohawk Paralegal Fees Book						
Date	Invoice number	Client	Fees billed	Disbursements billed	HST billed	Total billed

PUT IT INTO PRACTICE

Case Example: Special Journals

Ann Litigate has prepared the following invoices dated May 30, 20**:

Client Matter #21-xx:	$1,250.00 (Total Fees, Disbursements, and HST)
Fees Billed:	$1,000.00
Disbursement Recoverable:	$120.00, Court Filing Fees (no HST)
HST Billed:	$130.00

Client Matter #08-xx:	$583.20 (Total Fees, Disbursements, and HST)
Fees Billed:	$500.00
Disbursement Recoverable:	$16.10, Courier Fees (Speedy Courier)
HST Billed:	$67.10

Client Matter #11-xx:	$1,672.40 (Total Fees, Disbursements, and HST)
Fees Billed:	$1,440.00
Disbursement Recoverable:	$40.00, Travel Expense (Mileage)
HST Billed:	$192.40

Client Matter #29-xx:	$864.45 (Total Fees, Disbursements, and HST)
Fees Billed:	$750.00
Disbursement Recoverable:	$15.00, Photocopy Charges (Kwick Print)
HST Billed:	$99.45

Answer the following questions and list the steps that Ann will need to take for these transactions. Identify the appropriate special journals and ledgers.

1. How can Ann keep track of the balance owing by her clients once the invoices are issued?
2. When Ann receives payment on an invoice, how can she keep track of the payments made by her clients?
3. Suppose Ann paid $100 in disbursements or expenses on behalf of her client and wishes to recover the cost from the client.
   a. What entries should Ann make when the expense is incurred?
   b. What entries should Ann make when the expenses paid by Ann are not yet paid by the client?
   c. What entries should Ann make when the client subsequently pays the expense?

7

Trust Accounting

Difference Between a General Account and a Trust Account 158

Cash Receipts 160

Trust Bank Journal 161

Trial Balance 168

Matter-to-Matter Trust Transfer Journal 169

Valuable Property Record 171

Practice Audits 171

Chapter Summary 175

Key Terms 175

Further Reading 175

Review Questions 176

Practice Exercises 176

Put It into Practice 195

After reading this chapter, you should be able to:

LO1 Understand the difference between general accounts and trust accounts.

LO2 Be aware of the record-keeping requirements for trust accounts.

LO3 Create entries in a trust bank journal.

LO4 Post from the trust bank journal to the client trust ledgers.

LO5 Prepare a client trust listing and compare the total with the trust bank balance.

LO6 Incorporate trust information into the firm's financial statements.

LO7 Record matter-to-matter transfers.

LO8 Understand the valuable property record.

Keeping track of transactions affecting the **trust bank account** and maintaining all the trust records required by the LSO is like maintaining a parallel set of books for the firm (see Figure 7.1). Recording receipts and disbursements promptly and accurately ensures that you are able to meet your client trust obligations as they arise. Your trust records should always be up to date, and you should check clients' trust ledgers periodically to look for unusual or incorrect items. For example, was an amount entered in the wrong client's account?

Required for Trust Bank Account	Required for General Bank Account
Trust bank journal or trust receipts and disbursements journal	General journal or general receipts and disbursements journal
Trust transfer journal (matter-to-matter transfers)	Fees book
	General ledger
Client's trust ledger	Client's general ledger (recommended)
Valuable property record	
Book of duplicate cash receipts	Book of duplicate cash receipts
Trust bank reconciliation with trust listing	Bank reconciliation

FIGURE 7.1   Financial records maintained: trust bank account versus general bank account

Once all the records have been completed, the information will be merged into one set of financial reports showing a balance sheet for the firm in which the information from both the general and trust accounts is consolidated.

LO1 Difference Between a General Account and a Trust Account

Chapter 1 discussed the *general bank account* and the mixed trust account. Trust account records are subject to much more scrutiny by the LSO than general bank account records because these accounts hold money that belongs to clients, not to the firm. Trust records are not required if the firm does not receive any funds in trust for clients.

Trust accounting will need to be used in the following situations:

- *When money is received from another party on behalf of a client.* For example, a court case may have been settled in favour of the client, and funds are paid to the firm to be held in trust until the client signs a release and it is delivered to the other party's lawyer.
- *When money is received from a client to be paid to another party.* For example, a court case may have been settled and a client, having lost, brings funds into the firm to pay the judgment to the successful party.
- *When retainers are received from clients to pay for future legal services and future disbursements.* These receipts must be held in the mixed trust account.
- *When payments are made by the firm on behalf of its client.* These payments can be paid out of the trust account if the client has given a monetary retainer. For example, the client may have authorized the firm to pay a fine from funds held on her behalf in trust.
- *When reimbursement for proper expenses is paid out of the firm's general bank account on behalf of a client.* For example, the firm may have paid to issue a claim but did not have funds in trust for the client. Once the client brings in funds, the amount paid out by the firm from its general bank account can be transferred from trust to the general account to pay for the disbursement(s).
- *For payment on account after a bill has been sent to the client.* Once the client has been billed, funds can be transferred from the trust account to the general bank account to pay the amount owing, but only up to the amount held in trust for that particular client.

LO2 Deposits and Withdrawals from Trust

By-law 9, part I, section 1(3) of the LSO requires that cash, cheques negotiable by the licensee, cheques drawn by the licensee on the licensee's trust account, and credit card sales slips in the possession and control of the licensee are to be deposited in the trust account *no later than the following banking day.*

Trust cheques or bank drafts cannot be made payable to "cash" or "bearer," and cash should never be withdrawn from the trust account, because an audit trail is required. Deposit records kept by the firm must indicate the date on which funds were deposited, the firm's name, the bank account number, the source of each receipt, the name of the client, and the amount of the deposit (see Figure 7.2). Each deposit slip should be stamped by a bank teller. If funds are deposited using an automated teller machine, the ATM receipt needs to be attached to the corresponding deposit slip.

POTENTIAL PARALEGAL PITFALLS

- **Potential pitfall:** Holding business money in the trust account.
- **Possible fallout:** Losing track of which clients have trust balances; may appear to be a way to hide money earned or HST collected from CRA.
- **Proposed recommendation:** Remember to use trust accounts only for client trust money. Use the general bank account for all business money.

CREDIT ACCOUNT OF:			BUSINESS ACCOUNT DEPOSIT SLIP	

JUSTIN CASE, PARALEGAL
IN TRUST
ACCOUNT NUMBER   232017661

BANK OF MONEY
ONTARIO, CANADA

DATE:

DAY	MONTH	YEAR
03	OCT	20**

INITIALS:

DEPOSITOR'S	TELLER'S
JC	NM

LIST OF CHEQUES:

CHEQUE IDENTIFICATION	AMOUNT
1 HOWES, CLIFF	1,000.00
2 JONES, FRANK	500.00
3	
4	
5	
6	
7	
8	
CHEQUE SUBTOTAL	1,500.00
TOTAL # OF CHEQUES	2

CASH COUNT:

	X 5	
	X 20	
	X 20	
JONES 2	X 50	100.00
	X $1 COIN	
	X $2 COIN	
COIN TOTAL		
CASH COUNT		
CASH SUBTOTAL		100.00

DEPOSIT:

CASH SUBTOTAL	100.00
CHEQUE SUBTOTAL	1,500.00
DEPOSIT TOTAL	**$ 1,600.00**

FIGURE 7.2   Sample trust account deposit slip

Cash Receipts

By-law 9, part III, section 4(1) of the LSO contains a provision that a licensee shall not receive or accept from a person, in respect of any one client file, cash in an aggregate amount equal to or exceeding Cdn$7,500.

Exceptions to this requirement are found in section 6 of the by-law and deal mostly with funds received from public bodies or financial institutions. There is an exception if cash is received from a client for the purpose of paying a fine or penalty. There is also an exception if cash is received for fees, disbursements, expenses, or bail, provided that any refund out of such receipts is also made in cash.

As a minimum additional requirement to maintaining the usual records, a book of duplicate **cash receipts** must be kept with each receipt, identifying the date on which cash is received, the person from whom cash is received, the amount of cash received, the client for whom cash is received, and any file number in respect of which cash is received (see Figure 7.3). The signatures of the licensee or the person authorized by the licensee to receive cash, and of the person from whom cash is received, are also required (by-law 9, part V, section 19). The receipt book must be kept for a ten-year period pursuant to by-law 9, part V, section 23(2).

DUPLICATE CASH RECEIPT		NUMBER	1001
RECEIVED FROM	Frank Jones	DATE	03/10/20**
			dd/mm/yr
ON BEHALF OF		FILE NO.	2
AMOUNT	One hundred dollars	DOLLARS	(100.00)
Frank Jones		*Justin Case*	
Signature of Payor		Authorized signature on behalf of firm	
GST/HST REG. NO. RT12345			

FIGURE 7.3   Sample receipt

Remember that money received on behalf of a client for future services or future disbursements must be deposited into the mixed trust bank account, and all amounts received and paid out on behalf of clients must be tracked. A company's balance sheet includes two **trust control accounts**: the trust bank account (moneys received from clients) and the trust funds owed accounts (moneys owed to clients). These trust accounts provide a total of all moneys received in trust for each client and a total of all moneys owed to each client.

The same double-entry bookkeeping system that applies to general accounting also applies to trust accounting.

LO3 Trust Bank Journal

All the transactions recorded in previous chapters related to general journal entries. When recording amounts related to trust receipts and disbursements, it is faster and more practical to use a special **trust bank journal**, sometimes called a trust receipts and disbursements journal, in which all financial transactions related to the mixed trust bank account are entered. Keeping trust records in a separate journal helps to eliminate errors and makes it easier to reconcile bank balances at the end of each month. This chapter will teach you how to record transactions in the trust bank journal and how to post the entries to the individual **client ledgers**, also called **client trust ledgers**. Note that trust balances are incorporated into the financial statements for the firm using the two control accounts: Trust Bank Account (115, an asset account) and Trust Funds Owed (215, a liabilities account). (See the chart of accounts listed on the inside front cover of this textbook.) Some firms prefer to keep two different trust journals, one for trust receipts and one for trust disbursements, while other firms use a single journal for both receipts and disbursements.

Book of Original Entry

The trust records to be kept pursuant to the LSO's by-law 9, part V, section 18(1) include a book of original entry identifying the following transaction details:

- each date on which money is received in trust for a client;
- the method by which money is received;
- the person from whom money is received;
- the amount of money received;
- the purpose for which money is received; and
- the client for whom money is received in trust.

Steps in Using the Trust Bank Journal

1. Record the trust bank journal entry (see Examples 1 and 2).
2. Post trust receipts and disbursements to each individual client trust ledger.
3. Prepare the client trust listing (total balance is transferred/posted to Trust Funds Owed).
4. Post the total trust receipts and trust disbursements to the Trust Bank Account ledger (115) and the Trust Funds Owed ledger (215).

Recording Debits and Credits in the Trust Bank Journal

When funds are received by the firm and deposited into the trust bank account, the entry will be recorded as a debit to the account. This is because Trust Bank Account (115) is an asset account, and assets have a normal debit balance. A credit entry will also be made to the client's trust ledger account to show that the funds are owed to the client. At the end of each period, the amounts in the client trust ledgers are totalled and the amount is posted to the control account Trust Funds Owed (215) as a credit because this is a liability account. Trust funds owed to clients must be equal to the amount in the trust bank account. Funds held in the trust account are shown as an asset on the balance sheet. Trust funds owed to clients are shown in the liabilities section of the balance sheet.

The examples that follow show the steps in recording receipts and disbursements in a trust bank journal.

EXAMPLE 1

Recording a Trust Receipt

On October 2, Cliff Howes, client file no. 1, brought Justin Case a retainer in the amount of $1,000 (in the form of a money order) for a Small Claims Court action against his neighbour, dealing with a dispute over a fence.

STEP 1

Enter the date of the receipt.

STEP 2

In the Received From/Paid To column, show the amount as "Rec." and enter the name of the person from whom the funds were received.

STEP 3

Under Client/Description, indicate the client file name and the reason the funds were received.

STEP 4

In the Method of Payment column, indicate how the client paid—via a money order, cheque, credit card, or other means.

STEP 5

In the Dr. column, enter $1,000 because funds were received and had to be deposited into the trust bank account. Trust Bank Account (115) is an asset account, so it is debited to indicate an increase in the account.

STEP 6

Post the amount of $1,000 to the client's trust ledger sheet by entering the amount in the Receipts (Cr.) column in the Cliff Howes file no. 1 ledger sheet (Figure 7.5). Show that the amount was posted by filling in the file number in the File No. column of the journal.

						Trust Bank Account	
Date 20**		Received From/Paid To	File No.	Client/Description	Method of Payment	Dr.	Cr.
Oct.	2	Rec. Cliff Howes	1	Cliff Howes/Retainer	Money Order	1,000	

Justin Case, Paralegal — Trust Bank Journal — TJ1

EXAMPLE 2

Recording a Trust Disbursement

On October 3, Justin wrote a cheque on the Cliff Howes file to Deliveries Inc. to pay the amount of $20 to send a demand letter by courier to Howes' neighbour.

STEP 1

Enter the date of the cheque.

STEP 2

In the Received From/Paid To column, show the amount as "Pd." and enter the name of the company to which the funds were paid.

STEP 3

Under Client/Description, indicate the name of the client and the reason the funds were paid out.

STEP 4

In the Method of Payment column, indicate the trust cheque number used to pay the bill.

STEP 5

Leave the Dr. column blank.

STEP 6

In the Cr. column, enter the amount of $20 paid out of the trust account.

Justin Case, Paralegal Trust Bank Journal						TJ1
Date 20**		Received From/Paid To	File No.	Client/Description	Method of Payment	Trust Bank Account	
						Dr.	Cr.
Oct.	2	Rec. Cliff Howes	1	Cliff Howes/Retainer	Money Order	1,000	
	3	Pd. Deliveries Inc.	1	Cliff Howes/Courier	Chq. 1		20

Follow the same steps as in the examples above for the transactions that took place from October 5 to the end of the period. Figure 7.4 shows the trust bank journal entries for October once the totals have been posted to the client trust ledgers. Posting from the trust bank journal is discussed in the following section.

Transactions
On October 5, Frank Jones, client file no. 2, paid Justin a retainer in the amount of $600 using his credit card and cash for defence of charges under the *Highway Traffic Act*.
On October 15, Justin received a bank draft in the amount of $2,500 from the neighbour's firm, James Settlor, in full settlement of the claim made by Cliff Howes.
On October 16, the funds received in settlement were paid to Cliff Howes.
On October 20, Justin represented Frank Jones in court and negotiated a reduced fine of $300. He paid the Minister of Finance the amount of the fine from trust funds held on behalf of the client.

Justin Case, Paralegal Trust Bank Journal						TJ1

Date 20**		Received From/Paid To	File No.	Client/Description	Method of Payment	Trust Bank Account	
						Dr.	Cr.
Oct.	2	Rec. Cliff Howes	1	Cliff Howes/Retainer	Money Order	$1,000	
	3	Pd. Deliveries Inc.	1	Cliff Howes/Courier	Chq. 1		20
	5	Rec. Frank Jones	2	Frank Jones/Retainer	Credit Card 500 Cash 100	600	
	15	Rec. James Settlor	1	Cliff Howes/Settlement	Bank Draft	2,500	
	16	Pd. Cliff Howes	1	Cliff Howes/Settlement	Chq. 2		2,500
	20	Pd. Minister of Finance	2	Jones/Payment of Fine	Chq. 3		300
	31				Totals	$4,100	$2,820
						(115/215)	(115/215)

FIGURE 7.4   Trust bank journal entries for October (after posting)

LO4 Posting from the Trust Bank Journal

Now that all the transactions for the month of October have been entered, total the columns in the trust bank journal. Post the totals from the trust bank account Dr. and Cr. columns to the general ledger for the firm (Trust Bank Account No. 115). Post the individual amounts to each client trust ledger sheet.

The figures in the File No. column indicate that the individual amounts were posted to each client's trust ledger sheet. This should be done on a daily basis when the entries are recorded in the journal.

The numbers at the bottom of the trust bank account Dr. and Cr. columns (115/215) in Figure 7.4 indicate that the total deposits and cheques made to the trust account were posted to the general ledger.

The client trust ledgers in Figure 7.5 show how the information was posted from the trust bank journal to the client trust ledger accounts. Note that a running total of the balance in the client's trust ledger account was calculated after each transaction. In this way, the lawyer/paralegal will always know how much money each client has to his or her credit in the mixed trust bank account.

Although there is only one entry for each date in the trust bank journal, Figure 7.5 shows that double entries have been made. Each amount in the trust bank journal is transferred to the individual client ledger accounts in the client trust ledger. These transactions are posted on a daily basis.

Justin Case, Paralegal
Client Trust Ledgers

Account: HOWES, Cliff re Small Claims Court					File No. 001
			Client Trust Ledger		
Date 20**		Received From/Paid To Explanation	Disbursements (Dr.)	Receipts (Cr.)	Balance in Trust
Oct.	2	Retainer		1,000	1,000
	3	Deliveries Inc.	20		980
	15	James Settlor, Settlement		2,500	3,480
	16	Cliff Howes, Settlement Funds	2,500		980

Account: JONES, Frank re *Highway Traffic Act*					File No. 002
			Client Trust Ledger		
Date 20**		Received From/Paid To Explanation	Disbursements (Dr.)	Receipts (Cr.)	Balance in Trust
Oct.	5	Retainer		600	600
	20	Minister of Finance, Fine	300		300

FIGURE 7.5   Client trust ledgers after posting

Some general principles about posting from the trust bank journal:

1. The individual amounts in the Dr. column of the trust bank journal are posted to the Receipts (Cr.) column in the client's trust ledger on a daily basis. Thus, there is a debit entry and a credit entry, which balances the books. Each client ledger sheet is kept up to date at all times, as posting is done daily and a running total is calculated. The client file number is entered in the trust bank journal to show the client trust account to which the entry was posted.

Trust Bank Account Dr. = Client Trust Ledger Sheet Cr.

2. The individual amounts in the Cr. column of the trust bank journal are posted to the Disbursements (Dr.) column in the client's trust ledger on a daily basis, and the file number is entered in the trust bank journal to show that the entry has been posted. Again, there is a double entry—a credit entry reducing the balance in the bank account and a debit entry in the respective client's trust ledger sheet.

Trust Bank Account Cr. = Client Trust Ledger Sheet Dr.

3. The totals of the trust bank account debit and credit columns are posted to the trust bank account in the general ledger. This is usually done at the end of the month.

4. A list of balances owed to clients, called the *client trust listing*, is prepared showing the total amounts held by each client. This information is obtained from the individual client trust ledger accounts (Figures 7.5 and 7.6). This total amount is entered in the

general ledger account Trust Funds Owed (215). The balance in this account must be equal to the balance in the Trust Bank Account (115) (see Figure 7.7).

Trust Bank Account Balance = Total of Client Trust Listing
(115)   (215)

LO5 Proving That Debits Equal Credits

To prove that there are no errors in the trust bank journal after posting, check to make sure that the balance in the general ledger account Trust Bank Account (115) is the same as the total of the list of balances owed to clients prepared at the end of the period.

	Justin Case, Paralegal List of Balances Owed to Clients October 31, 20**	
File No.	Account	Balance Owed
1	HOWES, Cliff re Small Claims Court	$980
2	JONES, Frank re *Highway Traffic Act*	300
	Total Owed to Clients	$1,280

FIGURE 7.6   Client trust listing at October 31

The total amount in the client trust listing as of October 31 is $1,280, with the individual amounts shown in Figure 7.6. After posting to the general ledger, the balance in Trust Bank Account (115) is $1,280. This serves as proof that the amounts in the client ledgers are equal to the amount in the bank.

Trust Bank Account						Account No. 115	
Date 20**		Explanation	PR	Debit	Credit	Dr./Cr.	Balance
Oct.	31	Trust Totals for October	TJ1	4,100	2,820	Dr.	1,280

Trust Funds Owed						Account No. 215	
Date 20**		Explanation	PR	Debit	Credit	Dr./Cr.	Balance
Oct.	31	Howes, Cliff	001		980	Cr.	980
	31	Jones, Frank	002		300	Cr.	1,280

FIGURE 7.7   General ledger, trust bank account at October 31

Possible Error

An error to watch for when comparing the client trust listing with the trust bank account balance is whether an amount was accidentally posted to the wrong client ledger. The total client trust listing and the bank balance might be equal, but the amount debited or credited to an individual client could be incorrect.

[LO6] Trial Balance

A **trial balance** of the general ledger accounts after the trust posting is completed would be as shown in Figure 7.8.

	Justin Case, Paralegal Trial Balance October 31, 20**		
#	*Account*	*Debit*	*Credit*
100	General Bank Account	$7,100	
115	Trust Bank Account	1,280	
155	Computer Equipment (Hardware)	900	
158	Office Furniture and Equipment	2,250	
200	Accounts Payable/General Liabilities		$580
205	Personal Loan		4,000
210	Credit Card Debt		1,500
215	Trust Funds Owed		1,280
300	Justin Case, Capital		2,550
400	Fees Earned		3,000
535	Office Supplies/General Expense	580	
538	Rent Expense	500	
565	Telephone Expense	300	
		$12,910	$12,910

FIGURE 7.8 Trial balance including Trust Bank Account and Trust Funds Owed

Because the only changes made were to the trust bank account and trust funds owed to clients, this will have no effect on the firm's income statement or on the statement of owner's equity for the month of October, so these statements are not reproduced here. However, the balance sheet would show the trust bank account and the trust funds owed as in Figure 7.9.

The LSO requires licensees to maintain a record showing a comparison made monthly of the total balances held in the trust account or accounts and the total of all unexpended balances of funds held in trust for clients as they appear from the financial records. An explanation must be provided giving the reasons for any differences between the totals in the client ledger and the reconciled bank balance (by-law 9, part V, section 18(8)). This point will be discussed in greater detail when bank reconciliations are covered in Chapter 10.

Justin Case, Paralegal Balance Sheet October 31, 20**			
Assets		Liabilities	
General Bank Account	$ 7,100	Accounts Payable/General Liabilities	$580
Trust Bank Account	1,280	Credit Card Debt	1,500
Computer Equipment (Hardware)	900	Trust Funds	1,280
Office Furniture and Equipment	2,250	Personal Loan	4,000
		Total Liabilities	$ 7,360
		Owner's Equity	
		J. Case, Capital	4,170
Total Assets	$11,530	Total Liabilities and Owner's Equity	$11,530

FIGURE 7.9   Balance sheet including trust assets and trust liabilities

LO7 Matter-to-Matter Trust Transfer Journal

Whenever trust funds are moved from one client's trust ledger account to another client's trust ledger account, the transfer must be recorded in a **matter-to-matter trust transfer journal,** and the reason for the transfer must be explained (by-law 9, part IV, section 9(1)(4) and part V, section 18(4)). The special journal used to record these transactions is called the trust transfer journal.

Sometimes a client may instruct the firm to transfer funds held in trust on his or her behalf over to another file. This situation might arise if a parent has a file with the firm and a child is charged with an offence. The parent assumes responsibility for the child's defence and instructs the paralegal to use money held in trust in the parent's account to cover the cost.

POTENTIAL PARALEGAL PITFALLS

- **Potential pitfall:** Spending trust money for business purposes.
- **Possible fallout:** Your license can be suspended permanently if you are found to have spent client trust money for items not involving clients.
- **Proposed recommendation:** Never spend client money on anything that is not specifically for that client. Do not spend trust money on behalf of other clients or for your business or personal expenses.

EXAMPLE 3

On November 1, Cliff Howes, client file no. 1, has $980 left in his trust account after receiving the settlement paid in his court case. Also, on November 1, he instructs the firm to transfer $280 to a new file in the name of Larry Howes as a retainer to cover legal fees in defending his son's shoplifting case.

This transaction must be recorded in a matter-to-matter trust transfer journal showing that money was moved from one client to another:

Justin Case, Paralegal Trust Transfer Journal						
Date 20**		Received From/Paid To Reason for Transfer	File No.	Client	Allocated Amount	Transfer Amount
Nov.	1	Cliff Howes	1	Cliff Howes	−280	
	1	Larry Howes	3	Larry Howes	280	280
		To transfer funds to account of Larry Howes				

Clients' instructions should be obtained before transferring funds from one matter to another matter if the two matters are for the same client. If the transfer is made from one client to another client, these instructions should be obtained in writing prior to any transfer being made.

A new client ledger would have to be opened for the Larry Howes file, and the transfer would be posted in the client ledgers as follows:

Justin Case, Paralegal Client Trust Ledgers					
Account: HOWES, Cliff re Small Claims Court					**File No. 001**
Date 20**		Received From/Paid To Explanation	Disbursements (Dr.)	Receipts (Cr.)	Balance in Trust
Oct.	2	Retainer		1,000	1,000
	3	Deliveries Inc.	20		980
	15	James Settlor, Settlement		2,500	3,480
	16	Cliff Howes, Settlement Funds	2,500		980
Nov.	1	Cliff Howes, Transfer to File No. 3	280		700
Account: HOWES, Larry					**File No. 003**
Date 20**		Received From/Paid To Explanation	Disbursements (Dr.)	Receipts (Cr.)	Balance in Trust
Nov.	1	Transfer from Cliff Howes		280	280

Note that the total balance in the trust bank account has not been affected by this transaction, because funds were moved only between two client trust ledger accounts. No cheque needs to be written to complete this transaction; however, the transfer must be shown in the firm's records.

The client list of trust funds owed to clients will reflect this transaction at the end of November when the trust listing is prepared.

LO8 Valuable Property Record

Another trust record required by the LSO is the **valuable property record** (by-law 9, part V, section 18(9)). The record is used to record all property, other than money, held in trust for clients, and describes each item and identifies the date on which the licensee took possession, the person who had possession immediately before the licensee took possession, the value, the client for whom each item is held in trust, the date on which possession is given away, and the person to whom the item is given.

Valuable property can be anything of value held for clients, such as bond certificates, share certificates, jewellery, or collector's items. Anything that a paralegal could convert to cash on his or her own authority should be included. It would be wise to investigate any insurance implications before agreeing to hold valuable property for clients. And you would certainly need to have written instructions from everyone before getting involved in such a situation.

The valuable property record is not used to record any trust moneys because these must be shown in the financial accounting records. Items such as term deposits and bank accounts held at a financial institution must be reported in the financial records, not in the valuable property record. Pursuant to by-law 9, sections 18(9) and 23, the valuable property record must be kept for ten years plus the current year.

Although holding a client's valuable property does not typically fall within a paralegal's role, the following scenario is not an impossible one.

EXAMPLE 4

On October 20, Frank Jones brought a stamp collection in to the firm for safekeeping. This collection is still held by the firm. On November 1, Larry's parents made him turn over his hockey cards to Justin Case to ensure their son helped pay for his legal fees for the shoplifting charge. The parents insisted that if Larry did not work to contribute to his legal costs, Justin Case would be authorized to sell the cards and apply the proceeds to Larry's legal fees. Justin sold the cards on December 15 because Larry did not come up with the money as required. The proceeds from the sale would be deposited in the trust bank account to the credit of Larry Howes.

Justin Case, Paralegal Valuable Property Record						
Client	Description of Property	Date Received	Received From	Value of Property	Given To	Date Given
Jones, Frank	Stamp Collection	Oct. 20, 20**	Jones, Frank	200		
Howes, Larry	Hockey Cards	Nov. 1, 20**	Howes, Larry	60	Joe's Pawn Shop	Dec. 15, 20**

Practice Audits

Section 49.2 of the *Law Society Act*[1] authorizes spot audits of members with a view to ensuring that licencees engage in proper management practices. Audits include an assessment of financial record-keeping practices to ensure compliance with by-law 9. The primary goal of audits is to provide on-site guidance aimed at helping the licensee correct minor deficiencies with respect to record-keeping, and to address any deficiencies that could adversely affect

---

1   RSO 1990, c L.8.

service to clients. Where misconduct is found, reviewers are required to report that misconduct pursuant to rule 6.10(3) of the *Rules of Professional Conduct*.[2] Failure to meet minimum standards can result in suspension of membership until the LSO is satisfied that the licensee is meeting the minimum standards of professional competence. It is usual to receive a two-week advance notice of a spot audit. If members try to defer or cancel audit appointments, they will be required to fax a copy of the most recent trust bank reconciliation to the auditor. Failure to do so may result in an immediate unannounced visit.

PCLAW®

Using the Trust Bank Features to Record Receipts and Payments

Retainers and other trust funds received are entered in PCLaw® by recording the amount received using the trust bank receipt feature (Figure 7.10). Recording the amount received shows the amount in the trust bank account and records it in the client trust ledgers. The PCLaw® system creates a deposit slip when requested. Note that the system indicates how the client paid, whether it be by cash or credit card. There is also a hold receipt feature whereby the paralegal can place a hold on the deposit for a certain period of time. This feature is used to ensure cheques are not written against a deposit until the client's cheque has been honoured by the client's bank.

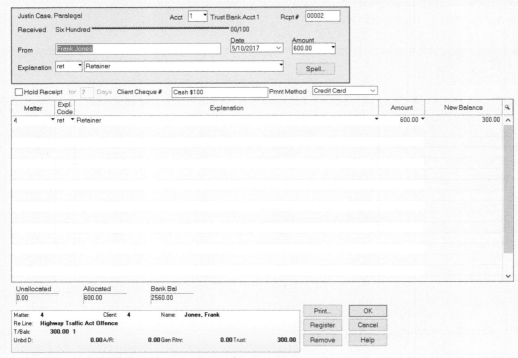

FIGURE 7.10 A trust bank receipt in PCLaw®

Disbursements from trust are recorded using the trust cheque feature in PCLaw® (Figure 7.11). Creating a trust cheque entry records the amount of the cheque as a credit to the trust bank account and as a debit to the specified client account.

---

2 Law Society of Ontario, *Rules of Professional Conduct* (1 October 2014; amendments current to 25 January 2018), online: <https://lso.ca/about-lso/legislation-rules/rules-of-professional-conduct>.

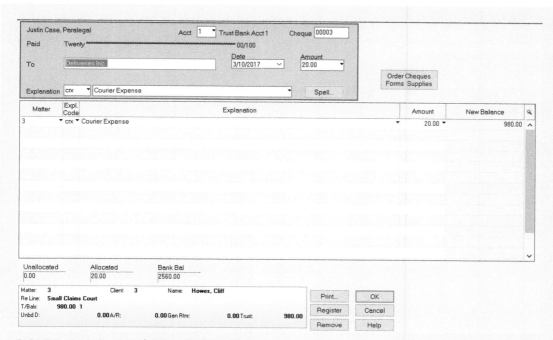

FIGURE 7.11   A trust cheque in PCLaw®

The system records deposits and cheques written on the trust bank account in the trust bank journal (Figure 7.12).

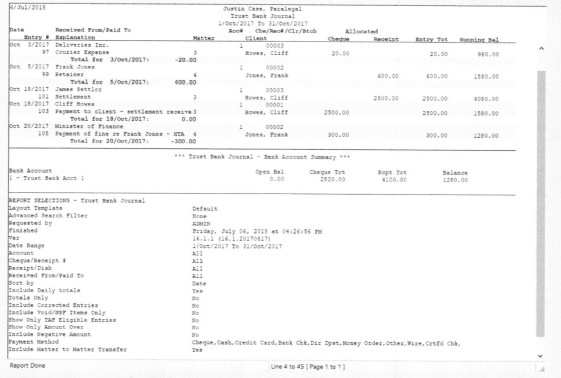

FIGURE 7.12   A trust bank journal in PCLaw®

Amounts entered in the trust bank journal are also automatically posted to the client ledgers (Figure 7.13). The client ledgers show all transactions affecting each account and provide totals so that the paralegal can always know what amount is held for each client in trust.

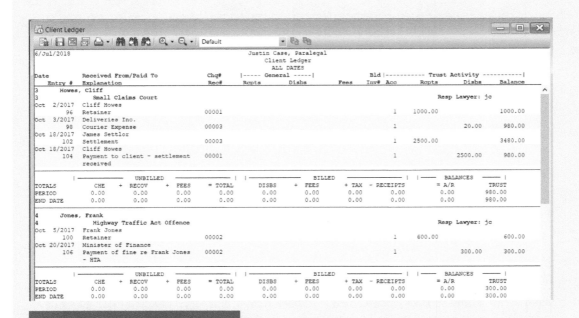

Client Ledger

Lists an accounting history by matter of Opening Balances, Disbursements, Time/Fees, Trust, Billing and Payments.

Run this report to:

- Provide an accounting record for the client file.
- List a matter's trust transactions for each trust account.
- Provide an accounting record for closed file records.
- Provide a year-end listing of each matter's transactions.

FIGURE 7.13   A client ledger in PCLaw®

CHAPTER SUMMARY

There are some similarities between trust accounting and general accounting: each has books of original entry and ledgers, and the double-entry bookkeeping system applies to both types of accounting. Trust accounting requires some additional records, whereas general accounting will incorporate information from the trust records into the financial statements for the firm. Most trust records must be maintained for a period of ten years plus the current year, whereas general records are required to be maintained for the most recent six full years plus the current year. See Chapter 10 for more discussion on this. All bank accounts, whether trust or general, must be reconciled at the end of each month.

In keeping with the LSO's mandate to protect the interests of the public, licensees must be vigilant in ensuring that the obligations set out by the *Law Society Act* and its by-laws and the *Rules of Professional Conduct* are followed. The LSO regularly conducts spot audits on members, and mishandling of trust funds can result in discipline or losing one's licence. If you purchase accounting software for a firm, it is wise to ensure that the system purchased can handle trust transactions and properly record transactions in a client ledger.

KEY TERMS

cash receipts, 160
client ledgers, 161
client trust ledgers, 161
matter-to-matter trust transfer journal, 169
trial balance, 168

trust bank account, 158
trust bank journal, 161
trust control accounts, 161
valuable property record, 171

FURTHER READING

Law Society of Ontario, *Bookkeeping Guide for Paralegals* (Toronto: LSO, December 2015), online: <https://lawsocietyontario.azureedge.net/media/lso/media/legacy/pdf/p/paralegal_bookkeeping_guide_final-s.pdf>. (See General Receipts Journal and General Disbursements Journal.)

Law Society of Ontario, By-Laws. "By-Law 9 – Financial Transactions and Records," online: <https://www.lso.ca/about-lso/legislation-rules/by-laws>. (See also the Appendix of this textbook.)

Law Society of Ontario, *Complete Paralegal Rules of Conduct*, online: <https://lso.ca/about-lso/legislation-rules/paralegal-rules-of-conduct/complete-paralegal-rules-of-conduct>.

Law Society of Ontario, *Paralegal Professional Conduct Guidelines*, online: <https://lso.ca/about-lso/legislation-rules/paralegal-professional-conduct-guidelines>.

REVIEW QUESTIONS

Short Answer

Give a full answer for each question:

1. A client bill is paid in part by trust moneys held on behalf of the client and in part by cheque. How will the paralegal record this transaction? **(LO3)**

2. If a client has two separate matters being handled by a paralegal, can that client authorize the transfer of funds from one trust account to the other? Explain. What if the transfer of funds is from a third-party trust account? Explain. **(LO7)**

3. When would a paralegal use a book of duplicate cash receipts? For how long would this record have to be maintained? **(LO2)**

4. How are monetary retainers recorded? Identify the appropriate journal and/or ledger. **(LO2)**

5. How can you verify that the trial balance after the trust posting is correct? **(LO6)**

6. Why is it important to review client ledgers from time to time? **(LO4)**

7. Which journal is used to track payments made from the trust bank account? **(LO3)**

8. A client entrusts to a paralegal her certificate of authenticity of a vintage coin collection that is the subject of a small claims dispute. How would the paralegal record and track this item? **(LO3)**

PRACTICE EXERCISES

Practice Exercise 7.1

Justin Case received the following amounts to be deposited into his trust account on March 1. **(LO2)**

- Justin received a cash payment from Victoria Hubert (file no. 35) in the amount of $245.50 on March 1 and deposited the amount in his trust account. The receipt consisted on the following denominations: four $50 bills, two $20 bills, one loonie, two toonies, and two quarters.
- Justin received a bank draft from Samuel Betts (file no. 50) as a retainer for $550 to be deposited on March 1.
- Justin received cheque #25 in the amount of $1,500 from Mike Dolan (file no. 45) as a retainer to be deposited on March 1.

a. Prepare the cash receipt using the forms provided.

b. Prepare the deposit slip using the forms provided.

DUPLICATE CASH RECEIPT   **NUMBER**   **150**

RECEIVED FROM   **DATE**

                                                        dd/mm/yr

ON BEHALF OF   **FILE NO.**

AMOUNT   **DOLLARS**

         Signature of Payor   Authorized signature on behalf of firm

TAX REG. NO.

CREDIT ACCOUNT OF: **BUSINESS ACCOUNT DEPOSIT SLIP**

JUSTIN CASE, PARALEGAL   **BANK OF MONEY**
IN TRUST   ONTARIO, CANADA
ACCOUNT NUMBER 232017661

DATE: **INITIALS:**

DAY	MONTH	YEAR

DEPOSITOR'S	TELLER'S

LIST OF CHEQUES:

CHEQUE IDENTIFICATION	AMOUNT
1	
2	
3	
4	
5	
6	
7	
8	
CHEQUE SUBTOTAL	
TOTAL # OF CHEQUES	

CASH COUNT:

X 5
X 20
X 20
X 50
X $1 COIN
X $2 COIN

COIN TOTAL

CASH COUNT

CASH SUBTOTAL

DEPOSIT:

CASH SUBTOTAL

CHEQUE SUBTOTAL

DEPOSIT TOTAL

Practice Exercise 7.2

The following transactions occurred during the month of August 20**, which affect the Ann Litigate trust account.

August 1–31, 20**:

1   L. Jones Bailey paid a retainer to Ann Litigate in the amount of $1,000 (money order).

1   R. Smythe paid a retainer to Ann Litigate in the amount of $1,000 (bank draft).

1   L. Forte paid a retainer to Ann Litigate in the amount of $500 (cheque #48).

3   Paid Quick Messenger $20.80 (HST included) with trust cheque #20 for deliveries on the L. Jones Bailey file.

5   Paid Ann Litigate $500 from the trust account (trust cheque #21) from the L. Jones Bailey account to pay the balance outstanding on invoice #401.

8   Paid Minister of Finance from the trust account, $100 (trust cheque #22) on the R. Smythe file to set matter down for trial.

10   Paid Ann Litigate out of trust account (trust cheque #23) on the L. Jones Bailey file to reimburse her for $120 paid for court filing fees on July 7 out of her General Bank Account.

    a. Prepare the appropriate Trust Bank Journal entries to record the transactions in the Trust Bank. (LO3)

    b. Post the transactions from the Trust Bank Journal in 7.2(a) to the Client Trust Ledgers provided. (LO4)

    c. Prepare a list of Balances Owed to Clients as of August 31 and enter the totals in Trust Funds Owed in the General Ledger (215). (LO5)

    d. Post the totals from the Trust Bank Journal to the Trust Bank Account in the General Ledgers provided. The total owed to clients and the total balance in the Trust Bank Account (115) should be the same. (LO5)

<table>
<tr><th colspan="6">Ann Litigate, Paralegal
Trust Bank Journal</th><th>TJ1</th></tr>
<tr><th rowspan="2">Date
20**</th><th rowspan="2">Received From/Paid To</th><th rowspan="2">File
No.</th><th rowspan="2">Client/Description</th><th rowspan="2">Method of
Payment</th><th colspan="2">Trust Bank Account</th></tr>
<tr><th>Dr.</th><th>Cr.</th></tr>
<tr><td></td><td></td><td></td><td></td><td></td><td></td><td></td></tr>
<tr><td></td><td></td><td></td><td></td><td></td><td></td><td></td></tr>
<tr><td></td><td></td><td></td><td></td><td></td><td></td><td></td></tr>
<tr><td></td><td></td><td></td><td></td><td></td><td></td><td></td></tr>
<tr><td></td><td></td><td></td><td></td><td></td><td></td><td></td></tr>
<tr><td></td><td></td><td></td><td></td><td></td><td></td><td></td></tr>
<tr><td>31</td><td>Totals</td><td></td><td></td><td></td><td></td><td></td></tr>
<tr><td></td><td></td><td></td><td></td><td></td><td>0.00</td><td>0.00</td></tr>
</table>

Ann Litigate, Paralegal
Client General Ledgers and Client Trust Ledger

Account: FORTE, L. — File No. 04

Date 20**	Received From/Paid To Explanation	Client General Ledger						Client Trust Ledger		
		Disbursements Expenses Paid	HST	Fees	Payments from Client	Balance Owed		Disbursements (Dr.)	Receipts (Cr.)	Balance in Trust

Account: BAILEY, L. JONES — File No. 05

Date 20**	Received From/Paid To Explanation	Client General Ledger						Client Trust Ledger		
		Disbursements Expenses Paid	HST	Fees	Payments from Client	Balance Owed		Disbursements (Dr.)	Receipts (Cr.)	Balance in Trust

Account: SMYTHE, R. — File No. 06

Date 20**	Received From/Paid To Explanation	Client General Ledger						Client Trust Ledger		
		Disbursements Expenses Paid	HST	Fees	Payments from Client	Balance Owed		Disbursements (Dr.)	Receipts (Cr.)	Balance in Trust

Ann Litigate, Paralegal
List of Balances Owed to Clients
June 30, 20**

File No.	Account	Balance Owed
	Total Owed to Clients	

Ann Litigate, Paralegal
General Ledger Accounts

General Bank Account — Account No. 100

Date 20**	Explanation	PR	Debit	Credit	Dr./Cr.	Balance

Trust Bank Account — Account No. 115

Date 20**	Explanation	PR	Debit	Credit	Dr./Cr.	Balance

HST Payable — Account No. 240

Date 20**	Explanation	PR	Debit	Credit	Dr./Cr.	Balance

Ann Litigate, Capital Account No. 300

Date 20**	Explanation	PR	Debit	Credit	Dr./Cr.	Balance

Fees Earned Account No. 400

Date 20**	Explanation	PR	Debit	Credit	Dr./Cr.	Balance

Salaries Expense Account No. 511

Date 20**	Explanation	PR	Debit	Credit	Dr./Cr.	Balance

Insurance—Professional Liability Account No. 527

Date 20**	Explanation	PR	Debit	Credit	Dr./Cr.	Balance

Rent Expense Account No. 538

Date 20**	Explanation	PR	Debit	Credit	Dr./Cr.	Balance

Delivery Expense						Account No. 550	
Date 20**		Explanation	PR	Debit	Credit	Dr./Cr.	Balance

PRACTICE
EXCEL

Practice Exercise 7.3

Ann Litigate had the following trust transactions in the month of June:

#	Date 20**	Transaction	Amount
1	June 1	Ann received a cheque (#91) from a new client, Jessica Palmer, file matter #6, as a retainer deposit in an immigration law matter.	$2,500
2	June 1	Ann wrote trust cheque #352 on the trust bank account in payment of invoice #518 previously sent to Karen Charles, file matter #4. Assume that on May 30, Charles had a balance of $4,500.	$4,000
3	June 8	There is an amount of $60 charged to Daniel Pitt, file matter #3 for photocopy charges incurred in the preparation of a document brief for use at an upcoming criminal trial. Invoice #519 was sent to Daniel Pitt, and Ann wishes to recover the charges for the disbursement from trust (trust cheque #353). Assume that on May 30, Pitt had a balance of $1,000.	$60
4	June 25	Louise Forte sent cheque #47 written on her personal bank account to the firm in the amount of $3,130, file matter #8. Ann deposited the cheque into the trust bank account and then wrote trust cheque #354 in payment of invoice #520 for $1,130 and held the balance remaining in trust as a retainer.	$3,130

Review the sample worksheet below and then using the worksheets provided:

a. Prepare the appropriate trust bank journal entries to record the transactions shown above. (LO3)

b. Post the entries to the client trust ledgers. (LO4)

c. Post the totals to the appropriate general ledger accounts. (LO4)

d. Complete the client trust listing at the end of the month. Does the listing match the amount in Account No. 215 (Trust Funds Owed)? (LO5)

Sample worksheets

On June 18, Paralegal receives $1,500 as a retainer from a new client, Anthony Johnston.

		Ann Litigate, Paralegal Trust Bank Journal				TJ1	
Date 20**		Received From/ Paid To	File No.	Client/Description	Method of Payment	Trust Bank Account	
						Dr.	Cr.
June	18	Rec. Anthony Johnston	01	Johnston, retainer	Cheque	1,500	
	30				Totals	1,500	0
						(115)	(115)

Sample client ledger after posting

		Ann Litigate, Paralegal Client Trust Ledgers			

Account: JOHNSTON, Anthony   **File No. 06**

Date 20**		Received From/Paid To Explanation	Client Trust Ledger		
			Disbursements (Dr.)	Receipts (Cr.)	Balance in Trust
June	18	Retainer		1,500	1,500

Worksheet a:

		Ann Litigate, Paralegal Trust Bank Journal				TJ1	
Date 20**		Received From/ Paid To	File No.	Client/Description	Method of Payment	Trust Bank Account	
						Dr.	Cr.
					Totals		

Worksheet b:

Ann Litigate, Paralegal Client Trust Ledgers					

Account:		File No.			
		CLIENT TRUST LEDGER			
Date 20**		Received From/Paid To Explanation	Disbursements (Dr.)	Receipts (Cr.)	Balance in Trust

Worksheet c:

Ann Litigate, Paralegal General Ledger Accounts						

Trust Bank Account						Account No. 115	
Date 20**		Explanation	PR	Debit	Credit	Dr./Cr.	Balance
May	30	Opening balance					5,500

Trust Funds Owed						Account No. 215	
Date 20**		Explanation	PR	Debit	Credit	Dr./Cr.	Balance
June	30	Total from client listing					

Worksheet d:

Ann Litigate, Paralegal List of Balances Owed to Clients June 30, 20**		
File No.	Account	Balance Owed
06	PALMER, J. re Immigration	
04	CHARLES, K.	
03	PITT, D.	
08	FORTE, L.	
	Total Owed to Clients	

Practice Exercise 7.4

You are a new paralegal with a general bank account balance of $8,000. On April 1 you set up a mixed trust account for your paralegal practice. The following events take place in your first two months of business, April and May 2014:

1. You are retained by Julie Moody in Matter 101. You receive $1,700 in trust to the credit of Matter 101 on April 1. Certified cheque #5489.

2. You are retained by Frances Buxton in Matter 107. You receive $500 in trust to the credit of Matter 107 on April 2. Certified cheque #277.

3. You pay for office rent to Mohawk Mall in the amount of $1,000 (plus HST) with general cheque #101 on April 3.

4. On April 4, you issue the plaintiff's claim for Julie Moody (Matter 101). You pay the court fee of $75 with trust cheque #1 payable to Small Claims Court.

5. On April 6, you issue the defendant's claim for Frances Buxton (Matter 107). You pay the court fee of $75 with trust cheque #2 payable to Small Claims Court.

6. On April 7, you file a defence for Frances Buxton (Matter 107). You pay the fee of $40 with trust cheque #3 payable to Small Claims Court.

7. You pay yourself $2,000 on April 30 with cheque #102.

8. You pay for office rent to Mohawk Mall in the amount of $1,000 (plus HST) with general cheque #103 on May 3.

9. You are retained by John Bender in Matter 112. You receive $2,000 in trust to the credit of Matter 112 on May 8. Certified cheque #310.

10. Matter 101 goes to settlement conference on April 10. No settlement is reached at the settlement conference, or within 30 days thereafter. On May 10, you request a date for trial. The court fee of $100 is paid out of the trust account with cheque #4 payable to Small Claims Court.

11. On May 12, you issue the defendant's claim for John Bender (Matter 112). You pay the court fee of $75 with trust cheque #5 payable to Small Claims Court.

12. You pay for Hydro in the amount of $150 plus HST, on May 14 with cheque #104.

13. On May 15, you deliver an interim invoice to Julie Moody. Your fees, excluding HST, are $1,100. The total amount of invoice #200, including HST, is $1,243. You transfer the funds from trust to pay the invoice.

14. On May 16, you deliver an interim invoice to Frances Buxton. Your fees, excluding HST, are $300. The total amount of invoice #201, including HST, is $339. You transfer the funds from trust to pay the invoice.

15. On May 17, you deliver an interim invoice to John Bender. Your fees, excluding HST, are $1,500. The total amount of invoice #202, including HST, is $1,695. You transfer the funds from trust to pay the invoice.

16. You pay yourself $2,000 on May 31 with cheque #105.

17. You are retained by Clark Morgans in Matter 120. You receive $1,600 in trust to the credit of Matter 120 on May 31. Certified cheque #886.

18. According to the Trust Account bank statement, the May 31 balance is $733. Trust cheques #4 and #5 were outstanding. Clark Morgans' trust receipt was also outstanding.

Complete the following:

a. Detailed duplicate trust deposit slips (LO2)
b. Trust Disbursements Journal (LO3)
c. Trust Receipts Journal (LO3)
d. Clients' Trust Ledgers (LO4)
e. Clients' General Ledgers (Chapter 6, LO2)
f. Fees Book (Chapter 6, LO2)
g. General Disbursements Journal (Chapter 6, LO4)
h. General Receipts Journal (Chapter 6, LO3)
i. Trust Reconciliation (LO5)
j. Client Trust Balances (LO5)

Bank of Hamilton			Credit Account of:
Date:			Mohawk Paralegal
Transit:	98765		**General Account**
Account number:	5345678991		
Cheques and Credit Card Vouchers		Details	Cash
		× $5	
		× $10	
		× $20	
		× $50	
		× $100	
		Cdn Cash Total	
Total		**Credit Card Vouchers and Cheques Forwarded**	

Trust Disbursements Journal				
Date	Method of payment/ Reference number	Paid to	Client	Amount

Mohawk Paralegal Trust Receipts Journal				
Date	Funds received from	Client	Method of payment	Amount

Mohawk Paralegal
Clients' Trust Ledger

Account: Julie Moody		**Re: Small Claims**		
Client matter no.:		101		
Date	Particulars	Receipts	Disbursements	Trust Balance

Account: Frances Buxton		**Re: Small Claims**		
Client matter no.:		107		
Date	Particulars	Receipts	Disbursements	Trust Balance

Account: John Bender		**Re: Small Claims**		
Client matter no.:		112		
Date	Particulars	Receipts	Disbursements	Trust Balance

Account: Clark Morgans		**Re: Small Claims**		
Client matter no.:		120		
Date	Particulars	Receipts	Disbursements	Trust Balance

Mohawk Paralegal
Fees' Book

Date	Invoice number	Client	Fees billed	Disbursements billed	HST Billed	Total Billed

Mohawk Paralegal
Clients' General Ledger

Account: Julie Moody — **Re: Small Claims**

Client matter no.: 101

Date	Particulars	Expenses paid	HST on expenses	Fees	HST on fees	Payment from client	Balance owing

Account: Frances Buxton — **Re: Small Claims**

Client matter no.: 107

Date	Particulars	Expenses paid	HST on expenses	Fees	HST on fees	Payment from client	Balance owing

Account: John Bender — **Re: Small Claims**

Client matter no.: 112

Date	Particulars	Expenses paid	HST on expenses	Fees	HST on fees	Payment from client	Balance owing

Account: Clark Morgans — **Re: Small Claims**

Client matter no.: 120

Date	Particulars	Expenses paid	HST on expenses	Fees	HST on fees	Payment from client	Balance owing

Mohawk Paralegal
General Disbursements Journal

Date	Paid to	Particulars	Method of payment/ Reference number	HST paid	Amount

Mohawk Paralegal
General Receipts Journal

Date	Funds received from	Particulars	Method of payment	Amount

Practice Exercise 7.5

You are a new paralegal with a general bank account balance of $12,000. On August 1 you set up a mixed trust account for your paralegal practice. The following events take place in your first two months of business, August and September 20**:

1. You pay for office rent to Jackson Mall in the amount of $950 (plus HST) with general cheque #200 on August 1.

2. You are retained by Carol Seaver in Matter 2050. You receive $2,500 in trust to the credit of Matter 2050 (Small Claims) on August 2. Certified cheque #658.

3. You are retained by Edna Garrett in Matter 2125. You receive $1,050 in trust to the credit of Matter 2125 (Small Claims) on August 3. Certified cheque #798.

4. On August 4, you issue the defendant's claim for Edna Garrett (Matter 2125). You pay the court fee of $75 with trust cheque #101 payable to Small Claims Court.

5. On August 6, you issue the plaintiff's claim for Carol Seaver (Matter 2050). You pay the court fee of $75 with trust cheque #102 payable to Small Claims Court.

6. On August 9, you file a defence for Edna Garrett (Matter 2125). You pay the fee of $40 with trust cheque #103 payable to Small Claims Court.

7. You pay yourself $2,300 on August 15 with cheque #201.

8. You pay for office rent to Jackson Mall in the amount of $950 (plus HST) with general cheque #202 on September 3.

9. You are retained by Tony Micelli in Matter 2226. You receive $3,400 in trust to the credit of Matter 2226 (Small Claims) on September 8. Certified cheque #359.

10. On September 13, you issue the defendant's claim for Tony Micelli (Matter 2226). You pay the court fee of $75 with trust cheque #104 payable to Small Claims Court.

11. Matter 2050 goes to settlement conference on August 14. No settlement is reached at the settlement conference, or within 30 days thereafter. On September 14, you request a date for trial. The court fee of $100 is paid out of the trust account with cheque #105 payable to Small Claims Court.

12. You pay Rogers Telephone for telephone expenses in the amount of $200, plus HST, on September 15 with cheque #203.

13. On September 16, you deliver an interim invoice to Edna Garrett. Your fees, excluding HST, are $400. The total amount of invoice #100, including HST, is $452.

14. On September 17, you transfer the funds (ET #987) from trust to pay invoice #100.

15. On September 18, you deliver an interim invoice to Carol Seaver. Your fees, excluding HST, are $900. The total amount of invoice #101, including HST, is $1,017.

16. On September 19, you transfer the funds (ET #654) from trust to pay invoice #101.

17. On September 20, you deliver an interim invoice to Tony Micelli. Your fees, excluding HST, are $1,400. The total amount of invoice #102, including HST, is $1,582.

18. On September 22, you transfer the funds (ET #321) from trust to pay invoice #102.

19. You pay yourself $1,800 on September 26 with cheque #204.

20. You are retained by Arnold Jackson in Matter 2389. You receive $2,000 in trust to the credit of Matter 2389 (Small Claims) on September 29. Certified cheque #144.

21. According to the Trust Account bank statement, the September 30 balance is $3,784. Trust cheques #102, #104, and #105 were outstanding. Arnold Jackson's trust receipt was also outstanding.

Complete the following on the worksheets provided:
a. Detailed duplicate trust deposit slips (LO2)
b. Trust Disbursements Journal (LO3)
c. Trust Receipts Journal (LO3)
d. Clients' Trust Ledgers (LO4)
e. Fees Book (Chapter 6, LO2)
f. Clients' General Ledgers (Chapter 6, LO2)
g. General Disbursements Journal (Chapter 6, LO4)
h. General Receipts Journal (Chapter 6, LO3)

Bank of Hamilton			Credit Account of:
Date:			Mohawk Paralegal
Transit:	98765		**General Account**
Account number:	5345678991		
Cheques and Credit Card Vouchers		Details	Cash
		× $5	
		× $10	
		× $20	
		× $50	
		× $100	
		Cdn Cash Total	
Total		**Credit Card Vouchers and Cheques Forwarded**	

Trust Disbursements Journal				
Date	Method of payment/ Reference number	Paid to	Client	Amount

Mohawk Paralegal Trust Receipts Journal				
Date	Funds received from	Client	Method of payment	Amount

Mohawk Paralegal
Clients' Trust Ledger

Account: Carol Seaver		Re: Small Claims		
Client matter no.:		2050		
Date	Particulars	Receipts	Disbursements	Trust Balance

Account: Edna Garrett		Re: Small Claims		
Client matter no.:		2125		
Date	Particulars	Receipts	Disbursements	Trust Balance

Account: Tony Micelli		Re: Small Claims		
Client matter no.:		2226		
Date	Particulars	Receipts	Disbursements	Trust Balance

Account: Arnold Jackson		Re: Small Claims		
Client matter no.:		2389		
Date	Particulars	Receipts	Disbursements	Trust Balance

		Mohawk Paralegal Fees Book				
Date	Invoice number	Client	Fees billed	Disbursements billed	HST Billed	Total Billed

Mohawk Paralegal
Clients' General Ledger

Account: Julie Moody   **Re: Small Claims**

Client matter no.:   101

Date	Particulars	Expenses paid	HST on expenses	Fees	HST on fees	Payment from client	Balance owing

Account: Frances Buxton   **Re: Small Claims**

Client matter no.:   107

Date	Particulars	Expenses paid	HST on expenses	Fees	HST on fees	Payment from client	Balance owing

Account: John Bender   **Re: Small Claims**

Client matter no.:   112

Date	Particulars	Expenses paid	HST on expenses	Fees	HST on fees	Payment from client	Balance owing

Account: Clark Morgans   **Re: Small Claims**

Client matter no.:   120

Date	Particulars	Expenses paid	HST on expenses	Fees	HST on fees	Payment from client	Balance owing

Mohawk Paralegal General Disbursements Journal					
Date	Paid to	Particulars	Method of payment/ Reference number	HST paid	Amount

Mohawk Paralegal General Receipts Journal				
Date	Funds received from	Particulars	Method of payment	Amount

PUT IT INTO PRACTICE

Case Example: LSO Rules

Ann Litigate operates a paralegal firm, operating under the name Ann Litigate Paralegal Services, and employs a part-time secretary. Ann works as a sole practitioner and deals with all professional, business, and administrative matters of the firm. For example, Ann does all the banking to ensure that she has control over her general and trust bank accounts in accordance with the rules and regulations of the LSO, and she does all the bookkeeping.

Ann is concerned about her record-keeping responsibilities because she is so busy with the day-to-day operations of the business as well as meeting deadlines and client expectations. Although Ann keeps all her source documents, she sometimes waits until the end of the month to complete the various journals and ledgers pursuant to section 18 of the LSO's by-law 9, and then she becomes overwhelmed. What best-practice strategies or tools can Ann use to meet all of her obligations? Discuss.

8 Adjusting Accounts for Financial Statements

Adjusting Entries 199

Preparing a Worksheet 199

Types of Adjusting Entries. 201

Preparing Adjusting Entries 204

Adjusted Trial Balance Column. 210

Income Statement and Balance Sheet Columns 210

Completing the Worksheet 211

Chapter Summary 214

Key Terms 214

Further Reading. 214

Review Questions 215

Practice Exercises 215

Put It into Practice. 219

After reading this chapter, you should be able to:

LO1 Record the trial balance in a worksheet.
LO2 Prepare adjusting entries at the end of a period.
LO3 Prepare an adjusted trial balance.
LO4 Complete the income statement and balance sheet portions of a worksheet.

Once the trial balance is prepared, the next step in the accounting cycle is to prepare a worksheet on which required adjustments are made before financial statements can be prepared. In this chapter you will learn how to prepare a *worksheet*, adjust entries, and prepare an *adjusted trial balance*. You will also use this information to complete the financial statements portion of the worksheet.

Figure 8.1 highlights these next steps in the accounting cycle.

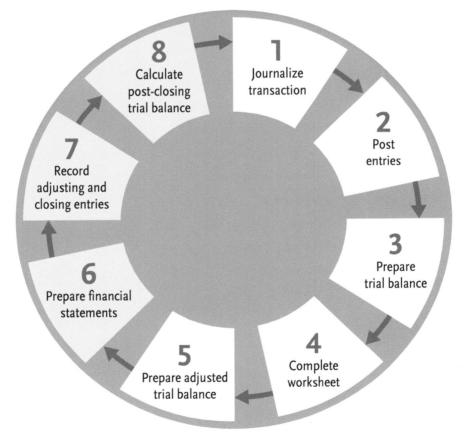

FIGURE 8.1   Steps in the accounting cycle

Adjusting Entries

At the end of the fiscal year, the firm is required to prepare an accurate and detailed statement of its revenues and expenses for income tax purposes. As discussed in Chapter 5, this is called an income statement and is used to calculate the profit (or loss) for the year. If the firm is a sole proprietorship, the business owner will have to include the amount of the profit on his or her personal income tax return. A worksheet enables the accountant to organize and check data, and make any necessary adjustments, before financial statements are prepared.

Before preparing his personal income tax return, Justin Case will want to ensure his records have been maintained in accordance with Canadian generally accepted accounting principles (GAAP). In particular, he will want to make certain that the **matching principle** has been respected, that is, that expenses incurred during the current accounting period are related to or have contributed toward the revenue that was generated during the same period. This principle is fundamental to the *accrual basis of accounting*.

Justin does not want to pay more income tax than he has to, so the statements will be reviewed and the entries adjusted with a view to ensuring that the numbers are accurate and that all expenses and deductions he is entitled to claim have been recorded. The reverse is also true: when reporting income for tax purposes, Justin must not understate his profit as a result of income or expenses not being recorded in the correct period.

The following is a sample of some of the adjusting entries needed in a firm. The adjustment process for Justin will include the following steps:

- Completing an accurate **office supplies inventory** and writing off supplies used as an expense.
- Calculating capital cost allowance or depreciation on Justin's assets and recording the amount of depreciation as an expense.
- Reviewing his accounts receivable to determine whether there are any bad debts to be written off.
- Reviewing the accuracy of his liabilities and making any necessary corrections.
- Ensuring there are no revenues and expenses that are to be carried over to the next operating year.
- Preparing an adjusted trial balance.

LO1 Preparing a Worksheet

The worksheet consolidates all adjustments to a firm's revenues and expenses. If the worksheet is prepared by hand, it can be completed in pencil because it is not a permanent record. Once the worksheet has been completed, the adjusting entries will be entered in the books of the firm using the general journal, and these entries will be posted to each of the ledger accounts affected.

The worksheet enables the bookkeeper to make sure that the books are balanced at each stage up to completion of the financial statements before starting the accounting cycle over again for the next period. A worksheet includes the following six column headings, as shown in Figure 8.2:

Account Titles	Trial Balance		Adjustments			Adjusted Trial Balance		Income Statement		Balance Sheet	
	Dr.	Cr.	Dr.		Cr.	Dr.	Cr.	Dr.	Cr.	Dr.	Cr.

FIGURE 8.2   Typical worksheet headings

1. *Account Titles*: The account numbers and names in the far left column of the worksheet are taken from the general ledger. The account number is not a requirement, but it can be included if the bookkeeper finds it helpful. For the purposes of this chapter, account numbers are included. The accounts are listed in the order of the trial balance: assets, liabilities, owner's equity, revenue, and expense.

2. *Trial Balance*: This section contains all of the account balances as found in the general ledger. Accounts with a zero balance are not listed. Additional account titles from the ledger will be added as they are needed once adjustments are made.

3. *Adjustments*: Each amount in the trial balance must be reviewed by the business owner, bookkeeper, or accountant to determine whether any adjustments are required. An adjusting entry can be recorded at the end of each accounting period, for example, each month. Some business owners may be satisfied with doing adjusting entries annually at the end of the fiscal year. Others may want to do them more often. Once the adjustments have been made, the debit and credit columns must be totalled to ensure that the adjusted debits are equal to the adjusted credits. The entries in the Adjustments column are assigned a letter for reference purposes, giving the corresponding debit and credit entries for a particular adjustment the same letter. This is helpful in tracking the entries that were made if you are looking for errors.

4. *Adjusted Trial Balance*: After the adjusting entries are recorded in the worksheet, the balance in each account is recalculated to arrive at the new balance for each account, and the amount is placed in the Adjusted Trial Balance column. Amounts from the trial balance that have not been adjusted are simply carried over to the Adjusted Trial Balance column. If there was an adjustment made to an account, a calculation of the new balance must be done. Debits are added to debits, credits are added to credits, and debits and credits are subtracted from one another. Once the horizontal calculations have been completed, the debit and credit column totals of the Adjusted Trial Balance column must be equal.

5. *Income Statement*: Extend the amounts for the income and expense accounts from the Adjusted Trial Balance column to the Income Statement column of the worksheet. These are the accounts with the numbers 400 to 599. Be careful to enter the amounts in the correct column for debit and credit. Revenue will normally be in the credit column, whereas expenses will normally be in the debit column. The difference between the income (credit) column and the expense (debit) column is the profit or loss for the period.

6. *Balance Sheet*: Extend the amounts of assets, liabilities, and owner's equity from the Adjusted Trial Balance column to the Balance Sheet column. The asset accounts are the accounts starting with the numbers 100 to 199, the liabilities are the accounts starting with the numbers 200 to 299, and the owner's equity accounts start with the numbers 300 to 399. Total the debit and credit columns once the entries have been copied from the Adjusted Trial Balance column. These totals will not be equal. The amount calculated as profit or loss from the income statement will be used to balance the debit and credit columns in the Balance Sheet column in the bottom portion of the worksheet.

Types of Adjusting Entries

Common adjustments include:

- prepaid expenses,
- amortization or depreciation,
- work in progress (WIP),
- accrued expenses, and
- accrued revenues.

Prepaid Expenses

Prepaid expenses represent items that have been paid for in advance. As the asset is used, the cost becomes an expense, and the amount used must be shifted from the balance in the asset account (Cr. the prepaid asset) to the expense section of the ledger (Dr. the expense). Common examples of prepaid expenses are prepaid insurance, office supplies, and prepaid rent.

Amortization or Depreciation

Amortization or **depreciation** refers to the estimated amount of a long-term asset that is *used up* during the period. The diminished value will be shown on the firm's balance sheet. The amount claimed for depreciation is an expense. Assets such as computers and office furniture have an extended life and are expected to be used by the firm for more than one accounting period. They cannot totally be written off as expenses in the year they are purchased. The cost of the item will be written off as an expense over the estimated useful life of the asset. This procedure complies with the matching principle in accounting. For income tax purposes, the amount expensed is called **capital cost allowance (CCA)**. When amortization expense is recorded, it is considered an operating expense, even though no cash is actually spent. (The cash was spent when the asset was acquired.)

There are some terms with which you need to be familiar when discussing depreciation:

- **Historical cost** refers to the original price paid for an item.
- **Class** refers to assets included in a particular account. For example, the account for office furniture will include desks, chairs, waiting room furniture, and so on.
- **Accumulated depreciation** refers to the total amount that has been expensed against a particular asset over time.
- **Depreciation expense** refers to the periodic write-off of long-term assets.
- **Book value** is the historical cost of the asset minus the accumulated depreciation. The number will decrease from period to period if no new assets have been added to the class.
- **Residual value** refers to the estimated value of the asset at the end of its useful life. Residual value is used when calculating depreciation expense.
- **Contra-asset account** is an account in the chart of accounts that has the opposite Dr./Cr. sign that is expected of its account type. In the case of accumulated depreciation, this contra-asset account records the depreciation of an asset. This account totals the amount of depreciation taken each period and is used to reduce the value of the asset on the balance sheet.

Depreciation will affect both the balance sheet and the income statement. The value of the asset on the balance sheet is being reduced by the amount of accumulated amortization taken. The expenses of the firm on the income statement are increased by the depreciation expense taken, resulting in lower income for the firm.

EXAMPLE 1

Depreciation

Suppose Justin Case purchased a photocopier costing $10,000 and took $79.17 depreciation in the month of December. The asset account would appear as follows on the balance sheet:

FIGURE 8.3   Depreciation of an asset

The amount of $79.17 will be posted as a debit to depreciation expense to balance the entry.

The value of the office equipment account shows the original cost of the photocopier. However, the accumulated depreciation for the period is linked to the office equipment account and the depreciation is subtracted (or credited) against the value. Once it is credited, the amount $9,920.83 represents the book value of the asset. Justin will know how much was originally paid for the photocopier because the historical cost does not change on the balance sheet. Amortization will increase from period to period, reducing the book value of the asset as time goes by.

Calculating Amortization

To depreciate an asset, how much of its cost is used up each period will need to be calculated. The CRA has specific rules that tell businesses in Canada how they can depreciate their assets for tax purposes. It is not necessary to use this calculation for financial reports because the value allowed by the CRA may be different from what the business owner feels is the useful life of an asset.

For the purposes of this textbook, two methods of calculating amortization on assets will be discussed, but the straight-line amortization method will be used for doing adjusting entries.

Straight-Line Amortization Method

The **straight-line amortization method** depreciates the value of an asset over its useful life after deducting its residual value, which refers to the estimated value of the asset at the end of its useful life. The amount of depreciation remains constant for each period.

The following formula is used to calculate the rate of amortization using the straight-line method:

$$\text{Depreciation} = \frac{\text{Cost of Equipment} - \text{Residual Value}}{\text{Estimated Useful Life}}$$

EXAMPLE 2

Suppose Justin purchased a photocopier that cost $10,000 and it was expected to last ten years, at which time he expected the residual value would be $500. The calculation of depreciation would be as follows:

$$\frac{\$10,000 - \$500}{10 \text{ years}} = \frac{\$9,500}{10 \text{ years}} = \$950 \text{ per year or } \$79.17 \text{ per month } (\$950/12)$$

The photocopier is depreciating at a constant rate of $950 per year or $79.17 per month ($950/12 months). Using the straight-line method for calculating depreciation on Justin's photocopier, the book value at the end of four years would be $6,200:

Office Equipment	Life	Historical Cost	Residual Value	Year	Depreciation 9,500/10 yrs.	Accumulated Depreciation	Book Value
Photocopier	10	10,000	500	1	950	950	9,050
		10,000	500	2	950	1,900	8,100
		10,000	500	3	950	2,850	7,150
		10,000	500	4	950	3,800	6,200

FIGURE 8.4 Calculation of depreciation using the straight-line method

Declining Balance Amortization Method

The CRA requires a business to calculate capital cost allowance using the declining balance method.[1] This means you claim CCA on the capital cost (original cost) of the property minus the CCA you claimed in previous years, if any. The remaining balance—the **undepreciated capital cost (UCC)**—declines over the years as CCA is claimed. The CRA prescribes the rates to be applied to each asset class as well as the formula used for calculating.

Work in Progress

Work in progress (WIP) refers to services that have not been completed or that have been performed in part but are still in progress and, therefore, not yet included as earned income or revenue. As mentioned in Chapter 2, paralegals may not exclude the value of work in progress from their income as is allowed for lawyers and accountants. An adjustment might be required to include as revenue the value of work in progress that has not yet been billed in income for the period. Usually, invoices are recorded when they are sent out and are shown as income. However, work in progress is recorded only when the invoice is sent. The **revenue recognition principle** of GAAP and the CRA rules governing paralegals require paralegals to include the value of work done on a file that has not yet been billed as revenue for the period. The balance sheet would also show the value of this work as an account receivable.

---

1 Canada Revenue Agency, "Claiming Capital Cost Allowance (CCA)," online: <http://www.cra-arc.gc.ca/tx/bsnss/tpcs/slprtnr/rprtng/cptl/menu-eng.html>.

Accrued Expenses

Accrued expenses refer to costs incurred in a period that are both unpaid and unrecorded. For example, a business could have **accrued interest expense** owing on an unpaid liability. Salaries often must be adjusted because the employee may be owed a certain number of days' pay at the end of the period, but payday is in the next period. Accrued vacation pay is a liability owing to the employee for which an adjustment may be required.

Accrued Revenues

Accrued revenues refer to income that has been earned but has not yet been received or recorded. For example, **accrued interest revenue** on an investment may have accumulated over the period, but may not have been received and not have been recorded in the records of the business. If Justin Case had a guaranteed investment certificate of $10,000 invested at the rate of 2 percent per annum, the daily interest accruing on the investment would be $10,000 × 2 percent per annum (365 days), or 55 cents a day. If he held the investment for 90 days, the adjustment would be $49.50.

TAX TIP

Value of Work in Progress

One of the adjustments that will need to be calculated for income tax purposes is the value of WIP if it has not already been included. The income statement prepared for the purposes of filing an income tax return must include all fees received for goods or services that were provided, whether money is received or will be received for it. A legal professional's income generally includes the value of their work in progress. Professional fees for the current year are the total of:

- all amounts received during the year for professional services, whether the services are provided before or during the current year or after the current year-end; plus
- all amounts receivable at the end of the current year for professional services provided during the current year; and
- the value of any WIP at the end of the current year for which amounts have not been received during the year; minus
- all amounts receivable at the end of the previous year-end; and
- the value of WIP that was included.

Preparing Adjusting Entries

Justin Case selected December 31 as his fiscal year-end. Once the accounting entries were completed, he prepared the trial balance as of December 31, and the balances were entered in the Trial Balance column of the completed worksheet in Figure 8.8 at the end of this chapter.

Adjusting Entries for Year-End

Upon reviewing the trial balance for his books at the end of December (Figure 8.5), Justin realizes that some transactions need to be adjusted before the financial statements for the year can be finalized. Each type of **adjusting entry** is demonstrated using the accounts described below.

Remember that even when doing adjusting entries, there must be a debit and a credit entry for the books to remain balanced. Each adjustment is identified with a letter of the alphabet (a, b, c, d, e, and so on) to track the corresponding debit and credit. Once an adjustment is completed, the rows across the page must be totalled to calculate the new balance in each account. This calculated amount is placed in the Adjusted Trial Balance column, as shown in Figure 8.6.

		Trial Balance	
	Justin Case, Paralegal **Worksheet** **for the Month Ended December 31, 20****		
	Account Titles	*Dr.*	*Cr.*
100	General Bank Account	$4,906.91	
115	Trust Bank Account	15,280.00	
120	Accounts Receivable	25,000.00	
125	Prepaid Insurance	600.00	
130	Office Supplies	630.00	
155	Computer Equipment (Hardware)	6,520.00	
158	Office Furniture and Equipment	2,250.00	
200	Accounts Payable/General Liabilities		$6,890.00
205	Personal Loan		3,000.00
210	Credit Card Debt		2,500.00
215	Trust Funds Owed		15,280.00
300	Justin Case, Capital		2,550.00
350	Justin Case, Drawings	1,800.00	
400	Fees Earned		31,580.00
511	Salaries Expense	960.00	
533	Meals and Entertainment Expense	350.00	
534	Membership/Professional Dues	1,343.75	
535	Office Supplies/General Expense	580.00	
538	Rent Expense	1,100.00	
565	Telephone Expense	479.34	
	Total	$61,800.00	$61,800.00

FIGURE 8.5   Trial balance at December 31

Adjustment (A): Prepaid Expenses

Justin has prepaid insurance of $600 on the trial balance. The insurance premiums cover one year; the policy starts on December 1 of this year and expires on November 30 next year. He must allocate the cost of the insurance over a 12-month period and cannot take the whole expense this year. This insurance covers liability for fire and theft on his premises.

The adjustment is calculated as follows:

$600/12 months = $50 per month

	Account Titles	Trial Balance Dr.	Trial Balance Cr.	Adjustments Dr.	Adjustments Cr.	Adjusted Trial Balance Dr.	Adjusted Trial Balance Cr.	Calculating the Balances in the Adjusted Trial Balance
100	General Bank Account	4,906.91				4,906.91		When there is no adjustment, simply place the trial balance amount in the Adjusted Trial Balance column, respecting Dr. and Cr.
125	Prepaid Insurance	600.00		+	50.00 (a)	550.00		Place the letter identifying the transaction in the column provided. Each transaction will have the same letter in two locations, one for the debit (see account 527 below) and one for the credit. Calculate the new balance: $600 Dr. – $50 Cr. = $550. Place the difference of $550 in the debit column, because the balance is a debit.
200	Accounts Payable		6,890.00	(d)			6,890.00	If the trial balance has a credit balance, and there are no adjustments, enter the amount in the credit column of the Adjusted Trial Balance column.
205	Personal Loan		3,000.00	+	100.00		3,100.00	If the trial balance has a credit balance and the adjustment is a credit, add the two credits together to obtain the new balance.
511	Salaries Expense	960.00	+	240.00 (e)		1,200.00		Add both debits together to get the new amount for salaries expense and place the total in the debit column of the Adjusted Trial Balance column.
	Total	61,800.00	61,800.00		Leave this space blank			Totals for the trial balance must be equal.
527	Insurance Expense			50.00 (a)		50.00		For the new accounts added at the end of the trial balance, the balance will be the amount entered in the Adjustments column. Place the amount in the Adjusted Trial Balance column, respecting Dr. and Cr. This is the entry that corresponds to entry "a" above.
	Totals			1,146.01	1,146.01	62,466.01	62,466.01	Total Dr. and Cr. for adjusting entries must be equal. Total Dr. and Cr. for the adjusted trial balance must be equal.

Justin must expense $50 for the month of December and leave the rest of the insurance premium in the prepaid insurance (asset) account. The adjusting entry required is a credit of $50 to the prepaid insurance account and a debit to the insurance expense account for $50. The adjusting entry required is as follows:

527	Insurance Expense	Dr.	$50
125	Prepaid Insurance	Cr.	$50

The steps followed to enter this adjustment in the worksheet are as follows (and are shown in Figure 8.7):

1. Enter $50 in the credit column of prepaid insurance and place the letter (a) next to the entry.
2. The account named Insurance Expense (527) is not listed in the trial balance. The account name must be added at the end of the list in the Account Titles column.
3. Enter the expense of $50 as a debit in the Adjustments column. Place the letter (a) next to the entry in the space provided.
4. Calculate the new account balance, taking the adjustments into consideration. The adjusted balance for prepaid insurance is $600 – $50, or $550. The insurance expense account has a new balance of $50. Calculate the new balances and place them in the Adjusted Trial Balance column in the correct column for debit or credit.

Adjustment (B): Office Supplies

Justin did an inventory of the supplies he has on hand in his supply cupboard. The amount remaining on December 31 is worth approximately $200. His trial balance shows a value of $630 in the office supplies account.

Calculation of the adjustment:

Inventory shown in trial balance	$630
Less: Amount left in stock	$200
Amount used over the period	$430

The goal of this adjustment is to show the correct value of what is left as an asset, which is $200, and to record the amount of $430 that was used as an expense.

Justin must record the amount of $430 as an expense, and he has to credit the asset account Office Supplies (130) to reduce the amount of the asset.

The adjusting entry required is as follows:

535	Office Supplies/General Expense	Dr.	$430
130	Office Supplies	Cr.	$430

The steps followed to enter this adjustment in the worksheet are as follows, and are shown in the completed worksheet in Figure 8.8 at the end of the chapter:

1. Enter $430 in the credit column of the asset account Office Supplies (130) and place the letter (b) next to the entry.
2. The account Office Supplies/General Expense (535) is listed in the Account Titles column, so it does not have to be added for this entry. Enter the expense of $430 as a debit in the Adjustments column. Place the letter (b) next to the entry in the space provided.
3. Calculate the new account balances after making the adjustments. The adjusted balance for Office Supplies (130) is $630 less the credit of $430, or $200. The adjusted balance for Office Supplies/General Expense (535) is $580 plus $430, or $1,010.

Adjustment (C): Depreciation

The account for Computer Equipment (Hardware) (155) has a value of $6,520 in the trial balance. Justin believes the assets have a useful life of about five years and that there will be no residual value for this equipment.

Calculation of depreciation using the straight-line method:

$$\frac{\text{Cost of Equipment} - \text{Residual Value}}{\text{Estimated Useful Life}} = \frac{\$6,520 - 0}{5} = \$1,304/12 \text{ months} = \$108.67$$

The annual depreciation of the equipment is $1,304. Suppose Justin has had the equipment in his business for only three months and wishes to take three months' worth of depreciation. He would multiply the monthly amount, or $108.67, by three months, for total depreciation of $326.01.

The adjusting entry required is as follows:

| 522 | Depreciation Expense | Dr. | $326.01 |
| 156 | Depreciation—Computer Equipment | Cr. | $326.01 |

The steps followed to enter this adjustment in the worksheet are as follows and are shown in Figure 8.8:

1. The account Depreciation Expense (522) is not listed in the Account Titles column, so the account name needs to be added below the last entry in the Account Titles column.
2. Enter the amount of depreciation expense ($326.01) as a debit in the Adjustments column. Place the letter (c) next to the entry.
3. The contra-asset account Depreciation—Computer Equipment (156) is not listed in the Account Titles column, so it also must be added. Add this below the account Depreciation Expense (522). Enter $326.01 as a credit in the Adjustments column and place the letter (c) next to the entry.
4. Calculate the new account balances after making the adjustments. The adjusted balance for Depreciation—Computer Equipment (156) is $326.01, and for Depreciation Expense (522) is $326.01.
5. Note that the account Computer Equipment (Hardware) (155) has not been changed. The value of this account has remained at $6,520, its historical value.

Adjustment (D): Personal Loan

Justin paid $1,000 to his father on the loan he accepted, but $100 of that was interest. His records show that he owes his father $3,000, but he in fact he owes his father $3,100 because the $100 for interest did not reduce the principal amount owing. Justin should have recorded the payment as a debit to Interest Expense (529) of $100 and $900 to the Personal Loan liability account (205). Because Justin's books show the amount of the loan outstanding at $3,000, he must correct this entry. He can do this using the following adjusting entry:

| 529 | Interest Expense | Dr. | $100 |
| 205 | Personal Loan | Cr. | $100 |

The steps required to enter this adjustment in the worksheet are as follows and are shown in Figure 8.8:

1. The account Interest Expense (529) is not listed in the Account Titles column, so the account name will need to be added below the last entry in the column.
2. Enter the amount of interest expense of $100 as a debit in the Adjustments column. Place the letter (d) next to the entry.
3. The personal loan secured by Justin was recorded in the account Personal Loan (205) in the liabilities section of the balance sheet. This account is listed on the trial balance, so the amount of $100 can be entered as a credit in the Adjustments column. Place the letter (d) next to the entry.
4. Calculate the new account balances after making the adjustments. The adjusted balance for Personal Loan (205) is $3,100, and Interest Expense (529) has a debit balance of $100. These amounts are shown in the Adjusted Trial Balance column.

POTENTIAL PARALEGAL PITFALLS

- **Potential pitfall:** Not completing adjusting journal entries at month, quarter, or year-end.
- **Possible fallout:** This will result in inaccurate financial information. Since paralegal sole proprietors pay income tax to the CRA based on their company net income, taxes may be over- or understated and an incorrect payment could be made to the CRA.
- **Proposed recommendation:** Analyze all trial balance accounts at year-end to determine if an adjustment is needed. For example, if there is a prepaid asset such as insurance or office supplies, consider if the prepaid asset was used up in the period and needs to be expensed. If the period-end adjustments are not well understood by the paralegal, consider hiring a bookkeeper or accountant to help.

Adjustment (E): Accrued Salaries Expense

Justin has a part-time employee who works five days a week, from Monday to Friday, and receives $80 a day, or $400 a week. She gets paid every two weeks on Friday. She was paid on December 12 and December 26, and she will receive her next paycheque on the next payday, which is January 9, next year. However, at the end of the fiscal period, December 31, the employee is owed three days' pay for December 29, 30, and 31. This payment will be made on January 9. An adjusting entry is therefore required to reflect the **accrued salaries expense** payable for three days at the rate of $80 a day for a total of $240. This can be done using the following adjusting entry:

| 511 | Salaries Expense | Dr. | $240 |
| 220 | Accrued Salaries Payable | Cr. | $240 |

The steps required to enter this adjustment in the worksheet are as follows and are shown in Figure 8.8:

1. The account Salaries Expense (511) is already listed in the Account Titles column. Debit the Adjustments column $240 to show the expense for salaries, and then place the letter (e) in the box next to the entry.
2. Accrued Salaries Payable (220) is not listed in the Account Titles column and must be added at the end.
3. Enter the amount of accrued salaries payable of $240 as a credit in the Adjustments column. Place the letter (e) in the box next to the entry.
4. Calculate the new account balances after making the adjustments. The adjusted balance for Salaries Expense (511) will be $1,200, and Accrued Salaries Payable (220) will have a credit balance of $240. These amounts are shown in the Adjusted Trial Balance column.

Checking the Adjusting Entries

To ensure that no mistakes were made in entering the adjusting entries, total the debit and credit columns of the Adjustments column in the worksheet (see Figure 8.8). The total debits must equal the total credits. If the totals are not equal, stop and look for errors using the same strategies for finding errors that were explained in Chapter 4. Do not proceed until these columns are balanced.

LO3 Adjusted Trial Balance Column

All account balances from the trial balance must be extended to the Adjusted Trial Balance column (see Figure 8.8). If the balances across the accounts were not already calculated as the adjustments were prepared, this is a good point to do it. Many people prefer to wait until all the adjustments are completed before calculating the adjusted trial balance. Remember to add debits together and to add credits together. Take the difference when calculating debits plus or minus credits and make sure the result is entered in the correct column. Keep in mind what the normal balance is supposed to be for each category of account (see Chapter 3).

If the balance is not the normal balance associated with that category of account, ask yourself, "why not?"

Looking for Errors

Consider the following potential errors:

- Calculation error: Two debits were not added together and instead were subtracted from one another or vice versa.
- Calculation error: The debits and credits were not subtracted.
- Entry in wrong column: The entry was put in the debit column instead of the credit column or vice versa.
- The balances from the trial balances were not carried over for the accounts that had no adjustment.

Once the debit and credit columns in the adjusted trial balance are equal, it is time to move on to the preparation of the financial statements.

LO4 Income Statement and Balance Sheet Columns

The totals from the adjusted trial balance should be carried over to the Income Statement column or the Balance Sheet column, depending on the category of account. Figure 8.7 shows the balances once they have been extended. Copy the amounts one by one from the adjusted trial balance over to the correct statement. Remember that the accounts numbered 100 to 399 belong in the Balance Sheet column and should be extended to the respective debit or credit columns. The accounts numbered 400 to 599 belong in the Income Statement column, so these amounts should be extended to the respective debit or credit columns.

Take care not to include the asset accounts listed at the bottom of the worksheet in the wrong category or statement. Pay particular attention to the contra-asset account for accumulated depreciation and the salaries payable account. These are credit balances that belong on the balance sheet.

Completing the Worksheet

Total the debit and credit columns of the Income Statement and Balance Sheet columns of the worksheet. The next task is to calculate the Income Statement and Balance Sheet columns.

Calculating Net Profit or Loss

Figure 8.7 shows the following steps (in superscript) in calculating the net profit or net loss:

	Income Statement		Balance Sheet		
	Dr.	Cr.	Dr.	Cr.	
	Totals	Totals	Totals	Totals	
Totals	[1]5,959.10	[1]31,580.00	[5]56,506.91	[5]30,886.01	
[4]Net Profit	[2]25,620.90			[6]25,620.90	
	[3]31,580.00	[3]31,580.00	[7]56,506.91	[7]56,506.91	[8]

Justin Case, Paralegal — Worksheet — for the Month Ended December 31, 20**

FIGURE 8.7   Completing the bottom portion of the worksheet

1. Total the Dr. and Cr. columns in the income statement section. They will not be equal.
2. Subtract the total credits and debits. If the credits on the income statement are higher than the debits, a net profit exists, but if the debits are higher than the credits, the result is a net loss. Enter the net loss in the space below whichever column has the smaller total.
3. Add the numbers at the bottom of the columns. The total debits should now equal the total credits at the bottom of the Income Statement column.
4. Write "Net Profit" or "Net Loss" in the Account Titles column.

Completing the Balance Sheet Portion of the Worksheet

Figure 8.7 shows the following steps (in superscript) in completing the balance sheet portion of the worksheet:

5. Total the Dr. and Cr. columns in the balance sheet portion of the worksheet. They will not be equal.
6. Place the amount of the net profit or loss from step 2 in the space below whichever column has the smaller total.
7. Add the balance sheet debit and credit columns on the last line of the worksheet. The debit and credit columns must be equal.
8. Rule the columns by placing a single line above and a double line below the totals.

A completed worksheet with all the adjustments and balances extended is shown in Figure 8.8.

Once the net profit or loss has been calculated and the result used to balance the columns under the balance sheet heading, all the information needed to prepare financial statements for the firm is now available.

Justin Case, Paralegal
Worksheet
for the Month Ended December 31, 20**

	Account Titles	Trial Balance		Adjustments		Adjusted Trial Balance		Income Statement		Balance Sheet	
		Dr.	Cr.	Dr.	Cr.	Dr.	Cr.	Dr.	Cr.	Dr.	Cr.
100	General Bank Account	4,906.91				4,906.91				4,906.91	
115	Trust Bank Account	15,280.00				15,280.00				15,280.00	
120	Accounts Receivable	25,000.00				25,000.00				25,000.00	
125	Prepaid Insurance	600.00			a 50.00	550.00				550.00	
130	Office Supplies	630.00			b 430.00	200.00				200.00	
155	Computer Equipment (Hardware)	6,520.00				6,520.00				6,520.00	
158	Office Furniture and Equipment	2,250.00				2,250.00				2,250.00	
200	Accounts Payable/ General Liabilities		6,890.00				6,890.00				6,890.00
205	Personal Loan		3,000.00		d 100.00		3,100.00				3,100.00
210	Credit Card Debt		2,500.00				2,500.00				2,500.00
215	Trust Funds Owed		15,280.00				15,280.00				15,280.00
300	Justin Case, Capital		2,550.00				2,550.00				2,550.00
350	Justin Case, Drawings	1,800.00				1,800.00				1,800.00	
400	Fees Earned		31,580.00				31,580.00		31,580.00		

	Account Titles	Trial Balance Dr.	Trial Balance Cr.	Adjustments	Adjustments Dr.	Adjustments Cr.	Adjusted Trial Balance Dr.	Adjusted Trial Balance Cr.	Income Statement Dr.	Income Statement Cr.	Balance Sheet Dr.	Balance Sheet Cr.
511	Salaries Expense	960.00		e	240.00		1,200.00		1,200.00			
533	Meals and Entertainment Expense	350.00					350.00		350.00			
534	Membership/Professional Dues	1,343.75					1,343.75		1,343.75			
535	Office Supplies/General Expense	580.00		b	430.00		1,010.00		1,010.00			
538	Rent Expense	1,100.00					1,100.00		1,100.00			
565	Telephone Expense	479.34					479.34		479.34			
	Total	61,800.00	61,800.00									
527	Insurance Expense			a	50.00		50.00		50.00			
522	Depreciation Expense			c	326.01		326.01		326.01			
156	Depreciation—Computer Equipment			c		326.01		326.01				326.01
529	Interest Expense			d	100.00		100.00		100.00			
220	Accrued Salaries Payable			e		240.00		240.00				240.00
	Totals				1,146.01	1,146.01	62,466.01	62,466.01	5,959.10	31,580.00	56,506.91	30,886.01
	Net Profit								25,620.90			25,620.90
	Totals								31,580.00	31,580.00	56,506.91	56,506.91

FIGURE 8.8   Completed worksheet

CHAPTER SUMMARY

The accrual basis of accounting requires that financial statements reflect revenues when earned and expenses when incurred so that they are reported in the correct accounting period. The adjustment process enables the record-keeper to adjust account balances to ensure that what is reported in the financial statements accurately reflects the financial position of the firm. A paralegal wishing to know how his or her business is doing will want to prepare an income statement fairly frequently. This practice tells the owner whether the company is making or losing money. The balance in the bank account is not always an indication of how your business is doing. The bank balance may show income from various sources, such as an investment by the owner, a transfer from the line of credit, or revenue earned.

Remember that a paralegal working as a sole proprietor does not receive a salary. Money is taken out of the firm by way of drawings. The income statement and balance sheet will tell the owner whether or not there is a profit from which a draw can be taken. Recording amortization on assets and preparing the common adjustments help to ensure that the financial records of the firm accurately reflect its financial position.

KEY TERMS

accrued interest expense, 204

accrued interest revenue, 204

accrued revenues, 204

accrued salaries expense, 209

accumulated depreciation, 201

adjusting entry, 204

amortization, 201

book value, 201

capital cost allowance (CCA), 201

class, 201

contra-asset account, 201

depreciation, 201

depreciation expense, 201

historical cost, 201

matching principle, 199

office supplies inventory, 199

prepaid expenses, 201

residual value, 201

revenue recognition principle, 203

straight-line amortization method, 202

undepreciated capital cost (UCC), 203

work in progress (WIP), 203

FURTHER READING

Canada Revenue Agency, "Accounting Methods," online: <http://www.cra-arc.gc.ca/tx/bsnss/tpcs/slprtnr/ccntng-eng.html>.

Canada Revenue Agency, "Claiming Capital Cost Allowance (CCA)," online: <http://www.cra-arc.gc.ca/tx/bsnss/tpcs/slprtnr/rprtng/cptl/menu-eng.html>.

Canada Revenue Agency, Guide RC4070(E) Rev. 17, *Information for Canadian Small Businesses*, online: <https://www.canada.ca/content/dam/cra-arc/formspubs/pub/rc4070/rc4070-17e.pdf>. See especially Chapter 5—Income Tax.

Canada Revenue Agency, Guide T4002(E) Rev. 17, *Self-Employed Business, Professional, Commission, Farming, and Fishing Income: 2017*, online: <https://www.canada.ca/content/dam/cra-arc/formspubs/pub/t4002/t4002-17e.pdf>.

Canada Revenue Agency, "Small Businesses and Self-Employed Income," online: <http://www.cra-arc.gc.ca/selfemployed>.

Michael Cooke, "External T.I. 2014-0531461E5—Paralegals and Work in Progress Election" (28 May 2014), online: <https://taxinterpretations.com/cra/severed-letters/2014-0531461e5>.

REVIEW QUESTIONS

True or False

_____ 1. The worksheet is an example of a financial statement. **(LO1)**

_____ 2. A contra-asset account reduces the value of an asset. **(LO2)**

_____ 3. An accrual is an adjustment that recognizes when cash is received or used to make a payment. **(LO2)**

_____ 4. Book value means the same thing as fair market value. **(LO2)**

_____ 5. Prepaid expense is an asset account reflected on the balance sheet. **(LO2)**

_____ 6. Paralegals can elect to exclude WIP in reporting income at the end of the financial year. **(LO2)**

_____ 7. Capital cost allowance is a tax reporting term used in the calculation of depreciating assets. **(LO2)**

_____ 8. Accumulated depreciation has a normal credit balance (Cr.). **(LO2)**

Short Answer

1. When Ann Litigate purchased $1,000 worth of stationery and supplies for the office, she recorded the purchases in the asset account Office Supplies (130). At the end of the year, she calculated the value of her office supply stock as $350. **(LO2)**

   a. What must Ann do to correctly reflect the accrued assets and expenses over the course of the past three months?

   b. Calculate the value of the office supplies used during the period.

   c. Which accounts need to be adjusted to record the office supplies used?

   d. If Ann does not make the necessary adjustment to her books, which account will be overstated and which will be understated?

   e. How would failure to make the adjustment affect:
      i.   the income statement?
      ii. the balance sheet?

2. What is the relationship between the adjusted trial balance and the income statement, balance sheet, and statement of owner's equity? **(LO3)**

PRACTICE EXERCISES

Practice Exercise 8.1

Complete the following table by calculating depreciation using the straight-line method for five years. **(LO2)**

Calculation of depreciation using the straight-line method							
Office Equipment	Life	Historical Cost	Residual Value	Year	Depreciation 3,500/10 yrs.	Accumulated Depreciation	Book Value
Computers	10	4,000	500	1	350	350	3,650
				2	350	700	3,300
				3			
				4			
				5			

Practice Exercise 8.2

Using the worksheet provided, prepare the adjusting entries for Ann Litigate's financial records, which her accountant will use in preparing her year-end financial statements. (LO2, LO3)

a. Dec. 31: Payment on account received (invoice #xx501, M. Arbor), $1,000.

b. Dec. 31: Prepaid professional insurance used up, $2,500 (one-year policy, from February of this year until February of next year, valued at $3,000).

c. Dec. 31: Rent expense recognized (Magnum Office Managers), $1,200.

d. Dec. 31: Office supplies used up, $200.

e. Dec. 31: Depreciation of computer equipment, $1,360/year based on the declining balance amortization calculation. Assume that Ann purchased the computer equipment for $6,800 in the previous year and that the annual depreciation being claimed is 20 percent.

	Account Titles	Trial Balance			Adjustments			Adjusted Trial Balance	
	Ann Litigate, Paralegal **Worksheet** **for the Month Ended December 31, 20****								
		Dr.	Cr.		Dr.	Cr.		Dr.	Cr.
100	General Bank Account	15,360							
115	Trust Bank Account	18,500							
120	Accounts Receivable	3,500							
125	Prepaid Insurance	3,000							
128	Prepaid Expense (Rent)	1,200							
130	Office Supplies	800							
155	Computer Equipment (Hardware)	6,800							
156	Depreciation—Computer Equipment								
200	Accounts Payable/General Liabilities		6,500						
210	Credit Card Debt		4,500						
215	Trust Funds Owed		18,500						
300	A. Litigate, Capital		12,500						
350	A. Litigate, Drawings	2,000							
400	Fees Earned		10,550						
511	Salaries Expense	1,000							
522	Depreciation Expense								
527	Insurance—Professional Liability								
534	Membership/Professional Dues	230							
535	Office Supplies/General Expense								
538	Rent Expense								
565	Telephone Expense	160							
	Totals	52,550	52,550						

PRACTICE EXCEL

Practice Exercise 8.3

Prepare the income statement and balance sheet portion of the worksheet from the adjusted trial balance for Ann Litigate's firm. (LO4)

		Ann Litigate, Paralegal Worksheet for the Month Ended December 31, 20**					
	Account Titles	Adjusted Trial Balance		Income Statement		Balance Sheet	
		Dr.	Cr.	Dr.	Cr.	Dr.	Cr.
100	General Bank Account	16,360					
115	Trust Bank Account	18,500					
120	Accounts Receivable	2,500					
125	Prepaid Insurance	500					
128	Prepaid Expense (Rent)	0					
130	Office Supplies	600					
155	Computer Equipment (Hardware)	6,800					
156	Depreciation—Computer Equipment		1,360				
200	Accounts Payable/General Liabilities		6,500				
210	Credit Card Debt		4,500				
215	Trust Funds Owed		18,500				
300	A. Litigate, Capital		12,500				
310	A. Litigate, Withdrawals	2,000					
400	Fees Earned		10,550				
511	Salaries Expense	1,000					
522	Depreciation Expense	1,360					
527	Insurance—Professional Liability	2,500					
534	Membership/Professional Dues	230					
535	Office Supplies/General Expense	200					
538	Rent Expense	1,200					
565	Telephone Expense	160					
	Totals	53,910	53,910				
	Net Profit						

Practice Exercise 8.4

Prepare the following adjusting entries for Peter Bitter's Legal Services firm and complete all columns of the worksheet. (LO2, LO3, LO4)

a. An adjustment for office supplies is required. The ending inventory as of December 31 is $300. Expense the office supplies used up over the period.

b. The landlord required prepayment of rent when Peter's firm moved into the premises. The amount of $1,200 has now been used up and needs to be written off as an expense.

c. At year-end, the firm owes three days' salary to the assistant at the rate of $90 per day.

d. The firm is taking $300 depreciation on office furniture and equipment.

Peter Bitter's Legal Services
Worksheet
for the Month Ended December 31, 20**

	Account Titles	Trial Balance		Adjustments		Adjusted Trial Balance		Income Statement		Balance Sheet	
		Dr.	Cr.	Dr.	Cr.	Dr.	Cr.	Dr.	Cr.	Dr.	Cr.
100	General Bank Account	5,230									
115	Trust Bank Account	3,200									
120	Accounts Receivable	3,500									
128	Prepaid Expense (Rent)	3,000									
130	Office Supplies	1,200									
158	Office Furniture and Equipment	22,000									
159	Dep. Office Furniture and Equipment		600								
200	Accounts Payable/General Liabilities		6,500								
215	Trust Funds Owed		3,200								
220	Accrued Salaries Payable										
300	Peter Bitters, Capital		13,170								
350	Peter Bitters, Drawings	6,000									
400	Fees Earned		29,000								
511	Salaries Expense	4,000									
522	Depreciation Expense	250									
527	Insurance—Professional Liability	450									
534	Membership/Professional Dues	230									
535	Office Supplies/General Expense	250									
538	Rent Expense	3,000									
565	Telephone Expense	160									
	Totals	52,470	52,470								
	Net Profit										

PUT IT INTO PRACTICE

Case Example: Financial Statements

Ann Litigate has scheduled a meeting with her small-business bank manager to discuss getting an additional line of credit. However, the bank manager has concerns about Ann's current debt ratio because this would be an additional credit facility. She has asked Ann to provide her with an interim financial statement. Ann does not understand why the bank manager needs this information because the bank produces statements for her general bank account and trust account each month. She thought that these bank statements, together with last year's tax return and financial statement, would be sufficient. Also, Ann does not know what information to provide to her accountant to prepare the interim financial statement, because she tends to contact the accountant only at the end of the year when she does her tax reporting.

1. Why would the bank manager need to see an interim, year-to-date financial statement as part of the bank approval process?
2. What are some of the things that Ann will need to discuss with her accountant? Which items on the balance sheet or income statement will likely require an adjustment? (Hint: Assess the before-adjustment and after-adjustment journal entries that may be required for such items on the balance sheet or income statement.)
3. What records will Ann need to review and update so that the accountant is in a good position to prepare the financial statement?

9 Final Steps in the Accounting Cycle

The Income Statement 223

The Statement of Owner's Equity. 223

The Balance Sheet. 224

Recording the Year-End Adjustments. 225

Preparing Closing Entries 226

Preparing the Post-Closing Trial Balance 229

General Ledger Accounts at the End of the Fiscal Year. 230

Chapter Summary 236

Key Terms 236

Further Reading. 236

Review Questions 237

Practice Exercises 237

Put It into Practice. 253

After reading this chapter, you should be able to:

LO1 Journalize and post adjusting entries to the general ledger.
LO2 Journalize and post closing entries.
LO3 Prepare a post-closing trial balance.

LEARNING OUTCOMES

Once the worksheet is completed, you have the information needed to prepare final financial statements for the period. In our case, we will prepare the statements as of the end of the year for Justin Case. The financial statements must be prepared in the following order:

1. Income statement
2. Statement of owner's equity
3. Balance sheet

Figure 9.1 highlights these final steps in the accounting cycle.

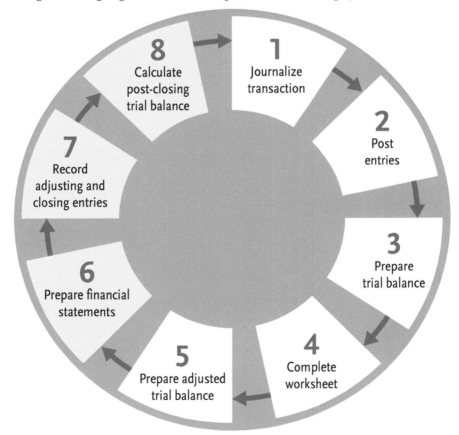

FIGURE 9.1   Steps in the accounting cycle

The worksheet prepared for Justin Case in Chapter 8 will be used for the preparation of the final income statement, the statement of owner's equity, and the balance sheet. The worksheet will also be used to record the adjusting entries in the general journal in order to make them part of the firm's permanent record.

The Income Statement

The information needed for preparing the income statement is found on the worksheet for the end of the period.

Justin Case, Paralegal Income Statement for the Period Ended December 31, 20**		
Income		
Fees Earned		$31,580.00
Expenses		
Meals and Entertainment Expense	$ 350.00	
Membership/Professional Dues	1,343.75	
Office Supplies/General Expense	1,010.00	
Rent Expense	1,100.00	
Salaries Expense	1,200.00	
Telephone Expense	479.34	
Insurance Expense—Professional Liability	50.00	
Depreciation Expense	326.01	
Interest Expense	100.00	
Total Expenses		5,959.10
Net Income		$25,620.90

FIGURE 9.2   Income statement

The Statement of Owner's Equity

The information that is needed to prepare the statement of owner's equity is found on the worksheet for the end of the period.

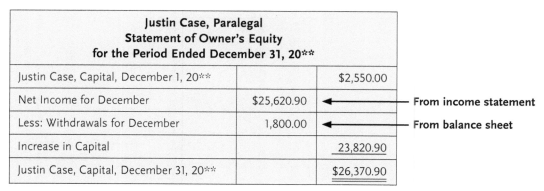

Justin Case, Paralegal Statement of Owner's Equity for the Period Ended December 31, 20**		
Justin Case, Capital, December 1, 20**		$2,550.00
Net Income for December	$25,620.90	← From income statement
Less: Withdrawals for December	1,800.00	← From balance sheet
Increase in Capital		23,820.90
Justin Case, Capital, December 31, 20**		$26,370.90

FIGURE 9.3   Statement of owner's equity

The Balance Sheet

Now that the owner's equity at the end of the period has been calculated, the balance sheet can be completed.

Once the financial statements have been completed, the books are ready to be closed for the year. The adjusting entries that were entered in the worksheet will need to be recorded, and the year-end **closing entries** will also need to be prepared.

Justin Case, Paralegal Balance Sheet December 31, 20**			
Assets			
Current Assets			
General Bank Account		$ 4,906.91	
Trust Bank Account		15,280.00	
Accounts Receivable		25,000.00	
Prepaid Insurance		550.00	
Office Supplies		200.00	
Total Current Assets			$45,936.91
Fixed Assets			
Computer Equipment (Hardware)	$6,520.00		
Less: Accumulated Depreciation on Computer Equipment	326.01	6,193.99	
Office Furniture and Equipment		2,250.00	
Total Fixed Assets			8,443.99
Total Assets			$54,380.90
Liabilities and Owner's Equity			
Liabilities			
Accounts Payable/General Liabilities		6,890.00	
Personal Loan		3,100.00	
Credit Card Debt		2,500.00	
Accrued Salaries Payable		240.00	
Trust Funds Owed		15,280.00	
Total Liabilities			28,010.00
Owner's Equity			
Justin Case, Capital			26,370.90
Total Liabilities and Owner's Equity			$54,380.90

← **From Statement of Owner's Equity**

FIGURE 9.4 Balance sheet

LO1 Recording the Year-End Adjustments

The year-end adjustments that were made on the worksheet must be recorded in the permanent records of the firm. These entries will be made using the general journal (see Figure 9.5).

Follow these steps to record adjusting entries:

1. Enter the title "Adjusting Entries" on the first line.
2. Copy the entry for each adjustment from the worksheet to the general journal, listing the debit entry first and the credit entry on the second line.
3. An explanation is not required because the "Adjusting Entries" title has been placed at the top of the column. Skip one line and enter the next adjusting entry.
4. Record the entries in the Adjustments column of the worksheet (a to e in this case) by repeating steps 2 and 3 for each entry until they have all been recorded.
5. Total the debits and credits in the general journal. The totals should be the same as the totals in the Adjustments column of the worksheet.
6. Once all the adjusting entries in the general journal have been entered, post each entry to the respective account in the general ledger, indicating that the entry is an adjusting entry in the description. Remember to complete the PR numbers in the general journal and in the reference in the general ledger account as each entry is posted.

		Justin Case, Paralegal General Journal			GJ4
Date 20**		Description	PR	Debit	Credit
		Adjusting Entries			
Dec.	31	Insurance—Professional Liability	527	50.00	
		Prepaid Insurance	125		50.00
	31	Office Supplies/General Expense	535	430.00	
		Office Supplies	130		430.00
	31	Depreciation Expense	522	326.01	
		Depreciation—Computer Equipment	156		326.01
	31	Interest Expense	529	100.00	
		Personal Loan	205		100.00
	31	Salaries Expense	511	240.00	
		Accrued Salaries Payable	220		240.00
		Totals		1,146.01	1,146.01

FIGURE 9.5   Adjusting entries

LO2 Preparing Closing Entries

Before starting to record transactions for the new year, the books for the previous fiscal period must be closed. **Balance sheet accounts** are referred to as **permanent accounts** because their balances carry over from one fiscal period to the next; the balance in the bank on December 31 will carry over to the next year—it does not disappear just because the fiscal year-end has arrived. This is true of all the assets. The same goes for any liabilities outstanding—they unfortunately do not disappear just because the end of the year has come. However, income, expense, and withdrawal accounts need to be zeroed out because each year needs to be started fresh. It is for this reason that these three categories of account are referred to as **temporary accounts**.

Closing entries are used to set the temporary account balances to zero at the end of the fiscal year. Closing entries:

- allow the paralegal to accumulate new data for the income, expense, and withdrawal accounts starting with the first day of the new fiscal year; and
- enable the paralegal to update the capital account going forward by transferring the net income or net loss to a permanent account (called income summary or retained earnings).

As illustrated in the journal entries shown below, there are four steps in the process for preparing closing entries:

1. Clear the balance in the income accounts and transfer the balance to the income summary.
   - Debit income accounts/credit income summary.
2. Clear the balance in the individual expense accounts and transfer the total to the income summary.
   - Debit income summary/credit expense accounts.
3. Clear the balance in the income summary (net income) account and transfer the balance to the capital account.
   - Debit income summary/credit capital (if net income).
4. Clear the balance in the drawings account and transfer the balance to the capital account.
   - Debit capital/credit drawings.

Step 1: Closing the Income (Revenue) Accounts

Use the information shown on the income statement to close accounts.

Close all accounts with a credit balance by debiting each **income account** with a credit balance to get a zero balance. For example, in the Justin Case income statement (Figure 9.2), the Fees Earned account has a credit balance of $31,580. Debit the Fees Earned account by that amount. To have a balanced entry, credit the **income summary account**.

General Journal					GJ5
Date 20**		Description	PR	Debit	Credit
		Closing Entries			
Dec.	31	Fees Earned	400	31,580	
		Income Summary	355		31,580
		To close income accounts			

FIGURE 9.6   General journal closing entries—income accounts

Step 2: Closing the Expense Accounts

Close all the accounts on the income statement with a debit balance (**expense accounts**) by crediting each account. This will bring each account down to zero. Debit the income summary account with the total debits. Remember that in the general journal, debits are entered on the first line and credits below so that the first line of your closing entry will be income summary, followed by a list of each expense account that is being closed. Each entry must be posted to the general ledger. Once the postings are completed, all the expense accounts should have a zero balance, and the income summary account will show the debits that when subtracted from the credits show the net profit.

General Journal					GJ5
Date 20**		Description	PR	Debit	Credit
Dec.	31	Income Summary	355	5,959.10	
		Depreciation Expense	522		326.01
		Insurance—Professional Liability	527		50.00
		Interest Expense	529		100.00
		Meals and Entertainment Expense	533		350.00
		Membership/Professional Dues	534		1,343.75
		Office Supplies/General Expense	535		1,010.00
		Rent Expense	538		1,100.00
		Salaries Expense	511		1,200.00
		Telephone Expense	565		479.34
		To close expense accounts			

FIGURE 9.7   General journal closing entries—expense accounts

Step 3: Closing the Income Summary Account

Once the closing entries for the income and expense accounts have been posted, the general ledger shows a credit balance in the income summary account. After posting, the balance in this account is equal to the net income (or net loss) of the firm. Figure 9.8 shows the income summary account after the closing entries for the income and expense accounts have been posted.

Income Summary						Account No. 355	
Date 20**		Explanation	PR	Debit	Credit	Dr./Cr.	Balance
Dec.	31	To close income accounts	GJ5		31,580.00		
	31	To close expense accounts	GJ5	5,959.10		Cr.	25,620.90

FIGURE 9.8   Income summary account in general ledger

In order to clear the net income amount from the income summary account, a closing entry must be created by debiting the income summary account and crediting the capital account.

The general journal closing entry made to close the income summary account is as shown in Figure 9.9.

General Journal					GJ5
Date 20**		Description	PR	Debit	Credit
Dec.	31	Income Summary	355	25,620.90	
		Justin Case, Capital	300		25,620.90
		To close income summary account			

FIGURE 9.9   Closing entries—income summary

Step 4: Closing the Drawings Account

Clear the balance in the drawings account and transfer the balance to the capital account. The owner of a sole proprietorship takes withdrawals for personal use over the course of the year, and this account needs to be cleared. As was seen on the statement of owner's equity, withdrawals decrease the owner's equity in the firm. For this reason, the amount taken by way of withdrawals will be transferred to the capital account and used to decrease the owner's equity in the firm. This account is cleared at the end of the fiscal year. Drawings taken in the subsequent year will start from zero and be accumulated over the next year.

The closing entry required to close the drawings account is as shown in Figure 9.10.

General Journal					GJ5
Date 20**		Description	PR	Debit	Credit
Dec.	31	Justin Case, Capital	300	1,800.00	
		Justin Case, Drawings	350		1,800.00
		To close drawings into capital			

FIGURE 9.10   General journal closing entries—drawings

Once the closing entries are posted, the general ledger capital and drawings accounts will appear as in Figure 9.11.

POTENTIAL PARALEGAL PITFALLS

- **Potential pitfall:** Paralegals may try to save money by doing their year-end accounting on their own
- **Possible fallout:** Mistakes can be made in completing general ledger postings, period-end adjustments, financial statements, and tax filings with the CRA.
- **Proposed recommendation:** Although it may be tempting for paralegals to complete their year-end accounting and tax return on their own (in order to save accounting fees), it is important to have complete and accurate financial information for every fiscal year. For this reason, it may be recommended that paralegals hire an accountant to complete their year-end work.

Justin Case, Capital						Account No. 300	
Date 20**		Explanation	PR	Debit	Credit	Dr./Cr.	Balance
Dec.	1	Balance Forward	✓		2,550.00	Cr.	2,550.00
	31	Closing Entry—Income Summary			25,620.90	Cr.	28,170.90
	31	Closing Entry—Drawings		1,800.00		Cr.	26,370.90

Justin Case, Drawings						Account No. 350	
Date 20**		Explanation	PR	Debit	Credit	Dr./Cr.	Balance
Dec.	1	Balance Forward	✓	1,800.00		Dr.	1,800.00
	31	Closing Entry	GJ5		1,800.00		0.00

Justin Case, Income Summary						Account No. 355	
Date 20**		Explanation	PR	Debit	Credit	Dr./Cr.	Balance
Dec.	31	Closing Entry—Income Account	GJ5		31,580.00	Cr.	31,580.00
	31	Closing Entry—Expense Accounts	GJ5	5,959.10		Cr.	25,620.90
	31	Closing Entry—Net Income transfer to Capital	GJ5	25,620.90			0.00

FIGURE 9.11 General ledger capital, drawings, and income summary accounts after posting

LO3 Preparing the Post-Closing Trial Balance

Once all the adjusting entries and closing entries have been recorded and posted, a **post-closing trial balance** must be prepared. All temporary accounts will have been closed, and the only balances remaining in the general ledger should be in the permanent accounts. Prepare a list of all the general ledger accounts with a balance. They have been placed in numerical order in the post-closing trial balance shown in Figure 9.12.

		Dr.	Cr.
	Justin Case, Paralegal **Post-Closing Trial Balance** **December 31, 20****		
100	General Bank Account	$ 4,906.91	
115	Trust Bank Account	15,280.00	
120	Accounts Receivable	25,000.00	
125	Prepaid Insurance	550.00	
130	Office Supplies	200.00	
155	Computer Equipment (Hardware)	6,520.00	
156	Depreciation—Computer Equipment		$ 326.01
158	Office Furniture and Equipment	2,250.00	
200	Accounts Payable/General Liabilities		6,890.00
205	Personal Loan		3,100.00
210	Credit Card Debt		2,500.00
215	Trust Funds Owed		15,280.00
220	Accrued Salaries Payable		240.00
300	Justin Case, Capital		26,370.90
	Totals	$54,706.91	$54,706.91

FIGURE 9.12   Post-closing trial balance

General Ledger Accounts at the End of the Fiscal Year

Figure 9.13 shows Justin's general ledger accounts at the end of December once the year-end was completed. Note that only those accounts from December 1 (where a balance forward was recorded) to the end of December are included here. The asset, liability, and capital accounts show a balance, but the drawings, income, and expense accounts are at zero, ready to start the new fiscal year.

		Justin Case, Paralegal **General Ledgers**					
General Bank Account						**Account No. 100**	
Date *20***		*Explanation*	*PR*	*Debit*	*Credit*	*Dr./Cr.*	*Balance*
Dec.	1	Balance Forward	✓	4,906.91		Dr.	4,906.91

Trust Bank Account **Account No. 115**

Date 20**		Explanation	PR	Debit	Credit	Dr./Cr.	Balance
Dec.	1	Balance Forward	✓	15,280.00		Dr.	15,280.00

Accounts Receivable **Account No. 120**

Date 20**		Explanation	PR	Debit	Credit	Dr./Cr.	Balance
Dec.	1	Balance Forward	✓	25,000.00		Dr.	25,000.00

Prepaid Insurance **Account No. 125**

Date 20**		Explanation	PR	Debit	Credit	Dr./Cr.	Balance
Dec.	1	Prepaid Insurance	✓	600.00		Dr.	600.00
Dec.	31	Adjusting Entry	GJ4		50.00	Dr.	550.00

Office Supplies **Account No. 130**

Date 20**		Explanation	PR	Debit	Credit	Dr./Cr.	Balance
Dec.	1	Balance Forward	✓	630.00		Dr.	630.00
	31	Adjusting Entry	GJ4		430.00	Dr.	200.00

Computer Equipment (Hardware) **Account No. 155**

Date 20**		Explanation	PR	Debit	Credit	Dr./Cr.	Balance
Dec.	1	Balance Forward	✓	6,520.00		Dr.	6,520.00

Depreciation—Computer Equipment **Account No. 156**

Date 20**		Explanation	PR	Debit	Credit	Dr./Cr.	Balance
Dec.	1	Adjusting Entry	GJ4		326.01	Cr.	326.01

Depreciation—Office Furniture and Equipment **Account No. 158**

Date 20**		Explanation	PR	Debit	Credit	Dr./Cr.	Balance
Dec.	1	Balance Forward	✓	2,250.00		Dr.	2,250.00

Accounts Payable/General Liabilities **Account No. 200**

Date 20**		Explanation	PR	Debit	Credit	Dr./Cr.	Balance
Dec.	1	Balance Forward	✓		6,890.00	Cr.	6,890.00

Personal Loan — Account No. 205

Date 20**		Explanation	PR	Debit	Credit	Dr./Cr.	Balance
Dec.	1	Balance Forward	✓		3,000.00	Cr.	3,000.00
	31	Adjusting Entry	GJ4		100.00	Cr.	3,100.00

Credit Card Debt — Account No. 210

Date 20**		Explanation	PR	Debit	Credit	Dr./Cr.	Balance
Dec.	1	Balance Forward	✓		2,500.00	Cr.	2,500.00

Trust Funds Owed — Account No. 215

Date 20**		Explanation	PR	Debit	Credit	Dr./Cr.	Balance
Dec.	1	Balance Forward	✓		15,280.00	Cr.	15,280.00

Accrued Salaries Payable — Account No. 220

Date 20**		Explanation	PR	Debit	Credit	Dr./Cr.	Balance
Dec.	31	Adjusting Entry	GJ4		240.00	Cr.	240.00

Justin Case, Capital — Account No. 300

Date 20**		Explanation	PR	Debit	Credit	Dr./Cr.	Balance
Dec.	1	Balance Forward	✓		2,550.00	Cr.	2,550.00
	31	Closing Entry—Income Summary	GJ5		25,620.90	Cr.	28,170.90
	31	Closing Entry—Drawings	GJ5	1,800.00		Cr.	26,370.90

Justin Case, Drawings — Account No. 350

Date 20**		Explanation	PR	Debit	Credit	Dr./Cr.	Balance
Dec.	1	Balance Forward	✓	1,800.00		Dr.	1,800.00
	31	Closing Entry	GJ5		1,800.00		0.00

Income Summary — Account No. 355

Date 20**		Explanation	PR	Debit	Credit	Dr./Cr.	Balance
Dec.	31	To close income accounts	GJ5		31,580.00	Cr.	31,580.00
	31	To close expense accounts	GJ5	5,959.10		Cr.	25,620.90
	31	To transfer balance to Capital	GJ5	25,620.90			0.00

Fees Earned | | | | | **Account No. 400**

Date 20**		Explanation	PR	Debit	Credit	Dr./Cr.	Balance
Dec.	1	Balance Forward	✓		31,580.00	Cr.	31,580.00
	31	Closing Entry	GJ5	31,580.00			0.00

Salaries Expense | | | | | **Account No. 511**

Date 20**		Explanation	PR	Debit	Credit	Dr./Cr.	Balance
Dec.	1	Balance Forward	✓	960.00		Dr.	960.00
	31	Adjusting Entry	GJ4	240.00		Dr.	1,200.00
	31	Closing Entry	GJ5		1,200.00		0.00

Depreciation Expense | | | | | **Account No. 522**

Date 20**		Explanation	PR	Debit	Credit	Dr./Cr.	Balance
Dec.	31	Adjustment—Computer Equipment	GJ4	326.01		Dr.	326.01
	31	Closing Entry	GJ5		326.01		0.00

Insurance—Professional Liability | | | | | **Account No. 527**

Date 20**		Explanation	PR	Debit	Credit	Dr./Cr.	Balance
Dec.	31	Adjusting Entry	GJ4	50.00		Dr.	50.00
	31	Closing Entry	GJ5		50.00		0.00

Interest Expense | | | | | **Account No. 529**

Date 20**		Explanation	PR	Debit	Credit	Dr./Cr.	Balance
Dec.	31	Adjusting Entry	GJ4	100.00		Dr.	100.00
	31	Closing Entry	GJ5		100.00		0.00

Meals and Entertainment Expense | | | | | **Account No. 533**

Date 20**		Explanation	PR	Debit	Credit	Dr./Cr.	Balance
Dec.	1	Balance Forward	✓	350.00		Dr.	350.00
	31	Closing Entry	GJ5		350.00		0.00

Membership/Professional Dues — Account No. 534

Date 20**		Explanation	PR	Debit	Credit	Dr./Cr.	Balance
Dec.	1	Balance Forward	✓	1,343.75		Dr.	1,343.75
	31	Closing Entry	GJ5		1,343.75		0.00

Office Supplies/General Expense — Account No. 535

Date 20**		Explanation	PR	Debit	Credit	Dr./Cr.	Balance
Dec.	1	Balance Forward	✓	580.00		Dr.	580.00
	31	Adjusting Entry	GJ4	430.00		Dr.	1,010.00
	31	Closing Entry	GJ5		1,010.00		0.00

Rent Expense — Account No. 538

Date 20**		Explanation	PR	Debit	Credit	Dr./Cr.	Balance
Dec.	1	Balance Forward	✓	1,100.00		Dr.	1,100.00
	31	Closing Entry	GJ5		1,100.00		0.00

Telephone Expense — Account No. 565

Date 20**		Explanation	PR	Debit	Credit	Dr./Cr.	Balance
Dec.	1	Balance Forward	✓	479.34		Dr.	479.34
	31	Closing Entry	GJ5		479.34		0.00

FIGURE 9.13   General ledgers after closing

Legal Requirements for Keeping Records

All records, such as paper documents as well as those stored in an electronic medium (such as on computer disk), must be kept in Canada or made available in Canada at the request of the CRA. The records must be in English or French.

A business is required to keep orderly records of all income received. All receipts, invoices, vouchers, and cancelled cheques indicating outlays of money must also be kept. Such outlays include:

- salaries and wages;
- operating expenses such as rent, advertising, and capital expenditures; and
- miscellaneous items such as charitable donations.

Records must be permanent and contain a systematic account of income, deductions, credits, and other information needed to file income tax and GST/HST returns. Incomplete records that use approximations instead of exact amounts are not acceptable. The records must:

- allow individuals to determine how much tax they owe, or the tax, duties, or other amounts to be collected, withheld, or deducted, or any refund or rebate they may claim; and
- be supported by vouchers or other necessary source documents.

If receipts or other vouchers are not kept to support expenses or claims, and there is no other evidence available, the CRA will probably reduce the expenses or claims that have been made.

The Six-Year Requirement

If tax returns are filed on time, records must be retained (other than certain documents for which there are special rules) for six years from the end of the last tax year to which they relate. Every record necessary for dealing with an objection or appeal must be kept until it is resolved and the time for filing any further appeal has expired, or until the six-year period has expired, whichever is later.

CHAPTER SUMMARY

In this chapter, you have completed the accounting cycle up to preparation of the post-closing trial balance. The post-closing trial balance serves as a check to ensure that the ledger accounts are in balance. All the temporary accounts have been cleared, and you are ready to begin the accounting cycle over again for the next fiscal period. The post-closing trial balance contains the balances for opening the books for the new fiscal year.

The financial statements were prepared for the end of the year. They can be prepared more frequently if you need to see how the business is doing or for submitting to a lender who requires the information.

KEY TERMS

balance sheet accounts, 226

closing entries, 224

expense accounts, 227

income account, 226

income summary account, 226

permanent accounts, 226

post-closing trial balance, 229

temporary accounts, 226

FURTHER READING

Canada Revenue Agency, *Business and Professional Income 2014*, online: <https://www.canada.ca/content/dam/cra-arc/formspubs/pbg/t2125/t2125-14e.pdf>. Financial reporting for sole proprietors.

Canada Revenue Agency, "General Index of Financial Information (GIFI)," online: <http://www.cra-arc.gc.ca/tx/bsnss/tpcs/crprtns/rtrn/wht/gifi-ogrf/menu-eng.html>. Corporate financial statements.

L Kenway, "Accounting and Bookkeeping Checklists," *Bookkeeping-Essentials.com*, online: <http://www.bookkeeping-essentials.com/bookkeeping-checklist.html>. Select the "Year End Accountant Checklist" link.

L Kenway, "Learn How to Read Your Internal Financial Reports," *Bookkeeping-Essentials.com*, online: <http://www.bookkeeping-essentials.com/accounting-training.html>. Select the "Balance sheet" and "Income statement" links.

MaRS Discovery District, online: <http://www.marsdd.com/collections/accounting/financial-statements>. See the following topics:

- "Accounting Mechanics: An Example of Financial Statements," online: <http://www.marsdd.com/mars-library/financial-statement-example>.
- "Reading a Financial Statement: The Balance Sheet (Assets, Liabilities and Equity)," online: <http://www.marsdd.com/mars-library/reading-financial-statement-balance-sheet-assets-liabilities-equity>.
- "Reading a Financial Statement: The Income Statement," online: <http://www.marsdd.com/mars-library/reading-financial-statement-income-statement>.

REVIEW QUESTIONS

True or False

_____ 1. Revenue and expenses are temporary accounts that reset to zero at the end of each fiscal year. (LO2)

_____ 2. At closing, all temporary and permanent account balances are brought to zero. (LO2)

_____ 3. The post-closing trial balance includes only the permanent accounts: assets, liabilities, and equity. (LO3)

_____ 4. To close the revenue accounts, you debit the revenue accounts. (LO2)

_____ 5. The income summary is a permanent account that is transferred to the opening balance in the next fiscal period. (LO2)

_____ 6. To close the expense account, you debit the expense account. (LO2)

_____ 7. To close the income summary account, you transfer the ending balance to the capital account. (LO2)

_____ 8. The ending balances on the general ledger and the post-closing trial balance become the opening balances in the new fiscal period. (LO3)

_____ 9. At the close of the fiscal year, the general ledger accounts must be updated to reflect all adjustments. (LO1)

_____ 10. The post-closing trial balance serves as a check to ensure that the ledger accounts are in balance. (LO3)

Short Answer

1. What happens to the drawings account at the end of the accounting cycle? (LO2)

2. What information does the general ledger report at the end of the accounting cycle? (LO1)

3. What are the four steps involved in closing the accounts at the end of the accounting cycle? (LO2)

4. Name two categories of accounts that are "permanent accounts." (LO2)

5. Name three categories of accounts that are "temporary accounts." (LO2)

PRACTICE EXERCISES

PRACTICE EXCEL

Practice Exercise 9.1

Following are the adjustments and the financial statements for Ann Litigate for the period ended December 31, 20**.

Dec. 31: Payment on account received (invoice #xx501, M. Arbor), $1,000.

Dec. 31: Prepaid professional insurance used up, $2,500 (one-year policy, from February of this year until February of next year, valued at $3,000).

Dec. 31: Rent expense recognized (Magnum Office Managers), $1,200.

Dec. 31: Office supplies used up, $200.

Dec. 31: Depreciation of computer equipment, $1,360/year based on the declining balance amortization calculation

Ann Litigate, Paralegal Income Statement for the Period Ended December 31, 20**		
Income		
Fees Earned		$10,550
Expenses		
Salaries Expense	$1,000	
Depreciation Expense	1,360	
Insurance—Professional Liability	2,500	
Membership/Professional Dues	230	
Office Supplies/General Expense	200	
Rent Expense	1,200	
Telephone Expense	160	
Total Expenses		6,650
Net Income		$3,900

Ann Litigate, Paralegal Statement of Owner's Equity for the Period Ended December 31, 20**		
Ann Litigate, Capital, December 1, 20**		$12,500
Net Income for December	$3,900	
Less: Withdrawals for December	2,000	
Increase in Capital		1,900
Ann Litigate, Capital, December 31, 20**		$14,400

Ann Litigate, Paralegal
Balance Sheet
December 31, 20**

Assets			
Current Assets			
General Bank Account		$16,360	
Trust Bank Account		18,500	
Accounts Receivable		2,500	
Prepaid Insurance		500	
Office Supplies		600	
Total Current Assets			$38,460
Fixed Assets			
Computer Equipment (Hardware)	$6,800		
Less: Accumulated Depreciation on Computer Equipment	1,360	5,440	
Total Fixed Assets			5,440
Total Assets			$43,900
Liabilities and Owner's Equity			
Liabilities			
Accounts Payable/General Liabilities		6,500	
Credit Card Debt		4,500	
Trust Funds Owed		18,500	
Total Liabilities			29,500
Owner's Equity			
Ann Litigate, Capital			14,400
Total Liabilities and Owner's Equity			$43,900

a. Using the December 31 adjustments and the financial statements, record the appropriate adjusting entries in Ann Litigate's general journal. (LO1)

Ann Litigate, Paralegal General Journal					GJ8
Date 20**		Description	PR	Debit	Credit
		Adjusting Entries			
Dec.	31				

b. Post the adjusting entries to the individual general ledger accounts for December 31, 20**. **(LO1)**

Ann Litigate, Paralegal
General Ledgers

General Bank Account — Account No. 100

Date 20**		Explanation	PR	Debit	Credit	Dr./Cr.	Balance
Dec.	31	Opening balance December 1	✓			Dr.	15,360

Trust Bank Account — Account No. 115

Date 20**		Explanation	PR	Debit	Credit	Dr./Cr.	Balance
Dec.	31	Opening balance December 1	✓			Dr.	18,500

Accounts Receivable — Account No. 120

Date 20**		Explanation	PR	Debit	Credit	Dr./Cr.	Balance
Dec.	31	Opening balance December 1	✓			Dr.	3,500

Prepaid Insurance — Account No. 125

Date 20**		Explanation	PR	Debit	Credit	Dr./Cr.	Balance
Dec.	31	Opening balance December 1	✓			Dr.	3,000

Prepaid Expense — Account No. 128

Date 20**		Explanation	PR	Debit	Credit	Dr./Cr.	Balance
Dec.	31	Opening balance December 1 (rent)	✓			Dr.	1,200

Office Supplies — Account No. 130

Date 20**		Explanation	PR	Debit	Credit	Dr./Cr.	Balance
Dec.	31	Opening balance December 1	✓			Dr.	800

Computer Equipment (Hardware)							Account No. 155
Date 20**		Explanation	PR	Debit	Credit	Dr./Cr.	Balance
Dec.	31	Opening balance December 1	✓			Dr.	6,800

Depreciation—Computer Equipment							Account No. 156
Date 20**		Explanation	PR	Debit	Credit	Dr./Cr.	Balance
Dec.	31	Opening balance December 1	✓				0

Accounts Payable/General Liabilities							Account No. 200
Date 20**		Explanation	PR	Debit	Credit	Dr./Cr.	Balance
Dec.	31	Opening balance December 1	✓			Cr.	6,500

Credit Card Debt							Account No. 210
Date 20**		Explanation	PR	Debit	Credit	Dr./Cr.	Balance
Dec.	31	Opening balance December 1	✓			Cr.	4,500

Trust Funds Owed							Account No. 215
Date 20**		Explanation	PR	Debit	Credit	Dr./Cr.	Balance
Dec.	31	Opening balance December 1	✓			Cr.	18,500

Ann Litigate, Capital							Account No. 300
Date 20**		Explanation	PR	Debit	Credit	Dr./Cr.	Balance
Dec.	31	Opening balance December 1	✓			Cr.	12,500

Ann Litigate, Drawings — Account No. 350

Date 20**		Explanation	PR	Debit	Credit	Dr./Cr.	Balance
Dec.	31	Opening balance December 1	✓			Dr.	2,000

Income Summary — Account No. 355

Date 20**		Explanation	PR	Debit	Credit	Dr./Cr.	Balance

Fees Earned — Account No. 400

Date 20**		Explanation	PR	Debit	Credit	Dr./Cr.	Balance
Dec.	31	Opening balance December 1				Cr.	10,550

Salaries Expense — Account No. 511

Date 20**		Explanation	PR	Debit	Credit	Dr./Cr.	Balance
Dec.	31	Opening balance December 1	✓			Dr.	1,000

Depreciation Expense — Account No. 522

Date 20**		Explanation	PR	Debit	Credit	Dr./Cr.	Balance
Dec.	31	Opening balance December 1	✓				0

Insurance—Professional Liability — Account No. 527

Date 20**		Explanation	PR	Debit	Credit	Dr./Cr.	Balance
Dec.	31	Opening balance December 1	✓				0

Membership/Professional Dues						Account No. 534	
Date 20**		Explanation	PR	Debit	Credit	Dr./Cr.	Balance
Dec.	31	Opening balance December 1	✓			Dr.	230

Office Supplies/General Expense						Account No. 535	
Date 20**		Explanation	PR	Debit	Credit	Dr./Cr.	Balance
Dec.	31	Opening balance December 1	✓				0

Rent Expense						Account No. 538	
Date 20**		Explanation	PR	Debit	Credit	Dr./Cr.	Balance
Dec.	31	Opening balance December 1	✓				0

Telephone Expense						Account No. 565	
Date 20**		Explanation	PR	Debit	Credit	Dr./Cr.	Balance
Dec.	31	Opening balance December 1	✓			Dr.	160

c. In the same general journal, once the adjusting entries have been posted, prepare the closing entries and post them to the general ledger. Use the same general journal and general ledgers you used for parts (a) and (b). (LO2)

d. Using the general journal and general ledgers from parts (b) and (c), close the income summary and drawings accounts to the Ann Litigate, Capital account. Then prepare the post-closing trial balance. (LO3)

	Ann Litigate, Paralegal Post-Closing Trial Balance December 31, 20**		
	Account Titles	Dr.	Cr.
100	General Bank Account		
115	Trust Bank Account		
120	Accounts Receivable		
125	Prepaid Insurance		
128	Prepaid Expense (Rent)		
130	Office Supplies		
155	Computer Equipment (Hardware)		
156	Depreciation—Computer Equipment		
200	Accounts Payable/General Liabilities		
210	Credit Card Debt		
215	Trust Funds Owed		
300	Ann Litigate, Capital		
	Totals		

Practice Exercise 9.2

Below is the adjusted trial balance for ABC Legal Services for the period ended December 31, 20**.

ABC Legal Services Adjusted Trial Balance December 31, 20**		
Account Titles	Dr.	Cr.
General Bank Account	$15,000	
Trust Bank Account	35,000	
Accounts Receivable	20,250	
Prepaid Insurance	700	
Prepaid Expense (Rent)	700	
Office Supplies	150	
Computer Equipment (Hardware)	4,750	
Depreciation—Computer Equipment		$950
Accounts Payable/General Liabilities		2,025
Personal Loan		6,000
Credit Card Debt		4,500
Trust Funds Owed		35,000
ABC, Capital		17,165
ABC, Drawings	5,000	
Fees Earned		23,000
Expense Recovery		750
Salaries Expense	1,700	
Depreciation Expense	950	
Insurance—Professional Liability	2,500	
Membership/Professional Dues	200	
Office Supplies/General Expense	500	
Rent Expense	1,800	
Telephone Expense	190	
Total	$89,390	$89,390

a.   Using the worksheet provided, prepare the closing entries for December 31, 20**. (LO2)

ABC Legal Services General Journal					GJ3
Date 20**		Description	PR	Debit	Credit
		Closing Entries			

b. Using the worksheet provided, post to the general ledgers at December 31, 20**. (LO2)

ABC Legal Services
General Ledgers
at December 31, 20**

General Bank Account — Account No. 100

Date 20**		Explanation	PR	Debit	Credit	Dr./Cr.	Balance
Dec.	31	Balance Forward	✓			Dr.	15,000

Trust Bank Account — Account No. 115

Date 20**		Explanation	PR	Debit	Credit	Dr./Cr.	Balance
Dec.	31	Balance Forward	✓			Dr.	35,000

Accounts Receivable — Account No. 120

Date 20**		Explanation	PR	Debit	Credit	Dr./Cr.	Balance
Dec.	31	Balance Forward	✓			Dr.	20,250

Prepaid Insurance — Account No. 125

Date 20**		Explanation	PR	Debit	Credit	Dr./Cr.	Balance
Dec.	31	Balance Forward	✓			Dr.	700

Prepaid Expense — Account No. 128

Date 20**		Explanation	PR	Debit	Credit	Dr./Cr.	Balance
Dec.	31	Balance Forward	✓			Dr.	700

Office Supplies — Account No. 130

Date 20**		Explanation	PR	Debit	Credit	Dr./Cr.	Balance
Dec.	31	Balance Forward	✓			Dr.	150

Computer Equipment (Hardware) | | | | | | **Account No. 155**

Date 20**		Explanation	PR	Debit	Credit	Dr./Cr.	Balance
Dec.	31	Balance Forward	✓			Dr.	4,750

Depreciation—Computer Equipment | | | | | | **Account No. 156**

Date 20**		Explanation	PR	Debit	Credit	Dr./Cr.	Balance
Dec.	31	Balance Forward	GJ3			Cr.	950

Accounts Payable/General Liabilities | | | | | | **Account No. 200**

Date 20**		Explanation	PR	Debit	Credit	Dr./Cr.	Balance
Dec.	31	Balance Forward	✓			Cr.	2,025

Personal Loan | | | | | | **Account No. 205**

Date 20**		Explanation	PR	Debit	Credit	Dr./Cr.	Balance
Dec.	31	Balance Forward	✓			Cr.	6,000

Credit Card Debt | | | | | | **Account No. 210**

Date 20**		Explanation	PR	Debit	Credit	Dr./Cr.	Balance
Dec.	31	Balance Forward	✓			Cr.	4,500

Trust Funds Owed | | | | | | **Account No. 215**

Date 20**		Explanation	PR	Debit	Credit	Dr./Cr.	Balance
Dec.	31	Balance Forward	✓			Cr.	35,000

ABC Legal Services, Capital							Account No. 300	
Date 20**		Explanation	PR	Debit	Credit	Dr./Cr.	Balance	
Dec.	31	Balance Forward	✓			Cr.	17,165	

ABC Legal Services, Drawings							Account No. 350	
Date 20**		Explanation	PR	Debit	Credit	Dr./Cr.	Balance	
Dec.	31	Balance Forward	✓			Dr.	5,000	

Income Summary							Account No. 355	
Date 20**		Explanation	PR	Debit	Credit	Dr./Cr.	Balance	

Fees Earned							Account No. 400	
Date 20**		Explanation	PR	Debit	Credit	Dr./Cr.	Balance	
Dec.	31	Balance Forward	✓			Cr.	23,000	

Expense Recovery							Account No. 410	
Date 20**		Explanation	PR	Debit	Credit	Dr./Cr.	Balance	
Dec.	31	Balance Forward	✓			Cr.	750	

Salaries Expense Account No. 511

Date 20**		Explanation	PR	Debit	Credit	Dr./Cr.	Balance
Dec.	31	Opening balance December 1	✓			Dr.	1,700

Depreciation Expense Account No. 522

Date 20**		Explanation	PR	Debit	Credit	Dr./Cr.	Balance
Dec.	31	Balance Forward	GJ3			Dr.	950

Insurance—Professional Liability Account No. 527

Date 20**		Explanation	PR	Debit	Credit	Dr./Cr.	Balance
Dec.	31	Balance Forward	GJ3			Dr.	2,500

Membership/Professional Dues Account No. 534

Date 20**		Explanation	PR	Debit	Credit	Dr./Cr.	Balance
Dec.	31	Balance Forward	✓			Dr.	200

Office Supplies/General Expense Account No. 535

Date 20**		Explanation	PR	Debit	Credit	Dr./Cr.	Balance
Dec.	31	Balance Forward	GJ3			Dr.	500

Rent Expense							Account No. 538
Date 20**		Explanation	PR	Debit	Credit	Dr./Cr.	Balance
Dec.	31	Balance Forward	GJ3			Dr.	1,800

Telephone Expense							Account No. 565
Date 20**		Explanation	PR	Debit	Credit	Dr./Cr.	Balance
Dec.	31	Opening balance December 1	✓			Dr.	190

c. Using the worksheet provided, prepare the post-closing trial balance. (LO3)

ABC Legal Services Post-Closing Trial Balance December 31, 20**		
Account Titles	Dr.	Cr.

PUT IT INTO PRACTICE

Case Example: Year-End Financial Statements

Ann Litigate had a meeting with her accountant, who advised her that there were some discrepancies in the information Ann provided. Consequently, the year-end financial statement will have to be adjusted and revised.

1. What steps can Ann take to ensure that the accountant has all the relevant information and that such information is accurate? Discuss. (LO1)
2. What are some common issues with financial statement preparation that Ann can avoid next time? Discuss. (LO1)

Petty Cash 256

Banking Procedures and Handling of Money 259

Reconciling a Bank Account 260

Reconciling the Mixed Trust Bank Account 266

Maintenance and Retention of General and Trust Records 271

Chapter Summary 273

Key Terms 273

Further Reading 273

Review Questions 274

Practice Exercises 275

Put It into Practice 281

After reading this chapter, you should be able to:

LO1 Establish and replenish a petty cash fund.
LO2 Reconcile a general bank account.
LO3 Reconcile a trust bank account.

LO1 Petty Cash

Because paying for small purchases by cheque can be time-consuming, inconvenient, and impractical, most businesses establish a fund for payment of incidental expenses. The **petty cash** fund is used to pay for minor expenses, such as postage and office supplies, or to make change if a client is paying with cash. The firm's policy regarding the types of expenditures that are acceptable for petty cash reimbursements should be clear and communicated to all members of the firm.

The petty cash system is one example of **cash controls** that protect against loss, misuse, or fraud in the handling of cash.[1] It ensures that funds from petty cash will not be used inappropriately—for example, to pay for an employee's lunch because he or she was short of money that day.

Establishing a Petty Cash Account

You will need to establish an account called Petty Cash on the chart of accounts in the Current Assets category. Justin Case has given it number 105, so it appears directly below account 100 (General Bank Account), and he will create a ledger in the general ledger called Petty Cash to track the money going in and out of Petty Cash.

Use a general journal entry to establish the petty cash fund. Justin has decided it would be reasonable to have a fund of $50. A cheque is issued from the general bank account and cashed for the predetermined amount, and the cash is placed in a safe location, usually a petty cash box with a lock on it. Figure 10.1 shows the general journal entry used to establish a petty cash fund.

| Justin Case, Paralegal
General Journal | | | | | GJ6 |
Date 20**		Description	PR	Debit	Credit
Jan.	5	Petty Cash	105	50	
		General Bank Account	100		50
		To establish petty cash fund			

FIGURE 10.1   General journal entry to establish fund

1   Law Society of Ontario, *The Bookkeeping Guide for Paralegals*, online: <https://lawsocietyontario.azureedge.net/media/lso/media/legacy/pdf/p/paralegal_bookkeeping_guide_final-s.pdf> at 59-67.

Recording Petty Cash Entries

A system should be established requiring pre-numbered written requests (vouchers) supported by original receipts for items to be paid out of petty cash to any person.

The information from the vouchers can be transferred to an auxiliary petty cash record, but that is not essential. It is sufficient to attach the purchase receipt to the petty cash voucher and keep the vouchers in the petty cash box until entries are made in the general journal. Figure 10.2 shows a sample voucher used for withdrawals from petty cash.

PETTY CASH VOUCHER NO.	1		
AMOUNT	$4.80		
DATE	January 8, 20**		
PAID TO	Tom's Office Supply		
FOR	Pens		
DEBIT ACCT. NAME	Office Supplies/General Expense	ACCT. NO.	535
APPROVED BY	Judith Wells, Assistant		
PAYMENT RECEIVED BY	Justin Case		

FIGURE 10.2   Petty cash voucher

At all times, the amount of cash plus the total amount of the vouchers should equal the total value of the fund, as shown in Figure 10.3.

Total paid out	$4.80
Cash in petty cash box	45.20
Total petty cash fund	$50.00

FIGURE 10.3   Balancing funds in a petty cash box

Replenishing a Petty Cash Account

In order to replenish the fund to bring the amount of petty cash back up to $50, Judith Wells, who as Justin's assistant is responsible for completing the petty cash vouchers, must record the expenses in the general journal and post the entries to the correct account. If she does not keep a record similar to the one in Figure 10.3, she will use the vouchers to create the general journal entries. Once the entries are made, she will write a cheque payable to herself (or to cash) for the total amount that was spent—in this case, $23.50—and summarize the vouchers as shown in Figure 10.4. At the bank, she will cash the petty cash cheque and return to the office and replenish the petty cash box back to $50.

Date 20**		Description	Account	Receipts	Paid Out	Balance
Jan.	5	Establish Fund	105	50.00		50.00
	9	Office Supplies/General Expense	535		4.80	45.20
	20	Postage Expense	563		6.00	39.20
	23	Maintenance and Repairs (cleaning products)	532		8.20	31.00
	30	Delivery Expense	550		4.50	26.50
		Total Spent $23.50				
	30	Replenish Fund, Cheque #25	105	23.50		50.00

FIGURE 10.4   Petty cash record tracking expenses

If Judith finds that the fund is too small and needs to be replenished too often, she can simply increase it by writing another cheque to increase the amount kept in petty cash. The journal entry would be similar to the entry that was made establishing the fund. The balance in the general ledger for petty cash usually remains constant at the amount at which the fund has been established. Figure 10.5 shows the journal entries that were made to establish the fund and then to replenish it.

Justin Case, Paralegal General Journal					GJ6
Date 20**		Description	PR	Debit	Credit
Jan.	5	Petty Cash	105	50.00	
		General Bank Account	100		50.00
		To establish petty cash fund			
Jan.	30	Office Supplies/General Expense	535	4.80	
		Postage Expense	563	6.00	
		Maintenance and Repairs (cleaning products)	532	8.20	
		Delivery Expense	550	4.50	
		Petty Cash	105		23.50
		To record payments from petty cash			
Jan	30	Petty Cash	105	23.50	
		General Bank Account	100		23.50
		To replenish petty cash fund			

FIGURE 10.5   General journal entries to establish and replenish petty cash fund

Cash Short and Over

A firm may use the petty cash or keep a separate float in the office for the purpose of making change if a client pays with cash. This float will consist of coins and small bills, usually totalling between $25 and $200, depending on the size of the firm. If for some reason the cash in the petty cash box does not equal the amount of the vouchers, the amount of cash short or the amount by which the cash is over should be recorded in a general ledger account called

cash short and over. If the cash is short, the Cash Short and Over account is debited, like an expense. If the cash is over, the Cash Short and Over account is credited.

Banking Procedures and Handling of Money

In addition to complying with the requirements of the LSO for setting up trust accounts and reporting to the LFO, certain internal cash controls should be in place to help run the practice more efficiently and to reduce the risk of errors and fraud.[2]

When a bank account is opened with a financial institution, the bank will require that a **signature card** be filled in as a safeguard against forgery of cheques or other instruments. The bank will provide a set of cheques and a deposit book containing deposit slips to be completed for banking transactions. It is a requirement to list each cheque that is being deposited, as well as any cash, and indicate the source of the funds on the deposit slip. (See Figure 7.2 for a sample trust account deposit slip.) Deposits to the general bank account will include similar information. When the deposit is made, the person making the deposit and the bank teller will initial the deposit slip, and the teller will stamp the copy of the deposit slip as proof of the transaction. When using an automated teller to make deposits, you should be aware of all the bank's terms and the risks involved in using an ATM. Make sure a receipt of the deposit is attached to the firm's deposit book.

Withdrawals are allowed from an ATM for the general bank account, but not for trust accounts. Ensure that the signature card for the trust account has been encoded for deposits only by your financial institution.

Debit and credit cards can be used to pay for general office expenses. If a debit card is used, the amount will be deducted directly from the firm's bank account. It is important to keep receipts for any credit or debit card payments because the bank or credit card statements are not sufficient evidence of purchases for tax purposes.

Cheque Endorsement

Endorsement refers to the signing or stamping of a cheque prior to depositing it. Cheques must be endorsed or signed by the person to whom the cheque is made payable before they can be deposited. Three common types of endorsement are as follows:

- *Blank endorsement*: Once the back of the cheque is signed by the person to whom it was made payable, it can be further endorsed and cashed by anyone else. This type of endorsement can be unsafe because anyone who gets a hold of a blank endorsed cheque could sign the back and cash it. Very few banking institutions will allow blank endorsement.
- *Full endorsement*: The person signing the back of the cheque indicates to whom the cheque may be made payable. For example, a cheque made payable to Justin Case could be endorsed by him, "Pay to the order of Judith Wells," at which point Judith would be entitled to cash the cheque. Very few banking institutions will allow full endorsement.
- *Restrictive endorsement*: This type of endorsement is the usual method used in law firms. It specifies that the cheque must be deposited to the firm's bank account. A stamp for endorsement purposes is often provided when a business bank account is first opened. If a stamp is not used, you will be required to endorse the back of the cheque with the account number to which the cheque is being deposited.

---

2 *Ibid.*

FIGURE 10.6   Endorsement using stamp

Cheques

Handwritten business cheques often come in a binder with a stub attached, which is used to keep track of the deposits made to the account, the cheques written, and the bank balance. The cheque stubs can be used to create journal entries. Terms that are encountered with regard to cheques include the following:

- **Drawer**: The person writing the cheque (sometimes referred to as the **payor**).
- **Drawee**: The financial institution on which the cheque is drawn.
- **Payee**: The person to whom the cheque is written.

Many firms use accounting software that simultaneously produces cheques when a bill is being paid, records the payment in the proper journal, and then posts the amount to the correct ledger accounts. This type of software is a great time saver and a useful tool for keeping all records current. Printable cheques can be purchased to print directly from the accounting software.

[LO2] Reconciling a Bank Account

Reconciliation is the process used to compare the bank statement balance with the balance in the bank shown in the firm's general ledger. Each month the firm will receive a bank statement for each of its bank accounts, showing the following information:

- the balance at the beginning of the month;
- all deposits that have been received in the account;
- all cheques that have been cleared through the account (cancelled cheques);
- all bank charges for the account; and
- the balance at the end of the month.

Banks no longer return cancelled cheques with the bank statement. Instead, for a fee, a scanned copy of the front and back of cheques is provided with the bank statement. The scanned copies show the particulars of when and where a cheque was cashed and by whom.

How to Reconcile the General and Trust Bank Balances

Although there is no formal requirement to reconcile a firm's general operating account with the bank statement, it is good business practice to ensure that the bank records and the accounting records agree.

When reconciling a bank balance, the following discrepancies should be looked for:

- A **deposit in transit** is one that appears on the firm's general ledger but does not appear on the bank statement. This can happen if the deposit was entered in the firm's books but not taken to the bank until the next day (on the day after the cut-off date for the bank statement).

- An **outstanding cheque** is one written by the firm that is not shown on the bank statement because it has not been cashed by the payee. Because it was not presented to the bank for payment, the bank does not show it on the statement; however, it has been deducted (credited) from the bank general ledger record.
- Bank **service charges** often vary from month to month and need to be recorded in the firm's books once the amount is determined.
- An **NSF cheque** is one that was deposited but did not go through because there were insufficient funds in the account of the drawer (typically a client). When this happens, the bank notifies the firm by sending a debit memorandum indicating that the deposit has been reversed. There are usually bank service charges associated with any returned cheques. The firm could also have one of its own cheques returned if there were insufficient funds in the bank account to cover it when it was presented for payment. NSF cheques are sometimes referred to as bounced cheques. The service charges for writing a bad cheque are substantial, sometimes as much as $25 for a single bounced cheque.

EXAMPLE 1

The ending bank balance as shown on the general bank statement for Justin's firm at the end of November is $5,414.31. However, the general ledger shows a balance of $5,366.91 at the end of November, a difference of $47.40. The goal is to find out why there is a difference and to make any corrections needed.

Financial institutions have their own format for preparing bank statements, but the information contained is similar for all banks. Figure 10.7 shows the general bank statement received by Justin Case for the month of November.

STEP 1

Complete the form on the back of the bank statement if there is one, or use a form designed by the firm for the purpose of reconciling the bank statements. The completed form used for reconciling a general bank account is shown in Figure 10.8. This form demonstrates the reconciliation of Justin's general bank balance for the month of November.

STEP 2

Fill in the date of reconciliation at the top of the form, in Justin's case, November 30, 20**.

STEP 3

Insert the bank balance at the end of the month from the bank statement on the "Balance per Bank Statement" line and place the balance from the general ledger account on the "Balance per General Bank Account Ledger" line near the bottom of the form.

STEP 4

Compare all of the cancelled cheques (those that have been cashed at the bank) on the bank statement, noting whether there are any discrepancies in the amounts shown on the bank statement and on the cheque images. Compare the cheques shown on the bank statement and those shown in the general disbursements journal. Place a check mark next to the cheque amount on the bank statement and a check mark next to the corresponding amount in the general disbursements journal. Any cheques that are not checked off in the disbursements journal are outstanding.

Justin Case, Paralegal
GENERAL BANK RECONCILIATION
as at November 30, 20**

GENERAL BANK ACCOUNT

Balance per Bank Statement	5,414.31
Less: Outstanding Cheques (See list below)	–113.00
Plus: Outstanding Deposits	50.00
Plus/Minus Bank Error	0.60
Reconciled General Bank Balance at November 30, 20**	5,351.91

Outstanding Cheques

Cheque Number	Date	Amount
#7	Nov. 6	22.60
#8	Nov. 15	90.40
Total Outstanding Cheques		113.00

BALANCE PER BOOKS

Balance per General Bank Account Ledger	5,366.91
Add: Deposits by Bank Not Shown in Books	
Deduct: Bank Charges	
Bank Errors	–15.00
NSF Cheque	
Adjusted Balance per Books at November 30, 20**	5,351.91

FIGURE 10.8   General bank reconciliation

ROYAL BANK OF MONEY
P.O. Box 5011, Station A
Montreal, QC H3C 3B8

General Bank Account Statement

Justin Case, Paralegal	November 1, 20** to November 30, 20**
135 Main Street	
Yourtown, Ontario K3P 1G9	Account number: 0216-520634

ACCOUNT SUMMARY FOR THIS PERIOD

Opening Balance on Nov. 1, 20**		$5,600.00
Total Deposits and Credits	+	$1,272.00
Total Cheques and Debits	–	$1,457.69
Closing Balance on Nov. 30, 20**	=	$5,414.31

ACCOUNT ACTIVITY DETAILS

Date	Description	Cheques and Debits	Deposits and Credits	Balance
Nov. 01	Opening Balance			5,600.00
Nov. 02	Chq. #4	339.00 ✓		5,261.00
Nov. 12	Deposit		700.00 ✓	5,961.00
Nov. 14	Chq. #5	303.69 ✓		5,657.31
Nov. 15	Deposit		300.00 ✓	5,957.31
Nov. 15	Bank Charges	15.00 o/s		5,942.31
Nov. 22	Deposit		272.00*	6,214.31
Nov. 22	Chq. #6	800.00 ✓		5,414.31
	Closing Balance			5,414.31

Please check this Account Statement without delay and advise us of any error or omission within 45 days of the statement date.
Royal Bank of Money GST Registration Number: R105248I028

* Bank error; should be 272.60.

FIGURE 10.7   General bank statement

Justin Case, Paralegal General Disbursements Journal							GDJ1
Date 20**	Method/ Ref. #	Paid To/Particulars Client/RE	PR	General Ledger Acct. Dr.	Client's General Ledger Dr.	HST Paid Dr.	General Bank Account Cr.
Nov. 1	chq #4	Lucky Landlord, Rent Exp.	538	300.00		39.00	339.00 ✓
4	chq #5	LSO re dues Oct. – Dec.	534	268.75		34.94	303.69 ✓
5	chq #6	J. Case, Drawings	350	800.00			800.00 ✓
6	chq #7	Quick Courier, Zimmer re Courier Exp.	4		20.00	2.60	22.60
15	chq #8	Unitel re Telephone Exp.	565	80.00		10.40	90.40
30		Totals		1,448.75	20.00	86.94	1,555.69

FIGURE 10.9 General disbursements journal checked off

STEP 5

Prepare a list of outstanding cheques. List these amounts on the bank reconciliation form in the "Outstanding Cheques" section. Sum the outstanding cheques and place the total on the "Less: Outstanding Cheques" line as shown in Figure 10.8.

STEP 6

Look for any amounts in the Cheques and Debits column of the bank statement that did not appear in the general disbursements journal. Deduct the amount in the "Balance per Books" section of the bank reconciliation. Add lines as required. These are items that are not yet recorded in the firm's accounting records.

STEP 7

Check to see if there were any cheques outstanding from the previous month that have still not cleared the bank. In Justin's case, there are none. If there were any, you would add those cheques to the outstanding list because they are still outstanding. You might also choose to do a follow-up at that point to see why the cheques had not been cashed.

STEP 8

Using the deposit book for the general bank account (see Figure 10.10), compare all deposits on the bank statement with those in the deposit book, checking off each item and noting any discrepancies in the amounts.

STEP 9

Outstanding deposits: Compare the total amount of the deposits on the bank statement to the total deposits shown in the general ledger for the month (Figure 10.11). In Justin's situation, there was a deposit of $50 made using the general journal on November 21 that does not appear on the bank statement. Enter the amount of the outstanding deposits on the "Plus: Outstanding Deposits" line on the bank reconciliation form. Add additional lines if there is more than one deposit outstanding.

STEP 10

Bank errors: These are relatively rare but do occur occasionally. Typical bank errors include an entry being made to another customer's account or incorrectly recording the amount of a deposit or cheque. Notify the bank if it has made an error and the bank will correct it. In Justin's case, a bank error can be noted in the deposits entered on the bank statement. The records of the firm show a deposit for $272.60 on November 22 (see Figure 10.10), but the bank recorded the amount as $272.00. The bank account is understated by $0.60, so the bank must add this amount to the bank balance. When this occurs, the bank should be contacted and asked to make the correction, and a bank memo requested to confirm the correction. Place the amount on the "Plus/Minus Bank Error" line.

STEP 11

Calculate the reconciled bank balance. In Justin's case, a total of $5,351.91 will be arrived at.

CURRENT ACCOUNT DEPOSIT SLIP

DATE			INITIALS	
12	11	✷✷	JC	RW
DD	MM	YR	Depositor	Tellers

CASH COUNT	COIN		
	X 5		
	X 10		
	X 20		
	X 50		
	X 100		
Cash Subtotal	$		

R#20552-004 ACC #216-520634

LIST OF CHEQUES

CHEQUE IDENTIFICATION

	NAME	CHEQUE	REF. #	AMOUNT
1	Howes	Tr. Chq. #4	File No. 1	700.00
2				
3				
4				
5				
			Cheque Subtotal $	700.00

CREDIT ACCOUNT OF JUSTIN CASE, PARALEGAL

DEPOSIT SUMMARY

Visa Vouchers	
Cash Subtotal	
Cheque Subtotal	700.00
Deposit Total $	700.00 ✓

CURRENT ACCOUNT DEPOSIT SLIP

DATE			INITIALS	
15	11	✷✷	JC	RW
DD	MM	YR	Depositor	Tellers

CASH COUNT	COIN		
	X 5		
	X 10		
	X 20		
	X 50		
	X 100		
Cash Subtotal	$		

R#20552-004 ACC #216-520634

LIST OF CHEQUES

CHEQUE IDENTIFICATION

	NAME	CHEQUE	REF. #	AMOUNT
1	Jones	Tr. Chq. # 5	File No. 2	300.00
2				
3				
4				
5				
			Cheque Subtotal $	300.00

CREDIT ACCOUNT OF JUSTIN CASE, PARALEGAL

DEPOSIT SUMMARY

Visa Vouchers	
Cash Subtotal	
Cheque Subtotal	300.00
Deposit Total $	300.00 ✓

FIGURE 10.10   Deposit slips for general bank account (continued on next page)

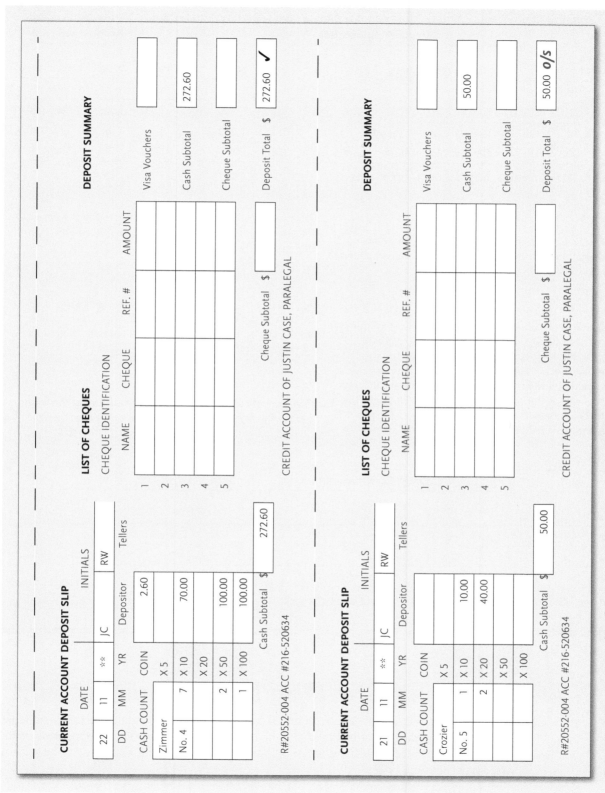

CURRENT ACCOUNT DEPOSIT SLIP

DATE			INITIALS		
22	11	※※	JC	RW	
DD	MM	YR	Depositor		Tellers

CASH COUNT	COIN		2.60	
Zimmer	X 5			
No. 4	7	X 10	70.00	
		X 20		
	2	X 50	100.00	
	1	X 100	100.00	
		Cash Subtotal $	272.60	

R#20552-004 ACC #216-520634

LIST OF CHEQUES

CHEQUE IDENTIFICATION

	NAME	CHEQUE	REF. #	AMOUNT
1				
2				
3				
4				
5				

Cheque Subtotal $

CREDIT ACCOUNT OF JUSTIN CASE, PARALEGAL

DEPOSIT SUMMARY

Visa Vouchers	
Cash Subtotal	272.60
Cheque Subtotal	
Deposit Total $	272.60 ✔

CURRENT ACCOUNT DEPOSIT SLIP

DATE			INITIALS		
21	11	※※	JC	RW	
DD	MM	YR	Depositor		Tellers

CASH COUNT	COIN			
Crozier	X 5			
No. 5	1	X 10	10.00	
	2	X 20	40.00	
		X 50		
		X 100		
		Cash Subtotal $	50.00	

R#20552-004 ACC #216-520634

LIST OF CHEQUES

CHEQUE IDENTIFICATION

	NAME	CHEQUE	REF. #	AMOUNT
1				
2				
3				
4				
5				

Cheque Subtotal $

CREDIT ACCOUNT OF JUSTIN CASE, PARALEGAL

DEPOSIT SUMMARY

Visa Vouchers	
Cash Subtotal	50.00
Cheque Subtotal	
Deposit Total $	50.00 **O/S**

FIGURE 10.10   Deposit slips for general bank account (concluded)

General Bank Account							Account No. 100
Date 20**		Explanation	PR	Debit	Credit	Dr./Cr.	Balance
Oct.	30		GJ2		500.00	Dr.	5,600.00
Nov.	21		GJ3	50.00		Dr.	5,650.00
	30	Totals from General Receipts Journal	GRJ1	1,272.60		Dr.	6,922.60
	30	Totals from General Disbursements Journal	GDJ1		1,555.69	Dr.	5,366.91

FIGURE 10.11   General bank account ledger sheet

STEP 12

The line indicating the adjusted balance per books at the end of the month must equal the reconciled general bank balance at the end of the month.

STEP 13

Bank charges or credits: The bank statement should be looked at to determine whether there are any bank charges that have not been recorded in the records. Note that there is a bank charge of $15. This amount must be deducted from the balance in the general ledger to arrive at the correct bank balance. Deduct $15 on the bank charges line. Because these bank charges were not recorded in the books of the firm, a general journal entry must be created and posted to the general ledger. The journal entry that would be made is shown in Figure 10.12.

STEP 14

Any credits made to the account by the bank should also be recorded. For example, if the bank had paid interest on the account, it would need to be entered. In Justin's case, there weren't any credits.

STEP 15

Compute the adjusted balance at the bottom of the form per the firm's books. This amount should equal the reconciled general bank balance shown in Figure 10.8.

Justin Case, General Journal					GJ3
Date 20**		Description	PR	Debit	Credit
Nov.	30	Bank Charges and Credit Card Expense	507	15.00	
		General Bank Account	100		15.00
		To record bank charges for November			

FIGURE 10.12   General journal entry to record bank charges

LO3 Reconciling the Mixed Trust Bank Account

Chapter 7 discussed how to enter data into the trust bank journal and post to the client trust and general ledgers. The individual doing the bookkeeping will need to have the bank statement and these records on hand when preparing the bank reconciliation statement for a mixed trust account.

By-law 9, part V, section 18(8) of the LSO requires that the monthly bank reconciliation statement be accompanied by a monthly **trust comparison** showing the amount of money held in trust for each client. This is done by preparing:

- a reconciliation of the trust bank balance; and
- a detailed listing showing the amount of money held in trust for each client and identifying each client for whom money is held in trust.

By-law 9, part V, section 22(2) requires that the trust bank reconciliation and trust comparison be completed by the 25th day of the following month for all trust funds held. The bank statement for the previous month is usually sent out before the end of the second week of the following month or is available earlier using online banking, so the 25th gives an individual plenty of time to prepare the reconciliation (see Figure 10.13). Any discrepancies discovered in the trust account records should be corrected as soon as they are discovered. Any bank or posting errors should be corrected before the month-end.

Bear in mind that each trust bank account operated by the firm, including interest-bearing accounts, GICs, and term deposits, must be reconciled every month—even if there was no activity in the account for a particular month.

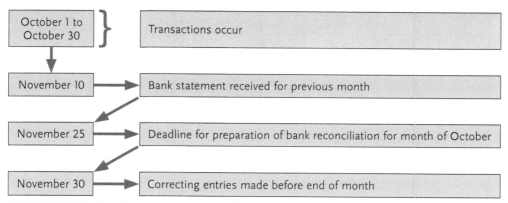

FIGURE 10.13   Timeline for mixed trust bank reconciliation

The process followed to complete the trust bank reconciliation statement is similar to reconciling the general bank account, but with a few added steps.

EXAMPLE 2

STEP 1

Compare the cheque images of the cancelled cheques with the entries shown on the trust bank statement (Figure 10.14) and note any discrepancies in the amounts shown. Verify whether the error was made by the bank or by the firm and make any necessary corrections.

STEP 2

Outstanding cheques: Compare the cheque entries on the trust bank statement with those in the trust bank journal in the accounting records or deposit book. Check off all cheques that cleared the bank in the records (we have used the trust bank journal; see Figure 10.15) and on the trust bank account statement (Figure 10.14). List any outstanding cheques, including the cheque number, date of issue, and amount on the bank reconciliation, and then place the total on the "Less: Outstanding Cheques" line (Figure 10.17).

ROYAL BANK OF MONEY
P.O. Box 5011, Station A
Montreal, QC H3C 3B8

Trust Bank Account Statement

Justin Case, Paralegal, Trust	October 1, 20** to October 31, 20**
135 Main Street	
Yourtown, Ontario K3P 1G9	Account number: 0216-520635

ACCOUNT SUMMARY FOR THIS PERIOD

Opening Balance on Oct. 1, 20**		$0.00
Total Deposits and Credits	+	$4,100.00
Total Cheques and Debits	−	$2,820.00
Closing Balance on Oct. 31, 20**	=	$1,280.00

ACCOUNT ACTIVITY DETAILS

Date	Description	Cheques and Debits	Deposits and Credits	Balance
Oct. 03	Deposit		1,600.00 ✓	1,600.00
Oct. 08	Chq. #1	20.00 ✓		1,580.00
Oct. 16	Deposit		2,500.00 ✓	4,080.00
Oct. 30	Chq. #2	2,500.00 ✓		1,580.00
	Closing Balance			1,580.00

Please check this Account Statement without delay and advise us of any error or omission within 45 days of the statement date.
Royal Bank of Money GST Registration Number: R1052481028

FIGURE 10.14   Trust bank account statement

Justin Case, Paralegal Trust Bank Journal						TJ1

Date 20**		Received From/ Paid To	File No.	Client/Description	Method of Payment	Trust Bank Account	
						Dr.	Cr.
Oct.	2	Rec. Cliff Howes	1	Cliff Howes/Retainer	Money Order	1,000 ✓	
	3	Pd. Deliveries Inc.	1	Cliff Howes/Courier	Chq. #1		20 ✓
	3	Rec. Frank Jones	2	Frank Jones/Retainer	Credit Card $500 Cash $100	600 ✓	
	15	Rec. James Settlor	1	Cliff Howes/Settlement	Bank Draft	2,500 ✓	
	16	Pd. Cliff Howes	1	Cliff Howes/Settlement	Chq. #2		2,500 ✓
	20	Pd. Minister of Finance	2	Jones/Payment of Fine	Chq. #3		300 o/s
	31	Totals				4,100	2,820
						(115)	(115)

FIGURE 10.15   Trust bank journal

	Justin Case, Paralegal List of Balances Owed to Clients October 31, 20**		
File No.	Account	Last Activity Date	Balance Owed
1	HOWES, Cliff re Small Claims Court	Oct. 15	980.00
2	JONES, Frank re *Highway Traffic Act*	Oct. 9	300.00
	Total Owed to Clients		1,280.00

FIGURE 10.16   Client trust listing

STEP 3

Outstanding deposits: Compare the entries on the bank statement with the entries in the trust bank journal or the deposit book for the trust bank account. Check off all corresponding deposits on the trust bank statement and trust bank journal, noting any discrepancies in the amounts. Note that in this example, the deposit $1,600 is shown as two entries in the trust bank journal but as one amount on the trust bank account statement. Any deposits for the previous month that are not recorded on the bank statement should be listed by date and amount. Enter the total amount of the outstanding deposits on the "Plus: Outstanding Deposits" line on the trust bank account reconciliation (Figure 10.17).

STEP 4

List any bank errors and/or posting errors individually by date of occurrence and provide a brief explanation. A copy of any supporting documentation, such as a bank memo, should be attached to the reconciliation.

STEP 5

Calculate the reconciled mixed trust balance on the bank reconciliation form. Enter this amount on the "Reconciled Mixed Trust Balance" line.

STEP 6

Client trust listing:

- Prepare a list of client balances from the client trust ledgers, identifying the clients for whom funds are held in trust at the end of the previous month.

- List the client names with the balance in the trust accounts, including the last activity date, to help monitor inactive or dormant accounts.

- Total the client trust listing as shown in Figure 10.16. Enter the information from the client trust listing in the "Client Trust Listing" section, as shown in Figure 10.17.

STEP 7

Trust comparison: Compare the reconciled trust bank balance (Figure 10.17) with the client trust listing total (Figure 10.16). The two amounts should be equal. If the amounts are not the same, the discrepancy must be found and corrected immediately.

Justin Case, Paralegal
TRUST BANK RECONCILIATION
as at October 31, 20**

TRUST BANK ACCOUNT

Balance per Bank Statement	1,580
Less: Outstanding Cheques (See list below)	300
Plus: Outstanding Deposits	
List:	
Plus/Minus Bank Error	
Reconciled Mixed Trust Balance at October 31, 20**	1,280

Outstanding Cheques

Cheque Number	Date	Amount
Chq. #3	Oct. 20, 20**	300
Total Outstanding Cheques		300

CLIENT TRUST LISTING
(from clients' trust ledger balances)
as at October 31, 20**

File Name	Last Activity Date		Amount
1. HOWES, Cliff re Small Claims Court	Oct. 15, 20**		980
2. JONES, Frank re *Highway Traffic Act*	Oct. 9, 20**		300
Total Trust Liabilities to Clients at October 31, 20**			1,280

TRUST COMPARISON
as at October 31, 20**

Reconciled Trust Bank Balance	1,280
Total of unexpected balances per client's trust ledger	1,280

FIGURE 10.17   Trust bank account reconciliation

POTENTIAL PARALEGAL PITFALLS

- **Potential pitfall:** Not reconciling the trust bank account monthly.
- **Possible fallout:** Client money could be spent inappropriately; shortfalls in trust may go unnoticed; paralegals could get in trouble with the LSO for not completing bank reconciliations.
- **Proposed recommendation:** Reconcile trust accounts monthly, get help from an accountant if needed, and resolve any reconciliation differences immediately upon discovery.

Reviewing the Trust Bank Reconciliation

When reviewing the monthly trust comparisons, the paralegal should:

- Ensure that the bank reconciliations are prepared before the 25th of the following month.
- List items that were reconciled, giving a clear explanation that can be traced to the bank statement. It is a requirement to provide this information to the LSO when the firm's annual report is filed.
- If there are any cheques that have remained uncashed for more than two months, follow up to see why they were not cashed. It might be necessary to put a stop payment on a cheque if it has been lost, and a replacement cheque will then need to be prepared.
- If a cheque is stale-dated (more than six months old), a stop payment should be placed on it. If this is done, a reversing entry will be required to place the funds back in the client's trust ledger account. It is necessary to inquire as to why the cheque was not cashed and provide a replacement cheque, if necessary.
- Ensure that the balance in each client's trust ledger is correct. If an amount was entered in the wrong client's account, this will not be revealed by the bank reconciliation process. The paralegal reviewing the client listing should notice if an amount shown on a client's trust ledger appears to be incorrect.
- Once work on a file has been finished, an invoice should be sent to the client. If funds remain in trust, a refund should also be sent.
- If the bank is taking bank charges out of the trust account, make sure that the bank is contacted and an arrangement is made for all bank charges to be taken out of the general bank account, as required by the LSO.

Maintenance and Retention of General and Trust Records

The financial records required to be maintained for general and trust accounts may be entered and posted by hand or electronic means, but if the records are entered and posted by hand, this should be done in ink.[3] If electronic records are maintained, a licensee must ensure that a paper copy of the record can be produced promptly on the LSO's request.[4] If records are kept electronically, it is important to back them up frequently in case of a computer crash. By-law 9 also requires that trust financial records be entered and posted so that they are current at all times.[5]

General Bank Records

The financial records required by the LSO related to general bank accounts must be kept for at least six years plus the current year.[6] These records include the fees book, general receipts and disbursements journals, general ledgers, and all related bank records such as passbooks,

---

3   By-law 9, part V, s 21(1).

4   *Ibid*, s 21(2).

5   *Ibid*, s 22(1).

6   *Ibid*, s 23(1).

cancelled cheques, trust transfer journals, and bank reconciliations. If money is received in cash, a book of duplicate receipts must be kept for the most recent six full years plus the current year.

Trust Bank Records

The financial records related to trust accounts required by the LSO must be kept for ten years plus the current year.[7] These records include the trust bank journal, the monthly trust reconciliation, valuable property record, and all bank passbooks, cashed cheques, signed electronic trust transfer requisitions, and printed confirmations of electronic transfers.

Dormant Accounts

Dormant accounts are funds held in trust on behalf of a client that are unclaimed. Perhaps a client paid a retainer and then disappeared, and you have been unable to contact her over a period of two years. Section 59.6 of the *Law Society Act* permits a licensee to apply for permission to transfer such funds to the LSO if the client cannot be located despite reasonable efforts after two years, or if the lawyer or licensed paralegal is unable to determine who is entitled to the money. The procedure for transferring such moneys to the LSO is set out in by-law 10.

TAX TIP

Documentation for a CRA Audit

Regardless of whether a paralegal's business is organized as a sole proprietorship, partnership, or corporation, there is a high likelihood that it will be audited by the CRA at some point.

The CRA auditor can examine books and records, documents, previous tax returns, and business records including ledgers, journals, invoices, receipts, contracts, and bank statements with bank reconciliations. Personal records such as bank statements, mortgage documents, and credit card statements, as well as personal or business records of a spouse or family member, may be included. Adjustments made by the bookkeeper or accountant to arrive at income for tax purposes can also be reviewed.

---

7 *Ibid.*

CHAPTER SUMMARY

The objective of this chapter has been to outline the obligations of a licensee with respect to reviewing the accounting records at the end of each month to ensure that the requirements of the LSO are being met. Reconciling the general bank account promptly each month is part of the month-end process before completing your financial statements. If the duties of operating and maintaining bank accounts are delegated to others, the reconciliation will enable the licensee to evaluate whether tasks are being performed correctly and in compliance with LSO rules. Any errors or differences identified by the reconciliation may alert you to a need for greater supervision of employees who may need additional training.

KEY TERMS

cash controls, 256

cash short and over, 259

deposit in transit, 260

dormant accounts, 272

drawee, 260

drawer, 260

endorsement, 259

NSF cheque, 261

outstanding cheque, 261

payee, 260

payor, 260

petty cash, 256

reconciliation, 260

service charges, 261

signature card, 259

trust comparison, 267

FURTHER READING

Canadian Bankers Association (CBA), "Cheques—What You Need to Know," online: <https://www.cba.ca/cheques-what-you-need-to-know>. See the section "Cheque Cashed by a Different Individual (Counter-Signed Cheques)." The CBA advises consumers to "check with your financial institution to find out if counter-signed cheques are accepted."

Law Society of Ontario, "Reconciling a Trust Account," online: <https://lso.ca/lawyers/practice-supports -and-resources/topics/managing-money/trust-accounts/reconciling-a-trust-account>.

Law Society of Ontario, *The Bookkeeping Guide for Paralegals* (Toronto: LSO, February 2014) at 70-71 ("Monthly Financial Review Checklist"), online: <https://lawsocietyontario.azureedge.net/media/lso/ media/legacy/pdf/p/paralegal_bookkeeping_guide_final-s.pdf>.

REVIEW QUESTIONS

True or False

_____ 1. By-law 9 of the LSO requires that the general bank ledger be reconciled by the 25th day of the following month after the date of the bank statement. (LO3)

_____ 2. The petty cash account balance is changed only when establishing, increasing, or decreasing the petty cash balance limit. (LO2)

_____ 3. Outstanding cheques are added to the bank statement balance. (LO2)

_____ 4. "Deposit to the Credit of" is an example of a full endorsement. (LO1)

_____ 5. Deposits in transit are added to the bank statement balance. (LO2)

_____ 6. Adjustments to the bank statement balance require an adjustment entry in the general journal. (LO2, LO3)

_____ 7. After preparing the trust bank reconciliation, any bank or posting errors should be corrected before the end of the month in which the most recent bank statement is received. (LO3)

_____ 8. The ending balances on the general bank ledger or trust bank ledger must equal the ending bank statement reconciled balance in order for the records to be reconciled. (LO2, LO3)

_____ 9. Petty cash is an expense account reflected on the income statement. (LO1)

_____ 10. The value of the petty cash account is equal to the petty cash voucher total and the remaining cash balance in the petty cash box. (LO1)

Short Answer

Give a full answer for each question:

1. Discuss the following statement: "It is important to keep receipts for any credit or debit card payments." (LO2)

2. What are some of the goals of internal controls for a business? What are some key considerations for paralegals? (See Law Society of Ontario, *The Bookkeeping Guide for Paralegals*, in Further Reading.) (LO2)

3. What are the record-keeping requirements for general bank account records and trust bank account records, as set out in by-law 9? For how long must the records be kept? (LO3)

4. What are the seven steps involved in reconciling the trust bank account against the trust bank ledger? (LO3)

PRACTICE EXERCISES

Practice Exercise 10.1 (LO1)

Ann Litigate advises her administrative assistant to establish a petty cash fund with a limit of $150 for minor and day-to-day expenses. Ann also advises the administrative assistant that, as custodian of the petty cash fund, she is to replenish the petty cash on a monthly basis.

a.   Prepare the general journal entry to show the establishment of the account (January 1, 20**).

b.   Based on the following petty cash expenses for the month, prepare the petty cash record tracking expenses:

> Jan. 6   Courier charges, Voucher #1 ($15)
>
> Jan. 10   Postage, Voucher #2 ($10.65)
>
> Jan. 12   Parking, Voucher #3 ($12.75)
>
> Jan. 17   Office supplies, miscellaneous, Voucher #4 ($33.50)
>
> Jan. 23   Courier charges, Voucher #5 ($18)
>
> Jan. 27   Postage, Voucher #6 ($10.65)
>
> Jan. 30   Parking, Voucher #7 ($12.75)

c.   Prepare the journal entries showing the expenses from the petty cash record tracking expenses and the replenishment of the petty cash fund (January 31, 20**).

Ann Litigate Paralegal Services General Journal				GJ3
Date 20**	Description	PR	Debit	Credit

> **HINT**
>
> Check and Balance Petty Cash Fund
> The amount of cash on hand plus the amount of all petty cash vouchers is equal to the total value of the fund.
>
> | Total paid out | $113.30 |
> |---|---|
> | Cash in petty cash box | 36.70 |
> | Total petty cash fund | $150.00 |

Practice Exercise 10.2 (LO2)

Review and compare Ann Litigate's general bank account ledger for January 20** and the general bank statement for the month-end January 31.

a.   Record and note any differences and discrepancies.

b.   Prepare the bank reconciliation using the worksheet provided.

c.   Prepare adjusting journal entries in the general journal in respect of any corrections.

General Bank Account							Account No. 100
Date 20**		Explanation	PR	Debit	Credit	Dr./ Cr.	Balance
Jan.	1	Opening Balance	GJ2			Dr.	6,300.00
	1	Cheque #11	GJ2		1,500.00	Dr.	4,800.00
	20	Transfer from Trust re Invoice #14-201	GJ2	800.00		Dr.	5,600.00
	30	Cheque #12	GJ2		1,300.00	Dr.	4,300.00
	31	Cheque #13	GJ2		118.73	Dr.	4,181.27
	31	Cheque #14	GJ2		450.00	Dr.	3,731.27

Bank Statement (General Bank Account)

Ann Litigate Paralegal Services
11 Any Street, Ottawa, ON K1A 0B0

ABC Bank
1000 Front St.
Ottawa, ON

Jan. 1 – Jan. 31, 20**

Date	Description	Reference	Debit	Credit		Balance
December 31, 20**	Balance Forward				Cr.	$6,300.00
January 1, 20**	Cheque #11	200	1,500.00		Cr.	$4,800.00
January 3, 20**	Deposit—Cheque	121		1,000.00	Cr.	$5,800.00
January 19, 20**	ATM W/D	004430	11.50		Cr.	$5,788.50
January 20, 20**	TFR FR 10002	JXY01		800.00	Cr.	$6,588.50
January 30, 20**	Cheque #12	203	1,300.00		Cr.	$5,288.50
January 31, 20**	Service Charge		23.00		Cr.	$5,265.50
	Total Debits and Credits		$2,834.50	$1,800.00		
	Closing Balance					$5,265.50

Note re bank statement: Debit (Withdrawal); Credit (Deposit)

Ann Litigate Paralegal Services
GENERAL BANK RECONCILIATION
as at January 31, 20**

GENERAL BANK ACCOUNT

Balance per Bank Statement

Less: Outstanding Cheques (See list below)

Plus: Outstanding Deposits

Plus/Minus Bank Error

Reconciled General Bank Balance at January 31, 20**

Outstanding Cheques

Cheque Number	Date	Amount

Total Outstanding Cheques

BALANCE PER BOOKS

Balance per General Bank Account Ledger

Add: Deposits by Bank Not Shown in Books

Deduct: Bank Charges

   ATM Withdrawals

   Bank Errors

   NSF Cheque

Adjusted Balance per Books at January 31, 20**

Ann Litigate Paralegal Services General Journal					GJ2
Date 20**		Description	PR	Debit	Credit

Practice Exercise 10.3 (LO3)

Review and compare Ann Litigate's trust bank account ledger for January 20** and the trust bank statement for the month-end January 31.

a. Record and note any differences and discrepancies. Note that an error was made by the bookkeeper when cheque #0138 was entered. The amount should have been entered as $280 instead of $260. This has resulted in a $20 overdraft in the B. Saul Client Trust Ledger Account. In addition, remember that the service charge should not be deducted from the trust account. The bank will need to be asked to reverse this entry. The error needs to be reconciled and the bank needs to be contacted to correct the account for bank charges.

b. Prepare the bank reconciliation using the worksheet provided.

c. Compare the reconciled trust bank balance with the client trust listing total.

d. Prepare the adjusting journal entry in the trust bank journal provided in respect of any corrections.

Trust Bank Account							Account No. 115
Date 20**		Explanation	PR	Debit	Credit	Dr./ Cr.	Balance
Jan.	1	Opening Balance	TJ2			Dr.	10,000.00
	1	Retainer Received— A. Paulo, Cheque #11225	TJ2	1,500.00		Dr.	11,500.00
	3	Refund to Client from Trust— B. Saul, Cheque #0138	TJ2		260.00	Dr.	11,240.00
	20	Transfer from Trust re Invoice #14-201	TJ2		800.00	Dr.	10,440.00
	30	Retainer Received— C. Charles, Cheque #002	TJ2	2,000.00		Dr.	12,440.00

Bank Statement (Trust Bank Account)

Ann Litigate Paralegal Services
11 Any Street, Ottawa, ON K1A 0B0

ABC Bank
1000 Front St.
Ottawa, ON

Jan. 1 – Jan. 31, 20**

Date	Description	Reference	Debit	Credit		Balance
December 31, 20**	Balance Forward				Cr.	$10,000.00
January 1, 20**	Deposit—Cheque	11225		1,500.00	Cr.	$11,500.00
January 3, 20**	Cheque	0138	280.00		Cr.	$11,220.00
January 20, 20**	TFR FR 10002	JXY01	800.00		Cr.	$10,420.00
January 31, 20**	Service Charge		23.00		Cr.	$10,397.00
	Total Debits and Credits		$1,103.00	$1,500.00		
	Closing Balance					$10,417.00

Note re bank statement: Debit (Withdrawal); Credit (Deposit)

Ann Litigate Paralegal Services
TRUST BANK RECONCILIATION
as at January 31, 20**

TRUST BANK ACCOUNT

Balance per Bank Statement

Less: Outstanding Cheques (See list below)

Plus: Outstanding Deposits

Plus/Minus Bank Error

Reconciled Mixed Trust Balance at January 31, 20**

Outstanding Cheques

Cheque Number	Date	Amount
Total Outstanding Cheques		

BALANCE PER BOOKS

Balance per Trust Bank Account Ledger

Add: Deposits by Bank Not Shown in Books

Deduct: Bank Charges

Bank Errors

NSF Cheque

Adjustments

Chq. #0138   January 3, 20**

Incorrect Entry per Books

Correct Entry per Bank Statement

Add to Trust Bank Ledger

Adjusted Balance per Books at January 31, 20**

Ann Litigate Paralegal Services List of Balances, Trust Funds Owed January 31, 20**		
File No./Account Name	Last Activity Date	Balance Owed
File No. 101, Moore, C.	Nov. 15, 20**	2,100.00
File No. 102, Abernathy, L.	Dec. 1, 20**	1,700.00
File No. 103, Pasec, S.	Dec. 15, 20**	200.00
File No. 104, Smith, A.L.	Dec. 29, 20**	3,000.00
File No. 105, Saul, B.	Jan. 3, 20**	(20.00)
File No. 106, Reuter, D.	Jan. 20, 20**	1,940.00
File No. 107, Charles, C.	Jan. 30, 20**	2,000.00
File No. 108, Paulo, A.	Jan. 1, 20**	1,500.00
Total Trust Funds Owed		$12,420.00

Ann Litigate Paralegal Services Trust Bank Journal					TJ2	
Date 20**		Received From/ Paid To	File No.	Client/Description	Method of Payment	Trust Bank Account
						Dr.	Cr.

PUT IT INTO PRACTICE

Case Example: Trust Bank Account Reconciliation

Ann Litigate compared her trust bank account statement against her trust bank journal and noticed a discrepancy. Review the following trust receipts and disbursements journals, trust bank account ledger, and trust bank statement for Ann Litigate for the month of May 20** and advise her on how to prepare a bank reconciliation by answering the following questions. (LO3)

- a. Are there any outstanding deposits for the period?
- b. Are there any outstanding cheques for the period?
- c. Are there any withdrawals improperly made from the trust bank account for such items as service and bank charges that need to be reversed by the bank?
- d. What is the bank balance at the end of the month shown on the trust bank statement?
- e. What is the bank balance shown in the trust bank account ledger?
- f. What needs to be done to reconcile the two amounts?
- g. What should the total of the client trust ledgers and the reconciled bank balance be?

Trust Receipts Journal				TRJ1
Date 20**	Received from	Description	Method of Payment	Amount
May 1	S. Bailey	S. Bailey—Retainer	Chq. #058	1,500
12	C. Smythe	C. Smythe—Retainer	Chq. #021	1,000
15	D. Pitt	D. Pitt—Retainer	Chq. #002	1,750
28	R. Park, Defendant	F. Moore—Settlement	Chq. #011	5,000
30	K. Thomas	K. Thomas—Retainer	Chq. #095	2,000
			Total	11,250
				(115)

Trust Disbursements Journal				TDJ1
Date 20**	Paid to	Description	Method of Payment	Amount
May 5	Ann Litigate	F. Moore—Courier charges recoverable	Trust Chq. #0023	40
12	Ann Litigate	B. Daley—Paid invoice #350	Trust Chq. #0024	1,100
30	F. Moore	F. Moore—Settlement	Trust Chq. #0025	5,000
			Total	6,140
				(115)

Trust Bank Account					Account No. 115	
Date 20**		Description	PR	Debit	Credit	Dr./Cr.	Balance
May	1	Opening Balance					0
	30	Trust Totals for May	TJ1	11,250	6,140	Dr.	5,110

ABC Credit Union Trust Bank Statement May 1 to May 30, 20**						
Date 20**		Description	Ref.	Debit (With-drawals)	Credit (Deposits)	Balance
		BALANCE FORWARD				0
May	1	Deposit			$1,500	$1,500
	5	Cheque	23	$40		$1,460
	12	Deposit			$1,000	$2,460
	15	Cheque	24	$1,100		$1,360
	15	Deposit			$1,750	$3,110
	28	Deposit			$5,000	$8,110
	30	Deposit			$2,000	$10,110
		Total Debits (Withdrawals) and Credits (Deposits)		$1,140	$11,250	
		Closing Balance				$10,110

Accounting for GST/HST, Payroll, and Income Tax

Goods and Services Tax 284

Payroll 288

Income Tax. 292

Chapter Summary 300

Key Terms 300

Further Reading. 300

Review Questions 301

Practice Exercises 302

Put It into Practice. 304

After reading this chapter, you should be able to:

LO1 Describe different methods for calculating GST/HST and making remittances to the Canada Revenue Agency.

LO2 Calculate, record, and remit payroll deductions.

LO3 Explain common income tax considerations.

LEARNING OUTCOMES

Goods and Services Tax

The **goods and services tax (GST)** is a multi-level, value-added tax that was introduced in Canada on January 1, 1991 by the then prime minister Brian Mulroney and his finance minister, Michael Wilson. Most Canadians and Canadian companies must pay **GST/HST** on their purchases, including legal fees. Some groups and organizations, such as diplomats, governments, and status Indians, are exempt from paying GST/HST. However, if a false claim for exemption is made by a client, and even if a fake exemption card is presented to avoid paying the tax, the business owner still must account for the tax that should have been collected.

The provinces of New Brunswick, Nova Scotia, Newfoundland and Labrador, Ontario, and Prince Edward Island—referred to as the participating provinces—harmonized their provincial sales tax with the GST to create the **harmonized sales tax (HST)**. The current rate for HST in Ontario is 13 percent, which includes the 5 percent federal goods and services tax and the 8 percent provincial retail sales tax.

As mentioned in Chapter 1, paralegals are considered a small supplier, exempted from collecting GST/HST if their total annual revenues from all of their businesses are $30,000 or less.

Remitting GST/HST to the Receiver General

To complete a GST/HST return, it is necessary to know the following amounts:

- The total fees and disbursements or other revenues on which GST/HST is charged.
- The amount of GST/HST charged (even if it was not yet collected).
- The amount of GST/HST the business owner paid or is payable on purchases made for the business. This is referred to as the input tax credit (ITC).
- Other amounts might also have to be included on the GST/HST report, such as installments paid during the year or other adjustments being claimed.

For a sole proprietor with a fiscal year-end of December 31 and an annual reporting period for GST/HST purposes, payment is due no later than April 30, although the return is not due until June 15. Payments may be made to the Receiver General using online banking, at a financial institution, or by mail. The CRA does not accept credit cards. A penalty plus interest is charged on any balance owing if the return is not received by the CRA on time. The penalty is calculated as 1 percent of the amount owing, plus 25 percent of that amount multiplied by the number of months the return is overdue, up to 12 months.

Maintenance of Records

Usually, all sales and purchase invoices and other **records** related to your business operations and the GST/HST need to be kept for six years from the end of the year to which they relate. If the business owner wants to destroy these records after six years, the CRA recommends that a written request be sent and to wait for written approval to do so. As a registrant, it is necessary that the invoices provided by the suppliers used show the correct information to support your **input tax credit (ITC)** claims. Registered businesses from which goods or services are purchased must provide invoices showing their GST/HST registration number and other required information. Verifying that a supplier has provided a valid GST/HST number can be done through the CRA's online GST/HST Registry. The CRA administers an audit program, during which auditors may ask to see a business owner's records. During an audit, the CRA will make sure that the business owner has charged and reported the GST/HST when required, and that the business owner is entitled to all the ITCs that have been claimed on the return.

Many rules apply to what can and cannot be claimed as an ITC. As a guideline, claim only those tax-deductible purchases that are authorized under the *Income Tax Act* on which GST/HST is charged. For example, under the *Income Tax Act*, the deduction for meals and entertainment expenses is limited to 50 percent of the cost of the meals and entertainment. Likewise, the ITCs claimed for this expense are also limited to 50 percent of the amount paid. If a business owner qualifies to claim home office expenses for income tax purposes, the ITCs applicable can be claimed to the portion of the home expenses allowed to be deducted from the business owner's income for calculating net income for tax purposes. A special calculation is required to claim GST/HST paid on the purchase of a vehicle. The amount allowed for GST/HST is based on what the business owner is entitled to claim based on the permissible capital cost allowance (CCA). It is advisable to check the CRA website information on claiming ITCs or speak to a tax professional to ensure the amounts being claimed are allowed.

LO1   Methods for Calculating GST/HST Remittance

There are three methods used for tracking GST/HST:
- the regular method,
- the simplified method, and
- the quick method.

The quick method will not be discussed here because persons who provide legal, accounting, or actuarial services in the course of their professional practice are not permitted to use it.

A paralegal may use either the regular or the simplified method for calculating the amount of GST/HST that must be remitted to the Receiver General.

Regular Method

If the regular method is to be used for submitting GST/HST remittances, it should be ensured that journals and ledgers are set up with the necessary columns for tracking GST/HST billed to clients and GST/HST paid or payable on purchases by the firm. This will provide the bookkeeper with the data needed for completing the returns. To use the regular method for calculating the amount of GST/HST that will need to be remitted, it is necessary to know the following:

- the total amount of fees billed to clients on which GST/HST was charged over the reporting period;
- the total amount of GST/HST charged to clients, whether or not it has been collected;
- the total amount the firm paid or is payable on tax-deductible purchases for GST/HST; and

- the difference between the amount of GST/HST collected from clients and the amount of GST/HST paid or payable for purchases. This is the amount of net tax that either needs to be remitted or for which the firm is entitled to a refund.

If legal or other software is being used for accounting purposes, the calculation of these amounts and preparation of a report is usually done automatically. Figure 11.1 shows the GST/HST return template that is available on the CRA website.[1]

Goods and Services Tax / Harmonized Sales Tax (GST/HST) Return Working Copy

Do not use this working copy to file your return or to make payments at your financial institution.

Name	Business number R T
Reporting period From Year Month Day to Year Month Day	Due date Year Month Day

Working copy (for your records)

► Copy your Business number, the reporting period, and the amounts from the highlighted line numbers in this worksheet to the corresponding boxes in your GST/HST return.

Enter your total **sales and other revenue**. Do not include provincial sales tax, GST or HST. If you are using the Quick Method of accounting, include the GST or HST.	101	00		

Net tax calculation

Enter the total of all **GST and HST amounts that you collected or that became collectible** by you in the reporting period.	103			
Enter the total amount of **adjustments** to be added to the net tax for the reporting period (for example, the GST/HST obtained from the recovery of a bad debt).	104			
Total GST/HST and adjustments for period (add lines 103 and 104) ➔			105	
Enter the GST/HST you paid or that is payable by you on qualifying expenses **(input tax credits – ITCs)** for the current period and any eligible unclaimed ITCs from a previous period.	106			
Enter the total amount of **adjustments** to be deducted when determining the net tax for the reporting period (for example, the GST/HST included in a bad debt).	107			
Total ITCs and adjustments (add lines 106 and 107) ➔			108	
Net tax (subtract line 108 from line 105)			109	

Other credits if applicable

Do not complete line 111 until you have read the instructions.

Enter any **instalment and other annual filer payments** you made for the reporting period. If the due date of your return is June 15, see the instructions.	110			
Enter the total amount of the GST/HST **rebates, only** if the rebate form indicates that you can claim the amount on this line. For filing, information, see instructions.	111			
Total other credits (add lines 110 and 111) ➔			112	
Balance (subtract line 112 from line 109)			113 A	

Other debits if applicable

Do not complete line 205 or line 405 until you have read the instructions.

Enter the total amount of the **GST/HST due on the acquisition of taxable real property**.	205			
Enter the total amount of **other GST/HST to be self-assessed**.	405			
Total other debits (add lines 205 and 405) ➔			113 B	
Balance (add lines 113 A and 113 B)			113 C	

Line 114 and line 115: If the result entered on line 113 C is a negative amount, enter the amount of the refund you are claiming on line 114. If the result entered on line 113 C is a positive amount, enter the amount of your payment on line 115.

Refund claimed	Payment enclosed
114	115

Instructions

Line 110
Annual filer with a June 15 due date: If you are an individual with business income for income tax purposes and have a December 31 fiscal year-end, the due date of your return is June 15. However, any GST/HST you owe is payable by April 30. This payment should be reported on line 110 of your GST/HST Tax Return.

Line 111: Some rebates can reduce or offset your amount owing. Those rebate forms contain a question asking you if you want to claim the rebate amount on line 111 of your GST/HST Tax Return. Tick **yes** on the rebate form(s) if you are claiming the rebate(s) on line 111 of your GST/HST Tax Return. If you file your return electronically, send the rebate application by mail to the Prince Edward Island Tax Centre.

Line 205: Complete this line **only** if you purchased taxable real property for use or supply primarily (more than 50%) in your commercial activities and you are a GST/HST registrant (other than an individual who purchases a residential complex) or you purchased the property from a non-resident. If you qualify for an input tax credit on the purchase, include this amount on line 108.

Line 405: Complete this line **only** if you are a GST/HST registrant who has to self-assess GST/HST on an imported taxable supply or who has to self-assess the provincial part of HST.

Personal information is collected under the *Excise Tax Act* to administer tax, rebates, and elections. It may also be used for any purpose related to the administration or enforcement of the Act such as audit, compliance and the payment of debts owed to the Crown. It may be shared or verified with other federal, provincial/territorial government institutions to the extent authorized by law. Failure to provide this information may result in interest payable, penalties or other actions. Under the *Privacy Act*, individuals have the right to access their personal information and request correction if there are errors or omissions. Refer to Info Source at cra.gc.ca/gncy/tp/nfsrc/nfsrc-eng.html, Personal Information Bank CRA PPU 241.

FIGURE 11.1 GST/HST return working copy

Reproduced with permission of the Minister of National Revenue, 2018.

1 Canada Revenue Agency, "Goods and Services Tax/Harmonized Sales Tax (GST/HST) Return Working Copy," online: <http://www.cra-arc.gc.ca/tx/bsnss/tpcs/gst-tps/bspsbch/rtrns/rtrnwkcpy-eng.pdf>.

Simplified Method

When the simplified method is being used, the bookkeeping records do not need to show the purchase price of goods and GST/HST paid separately. To be eligible to use this method, annual fees income and purchases must be $1 million or less. To calculate the GST/HST, add up the ITC-eligible **business expenses**, including the GST/HST paid. Expenses on which no GST/HST is payable, such as salaries, may not be included; only GST/HST charged on purchases deductible as legitimate business expenses under the *Income Tax Act* can be claimed. For example, for those living in Ontario, which has a combined GST/HST rate of 13 percent (5 percent federal and 8 percent provincial), the simplified method calculation would be as follows:

Description	Expenses
Rent (includes HST)	$1,070.00
Salaries (HST does not apply)	3,000.00
Insurance (HST does not apply)	50.00
Advertising (HST included)	214.00
Office supplies (HST included)	230.00
Total purchases and expenses	$4,564.00
Step 1	
• Add all purchases and expenses including the HST (GST and PST)	$4,564.00
• Subtract non-taxable items (salaries and insurance)	–3,050.00
Taxable expenses	$1,514.00
Step 2	
• Multiply taxable expenses on which you paid 13 percent HST by 13/113 to calculate the input tax credit	$174.18

FIGURE 11.2   Simplified calculation of GST/HST

Calculate the net tax for each GST/HST reporting period and report this on the GST/HST return. To do so, calculate:

- the GST/HST collected or that became collectible on the fees billed during the reporting period;
- the GST/HST payable using the simplified calculation above; and then
- take the difference between these two amounts, including any adjustments, to arrive at the net tax.

A positive amount must be remitted to the Receiver General. If the GST/HST paid is more than the GST/HST the firm has charged or collected, a claim for a refund for the difference can be made.

Note that the GST/HST rate used above is for Ontario, and the multiplier of 13/113 will vary with the GST/HST rates for each province.

Deciding which method is best for calculating GST/HST is complicated. The business owner may wish to speak to an accountant when making a decision.

Remitting GST/HST

Before the end of each GST/HST reporting period, the business owner will receive a form to complete from the CRA that must be filled in and returned along with any payment owing. If the business owner files quarterly, the return must be sent along with the amount owing before the end of the following month. That is, a report covering January to March would have to be filed before the end of April. If the business owner files annually, the report must be sent within three months after the end of the one-year period. Returns and remittances (payments) may be made by filing online, at a financial institution, or by mail.

LO2 Payroll

Salaries can represent a large part of the operating expenses for a firm. Employers are responsible for deducting CPP contributions, EI premiums, and income tax from remuneration paid to employees and for remitting the deductions to the CRA along with the required reports. If a firm does not fulfill its obligations or comply with payroll requirements, it may be assessed a penalty with interest, or incur other consequences. On prosecution, a person can be fined from $1,000 to $25,000 or fined and imprisoned for a term of up to 12 months. The CRA can assess a penalty of 10 percent of the amount of CPP, EI, and income tax that was not deducted and will apply a penalty of 20 percent to second or later failures under certain circumstances.

When an employee is hired, the business owner must:

- obtain the employee's social insurance number (SIN), and
- obtain from the employee a completed Form TD1, Personal Tax Credits Return.[2]

The Payroll Process

Employee pay will be established with the employee at the time of hire. It may be a salary based on various pay periods, usually weekly, biweekly, or monthly. When hiring an employee, ensure there is a clear understanding of the rate being paid, the hours of work, and other benefits, such as sick days and vacation time.

Suppose Justin Case hires an assistant who will work from 8:30 to 5:00 every day (with one hour off for lunch) at an hourly rate of $20 per hour. That would make for a 7.5-hour day, or 37.5 hours a week. At the rate of $20 an hour, this would yield a **gross pay** of $750 a week. Gross pay is the full amount of the employee's earnings, before taking (or "withholding") any deductions for CPP, EI, and income tax. Justin will need to determine how frequently the employee will be paid to determine the gross pay for each pay period before the **payroll deductions** at source can be calculated.

---

2 Canada Revenue Agency, "Filing Form TD1, Personal Tax Credits Return," online: <https://www.canada.ca/content/dam/cra-arc/formspubs/pbg/td1/td1-fill-18e.pdf>.

Gross pay	$750 per week x 52 weeks	$39,000
Weekly	$39,000/52 pay periods	$750
Bi-weekly	$39,000/26 pay periods	$1,500
Twice a month	$39,000/24 pay periods	$1,625
Monthly	$39,000/12 pay periods	$3,250

FIGURE 11.3   Calculation of gross pay

TD1 Form

When hiring an employee, the employee's social insurance number must be recorded and the employee must fill in the TD1 form. This form is used to determine the employee's claim code to calculate the amount of income tax to be deducted from an individual's employment income. There are two forms that must be completed: one federal and one provincial or territorial. Employees complete the forms and give them to their employer, who should keep a completed form with their records.

For the purposes of this chapter, assume that Justin's assistant, Judith Wright, has completed the TD1 form and arrived at a claim code 1, because she was previously unemployed and has **personal deductions** she could claim, such as tuition fees and childcare expenses.

Payroll Calculator

The easiest way for an employer to calculate source deductions that must be taken from the employee's paycheque and the amounts that will need to be remitted (as employer) is to use the Payroll Deductions Online Calculator on the CRA website, online at: <https://www.canada.ca/en/revenue-agency/services/e-services/e-services-businesses/payroll-deductions-online-calculator.html>. The CRA also has tables that can be used manually to look up the amount that must be deducted, although this manual method can be cumbersome.

EXAMPLE 1

Justin Case went to the CRA website and used the payroll calculator to find out what deductions had to be taken and how much he would have to remit to the CRA for the pay period. Figure 11.4 shows the report obtained using the payroll calculator.

The report indicates that on a gross paycheque of $1,625, the amount of $147.45 must be deducted for federal taxes and $73.97 for provincial taxes, totalling $221.42. Claim Code 1 from the TD1 Form was used for the purposes of this calculation. The deduction from gross pay for CPP is $73.22 and for EI is $26.98. The total deductions come to $321.62, and Judith will receive a paycheque of $1,303.38.

Figure 11.5 shows the general journal entries required to record the salaries expense, the employer's payroll contributions, and the employer's remittance to the Receiver General for the salaries paid on December 15. The payroll deductions calculations from Figure 11.4 provide the information that is needed to make these entries.

Employee's name: Judith Wright			
Employer's name: Justin Case, Paralegal			
Pay period frequency: Twice a month (24 pay periods a year)			
Date the employee is paid: 2018-12-15			
Province of employment: Ontario			
Federal amount from TD1: Minimum—11,809.00 (Claim code 1)			
Provincial amount from TD1: Minimum—10,354.00 (Claim code 1)			
Salary or wages income (assume $750 gross/week)		1,625.00	
Total cash income			1,625.00
Taxable income for the pay period		1,625.00	
Pensionable earnings for the pay period		1,625.00	
Insurable earnings for the pay period		1,625.00	
Federal tax deduction (Payroll Tax Table, D)	147.45		
Provincial tax deduction (Payroll Tax Table, E)	73.97		
Total tax deductions		221.42	
CPP deductions (Payroll Tax Table, B)		73.22	
EI deductions (Payroll Tax Table, C) *The employer's EI premium is equal to 1.4 times the employee's premium, unless a reduced rate applies.*		26.98	
Total deductions			321.62
Net amount			1,303.38
Employer Remittance Summary			
Employee CPP contributions	73.22		
Employer CPP contributions	73.22		
Subtotal of Canada Pension Plan (CPP)		146.44	
Employee EI contributions	26.98		
Employer EI contributions	37.77		
Subtotal of Employment Insurance (EI)		64.75	
Tax deductions		221.42	
For this calculation, remit this amount		**432.61**	

FIGURE 11.4   Payroll deductions online calculation

STEP 1

December 15—This entry reflects that Judith Wright was paid $1,625 but received a cheque for $1,303.38 because the source deductions for income tax and her share of CPP and EI were taken off her paycheque. However, the firm is entitled to write off $1,625 as a salaries expense because that is its cost.

STEP 2

December 15—The firm contributes the employer's share of EI and CPP for Judith and is entitled to write those expenses off as a tax-deductible expense. Because the remittance is not sent immediately, it is posted to payroll liability accounts.

STEP 3

December 31—When the firm forwards the source deductions taken from Judith's salary on the 15th plus the employer's share it owes, the liability accounts (CPP, EI, income tax payable) are debited, thus reducing the balances to zero, and a cheque payable to the Receiver General for the amount owing to the CRA is credited to the general bank account.

Date 20**		Justin Case, Paralegal General Journal			GJ6
		Description	PR	Debit	Credit
Dec.	15	Salaries Expense	511	1,625.00	
		Income Taxes Payable	217		221.42
		CPP Payable	218		73.22
		EI Payable	219		26.98
		General Bank Account	100		1,303.38
		To record payroll for Dec. 15			
	15	CPP Expense	518	73.22	
		EI Expense	517	37.77	
		CPP Payable	218		73.22
		EI Payable	219		37.77
		To record employer's payroll contributions			
	31	Income Taxes Payable	217	221.42	
		CPP Payable	218	146.44	
		EI Payable	219	64.75	
		General Bank Account	100		432.61
		To record remittance to Receiver General for December			
		Totals		2,168.60	2,168.60

FIGURE 11.5   General journal entries recording payroll

Vacation Pay and Vacation Time

Employees are entitled to be paid vacation pay after their first full year of employment. Typically, in Ontario, an employee is entitled to a minimum payment of 4 percent of gross annual earnings. The employee accrues vacation pay as he or she earns wages regardless of vacation time taken, not taken, or carried over.

Normally, employees take the time off and receive a regular paycheque while they are away. However, if their employment is terminated and vacation pay is owed, this must be paid and will be subject to the source deductions and employer contributions to CPP and EI described above.

The normal minimum vacation time is two weeks in each year that the employee is employed, which represents 4 percent of the year. The employment contract or policy agreement should explain how to handle vacation time that is not taken or is carried over past the prescribed or agreed-upon deadline to take such vacation.[3]

Taxable Benefits

Some employers provide **taxable benefits** for their employees, such as medical and dental coverage, life insurance premiums, and company cars. Some of these benefits are deemed to be taxable benefits in the hands of an employee and will be included on the T4 slip issued to the employee at the end of the year.

T4 Information Return

On or before the last day of February in each year, a T4 **information return** must be filed with the CRA, and each employee must be provided with a T4 slip for their personal income tax purposes. A copy of each T4 slip prepared, as well as a T4 summary of remuneration paid, must be sent to the CRA. These forms can be obtained online at the CRA website.

LO3 Income Tax

Legal Requirements for Keeping Records

All records for **income tax** purposes, such as paper documents as well as those stored in an electronic medium (such as on computer hard drive or USB flash drive), must be kept in Canada or made available in Canada at the request of the CRA. The records must be in English or French.

A business is required to keep orderly records of all income received. All receipts, invoices, vouchers, and cancelled cheques indicating outlays of money must also be kept. Such outlays include:

- salaries and wages;
- operating expenses such as rent, advertising, and capital expenditures; and
- miscellaneous items such as charitable donations.

Records must be permanent and contain a systematic account of income, deductions, credits, and other information needed to file income tax and GST/HST returns. Incomplete records that use approximates instead of exact amounts are not acceptable. The records must:

- allow a business owner to determine how much tax is owed, or the tax, duties, or other amounts to be collected, withheld, or deducted, or any refund or rebate that may be claimed; and
- be supported by vouchers or other necessary source documents.

If receipts or other vouchers are not kept to support business expenses or claims, and there is no other evidence available, the CRA will likely deny the expenses or claims that have been made.

---

3   Ontario Ministry of Labour, "Vacation Time and Vacation Pay," online: <http://www.labour.gov.on.ca/english/es/pubs/guide/vacation.php>.

The Six-Year Requirement

If tax returns are filed on time, records must be retained (other than certain documents for which there are special rules) for six years from the end of the last **tax year** to which they relate. Every record necessary for dealing with an objection or appeal must be kept until it is resolved and the time for filing any further appeal has expired, or until the six-year period mentioned above has expired, whichever is later.

Types of Operating Expenses

Personal or Living Expenses

In most cases, personal and living expenses cannot be deducted, except for travelling expenses incurred in the course of carrying on a business while away from home. The general rule is that business owners cannot deduct outlays or expenses that are not directly related to earning business income.

Prepaid Expenses

A prepaid expense is an expense you pay ahead of time. If the accrual method of accounting is being used, claim any expense that is prepaid in the year or years in which the related benefit is received. For instance, if the annual business insurance is prepaid, only the portion of the expense that relates to the months that occurred in the current fiscal year can be claimed.

Accounting and Legal Fees

Fees incurred for external professional business advice or services, including consulting fees can be deducted, as can accounting and legal fees incurred to get advice and help in keeping records as well as fees incurred for preparing and filing income tax and GST/HST returns.

Advertising Expenses

Expenses for advertising, including advertisements in Canadian newspapers and on Canadian television and radio stations, can be deducted.

Bad Debts

A **bad debt** is an amount owing from a client that a business owner will not receive payment for. This can arise as a result of client bankruptcy. An amount for a bad debt can be deducted if:

- it's determined that an account receivable is a bad debt in the year, and
- the amount of revenue had already been included in the income.

For more information, see Interpretation Bulletin IT-442R, "Bad Debts and Reserves for Doubtful Debts."[4] This bulletin may be replaced by the CRA with "Folio 9 Bad Debts & Debt Forgiveness"[5] at some future date.

---

4 Canada Revenue Agency, "Bad Debts and Reserves for Doubtful Debts," online: <http://www.cra-arc.gc.ca/E/pub/tp/it442r/it442r-e.html>.

5 Canada Revenue Agency, "Folio 9 Bad Debts & Debt Forgiveness," Income Tax Folio Index, online: <https://www.canada.ca/en/revenue-agency/services/tax/technical-information/income-tax/income-tax-folios-index.html#S4>.

Business Tax, Fees, Licences, and Dues

Annual licence fees, law association membership dues, and any business taxes incurred to run the business can be deducted. However, club membership dues (including initiation fees) cannot be deducted if the main purpose of the club is to provide dining, recreational, or sporting facilities for its members.

Insurance Expenses

All regular commercial insurance premiums incurred on any buildings, machinery, and equipment that are used for the business can be deducted. Life insurance premiums are generally not deductible.

Interest and Bank Charges

The interest incurred on money borrowed to run the business can be deducted. There is a limit on the interest that can be deducted on money that is borrowed to buy a passenger vehicle.

Maintenance and Repairs Expenses

The cost of labour and materials for any minor repairs or maintenance done to property that is used to earn income can be deducted. However, business owners cannot deduct the value of their own labour. Costs that are incurred for repairs that are capital in nature cannot be deducted, but the business owner may be able to claim CCA on the repaired property. A capital expense generally gives a lasting benefit or advantage, thereby extending the estimated life of the asset. For example, the cost of putting vinyl siding on the exterior walls of a wooden house is a capital expense.

Meals and Entertainment Expenses

The maximum that can be claimed for food, beverages, and entertainment expenses is 50 percent of either the amount spent or an amount that is reasonable in the circumstances, whichever is less.

The 50 percent limit also applies to the cost of meals when business owners or their employees travel or go to a convention, conference, or similar event. However, special rules can affect the claim for meals in these cases. The 50 percent limit does not apply if meal and entertainment expenses are incurred to provide a Christmas party or similar event and all the employees from a particular location are invited; however, business owners are limited to six of these events each year. Also, the 50 percent limit does not apply to meal and entertainment expenses incurred for a fundraising event that was mainly for the benefit of a registered charity.

Entertainment expenses include tickets and entrance fees to an entertainment or sporting event, gratuities, cover charges, and room rentals such as for hospitality suites. For more information, see Interpretation Bulletin IT-518R, "Food, Beverages and Entertainment Expenses."[6]

---

6 Canada Revenue Agency, "Food, Beverages and Entertainment Expenses," online: <http://www.cra-arc .gc.ca/E/pub/tp/it518r/it518r-e.pdf>.

Motor Vehicle Expenses

When claiming motor vehicle expenses, note that travel from home to the office is not considered travel for business purposes. It is the responsibility of the individual to get to and from work each day, not the responsibility of the business.

Expenses incurred to run a motor vehicle that is used to earn business income can be deducted. However, several factors can affect the deduction. The kind of vehicle owned can affect the expenses deducted. Motor vehicle expenses can be deducted only when they are considered reasonable and the business owner has receipts to support them. The types of deductible expenses include the following:

- fuel and oil;
- maintenance and repairs;
- insurance;
- licence and registration fees;
- capital cost allowance;
- interest paid on a loan used to buy the motor vehicle; and
- leasing costs.

Figure 11.6 shows the calculation of motor vehicle expenses for Justin Case. The deductible business portion of Justin's vehicle expenses is $4,770. He can also include additional fees he pays for business, such as parking fees of $40 or a supplementary business insurance cost of $100, to increase his deduction to $4,910.

Calculation of Motor Vehicle Expenses	
Kilometres driven to earn business income	27,000
Total kilometres driven in the year	30,000
Percentage for business use: 27,000/30,000 x 100	90%
Expenses:	
Gas and oil	2,400
Insurance	1,900
Interest	800
Maintenance and repairs	200
Total expenses for the car	5,300
Calculation of deduction for tax purposes: $5,300 x 90%	4,770

FIGURE 11.6 Calculating vehicle expenses

To get the full benefit of a vehicle claim, a record of the total kilometres driven for personal use and the kilometres driven to earn business income must be kept. For each business trip, list the date, destination, purpose, and number of kilometres driven. Record the odometer reading of the vehicle at the start and end of the fiscal period.

Capital cost allowance is claimable on the cost of the vehicle up to a maximum value of $30,000. The rate of depreciation allowed is 30 percent with an adjustment in the year of acquisition, which reduces the allowed deductible amount for CCA by one-half.

Leasing Costs for a Passenger Vehicle

Amounts incurred to lease a motor vehicle that is used to earn income can be deducted. When a passenger vehicle is used to earn income, there is a limit on the amount of the leasing costs that can be deducted. If the lease agreement for the passenger vehicle includes items such as insurance, maintenance, and taxes, they can be included as part of the lease charges.

Work Space in Home Expenses

If a business owner rents a home in which there is a home office that is used, the part of the rent and any expenses incurred that relate to the work space can be deducted. The amount that can be deducted for business-use-of-home expenses, regardless of whether the home is rented or owned, cannot be more than the net income from the business before these expenses are deducted. In other words, these expenses cannot be used to increase or create a business loss.

EXAMPLE 2

Justin has space in his home devoted to the sole purpose of running his business. The business uses an area of 35 square metres. The house has 800 square metres, and the annual household expenses are $5,800.

The calculation to determine the tax deduction for use of the space is as follows:

$$35/800 \text{ square metres} \times \$5,800 \text{ expenses} = \$253.75$$

Justin can deduct a total of $253.75 for work space in home expenses. Because capital gain and recapture rules will apply if he deducts CCA on the business-use part of his home if he owns the home and he later sells it, he should seek professional advice before doing this.

Computer and Other Equipment Expenses

If computers, cellular telephones, fax machines, and other equipment are being leased, the percentage of the lease costs that reasonably relate to earning business income can be deducted. The percentage of airtime expenses for a cellular telephone that reasonably relate to earning business income can also be deducted. If a computer, cellular telephone, fax machine, or other such equipment is bought, the actual cost of these items cannot be deducted in the first year, as presumably the asset will be used for a few years. But CCA can be deducted as well as interest paid on money borrowed to buy this equipment that reasonably relates to earning business income.

POTENTIAL PARALEGAL PITFALLS

- **Potential pitfall:** Not filing GST/HST, payroll deductions, and tax returns on time.
- **Possible fallout:** The paralegal will be charged penalties and interest. The paralegal may also be denied a loan or other form of credit as potential creditors may ask to see the notices of assessment indicating that the paralegal is not behind on filing returns and making payments.
- **Proposed recommendation:** The paralegal must manage their money carefully so as to not miss CRA payments. The paralegal should hire an accountant to help file returns, if needed.

Convention Expenses

Business owners can deduct the cost of going to a maximum of two conventions a year. The conventions must:

- relate to the business or professional activity; and
- be held by a business or professional organization within the geographical area where the organization normally conducts its business.

This second requirement may not apply if an organization from another country sponsors the convention and the convention relates to the business or professional activity.

Sometimes, convention fees include the cost of food, beverages, or entertainment. However, the convention organizer may not show these amounts separately on its bill. If this is the case, business owners should subtract $50 from the total convention fee for each day the organizer provides food, beverages, or entertainment. Business owners can deduct this daily $50 amount as a meal and entertainment expense. However, the 50 percent limit applies to the daily $50 amount.

EXAMPLE 3

Justin attended a two-day convention in May that cost him $600. The organizer did not indicate what part of the $600 fee was for food and entertainment. The CRA allows business owners to claim the following convention expenses:

Cost of meals and entertainment
    Two days at $50/day = $100 allowed at 50% $50   } Total deduction $550
Cost of convention ($600 − $100 meals) $500 }

Office Expenses

The cost of office expenses, which include small items such as pens, pencils, paper clips, stationery, and stamps can be deducted. Office expenses do not include larger items such as filing cabinets, chairs, and desks, which are capital items and can be claimed using CCA since they will be used in future years as well as the current year.

Salaries, Including Employer's Contributions

Salaries and the employer's share of contributions paid to employees can be deducted. These salaries are reported by the end of February on a T4 slip (statement of remuneration paid) or T4A slip (statement of pension, retirement, annuity, and other income).

Amounts paid or payable to business owners or their business partners are not deductible and cannot be expensed. They are considered drawings. A drawing is any withdrawal of cash, other assets, or services of a business by the proprietor or partners. This includes such transactions by the proprietor or partners (or family members) as withdrawing cash for non-business use and using business assets or services for personal use. Professionals must include the cost or value of personal use of business assets or services in their drawings for the year rather than showing them as expenses in their books. Drawings are not an expense of the business; they represent a reduction in the owner's equity of the business.

Salaries Paid to Family Members

Salaries paid to business owners' children or spouses (including common law partners) can be deducted as long as all these conditions are met:

- the salary is actually paid;
- the work the child or spouse does is necessary for earning business or professional income; and
- the salary is reasonable when considering the child's age, and that the amount paid is what would be paid to someone else.

The business owner must keep documents to support the salary paid to their child. If the child is paid by cheque, keep the cancelled cheque. If the child is paid with cash, have the child sign a receipt. The salary a business owner pays to their spouse can also be deducted. When business owners pay their spouse a salary, they should use the same rules that apply to paying their child. Salaries paid to a business owner's children and spouse need to be reported on T4 slips, the same as is done for other employees. However, business owners cannot claim as an expense the value of board and lodging that is provided to their dependent children or spouse.

Telephone and Utilities Expenses

Expenses for telephone and utilities, such as gas, oil, electricity, and water, can be deducted, if the expenses are incurred to earn income. Expenses for utilities that are related to the business use of workspace in the business owner's home can also be claimed.

Deductions and Remittances

To be able to deduct a business expense, business owners must have carried on a business in the fiscal period in which the expense was incurred. Because of this, business owners must be very clear about the date their business started. Determining exactly what can be claimed as a start-up expense can be difficult.

Capital Gains

If you sell an asset for more than it cost, you may have a capital gain, which is taxable.

TAX TIP

Tax Information Videos

The CRA has a number of tax information videos for individuals and small businesses on topics such as preparing income tax and benefit returns, and reporting business income and expenses. To watch these videos, go to <https://www.canada.ca/en/revenue-agency/news/cra-multimedia-library.html>. Videos that provide helpful information on filing of HST/GST for new businesses are found online at <https://www.canada.ca/en/revenue-agency/news/cra-multimedia-library/businesses-video-gallery/gst-q-a.html>.

TAX TIP

Applying GST/HST to Client Accounts

Rule 8.01(2) of the LSO's *Paralegal Rules of Conduct* requires licensees to promptly meet all financial obligations incurred in the course of practice. One responsibility is to collect and remit HST to the CRA. Licensees must confirm how GST/HST applies to the specific legal services and disbursements they provide. They should consult with an accounting or tax professional to discuss how to implement HST properly within their internal accounting and invoicing systems.

The CRA has published a policy to deal with GST/HST on disbursements, which would also apply to paralegals. Its GST/HST Policy Statement P-209R can be found at <https://www.canada.ca/en/revenue-agency/services/forms-publications/publications/p-209r.html>. This policy expands on the obligation of the firm to pay GST/HST on disbursements paid on behalf of its clients. The disbursements described in this policy statement are characterized as either "incurred as agent" or "not incurred as agent."

The phrase "incurred as agent" indicates that the disbursement described is generally incurred in a lawyer's capacity as agent for a particular client. As such, no GST/HST is exigible (able to be charged) on the subsequent reimbursement by the client. The phrase "not incurred as agent" indicates that the disbursement described is generally incurred otherwise than in a lawyer's capacity as agent for a particular client, so GST/HST is eligible on the subsequent reimbursement by the client.

For example, in the area of civil litigation practice, common disbursements considered to be incurred as agent are court fees to start a legal proceeding, motion fees, court filing fees, or notice of trial fees. Because these fees are deemed by the CRA to be incurred as agent for a particular client, GST/HST is not charged on the disbursements when the client is invoiced.

However, in civil litigation practice, payment of witness fees, fees for recording services, transcript production or special examiner fees, service of document fees, and fees paid to have an expert prepare a report in respect of a particular proceeding or to have the expert appear at trial are all subject to GST/HST because they are considered "not incurred as agent."

The CRA considers disbursements not incurred as agent to include such items as payment made for telephone charges, photocopy charges, courier costs, costs for travel by the licensee, and postage. GST/HST is charged on these amounts even though GST/HST may have been charged on the original invoice to the firm.

CHAPTER SUMMARY

Taxes are a fact of life that most of us have come to accept, but who knew that working as a paralegal would turn you into a tax collector? In this chapter, we have examined your responsibilities with regard to collection and remittance of GST/HST, collection and remittance of payroll deductions, and payment of income taxes. These tasks are time-consuming, and you must keep yourself informed because tax laws change frequently. Although rates may change, the basic principles remain fairly constant.

Remember that although you are not paid to collect and remit taxes for the government, you will certainly be penalized if you fail to complete these tasks in a correct and timely manner. It is advisable for licensees to consult with an accountant when the time comes to file tax returns each year.

KEY TERMS

bad debt, 293

business expenses, 287

goods and services tax (GST), 284

gross pay, 288

GST/HST, 284

harmonized sales tax (HST), 284

income tax, 292

information return, 292

input tax credit (ITC), 285

payroll deductions, 288

personal deductions, 289

records, 285

taxable benefits, 292

tax year, 293

FURTHER READING

Canada Revenue Agency, "Business Video Gallery," online: <https://www.canada.ca/en/revenue-agency/news/cra-multimedia-library/businesses-video-gallery/gst-q-a.html>.

Canada Revenue Agency, Form T2125, "Statement of Business or Professional Activities," online: <https://www.canada.ca/content/dam/cra-arc/formspubs/pbg/t2125/t2125-fill-17e.pdf>.

Canada Revenue Agency, Guide RC4070(E) Rev.17, "Information for Canadian Small Businesses," 2018, online: <https://www.canada.ca/content/dam/cra-arc/formspubs/pub/rc4070/rc4070-17e.pdf>.

REVIEW QUESTIONS

True or False

_____ 1. GST/HST is remitted on the total amount of GST/HST charged and collected. (LO1)

_____ 2. The simplified method of calculating GST/HST payable does not need to show the purchase price of goods and GST/HST paid separately but is based on eligible business expenses based on a prescribed formula. (LO1)

_____ 3. Paralegals have the option of using the quick method to calculate the amount of GST/HST to be paid. (LO1)

_____ 4. Legal and accounting fees incurred by a business owner for external business-related advice can be deducted as a business expense. (LO3)

_____ 5. Business records should be maintained for a minimum period of six years from the end of the last tax year to which such records relate. (LO3)

_____ 6. Payroll calculations include the withdrawals made by the business owner from the business. (LO2, LO3)

_____ 7. Input tax credits can be claimed only on purchases made by the business. (LO1)

_____ 8. Salaries and the employer's share of contributions paid to employees can be deducted as business expenses. (LO2)

_____ 9. A small supplier for GST/HST purposes is required to register for GST/HST as soon as it commences operation, regardless of its total annual revenue. (LO1)

_____ 10. A business can claim only those expenses or portions of such expenses that are related or attributed to earning income for the business. (LO3)

Short Answer

Give a full answer for each question:

1. What are the record-keeping requirements for business records as stated by the CRA? (LO3)

2. What are some examples of ineligible business expenses? (LO3)

3. What are the steps involved in calculating GST/HST payable using the regular method? (LO1)

4. What are the steps involved in calculating payroll? (LO2)

PRACTICE EXERCISES

Practice Exercise 11.1 (LO1)

Based on the entries below in the fees journal and general disbursements journal, prepare a GST/HST worksheet for the month of January 20** according to the regular method. The worksheet is based on the GST/HST return working copy shown in Figure 11.1.

			Fees Journal (Service Revenue)			
Date 20**	Invoice #	Client	Fees Billed	Disbursements Billed	HST Billed (13% ON)	Total Amount Billed
Jan. 1	400	L. Forte	500.00	60.00	72.80	632.80
3	401	L. Bailey	1,000.00	120.00*	130.00	1,250.00
5	402	R. Smythe	0.00	120.00*	0.00	120.00
10	403	C. Schultz	5,000.00	0.00	650.00	5,650.00
15	405	L. Pepino	1,500.00	0.00	195.00	1,695.00
18	406	R. Saunders	800.00	300.00	143.00	1,243.00
25	407	B. Enders	2,400.00	160.00	332.80	2,892.80
Totals:			11,200.00	760.00	1,523.60	13,483.60

* HST not applicable

			General Disbursements Journal			
Date 20**	Paid To	Description	Method of Payment	Amount Paid	HST Paid/ Payable (13% ON)	Total Amount Paid
Jan. 1	Magnum Office Manager	A. Litigate—Paid rent, invoice #1001	Chq. #217	1,000.00	130.00	1,130.00
7	ATB Web Services	A. Litigate—Paid invoice #A0-111	Chq. #218	120.00	15.60	135.60
15	A. Booth, secretary	A. Litigate—Paid salary expense*	Chq. #219	1,000.00	0.00	1,000.00
15	ABC Insurance	A. Litigate—Paid invoice #501	Chq. #220	165.00	21.45	186.45
25	Centrum Parking	A. Litigate—Paid monthly parking invoice #AA123	Chq. #221	100.00	15.00	115.00
29	SSI Computers and Electronics	A. Litigate—Paid for computer equipment	Chq. #223	700.00	105.00	805.00
30	A. Booth, secretary	A. Litigate—Paid salary expense*	Chq. #224	1,000.00	0.00	1,000.00
31	AAA Advertising	A. Litigate—Paid invoice #A0-112	Chq. #226	85.00	12.75	97.75
Totals:				4,170.00	299.80	4,469.80

* HST not applicable

Net GST/HST Tax Payable	
Total Fees Billed	
Total Disbursements Billed	
Total GST/HST Charged	
Total Purchases (tax-deductible, ITCs)	
Total GST/HST paid or payable on tax-deductible purchases	
Net GST/HST Tax	

GST/HST Worksheet, Net GST/HST Calculation (for the Month of January 20**)				
Total GST/HST Collected or Collectible	Line 103	$		complete
Adjustments	Line 104	$		complete, if applicable
	Line 105		$	add Lines 103 and 104
Total GST/HST Paid or Payable for Eligible Expenses	Line 106	$		complete
Adjustments	Line 107	$		complete, if applicable
Total ITCs	Line 108		$	add Lines 106 and 107
Net GST/HST	Line 109		$	subtract Line 108 from Line 105

Practice Exercise 11.2 (LO2)

Ann Litigate hired a law clerk and wishes to issue her first paycheque. The clerk's annual salary is $39,000 per year, and the TD1 Form indicated that claim code 2 applies. Salary is paid twice a month on the 15th and on the last day of the month. Vacation pay is paid when the clerk takes holidays. Using the CRA payroll calculator, calculate the payroll deductions for the clerk's first paycheque as of May 15. Complete the table that follows:

a	Gross salary (taxable income) due on May 15, 20**	
b	Federal Tax deductible	
c	Provincial Tax deductible	
d	Total tax deductions	
e	CPP deduction	
f	EI deduction	
g	Employer CPP contributions	
h	Employer EI contributions	

PUT IT INTO PRACTICE

Case Example: Employer, Small Business, and Professional Responsibilities

Review the online CRA resource "Checklist for New Small Businesses" (<https://www.canada.ca/en/revenue-agency/services/tax/businesses/small-businesses-self-employed-income/checklist-small-businesses.html>) and help Ann Litigate create a customized checklist for her CRA filings as an employer and as a small business proprietor and legal professional. (LO1, LO2)

12

Computerized Time and Money Management

Getting Started with Legal Accounting Software. 307

Setting Up the Firm. 307

Creating Opening Entries 307

Time Entries and Billing 308

Trust Receipts and Disbursements 310

Recording Receipts and Disbursements 311

Billing Requirements. 312

End-of-Period Functions 312

Maintaining Electronic Records 312

Chapter Summary 313

Key Terms 313

Further Reading. 313

Review Questions 314

Put It into Practice. 315

LEARNING OUTCOMES

After reading this chapter, you should be able to:

LO1 Use legal accounting software to enter the opening balance sheet.

LO2 Use legal accounting software to manage client files.

LO3 Record time and fees and prepare invoices.

LO4 Record trust receipts and disbursements.

LO5 Enter general receipts and disbursements.

LO6 Recover client costs.

LO7 Understand billing requirements.

Large law firms usually have a centralized accounting department to perform all accounting functions, but smaller firms may use a system in which the licensee and his or her support staff all participate in performing these functions. The systems implemented may range from a manual system (by hand), to spreadsheet software, to general or **legal accounting software**. Most legal firms use some sort of accounting software, whether it is generic or a dedicated legal accounting program.

Before purchasing accounting software, you should have a good idea of what tasks you want the software to perform. Are you just looking for **time entry and billing**? Do you need software that will do all journal entries for both trust and general accounts, automatically post them and then prepare reports and financial statements? What kinds of reports would be useful in your practice? Do you want productivity reports showing how time is being managed, and reports that prepare GST/HST returns? A major consideration for paralegals starting out will be the cost of the system or software, including the cost of updates, support, and renewal fees. Is the system being investigated easy to use, or does it require extensive training? Do you want to be able to access the software through a mobile device when away from the office? The system you select will be determined by the size of the firm and whether the system needs to be centralized or accessed by various individuals.

A few of the popular software providers for legal services firms are Amicus Attorney, Clio, ESILAW, PCLaw®, and Intuit QuickBooks. Some software companies store data on a web server, while others store data on your desktop. We are not recommending the use of any particular accounting software, and this chapter will focus generally on software specifically designed for use in legal practices. The main functions we will review are file management, general and trust accounting, and time and billing.

When starting your own practice, you may find the cost of purchasing specialized legal software daunting. However, keep in mind that the time and effort used to set up a good accounting system will save time and money down the road. It is amazing how a bill generated by a computer can look so much more professional and as a result be less likely to be questioned than one produced by other means.

A good system pays off in other ways. Legal software programs have been developed that keep the requirements of the LSO in mind and with a view to helping licensees comply with by-law 9. You should be able to produce the records required by the LSO seamlessly, practically at the press of a button. However, the old adage "garbage in, garbage out" applies even with the best of software. The information produced by your system will only be as good as the information that is put into it. It is important to establish good bookkeeping practices at the outset.

Getting Started with Legal Accounting Software

Once the paralegal has selected the accounting system that meets their needs, time needs to be taken to set it up properly. Or, the paralegal may be employed by a firm that uses particular software, and the paralegal will be expected to learn to use it correctly. Although the paralegal may experience some initial frustration, the time and effort required to learn any new software will be well spent because they will learn how to gain maximum benefit from its features.

We will use the PCLaw® Experimental Set of Books for Reif, Black, and Brito to provide practice exercises to demonstrate how to use the PCLaw® software. Be aware that the main toolbar has a Help feature that the user can access to get clarification on any issues they are having with the software. The user should not hesitate to browse the Help menus provided to locate specific information about any system they may be using.

Setting Up the Firm

The firm network administrator will usually set up the firm before the paralegal starts using any accounting software. For the purposes of this textbook, the names of the lawyers, paralegals, or law clerks have to be entered into the system along with other firm information, such as rates to be charged by each user.

If PCLaw® software is being used, use the PCLaw® Tutorial 12.1 to set up the firm Reif, Black, and Brito.

LO1 Creating Opening Entries

When accounting records for a practice are being set up, the opening balance sheet is entered into the books to record the opening balances for the firm. PCLaw® uses the Startup feature for this purpose. A sample of opening entries for Justin Case's firm using PCLaw® was shown in Chapter 3 (see Figure 3.8).

Use PCLaw® Tutorial 12.2 to enter the opening balance sheet for Reif, Black, and Brito.

LO2 Managing Client Files

The system provides two numbers on file opening: a **client number** and a **client matter** or file number. The client number identifies the name and contact information of the client. The file or client matter number describes particulars about the area of law for which the firm has been retained. When a new client file is opened for an existing client, the original client number is used.

Once all the information is entered into the system, print labels for the client file. The label contains information about the file, such as the client name, description, client and file numbers, contact information for the client, responsible lawyer, and date the file was opened.

Type of Law

The system will ask for the type of law that applies to the matter. Classifications of law generally include such topics as provincial offences, litigation, corporate, or miscellaneous. Selecting this feature allows the firm to track useful information regarding the sources of the firm's income. These classifications are also helpful for collecting statistics for preparation of the licensee's annual report to the LSO, which asks for a breakdown of the percentage of time spent on various types of law.

Use PCLaw® Tutorial 12.3 to open client files for clients that we will be using in the tutorials that follow.

Conflict of Interest Search

Rule 1.02 of the *Paralegal Rules of Conduct* defines **conflict of interest** as the existence of a substantial risk that a paralegal's loyalty to or representation of a client would be materially and adversely affected by the paralegal's own interest or duties to another client, a former client, or a third person. The risk must be more than a mere possibility; there must be a genuine, serious risk to the duty of loyalty or to client representation arising from the retainer.

When a new client approaches a firm, it is important to conduct a **conflict search** that checks all of the firm's clients, files, calendars, and vendors to determine if there are any previous contacts with a potential client or file that could lead to a conflict of interest. Nothing is more frustrating, embarrassing, and perhaps expensive to a firm than having to withdraw from a file because a conflict of interest was not discovered in a timely manner. If no conflict of interest is found, the firm may then accept the retainer and open a client file.

Use PCLaw® Tutorial 12.4 to conduct a conflict search.

Closing Client Files

Archiving files is a job that often suffers the indignity of procrastination. But archiving regularly helps to keep records accurate. It is important to be vigilant when it comes time to close client files. Legal accounting software will assign and track a closed file number for archived files to make it easy to retrieve the file if it is ever required. Closing the file when the matter is finished helps to produce client reports that are accurate and reliable. Producing a client listing that contains files that were finished but not closed on the system years ago is frustrating and not helpful. When a list of current clients needs to pulled up, no one wants the list to include the names and balances for inactive files. The anticipated date for destruction of a file can be entered when the file is closed.

Files that are to be destroyed should be shredded to protect confidential information contained in them, and a certificate of destruction should be obtained from the company after shredding. The experimental books in PCLaw® do not allow us to close client files, so no tutorial is provided for this purpose.

LO3 Time Entries and Billing

The time and billing function of accounting software uses explanation codes to indicate the activity that was performed by the licensee. Examples of some commonly used explanation codes are shown in Figure 12.1.

Explanation Codes					
att	attendance at	ct	correspondence to	lr	legal research
cf	correspondence from	dr	drafting	mwc	meeting with client

FIGURE 12.1 Explanation codes

Effort can be saved when entering time by using an explanation code such as "att" and allowing the system to autofill the phrase to "attendance at." Other information can then be added to the explanation such as attendance at "court." In addition to being a time-saving device, explanation codes avoid typographical errors. Codes can be added or deleted when the time and billing system is set up to autofill the description of work that is most commonly billed to a file. The paralegal is not required to use the codes, but once these shortcuts become familiar, the paralegal will benefit from the time saved and errors avoided.

Recording Time Entries

There are several different ways software can be used to charge fees to a matter:

- enter time recorded by hand on a time slip;
- use the time-tracking function of the software to track meetings, telephone calls, and so on;
- charge a **flat rate**; and
- convert appointments and phone calls into time entries.

Firms usually bill clients based on the amount of time spent working on a file or based on a flat rate or fee. A flat fee is common in files such as traffic court, where the time that will be required is easy to estimate.

When time is being billed by the hour, it is usual to bill in tenths of an hour. Most firms bill time out in six-minute blocks, with each block representing one-tenth of an hour. This makes the calculation of the hourly rate straightforward and has been recognized as reasonable by the profession. It is hard to imagine anyone interrupting what they are doing, taking a phone call, then making a note on the file in less than six minutes. This compromise seems to be acceptable to clients and works for the office. Most time and billing software will round time entries up to the nearest tenth of an hour by default, but this standard can be changed if desired. Figure 12.2 shows a minutes-to-decimal conversion chart to help you calculate blocks of one-tenth of an hour when making time entries. The **billable rate**, which is the hourly rate charged on a file, is multiplied by the time spent working on the file. Each legal professional working in the firm may have a number of hourly rates charged, depending on the type of matter and the client retainer that was entered into.

Minutes	Decimals
1–6	0.1
7–12	0.2
13–18	0.3
19–24	0.4
25–30	0.5
31–36	0.6
37–42	0.7
43–48	0.8
49–54	0.9
55–60	1.0

FIGURE 12.2   Minutes-to-decimal conversion chart

EXAMPLE

If Justin Case worked for 53 minutes on a file at an hourly rate of $80, the software would calculate the amount to bill as follows:

STEP 1

Convert 53 minutes to tenths of an hour, or 0.9, then multiply 0.9 × $80/hour = $72.

STEP 2

To create time entries, go to the time entry section in the software, enter the date and file number, select the name of the person who did the work, enter the time and rate if not automatically selected, and let the software calculate the dollar amount to bill.

STEP 3

An explanation of the work that was done is entered using the explanation code and any additional description the paralegal wishes to use.

STEP 4

Once all the time entries are completed, this information will be used to produce the invoice to the client. It is important to spellcheck the entries before saving to correct any typographical errors, because no one wants any errors or types to show on the final invoice to the client. Remember, when recording time entries, what is typed in the explanation section will appear on the bill.

Use PCLaw® Tutorial 12.5 to enter time entries on various client files and to print a productivity report with a time listing for the period.

LO4 Trust Receipts and Disbursements

A trust receipt can be entered as a deposit to the trust bank account in the system. A deposit slip is printed containing all the information required by the LSO, such as from whom the money was received, the amount of the deposit, and the method of payment (number on the client's cheque). This slip can be taken to the bank and stamped by the teller, along with the firm's deposit book. The amount of the deposit is posted as a debit to the trust bank account and credited to the individual client's trust ledger sheet, enabling the paralegal to know the current balance of funds held in trust for each client at all times.

Just as with general cheques, trust cheques can also be recorded and printed using legal accounting software. Once a cheque is entered into the system, the trust bank account will be credited and the client trust ledger will be debited. Some software is programmed to safeguard against anyone writing a cheque against a client's trust ledger if there are insufficient funds in that particular client's account. The system produces a warning that there are insufficient funds in the account. When preparing the trust bank reconciliation, which can also be done using the software, the system will produce the client trust listing for comparison with the trust bank balance. However, the bank reconciliation feature is not available for experimental books.

Use PCLaw® Tutorial 12.6 to record retainers received from clients and print a trust listing.

POTENTIAL PARALEGAL PITFALLS

- **Potential pitfall:** As paralegals and lawyers become busy in their practice, it may become difficult for them to keep up with day-to-day bookkeeping.
- **Possible fallout:** Incomplete accounting information can cause many problems for businesses, such as missed due dates to the CRA or the LSO, poor decisions made based on a lack of information, unbilled billable hours, overdue balances owing from clients, and losing track of receipts from clients.
- **Proposed recommendation:** In order to ensure accounting information is always up to date, paralegals should schedule the task of updating financial information into the accounting system into a calendar, to be completed on a daily, weekly, biweekly, and/or monthly basis, regardless of whether it is tracked electronically or in a manual set of books. If the task becomes overwhelming due to the difficulty of the work or the busyness of the practice, a bookkeeper or accountant should be hired on a contract, part-time, or full-time basis.

LO5 Recording Receipts and Disbursements

Legal accounting software should allow the paralegal to write general or trust cheques and make deposits in the program, then print the required cheque or deposit slip. Special printable cheques will need to be purchased to use this function. If the office does not purchase pre-formatted cheques, cheques can be written by hand and then entered into the system without printing.

The many advantages of a program that records deposits and cheques in journals and simultaneously posts them to the proper general, special, and client ledger accounts include the following:

- Deposit and cheque balances will always be current.
- Deposits are automatically posted to the individual client's ledger sheet, and the bank account is debited.
- GST/HST is recorded and tracked for preparation of the GST/HST report. The amount of the payment is posted directly to the account to be charged. For example, if Justin Case wrote a $565 cheque for rent, which includes $65 for GST/HST and $500 for payment of rent, the system automatically journalizes the entries and posts $500 to the rent expense account and $65 to the GST/HST input tax credits account, and also credits the general bank account for $565. All this happens when the cheque is written. If explanation codes are used for writing the cheque—for example, "rnt" for rent expense—the system automatically knows the number of the account where rent expense is to be posted. There is no need to look up the account number on the chart of accounts.
- Even if cheques are manually prepared, they can be entered into the system by completing the pro forma cheque on the system, and the cheque is simply not printed.

Use PCLaw® Tutorial 12.7 to enter cheques for payment of disbursements for the firm and payments made from trust for client expenses.

LO6 Recovering Client Costs

Some costs incurred in an office on behalf of clients are not paid for by cheque. Photocopies, faxes, and postage are examples of amounts that get billed to a client without a corresponding bill being received by the firm for that expense. Some photocopiers, facsimile machines, and postage meters are equipped to provide a printout summarizing photocopies and faxes to be charged to a particular client file. In order to recover these expenses from the client, they must be entered into the system, either periodically or at the time of billing.

Because the expense for these items can be substantial, it is worth taking the time to track and bill them. These entries may appear in a special journal called a **client cost recovery journal** and also in the client ledger. Once entered, they will show up on the invoice produced when the client bill is prepared.

Use PCLaw® Tutorial 12.8 to enter disbursements being charged to the client by the firm.

LO7 Billing Requirements

It is important to develop good billing practices. The LSO requires that a bill be rendered prior to payment being deposited into the General Bank Account for services rendered. Failure to provide invoices to clients on a regular basis can cause cash flow problems. Clients should be informed of the cost of services rendered on a regular basis to prevent surprises when the bill is delivered to the client. Quick bills are convenient to use for walk-in clients. The Create Bill function is used to provide an invoice to the client for services rendered after the pre-bill has been reviewed and approved.

Use PCLaw® Tutorial 12.9 to prepare a Quick Bill and to Create a Bill.

End-of-Period Functions

Legal accounting software can produce the financial statements for any period that is requested, making it easy to get an income statement and balance sheet showing the results from the paralegal's practice on a regular basis. The software also provides bank reconciliation features for reconciling general and trust bank accounts.

Use PCLaw® Tutorial 12.10 to prepare an HST Report and Financial Statements.

Maintaining Electronic Records

If electronic records are kept, be sure to have backups of the system. The paralegal may be required to produce printed copies of information by the LSO. Having to go back and re-create a set of books because of a computer crash, or even a break-in during which office computers are stolen, is a hardship that is easily avoided. Most insurance companies will not cover the cost of paying someone to re-enter all the data; they cover only the cost of restoring the backup.

TAX TIP

Electronic Records

The CRA requires all taxpayers to retain their business records in an electronically readable format. The retained records must provide the information necessary to determine the person's liabilities and obligations, or their entitlement to any refund or rebate under the *Income Tax Act*. The taxpayer is not relieved of this responsibility because of the utilization of a third party, such as an accountant or other service provider. All retained records must be clearly labelled and stored in a secure environment in Canada.

CHAPTER SUMMARY

Legal software can take care of many functions in a firm, such as tracking calendar appointments, tickler systems, and phone calls, as well as maintaining financial records. Many systems have applications that can be accessed from a mobile device, so entries can be made from any location. Some licensees have found this to be a very convenient feature. Maintaining accurate and up-to-date accounting records is a requirement of the LSO. By implementing a good legal accounting system that has billing and accounting features, you will meet the LSO's requirements and be more productive. It is important to be familiar with how legal software works because, at the very least, employees hired by legal firms are usually expected to be familiar with relevant software applications used in the management of a law practice.

KEY TERMS

billable rate, 309

client cost recovery journal, 312

client matter, 307

client number, 307

conflict of interest, 308

conflict search, 308

flat rate, 309

legal accounting software, 306

time entry and billing, 306

FURTHER READING

Law Society of Ontario, "Guide to Opening Your Practice for Paralegals," online: <https://lso.ca/paralegals/practice-supports-and-resources/topics/opening,-operating-or-closing-a-practice/guide-to-opening-your-practice-for-paralegals>.

Law Society of Ontario, "Practice Management Guidelines," online: <https://lso.ca/lawyers/about-your-licence/practice-review/practice-management-guidelines?lang=en-ca>.

REVIEW QUESTIONS

Short Answer

Give a full answer for each question:

1. How do you determine what the best legal accounting system or software is for your practice? (LO1)

2. What are some of the advantages of having a computerized legal accounting system? (LO1)

3. What are the rules established under by-law 9 regarding the maintenance of electronic records? (LO5)

4. What are the key considerations in opening a new client file? (LO1)

5. Why should you close files in a timely and systematic manner? (LO1)

PUT IT INTO PRACTICE

Case Example: Simulation Exercises

The following simulation exercises can be used to practise making entries using various types of legal accounting software. If you are using PCLaw®, tutorials specific to PCLaw® software are provided below. The entries should be adapted as needed to correspond with the features of the legal software being used. Although the LSO does not require paralegals to learn how to use legal accounting software for licensing purposes, students may find themselves employed in a firm that uses such software, so it is useful to get some practice. Students may wish to inquire about getting a free download from an accounting software provider to try out a system. Your role as a paralegal or law clerk should be entered when setting up the information regarding the firm.

The exercises are designed to demonstrate the following features:

- perparing the accounting system by entering accounting, lawyer, paralegal, and law clerk information;
- opening files for new clients;
- perparing time entries on client files;
- recording receipts and disbursements in general and trust accounts;
- conducting conflict searches for new clients;
- recovering costs for client disbursements such as photocopies and faxes;
- perparing invoices and transfer of funds from trust to general bank accounts;
- closing a client file; and
- preparing financial reports.

Simulation Exercise 12.1: Preparing the Accounting System (LO1)

Set up your system by inserting the name, address, and telephone numbers of the law firm. You should also enter a GST registration number such as RT 112233. Make any other adjustments to the system settings that your instructor thinks are necessary.

The names of any paralegals, lawyers, and law clerks working in the firm should be added to the system, as well as their billable rates for various files.

Simulation Exercise 12.2: Creating a Matter for a New Client (LO2)

You should learn the terminology that applies to the software you are using. Help resources are usually available and should be consulted as needed. You must create a file for each new client. New files are often referred to as "matters," and each client matter is given a unique number. Client matters or files are usually numbered consecutively, and the numbers are assigned by the system. Each new client will also have an assigned client number, which is used for all matters related to that particular client. So client no. 1 might have several matters or files, each with a different matter number. It is useful to have a client number because this avoids having to rekey the client's name and address each time a new matter or file is opened for that particular client.

a. Create a new client matter on your system titled "*Karen Fisher v Reveal Cosmetics*." Karen Fisher has come to Justin Case to see about launching a product liability suit against Reveal Cosmetics. Justin feels she has a good case. The type of law is litigation, and you should select the rate at which the file is to be billed. Fill in the description box for the file by naming the client and the defendant. The description will be the reference line used on the invoice sent to the client; it also appears on the file label. Enter the client's name, address, and telephone number in the areas provided by your system. The system will assign Fisher client no. 1.

Karen Fisher has asked the firm to represent her in a second matter against James King regarding an encroachment on her property. Open a second file for this client, not allowing the system to allocate a new client number. Keep the same client number and allow the system to create a new matter or file number. The firm has quoted a flat rate for this matter of $3,500. Enter this information into your system.

b. Using what you have learned, create a new client matter for a second client, Robert Crookshank. Title it "Robert Crookshank re Traffic Court." Crookshank will be represented in this matter by a different paralegal in the firm at a different rate. The client's address is 123 York Street, Yourtown, Ontario, and his telephone number is (555) 235-2323. The system will automatically assign client no. 2 to Crookshank because no. 1 is taken up by Karen Fisher, and it will allocate file no. 3 to the matter.

Once you have completed this exercise, prepare a list of clients using your software.

Simulation Exercise 12.3: Recording Time and Fees (LO3)

This exercise describes how to enter hours recorded on a time slip using legal accounting software. When entering time, use the minutes-to-decimal conversion chart provided in this chapter. Use explanation codes, if available, to describe the work done, such as "mwc" for "meeting with client." You can add to the description by including further information such as "to discuss liability suit." You may wish not to charge for the initial interview. The software will allow you to show no charge. It is a good idea to enter this time and show it as not being charged so that the client will be able to appreciate the fact that she received a free consultation.

Enter the following time entries for Justin Case on the *Karen Fisher v Reveal Cosmetics* file using appropriate dates. Remember to convert time to tenths of an hour when recording time entries.

Month	3	Meeting with client to discuss liability suit—½ hour at no charge
	5	Instructing legal staff—20 minutes
	9	Legal research by the law clerk for 1 hour and 15 minutes
	15	Review correspondence from opposite party with offer to settle—15 minutes
	18	Meeting with client to discuss settlement offer—35 minutes

Justin has also provided a time slip setting out the following services performed on the Robert Crookshank file. Record the time entries.

Month	4	Meeting with client to discuss traffic charge—½ hour
	5	Review of HTA sections and legal research—1 hour and 15 minutes
	9	Attendance at traffic court and negotiation of plea—2 hours

Justin also worked on the *Karen Fisher v J King* easement dispute file. Record the time entries.

Month	5	Researching cases on easements—2 hours and 20 minutes
	15	Correspondence with opposite party—½ hour
	20	Response with offer to settle for $3,000—15 minutes
	25	Meeting with client to sign minutes of settlement—20 minutes
	30	Report to client—20 minutes

Produce a report to show the time entries you have made. Your system should allow you to re-enter the system to make corrections to any incorrect time entries.

Simulation Exercise 12.4: Recording Trust Receipts and Retainers (LO4)

Before a retainer can be entered into a client file or matter, a file must be opened for that client matter on the system. If you do not already have a file for a client, open a file. Then enter the retainers received by depositing the funds to the trust bank account.

The following retainers were received and new files opened by the firm. Conduct a conflict search and create a new client file for the following persons: Susan Silver, David Silver, Angela Finelli, Stephen Bell, and Peter Stubbs. You or your instructor can make up the description, address, and telephone number for each client. Use the preferred default rate for all new files.

Date 20**		Transaction Details	Amount	Method	Total
Month	1	*Karen Fisher v J King* re easement—retainer	800	cheque	800
	3	Susan Silver re traffic retainer	900	cr. card	900
	3	Robert Crookshank re traffic court—retainer	700	cert. cheque	700
	3	David Silver re Small Claims Court—retainer	100	cr. card	100
	8	Angela Finelli re traffic—no retainer received	Open client file only		
	10	Stephen Bell, Small Claims Court—no retainer received	Open client file only		
	11	Peter Stubbs re Small Claims Court—retainer	200	cash	200
	30	Received from J. King—settlement on *Karen Fisher v J King* file	3,000	bank draft	3,000

Simulation Exercise 12.5: Recording General and Trust Disbursements (LO5)

Record the following transactions in your legal software, being careful to use the correct bank account for each transaction. If funds are available in trust for any client, use trust funds; if not, you need to use the general bank account.

Date 20**		Transaction Details	Amount	HST	Total
Month	1	Paid rent to Minto Management (chq. #G198)	1,200	156	1,356
	3	Paid membership dues to the Law Society of Ontario (chq. #G199)	600	78	678

	6	Expense recovery. The following charges were recorded for disbursements made in the office, which are to be billed to clients:
		
		• Photocopies: (.25 each)
		  – David Silver 20 copies
		  – Stephen Bell 10 copies
		  – Crookshank 30 copies
		
		• Faxes: (.30 each)
		  – David Silver 3 pages
		  – Stephen Bell 8 pages
		  – Peter Stubbs 2 pages
			Calculate and enter under expense recovery		

	12	Paid traffic ticket to Minister of Finance on behalf of Susan Silver (chq. #T10)	90	0	90
	26	Paid Royal Bank—interest on loan (chq. #G200)	120	0	120
	26	Paid Minister of Finance to file statement of defence re David Silver (chq. #T11)	40	0	40
	27	Paid fine on behalf of Robert Crookshank to Minister of Finance (chq. #T12)	500	0	500
	27	Paid Minister of Finance to issue notice of garnishment on Stubbs file (chq. #T13)	100	0	100
	28	Paid to issue claim re Stephen Bell (chq. #G201) (no retainer)	75	0	75

Simulation Exercise 12.6: Preparing Invoices to Clients (LO6, LO7)

Prepare invoices for the following client files:
- *Karen Fisher v Reveal Cosmetics*
- *Karen Fisher v J King*
- Robert Crookshank re Traffic Court
- Peter Stubbs re Small Claims Court: you have been asked to prepare a quick bill and charge the client $250 for services rendered plus $3.50 for disbursements incurred but not yet recorded. Record the disbursement at the time it is entered on the bill.

Simulation Exercise 12.7: Conducting a Conflict Search and Closing a Client File (LO2)

John King has called your office to set up an appointment regarding starting an action against Peter Silver. Conduct a conflict search to determine whether there is a potential conflict of interest.

You have completed all work to be done on the *Karen Fisher v J King* file. Close the file on your system

Simulation Exercise 12.8: Reconciling the Bank Statement and Preparing Reports (LO4, LO5)

Using the bank statement for Justin Case's trust account for the month, reconcile the bank statement with your records.

ROYAL BANK OF MONEY
P.O. Box 5011, Station A
Montreal, QC H3C 3B8

Trust Bank Account Statement

Justin Case, Paralegal 135 Main Street Yourtown, Ontario K3P 1G9	Month 1, 20** to Month 3*, 20**
	Account number: 0216-520635

ACCOUNT SUMMARY FOR THIS PERIOD

Opening Balance at Beginning of Month		$1,000.00
Total Deposits and Credits	+	$5,800.00
Total Cheques and Debits	−	$730.00
Closing Balance at End of Month	=	$6,070.00

ACCOUNT ACTIVITY DETAILS

Date	Description	Cheques and Debits	Deposits and Credits	Balance
Mo. 01	Deposit		800.00	1,800.00
Mo. 03	Deposit		900.00	2,700.00
Mo. 03	Deposit		800.00	3,500.00
Mo. 03	Deposit		100.00	3,600.00
Mo. 12	Deposit		200.00	3,800.00
Mo. 18	Chq. #T10	90.00		3,710.00
Mo. 24	Chq. #T11	40.00		3,670.00
Mo. 27	Chq. #T12	500.00		3,170.00
Mo. 27	Chq. #T13	100.00		3,070.00
Mo. 30	Deposit		3,000.00	6,070.00
	Closing Balance			6,070.00

Please check this Account Statement without delay and advise us of any error or omission within 45 days of the statement date.
Royal Bank of Money GST Registration Number: R1052481028

On your system, prepare a GST/HST report for last month.
Prepare an income statement and a balance sheet for the month.

Appendix

BY-LAW 9
Financial Transactions and Records

Made: May 1, 2007

Amended: June 28, 2007

            January 24, 2008

            February 21, 2008

            March 20, 2009 (editorial changes)

            September 29, 2009 (editorial changes)

            April 28, 2011

            May 3, 2011 (editorial changes)

            October 19, 2015 (editorial changes)

Law Society of Ontario, *By-Laws*, online: <https://lso.ca/about-lso/legislation-rules/by-laws>.

PART I
INTERPRETATION

Interpretation

1. (1) In this By-Law,

"arm's length" has the same meaning given it in the *Income Tax Act* (Canada);

"cash" means current coin within the meaning of the *Currency Act* (Canada), notes intended for circulation in Canada issued by the Bank of Canada pursuant to the *Bank of Canada Act* and current coin or banks notes of countries other than Canada;

"charge" has the same meaning given it in the *Land Registration Reform Act*;

"client" means a person or group of persons from whom or on whose behalf a licensee receives money or other property;

"firm of licensees" means,

 (a) a partnership of licensees and all licensees employed by the partnership,

 (b) a professional corporation established for the purpose of practising law in Ontario and all licensees employed by the professional corporation,

 (c) a professional corporation established for the purpose of providing legal services in Ontario and all licensees employed by the professional corporation, or

 (d) a professional corporation established for the purpose of practising law and providing legal services in Ontario and all licensees employed by the professional corporation;

"holiday" means,

 (a) any Saturday or Sunday;

 (b) New Year's Day, and where New Year's Day falls on a Saturday or Sunday, the following Monday;

 (c) Family Day;

 (d) Good Friday;

 (e) Easter Monday;

 (f) Victoria Day;

 (g) Canada Day, and where Canada Day falls on a Saturday or Sunday, the following Monday;

 (h) Civic Holiday;

 (i) Labour Day;

 (j) Thanksgiving Day;

 (k) Remembrance Day, and where Remembrance Day falls on a Saturday or Sunday, the following Monday;

 (l) Christmas Day, and where Christmas Day falls on a Saturday or Sunday, the following Monday and Tuesday, and where Christmas Day falls on a Friday, the following Monday;

 (m) Boxing Day; and

 (n) any special holiday proclaimed by the Governor General or the Lieutenant Governor;

"lender" means a person who is making a loan that is secured or to be secured by a charge, including a charge to be held in trust directly or indirectly through a related person or corporation;

"licensee" includes a firm of licensees;

"money" includes cash, cheques, drafts, credit card sales slips, post office orders and express and bank money orders;

"related" has the same meaning given it in the *Income Tax Act* (Canada);

"Teranet" means Teranet Inc., a corporation incorporated under the *Business Corporations Act*, acting as agent for the Ministry of Consumer and Business Services.

Time for doing an act expires on a holiday

(2) Except where a contrary intention appears, if the time for doing an act expires on a holiday, the act may be done on the next day that is not a holiday.

When deemed in trust

(3) For the purposes of subsections 9(1), (2) and (3) and section 14, cash, cheques negotiable by the licensee, cheques drawn by the licensee on the licensee's trust account and credit card sales slips in the possession and control of the licensee shall be deemed from the time the licensee receives such possession and control to be money held in a trust account if the cash, cheques or credit card sales slips, as the case may be, are deposited in the trust account not later than the following banking day.

PART II
HANDLING OF MONEY BY BANKRUPT LICENSEE

Handling of money by bankrupt licensee

2.   (1)   Subject to subsections (2) and (3), a licensee who is bankrupt within the meaning of the *Bankruptcy and Insolvency Act* (Canada) shall not receive from or on behalf of a person or group of persons any money or other property and shall not otherwise handle money or other property that is held in trust for a person or group of persons.

Exception

(2)   A licensee who is bankrupt within the meaning of the *Bankruptcy and Insolvency Act* (Canada) may receive from or on behalf of a person or group of persons money,

(a)   in payment of fees for services performed by the licensee for the person or group; or

(b)   in reimbursement for money properly expended, or for expenses properly incurred, on behalf of the person or group.

Same

(3)   A licensee who is bankrupt within the meaning of the *Bankruptcy and Insolvency Act* (Canada) may apply in writing to the Society for permission to receive from or on behalf of a person or group of persons any money or other property, other than as permitted under subsection (2), or for permission to handle money or other property that is held in trust for a person or group of persons, and the Society may permit the licensee to do so, subject to such terms and conditions as the Society may impose.

PART II.1
HANDLING OF MONEY BY LICENSEE WHOSE LICENCE IS SUSPENDED

Interpretation

2.1   In this Part,

"suspended licensee" means a licensee who is the subject of a suspension order; "suspension order" means an order made under the Act suspending a licensee's licence to practise law in Ontario as a barrister and solicitor or to provide legal services in Ontario, regardless of whether the suspension begins when the order is made or thereafter.

Handling of money by suspended licensee

2.2   (1)   Subject to subsection (2) and section 2.3, a suspended licensee shall not, during the suspension receive from or on behalf of a person or group of persons any money or other property and shall not otherwise handle money or other property that is held in trust for a person or group of persons.

Exception

(2)   A suspended licensee may receive from or on behalf of a person or group of persons money,

(a)   in payment of fees for services performed by the suspended licensee for the person or group; or

(b)   in reimbursement for money properly expended, or for expenses properly incurred, on behalf of the person or group.

Trust account

2.3   (1)   A suspended licensee shall, within 30 days of the beginning of the suspension,

(a)   withdraw from every trust account kept in the name of the suspended licensee, or in the name of the firm of licensees of which the suspended licensee is a partner or by which the suspended licensee is employed, and, as required, pay to the appropriate person,

(i)   money properly required for payment to a person on behalf of a client,

(ii)   money required to reimburse the suspended licensee for money properly expended, or for expenses properly incurred, on behalf of a client,

(iii)   money required for or toward payment of fees for services performed by the suspended licensee, and

(iv)   all other money that belongs to the suspended licensee or to a person other than a client;

(b)   after complying with clause (a), withdraw from every trust account kept in the name of the suspended licensee, or in the name of the firm of licensees of which the suspended licensee is a partner or by which the suspended licensee is employed, all money belonging to a client and pay the money to,

    (i)   the client,

    (ii) another licensee to whom the client has directed the suspended licensee to make payment, or

    (iii) another licensee who has agreed with the suspended licensee to accept payment in the event that the suspended licensee is unable to comply with subclause (i) or (ii); and

(c)   after complying with clauses (a) and (b),

    (i)   close every trust account that was kept in the name of the suspended licensee, and

    (ii) cancel or cause to be cancelled the suspended licensee's signing authority on every trust account that was kept in the name of the firm of licensees of which the suspended licensee is a partner or by which the suspended licensee is employed.

Compliance with clause (1)(b) not required

(2)   A suspended licensee is not required to comply with clause (1)(b) if the client's file is transferred, in accordance with Part IV of By-Law 7.1, to another licensee in the firm of licensees of which the suspended licensee is a partner or by which the suspended licensee is employed.

Application of sections of Part IV

(3)   Subsection 9(3) and sections 10, 11 and 12 apply to the withdrawal of money from a trust account under this section.

Report to Society on compliance

(4)   A suspended licensee shall, not later than thirty days after the suspension begins, complete and file with the Society, in a form provided by the Society, a report confirming and providing details of the suspended licensee's compliance with this section.

Permission to be exempt from requirement

2.4 A suspended licensee may apply in writing to the Society for an exemption from or a modification of a requirement mentioned in this Part, and the Society may exempt the suspended licensee from or modify the requirement, subject to such terms and conditions as the Society may impose.

PART III
CASH TRANSACTIONS

Definition

3.   In this Part,

"funds" means cash, currency, securities and negotiable instruments or other financial instruments that indicate the person's title or interest in them; "public body" means,

(a)   a department or agent of Her Majesty in right of Canada or of a province;

(b)   an incorporated city, metropolitan authority, town, township, village, county, district, rural municipality or other incorporated municipal body or an agent of any of them; and

(c)   an organization that operates a public hospital and that is designated by the Minister of National Revenue as a hospital under the *Excise Tax Act* (Canada) or agent of the organization.

Cash received

4.   (1)   A licensee shall not receive or accept from a person, in respect of any one client file, cash in an aggregate amount of 7,500 or more Canadian dollars.

Foreign currency

(2)   For the purposes of this section, when a licensee receives or accepts from a person cash in a foreign currency the licensee shall be deemed to have received or accepted the cash converted into Canadian dollars at,

(a)   the official conversion rate of the Bank of Canada for the foreign currency as published in the Bank of Canada's Daily Noon Rates that is in effect at the time the licensee receives or accepts the cash; or

(b)   if the day on which the licensee receives or accepts cash is a holiday, the official conversion rate of the Bank of Canada in effect on the most recent business day preceding the day on which the licensee receives or accepts the cash.

Application

5.   Section 4 applies when, in respect of a client file, a licensee engages in or gives instructions in respect of the following activities:

   1.   The licensee receives or pays funds.

   2.   The licensee purchases or sells securities, real properties or business assets or entities.

   3.   The licensee transfers funds by any means.

Exceptions

6.   Despite section 5, section 4 does not apply when the licensee,

   (a)   receives cash from a public body, an authorized foreign bank within the meaning of section 2 of the *Bank Act* (Canada) in respect of its business in Canada or a bank to which the *Bank Act* (Canada) applies, a cooperative credit society, savings and credit union or caisse populaire that is regulated by a provincial Act, an association that is regulated by the *Cooperative Credit Associations Act* (Canada), a company to which the *Trust and Loan Companies Act* (Canada) applies, a trust company or loan company regulated by a provincial Act or a department or agent of Her Majesty in right of Canada or of a province where the department or agent accepts deposit liabilities in the course of providing financial services to the public;

   (b)   receives cash from a peace officer, law enforcement agency or other agent of the Crown acting in an official capacity;

   (c)   receives cash pursuant to an order of a tribunal;

   (d)   receives cash to pay a fine or penalty; or

   (e)   receives cash for fees, disbursements, expenses or bail provided that any refund out of such receipts is also made in cash.

PART IV
TRUST ACCOUNT

TRUST ACCOUNT TRANSACTIONS

Money received in trust for client

7.   (1)   Subject to section 8, every licensee who receives money in trust for a client shall immediately pay the money into an account at a chartered bank, provincial savings office, credit union or a league to which the *Credit Unions and Caisses Populaires Act, 1994* applies or registered trust corporation, to be kept in the name of the licensee, or in the name of the firm of licensees of which the licensee is a partner, through which the licensee practises law or provides legal services or by which the licensee is employed, and designated as a trust account.

Interpretation

   (2)   For the purposes of subsection (1), a licensee receives money in trust for a client if the licensee receives from a person,

   (a)   money that belongs in whole or in part to a client;

   (b)   money that is to be held on behalf of a client;

   (c)   money that is to be held on a client's direction or order;

   (d)   money that is advanced to the licensee on account of fees for services not yet rendered; or

   (e)   money that is advanced to the licensee on account of disbursements not yet made.

Money to be paid into trust account

   (3)   In addition to the money required under subsection (1) to be paid into a trust account, a licensee shall pay the following money into a trust account:

   1.   Money that may by inadvertence have been drawn from a trust account in contravention of section 9.

   2.   Money paid to a licensee that belongs in part to a client and in part to the licensee where it is not practical to split the payment of the money.

Money to be paid into trust account: money received before licence issued

(3.1) If a licensee who holds a Class P1 licence receives from a person, prior to being issued the licence, money for services yet to be rendered to a client and the licensee does not perform the services for the client by May 2, 2010, the licensee shall on May 3, 2010 pay the money into a trust account.

Withdrawal of money from trust account

(4) A licensee who pays into a trust account money described in paragraph 2 of subsection (3) shall as soon as practical withdraw from the trust account the amount of the money that belongs to him or her.

One or more trust accounts

(5) A licensee may keep one or more trust accounts.

Money not to be paid into trust account

8. (1) A licensee is not required to pay into a trust account money which he or she receives in trust for a client if,

(a) the client requests the licensee in writing not to pay the money into a trust account;

(b) the licensee pays the money into an account to be kept in the name of the client, a person named by the client or an agent of the client; or

(c) the licensee pays the money immediately upon receiving it to the client or to a person on behalf of the client in accordance with ordinary business practices.

Same

(2) A licensee shall not pay into a trust account the following money:

1. Money that belongs entirely to the licensee or to another licensee of the firm of licensees of which the licensee is a partner, through which the licensee practises law or provides legal services or by which the licensee is employed, including an amount received as a general retainer for which the licensee is not required either to account or to provide services.

2. Money that is received by the licensee as payment of fees for services for which a billing has been delivered, as payment of fees for services already performed for which a billing will be delivered immediately after the money is received or as reimbursement for disbursements made or expenses incurred by the licensee on behalf of a client.

Record keeping requirements

(3) A licensee who, in accordance with subsection (1), does not pay into a trust account money which he or she receives in trust for a client shall include all handling of such money in the records required to be maintained under Part V.

Withdrawal of money from trust account

9. (1) A licensee may withdraw from a trust account only the following money:

1. Money properly required for payment to a client or to a person on behalf of a client.

2. Money required to reimburse the licensee for money properly expended on behalf of a client or for expenses properly incurred on behalf of a client.

3. Money properly required for or toward payment of fees for services performed by the licensee for which a billing has been delivered.

4. Money that is directly transferred into another trust account and held on behalf of a client.

5. Money that under this Part should not have been paid into a trust account but was through inadvertence paid into a trust account.

Permission to withdraw other money

(2) A licensee may withdraw from a trust account money other than the money mentioned in subsection (1) if he or she has been authorized to do so by the Society.

Limit on amount withdrawn from trust account

(3) A licensee shall not at any time with respect to a client withdraw from a trust account under this section more money than is held on behalf of that client in that trust account at that time.

Manner in which certain money may be withdrawn from trust account

10.   A licensee shall withdraw money from a trust account under paragraph 2 or 3 of subsection 9(1) only,

(a)   by a cheque drawn in favour of the licensee;

(b)   by a transfer to a bank account that is kept in the name of the licensee and is not a trust account; or

(c)   by electronic transfer.

Withdrawal by cheque

11.   A cheque drawn on a trust account shall not be,

(a)   made payable either to cash or to bearer; or

(b)   signed by a person who is not a licensee except in exceptional circumstances and except when the person has signing authority on the trust account on which a cheque will be drawn and is bonded in an amount at least equal to the maximum balance on deposit during the immediately preceding fiscal year of the licensee in all the trust accounts on which signing authority has been delegated to the person.

Withdrawal by electronic transfer

12.   (1)   Money withdrawn from a trust account by electronic transfer shall be withdrawn only in accordance with this section.

When money may be withdrawn

(2)   Money shall not be withdrawn from a trust account by electronic transfer unless the following conditions are met:

1.   The electronic transfer system used by the licensee must be one that does not permit an electronic transfer of funds unless,

   i.   one person, using a password or access code, enters into the system the data describing the details of the transfer, and

   ii.   another person, using another password or access code, enters into the system the data authorizing the financial institution to carry out the transfer.

2.   The electronic transfer system used by the licensee must be one that will produce, not later than the close of the banking day immediately after the day on which the electronic transfer of funds is authorized, a confirmation from the financial institution confirming that the data describing the details of the transfer and authorizing the financial institution to carry out the transfer were received.

3.   The confirmation required by paragraph 2 must contain,

   i.   the number of the trust account from which money is drawn,

   ii.   the name, branch name and address of the financial institution where the account to which money is transferred is kept,

   iii.   the name of the person or entity in whose name the account to which money is transferred is kept,

   iv.   the number of the account to which money is transferred,

   v.   the time and date that the data describing the details of the transfer and authorizing the financial institution to carry out the transfer are received by the financial institution, and

   vi.   the time and date that the confirmation from the financial institution is sent to the licensee.

4.   Before any data describing the details of the transfer or authorizing the financial institution to carry out the transfer is entered into the electronic trust transfer system, an electronic trust transfer requisition must be signed by,

   i.   a licensee, or

   ii.   in exceptional circumstances, a person who is not a licensee if the person has signing authority on the trust account from which the money will be drawn and is bonded in an amount at least equal to the maximum balance on deposit during the immediately preceding fiscal year of the licensee in all trust accounts on which signing authority has been delegated to the person.

5. The data entered into the electronic trust transfer system describing the details of the transfer and authorizing the financial institution to carry out the transfer must be as specified in the electronic trust transfer requisition.

Application of para. 1 of subs. (2) to sole practitioner

(3) Paragraph 1 of subsection (2) does not apply to a licensee who practises law or provides legal services without another licensee as a partner, if the licensee practises law or provides legal services through a professional corporation, without another licensee practising law or providing legal services through the professional corporation and without another licensee or person as an employee, if the licensee himself or herself enters into the electronic trust transfer system both the data describing the details of the transfer and the data authorizing the financial institution to carry out the transfer.

Same

(4) In exceptional circumstances, the data referred to in subsection (3) may be entered by a person other than the licensee, if the person has signing authority on the trust account from which the money will be drawn and is bonded in an amount at least equal to the maximum balance on deposit during the immediately preceding fiscal year of the licensee in all trust accounts on which signing authority has been delegated to the person.

Additional requirements relating to confirmation

(5) Not later than the close of the banking day immediately after the day on which the confirmation required by paragraph 2 of subsection (2) is sent to a licensee, the licensee shall,

(a) produce a printed copy of the confirmation;

(b) compare the printed copy of the confirmation and the signed electronic trust transfer requisition relating to the transfer to verify whether the money was drawn from the trust account as specified in the signed requisition;

(c) indicate on the printed copy of the confirmation the name of the client, the subject matter of the file and any file number in respect of which money was drawn from the trust account; and

(d) after complying with clauses (a) to (c), sign and date the printed copy of the confirmation.

Same

(6) In exceptional circumstances, the tasks required by subsection (5) may be performed by a person other than the licensee, if the person has signing authority on the trust account from which the money will be drawn and is bonded in an amount at least equal to the maximum balance on deposit during the immediately preceding fiscal year of the licensee in all trust accounts on which signing authority has been delegated to the person.

Electronic trust transfer requisition

(7) The electronic trust transfer requisition required under paragraph 4 of subsection (2) shall be in Form 9A.

Definitions

13. (1) In this section,

"closing funds" means the money necessary to complete or close a transaction in real estate; "transaction in real estate" means,

(a) a charge on land given for the purpose of securing the payment of a debt or the performance of an obligation, including a charge under the *Land Titles Act* and a mortgage, but excluding a rent charge, or

(b) a conveyance of freehold or leasehold land, including a deed and a transfer under the *Land Titles Act*, but excluding a lease.

Withdrawal by electronic transfer: closing funds

(2) Despite section 12, closing funds may be withdrawn from a trust account by electronic transfer in accordance with this section.

When closing funds may be withdrawn

(3) Closing funds shall not be withdrawn from a trust account by electronic transfer unless the following conditions are met:

1. The electronic transfer system used by the licensee must be one to which access is restricted by the use of at least one password or access code.

2. The electronic transfer system used by the licensee must be one that will produce immediately after the electronic transfer of funds a confirmation of the transfer.

3.   The confirmation required by paragraph 2 must contain,

i.   the name of the person or entity in whose name the account from which money is drawn is kept,

ii.   the number of the trust account from which money is drawn,

iii.   the name of the person or entity in whose name the account to which money is transferred is kept,

iv.   the number of the account to which money is transferred, and

v.   the date the transfer is carried out.

4.   Before the electronic transfer system used by the licensee is accessed to carry out an electronic transfer of funds, an electronic trust transfer requisition must be signed by,

i.   the licensee, or

ii.   in exceptional circumstances, a person who is not the licensee if the person has signing authority on the trust account from which the money will be drawn and is bonded in an amount at least equal to the maximum balance on deposit during the immediately preceding fiscal year of the licensee in all trust accounts on which signing authority has been delegated to the person.

5.   The data entered into the electronic transfer system describing the details of the electronic transfer of funds must be as specified in the electronic trust transfer requisition.

Additional requirements relating to confirmation

(4)   Not later than 5 p.m. on the day immediately after the day on which the electronic transfer of funds is carried out, the licensee shall,

(a)   produce a printed copy of the confirmation required by paragraph 2 of subsection (3);

(b)   compare the printed copy of the confirmation and the signed electronic trust transfer requisition relating to the transfer to verify whether the money was drawn from the trust account as specified in the signed requisition;

(c)   indicate on the printed copy of the confirmation the name of the client, the subject matter of the file and any file number in respect of which money was drawn from the trust account; and

(d)   after complying with clauses (a) to (c), sign and date the printed copy of the confirmation.

Same

(5)   In exceptional circumstances, the tasks required by subsection (4) may be performed by a person other than the licensee, if the person has signing authority on the trust account from which the money will be drawn and is bonded in an amount at least equal to the maximum balance on deposit during the immediately preceding fiscal year of the licensee in all trust accounts on which signing authority has been delegated to the person.

Electronic trust transfer requisition: closing funds

(6)   The electronic trust transfer requisition required under paragraph 4 of subsection (3) shall be in Form 9C.

Requirement to maintain sufficient balance in trust account

14.   Despite any other provision in this Part, a licensee shall at all times maintain sufficient balances on deposit in his or her trust accounts to meet all his or her obligations with respect to money held in trust for clients.

AUTOMATIC WITHDRAWALS FROM TRUST ACCOUNTS

Authorizing Teranet to withdraw money from trust account

15.   (1)   Subject to subsection (2), a licensee may authorize Teranet to withdraw from a trust account described in subsection 16(1) money required to pay the document registration fees and the land transfer tax, if any, related to a client's real estate transaction.

Conditions

(2)   A licensee shall not authorize Teranet to withdraw from a trust account described in subsection 16(1) money required to pay the document registration fees and the land transfer tax, if any, related to a client's real estate transaction unless Teranet agrees to provide

to the licensee in accordance with subsection (3) a confirmation of the withdrawal that contains the information mentioned in subsection (4).

Time of receipt of confirmation

(3)   The confirmation required under subsection (2) must be received by the licensee not later than 5 p.m. on the day immediately after the day on which the withdrawal is authorized by the licensee.

Contents of confirmation

(4)   The confirmation required under subsection (2) must contain,

(a)   the amount of money withdrawn from the trust account;

(b)   the time and date that the authorization to withdraw money is received by Teranet; and

(c)   the time and date that the confirmation from Teranet is sent to the licensee.

Written record of authorization

(5)   A licensee who authorizes Teranet to withdraw from a trust account described in subsection 16(1) money required to pay the document registration fees and the land transfer tax, if any, related to a client's real estate transaction shall record the authorization in writing.

Same

(6)   The written record of the authorization required under subsection (5) shall be in Form 9B and shall be completed by the licensee before he or she authorizes Teranet to withdraw from a trust account described in subsection 16(1) money required to pay the document registration fees and the land transfer tax, if any, related to a client's real estate transaction.

Additional requirements relating to confirmation

(7)   Not later than 5 p.m. on the day immediately after the day on which the confirmation required under subsection (2) is sent to a licensee, the licensee shall,

(a)   produce a paper copy of the confirmation, if the confirmation is sent to the licensee by electronic means;

(b)   compare the paper copy of the confirmation and the written record of the authorization relating to the withdrawal to verify whether

money was withdrawn from the trust account by Teranet as authorized by the licensee;

(c)   indicate on the paper copy of the confirmation the name of the client and any file number in respect of which money was withdrawn from the trust account, if the confirmation does not already contain such information; and

(d)   after complying with clauses (a) to (c), sign and date the paper copy of the confirmation.

Special trust account

16.   (1)   The trust account from which Teranet may be authorized by a licensee to withdraw money shall be,

(a)   an account at a chartered bank, provincial savings office, credit union or league to which the *Credit Unions and Caisses Populaires Act, 1994* applies or a registered trust corporation kept in the name of the licensee or in the name of the firm of licensees of which the licensee is a partner, through which the licensee practises law or by which the licensee is employed, and designated as a trust account; and

(b)   an account into which a licensee shall pay only,

(i)   money received in trust for a client for the purposes of paying the document registration fees and the land transfer tax, if any, related to the client's real estate transaction; and

(ii)   money properly withdrawn from another trust account for the purposes of paying the document registration fees and the land transfer tax, if any, related to the client's real estate transaction.

One or more special trust accounts

(2)   A licensee may keep one or more trust accounts of the kind described in subsection (1).

Payment of money into special trust account

(3)   A licensee shall not pay into a trust account described in subsection (1) more money than is required to pay the document registration fees and the land transfer tax, if any, related to a client's real estate transaction, and if more money is, through inadvertence, paid into the trust account, the licensee shall transfer from the trust account described in subsection (1) into another

trust account that is not a trust account described in subsection (1) the excess money.

Time limit on holding money in special trust account

(4) A licensee who pays money into a trust account described in subsection (1) shall not keep the money in that account for more than five days, and if the money is not properly withdrawn from that account by Teranet within five days after the day on which it is paid into that account, the licensee shall transfer the money from that account into another trust account that is not a trust account described in subsection (1).

Interpretation: counting days

(5) In subsection 16(4), holidays shall not be counted in determining if money has been kept in a trust account described in subsection 16(1) for more than five days.

Application of ss. 9, 11, 12 and 14

17. Sections 9, 11, 12 and 14 apply, with necessary modifications, to a trust account described in subsection 16(1).

PART V
RECORD KEEPING REQUIREMENTS

REQUIREMENTS

Requirement to maintain financial records

18. Every licensee shall maintain financial records to record all money and other property received and disbursed in connection with the licensee's professional business, and, as a minimum requirement, every licensee shall maintain, in accordance with sections 21, 22 and 23, the following records:

1. A book of original entry identifying each date on which money is received in trust for a client, the method by which money is received, the person from whom money is received, the amount of money received, the purpose for which money is received and the client for whom money is received in trust.

2. A book of original entry showing all disbursements out of money held in trust for a client and identifying each date on which money is disbursed, the method by which money is disbursed, including the number or a similar

identifier of any document used to disburse money, the person to whom money is disbursed, the amount of money which is disbursed, the purpose for which money is disbursed and the client on whose behalf money is disbursed.

3. A clients' trust ledger showing separately for each client for whom money is received in trust all money received and disbursed and any unexpended balance.

4. A record showing all transfers of money between clients' trust ledger accounts and explaining the purpose for which each transfer is made.

5. A book of original entry showing all money received, other than money received in trust for a client, and identifying each date on which money is received, the method by which money is received, the amount of money which is received and the person from whom money is received.

6. A book of original entry showing all disbursements of money, other than money held in trust for a client, and identifying each date on which money is disbursed, the method by which money is disbursed, including the number or a similar identifier of any document used to disburse money, the amount of money which is disbursed and the person to whom money is disbursed.

7. A fees book or a chronological file of copies of billings, showing all fees charged and other billings made to clients and the dates on which fees are charged and other billings are made to clients and identifying the clients charged and billed.

8. A record showing a comparison made monthly of the total of balances held in the trust account or accounts and the total of all unexpended balances of funds held in trust for clients as they appear from the financial records together with the reasons for any differences between the totals, and the following records to support the monthly comparisons:

   i. A detailed listing made monthly showing the amount of money held in trust for each client and identifying each client for whom money is held in trust.

    ii.   A detailed reconciliation made monthly of each trust bank account.

9.   A record showing all property, other than money, held in trust for clients, and describing each property and identifying the date on which the licensee took possession of each property, the person who had possession of each property immediately before the licensee took possession of the property, the value of each property, the client for whom each property is held in trust, the date on which possession of each property is given away and the person to whom possession of each property is given.

10.   Bank statements or pass books, cashed cheques and detailed duplicate deposit slips for all trust and general accounts.

11.   Signed electronic trust transfer requisitions and signed printed confirmations of electronic transfers of trust funds.

12.   Signed authorizations of withdrawals by Teranet and signed paper copies of confirmations of withdrawals by Teranet.

Record keeping requirements if cash received

19.   (1)   Every licensee who receives cash shall maintain financial records in addition to those required under section 18 and, as a minimum additional requirement, shall maintain, in accordance with sections 21, 22 and 23, a book of duplicate receipts, with each receipt identifying the date on which cash is received, the person from whom cash is received, the amount of cash received, the client for whom cash is received and any file number in respect of which cash is received and containing the signature of the licensee or the person authorized by the licensee to receive cash and of the person from whom cash is received.

No breach

    (2)   A licensee does not breach subsection (1) if a receipt does not contain the signature of the person from whom cash is received provided that the licensee has made reasonable efforts to obtain the signature of the person from whom cash is received.

Record keeping requirements if mortgages and other charges held in trust for clients

20.   Every licensee who holds in trust mortgages or other charges on real property, either directly or indirectly through a related person or corporation, shall maintain financial records in addition to those required under section 18 and, as a minimum additional requirement, shall maintain, in accordance with sections 21, 22 and 23, the following records:

1.   A mortgage asset ledger showing separately for each mortgage or charge,

    i.   all funds received and disbursed on account of the mortgage or charge,

    ii.   the balance of the principal amount outstanding for each mortgage or charge,

    iii.   an abbreviated legal description or the municipal address of the real property, and

    iv.   the particulars of registration of the mortgage or charge.

2.   A mortgage liability ledger showing separately for each person on whose behalf a mortgage or charge is held in trust,

    i.   all funds received and disbursed on account of each mortgage or charge held in trust for the person,

    ii.   the balance of the principal amount invested in each mortgage or charge,

    iii.   an abbreviated legal description or the municipal address for each mortgaged or charged real property, and

    iv.   the particulars of registration of each mortgage or charge.

3.   A record showing a comparison made monthly of the total of the principal balances outstanding on the mortgages or charges held in trust and the total of all principal balances held on behalf of the investors as they appear from the financial records together with the reasons for any differences between the totals, and the following records to support the monthly comparison:

    i.   A detailed listing made monthly identifying each mortgage or charge and showing for each the balance of the principal amount outstanding.

    ii.   A detailed listing made monthly identifying each investor and showing the balance of the principal invested in each mortgage or charge.

Financial records to be permanent

21. (1) The financial records required to be maintained under sections 18, 19 and 20 may be entered and posted by hand or by mechanical or electronic means, but if the records are entered and posted by hand, they shall be entered and posted in ink.

Paper copies of financial records

(2) If a financial record is entered and posted by mechanical or electronic means, a licensee shall ensure that a paper copy of the record may be produced promptly on the Society's request.

Financial records to be current

22. (1) Subject to subsection (2), the financial records required to be maintained under sections 18, 19 and 20 shall be entered and posted so as to be current at all times.

Exceptions

(2) The record required under paragraph 8 of section 18 and the record required under paragraph 3 of section 20 shall be created within twenty-five days after the last day of the month in respect of which the record is being created.

Preservation of financial records required under ss. 18 and 19

23. (1) Subject to subsection (2), a licensee shall keep the financial records required to be maintained under sections 18 and 19 for at least the six year period immediately preceding the licensee's most recent fiscal year end.

Same

(2) A licensee shall keep the financial records required to be maintained under paragraphs 1, 2, 3, 8, 9, 10 and 11 of section 18 for at least the ten year period immediately preceding the licensee's most recent fiscal year end.

Preservation of financial records required under s. 20

(3) A licensee shall keep the financial records required to be maintained under section 20 for at least the ten year period immediately preceding the licensee's most recent fiscal year end.

Record keeping requirements when acting for lender

24. (1) Every licensee who acts for or receives money from a lender shall, in addition to maintaining the financial records required under sections 18 and 20, maintain a file for each charge, containing,

    (a)   a completed investment authority, signed by each lender before the first advance of money to or on behalf of the borrower;

    (b)   a copy of a completed report on the investment;

    (c)   if the charge is not held in the name of all the lenders, an original declaration of trust;

    (d)   a copy of the registered charge; and

    (e)   any supporting documents supplied by the lender.

Exceptions

(2) Clauses (1)(a) and (b) do not apply with respect to a lender if,

    (a)   the lender,

        (i)   is a bank listed in Schedule I or II to the Bank Act (Canada), a licensed insurer, a registered loan or trust corporation, a subsidiary of any of them, a pension fund, or any other entity that lends money in the ordinary course of its business,

        (ii)   has entered a loan agreement with the borrower and has signed a written commitment setting out the terms of the prospective charge, and

        (iii)   has given the licensee a copy of the written commitment before the advance of money to or on behalf of the borrower;

    (b)   the lender and borrower are not at arm's length;

    (c)   the borrower is an employee of the lender or of a corporate entity related to the lender;

(d) the lender has executed the Investor/Lender Disclosure Statement for Brokered Transactions, approved by the Superintendent under subsection 54(1) of the *Mortgage Brokerages, Lenders and Administrators Act, 2006*, and has given the licensee written instructions, relating to the particular transaction, to accept the executed disclosure statement as proof of the loan agreement;

(e) the total amount advanced by the lender does not exceed $6,000; or

(f) the lender is selling real property to the borrower and the charge represents part of the purchase price.

Requirement to provide documents to lender

(3) Forthwith after the first advance of money to or on behalf of the borrower, the licensee shall deliver to each lender,

(a) if clause (1)(b) applies, an original of the report referred to therein; and

(b) if clause (1)(c) applies, a copy of the declaration of trust.

Requirement to add to file maintained under subs. (1)

(4) Each time the licensee or any licensee of the same firm of licensees does an act described in subsection (5), the licensee shall add to the file maintained for the charge the investment authority referred to in clause (1)(a), completed anew and signed by each lender before the act is done, and a copy of the report on the investment referred to in clause (1)(b), also completed anew.

Application of subs. (4)

(5) Subsection (4) applies in respect of the following acts:

1. Making a change in the priority of the charge that results in a reduction of the amount of security available to it.

2. Making a change to another charge of higher priority that results in a reduction of the

amount of security available to the lender's charge.

3. Releasing collateral or other security held for the loan.

4. Releasing a person who is liable under a covenant with respect to an obligation in connection with the loan.

New requirement to provide documents to lender

(6) Forthwith after completing anew the report on the investment under subsection (4), the licensee shall deliver an original of it to each lender.

Requirement to add to file maintained under subs. (1): substitution

(7) Each time the licensee or any other licensee of the same firm of licensees substitutes for the charge another security or a financial instrument that is an acknowledgment of indebtedness, the licensee shall add to the file maintained for the charge the lender's written consent to the substitution, obtained before the substitution is made.

Exceptions

(8) The licensee need not comply with subsection (4) or (7) with respect to a lender if clause (2)(a), (b), (c), (e) or (f) applied to the lender in the original loan transaction.

Investment authority: Form 9D

(9) The investment authority required under clause (1)(a) shall be in Form 9D.

Report on investment: Form 9E

(10) Subject to subsection (11), the report on the investment required under clause (1)(b) shall be in Form 9E.

Report on investment: alternative to Form 9E

(11) The report on the investment required under clause (1)(b) may be contained in a reporting letter addressed to the lender or lenders which answers every question on Form 9E.

Glossary

accountant   professional who maintains, inspects, or interprets financial accounts. The accountant prepares the various reporting and financial statements required for the business.

accounting cycle   process of recording the accounting events of a company. The cycle begins when a transaction occurs and ends with its inclusion in the financial statements. The eight steps of the accounting cycle are: (1) journalize the transaction; (2) post entries; (3) prepare the trial balance; (4) prepare the worksheet; (5) prepare the adjusted trial balance; (6) prepare the financial statements; (7) prepare the closing entries; and (8) calculate the post-closing trial balance. See Figure 3.1.

accounting equation   an equation based on the balance sheet accounts (assets, liabilities, and owner's equity) in which the left-hand side of the balance sheet must equal the right-hand side (debits = credits), as follows:

$$\text{Assets} = \text{Liabilities} + \text{Owner's Equity}$$

accounting period   any monthly, quarterly, or annual period that marks the beginning and end of financial reporting.

accounting standards   a set of principles that govern the reporting of financial information in a consistent, ethical, and accurate manner. Accounting standards vary by jurisdiction, but in an increasingly global economy, they are becoming more and more uniform in their application. In Canada, accounting standards include generally accepted accounting principles (GAAP); international financial reporting standards (IFRS); accounting standards for private enterprises (ASPE); public sector accounting standards (PSAS); and accounting standards for not-for-profit organizations (ASNPO).

accrual basis of accounting   the principle that revenue is recorded when it is earned regardless of whether or not payment has been received, and expenses are recorded when incurred. This is the approach used by paralegals as required under the *Income Tax Act*; compare **cash basis of accounting**.

accrued interest expense   interest expense on a loan or other debt that has not yet been paid.

accrued interest revenue   interest revenue earned because of an outstanding debt owed to the business owner by way of an accounts receivable.

accrued revenues   revenues that are earned in a period but not yet billed or paid.

accrued salaries expense   salary expenses that occur after the pay period end but before the end of the reporting period.

accumulated depreciation   the total amount that has been written off as an expense against a particular asset over time. Depreciation is calculated in the contra-asset account.

adjusted trial balance   the balance that shows the updated income statement and balance sheet entries on the worksheet.

adjusting entries   updates to accounts made as a result of changes to the account balance from the last reporting period. For example, when payment is made on accrued expense or revenue accounts, an adjustment is made to reflect the change to the balance sheet account, the income statement account, or both. However, the cash or bank account would not be adjusted; instead, the appropriate account would be adjusted on the opposite balance of that account. Typical adjustments are prepaid accounts and depreciation.

adjustment   a change made to the journal entries and general ledger at the end of an accounting period after the initial trial balance is prepared. Often, these adjustments have been accruing over the accounting period because it is more efficient to recognize the change at the end of the period.

amortization   the calculation of the decline in value of an asset from its original value to its residual or remaining value.

assets   all the cash, property, and other valuable items that a business or a person owns or is entitled to.

bad debt   money owed to a company that has not been successfully collected. Also known as a "write-off" because it is "written off" as a loss.

balance sheet   a financial statement showing the assets, liabilities, and capital of a business at a particular date.

balance sheet account   one of two types of general ledger accounts. (Income statement accounts are the other types.) Balance sheet accounts are used to sort and store transactions involving assets, liabilities, and owner's equity.

barter transaction   an exchange of goods or services that does not involve money. The goods or services received could be considered proceeds from a business operation and must be included in income. Barter transactions may also have GST/HST implications.

billable rate   the rate that a professional charges a client; for paralegals, this is typically based on the amount of time spent working on a file at an hourly rate (e.g., $80/h). The time billed must be time spent working on the file to move the matter forward, providing legal advice, researching, drafting, and conducting meetings with clients and third parties (including telephone calls). If the hourly billable rate changes during the retainer, the client must be notified or a new retainer agreement should be negotiated.

billable work   work performed on a file that will be billed to a client, such as court attendances, legal document preparation, correspondence, and telephone calls.

book value   the historical cost of an asset minus accumulated depreciation.

bookkeeper   person who records the day-to-day transactions of the accounting process. A bookkeeper is not an accountant, but an accountant may perform some of the tasks associated with bookkeeping. Having a bookkeeper enter and track data is typically more cost-effective than having an accountant do so.

bookkeeping   the system and tools used to analyze and record the day-to-day and cyclical financial transactions specific to a business.

business expenses   costs that are considered reasonable for a particular type of business and that are incurred for the purpose of earning income; also known as operating expenses. Business expenses can be deducted for tax purposes. Non-business-related expenses, which are either personal in nature or not related to earning business income, are not tax-deductible.

business number (BN)   a number that identifies a business to the government for all business purposes, including remittances of GST/HST, corporate income tax, and payroll.

Canada Revenue Agency (CRA)   the agency responsible for administering the tax laws for the Government of Canada and most of Canada's provinces and territories.

capital account   the investment by the owner in a business. Capital is not always cash; it can be assets that the owner chooses to invest in the company. The capital account includes the owner's beginning investment plus or minus the profits or losses earned by the firm.

capital cost allowance (CCA)   the means by which Canadian businesses may claim depreciation expense for calculating taxable income under the *Income Tax Act*.

cash basis of accounting   the principle that recognizes revenue only when the revenue is actually received and expenses only when payment has actually been made; compare **accrual basis of accounting**.

cash controls   internal systems to protect against the loss, misuse, or fraud of cash, including cash payment and receipt systems. Petty cash is an example of a cash payment and receipt system that has rules and procedures to safeguard against internal abuse.

cash receipts   a book of duplicate receipts maintained as proof of financial transactions; a requirement for paralegals in accordance with by-law 9, part V, section 19(1) of the Law Society of Ontario. Cash receipts in this context should not be confused with the cash received and documented on a general receipts journal, which is a special journal.

cash short and over   cash short is an income statement account that records shortages and overages in petty cash on hand and petty cash disbursements. When cash is short, debit this account to show the increase in expenses as a result of the shortage. When cash is over, credit this account to show the increase in income as a result of the overage. *Example:*

20**		Dr.	Cr.
Jan. 1	Expense Accounts	X	
– –			
Jan. 31	Cash Short and Over	X (short)	X (over)
Jan. 31	General Bank Account		X
	To replenish the petty cash fund ($100 limit)		

chart of accounts   a customized, detailed chart that creates a unique identification number for each business account, typically used in a firm's operation over the accounting cycle. This helps to reduce the number of entries and posting descriptions. New accounts can be added to the chart, but the chart should be ordered in a logical sequence similar to the balance sheet, the statement of owner's equity, and the income statement.

chartered professional accountant   designation given to members of the accounting profession regulated under the *Chartered Professional Accountants of Ontario Act, 2017*, RSO 2017, c 8

class   assets included in a particular account. For example, the account for office furniture will include desks, chairs, and other types of furniture.

client cost recovery journal   journal in which are entered expenses on behalf of clients that are recoverable from them. Such costs are typically recorded as a disbursements recoverable journal entry and are included as disbursements on the client invoice and in the fees book. Also, funds can be transferred from the trust account provided that the expense has been incurred and the client agrees to the expense (by way of the client's written authorization or a written retainer agreement).

client general ledger   *See* **client ledgers**.

client ledgers   the records of a firm's ongoing transactions, organized by client matter or file number, in respect of all receipts and disbursements made on behalf of or in regard to the firm's clients. The client trust ledger records payments taken by the firm for invoices sent to the client; disbursements paid from the trust account on behalf of the client; and the balance remaining in trust. The client general ledger records fees and disbursements received from the client; balance owing; and disbursements paid by the firm on behalf of the client when no trust funds are available. This ledger is especially useful if you need to report to a client the amounts that have been received by the firm as payments and those that remain outstanding in respect of funds that are not held in trust.

client matter   the descriptor for each client file, indicating the area of law and the particulars of the subject matter. *Example:* Client—Ann Smith, Matter re Small Claims (Smith ats Brown) File No. 101-0001.

client number   identifies the client by assigning a unique number associated with the client's name and contact information. *Example:* Client number 101 (Ann Smith, 123 Avenue Road, Toronto, ON).

client trust ledger   *See* **client ledgers**.

close the books   to "zero out" the income, expense, and withdrawal accounts by transferring the net amounts to the capital account and starting these accounts at a $0 balance in the new accounting period. *See* **closing entries**.

closing balance   the total balance for each account at the end of an accounting period, which becomes the opening balance for the next period.

closing entries   journal entries that record temporary account balances at the end of a reporting period (revenue, expenses, withdrawals, and income summary accounts) and the transfer of such balances to the capital account.

compound entry   a situation in which there are more than two entries for each transaction, such as when there are two debit entries and only one credit entry, or vice versa.

conflict of interest   an interest, financial or otherwise, that might adversely affect a licensee's judgment or loyalty with regard to a client or prospective client, or that would cause a licensee to prefer a third party's interests over those of a client or prospective client. (See rule 1.02 of the *Paralegal Rules of Conduct* of the Law Society of Ontario.)

conflict search   a search of a firm's client database or manual list that checks all of the firm's current and former clients, files, and vendors against related or opposing parties and former clients of former firm affiliations to determine whether there are any previous contacts with a potential client or file that could lead to a conflict of interest.

contra-asset account   an account linked to a long-term asset account that tracks and records the decrease in value of the asset without affecting its original value. It is called "contra" because although it is shown on the balance sheet as an asset account, and it represents an "opposite" normal balance for an asset account.

credit (Cr.)   an account entry that is found on the right side of a financial statement, journal, or ledger.

current assets   cash, or assets that will be converted into cash within one year. *Examples:* cash in bank accounts, accounts receivable, prepaid insurance.

DEAD CLIC   a memory device for determining which accounts show a normal debit balance and which have a normal credit balance—that is, **D**ebit **E**xpenses **A**ssets **D**rawings; **C**redit **L**iabilities **I**ncome **C**apital.

debit (Dr.)   an account entry that is found on the left side of a financial statement, journal, or ledger.

deposit in transit   a deposit made by the firm but not reflected on the bank statement by the statement cut-off date. To balance the internal records with the bank statement, this deposit amount (typically an outstanding cheque) would have to be added to the bank balance on the bank reconciliation statement.

depreciation   the calculation of the cost or expense of a long-term asset (such as property, plant, equipment, or intangibles) over the course of its useful life, representing the asset's decline in value.

depreciation expense   the periodic write-off of long-term assets.

dormant account   funds remaining in trust that are unclaimed by a client for more than two years. When this occurs, the paralegal can apply to the Law Society of Ontario for permission to transfer such funds to the LSO. (See section 59.6 of the *Law Society Act* and by-law 10.)

double-entry bookkeeping   an essential component of the accounting system, requiring that there be a check and balance of debits and credits. Every transaction must have at least two entries—a debit entry and a credit entry.

drawee   the financial institution on which a cheque is drawn.

drawer   the person who writes a cheque.

endorsement   the signing or stamping of a cheque by the payee (the person to whom a cheque is made payable), thereby transferring the rights of the cheque to the payee from the payor. See Figure 10.6.

expanded accounting equation   an equation that correlates the balance sheet assets with the income statement accounts (income and expenses) and the statement of owner's equity (increases and decreases to the capital account), as follows:

$$\text{Assets} = \text{Liabilities} + \text{Capital} - \text{Withdrawals} + (\text{Income} - \text{Expenses})$$

See Figure 2.4.

expense   day-to-day, regularly occurring costs, charges, and items that are consumed or used up; the costs of doing business.

expense account   all the expense accounts on the income statement that have a normal debit balance.

expense recovery   reimbursement for expenses incurred on behalf of clients in furtherance of their legal matters. Such expenses (e.g., photocopy, printing, faxing, courier, and court filing costs) should be described and disclosed in a retainer agreement. Some expenses are not subject to GST/HST and some have tax already included. Paralegals should be sure to apply HST only where required.

external users   stakeholders that are interested in a firm's financial accounting.

fees book   the record of a firm's billings for all clients, including fees for legal services, disbursements, and GST/HST.

fees journal   *See* **fees book**.

financial statements   a point-in-time reporting of the financial position of a business for each accounting period (monthly, quarterly, or annually), including the income statement, the statement of owner's equity, and the balance sheet.

fiscal period   the accounting period over which a firm reports its business or professional income.

fiscal year   any 12-month period selected by a firm to mark the beginning and the end of its financial reporting and tax reporting year (e.g., January 1 – December 31). For a sole proprietorship or partnership, the fiscal period is based on the calendar year; for a corporation, it may be any 12-month period (that coincides with the cycle of its business operation). The firm usually establishes its fiscal period when it files its first income tax return or when it registers a business account with the Canada Revenue Agency.

fixed or capital assets   assets that have a long life. They may be purchased with cash or on credit. *Examples:* land, buildings, equipment, vehicles.

flat rate   a charge that is the same in all cases. Paralegals can bill on a flat-fee basis when the time that will be required is easy to estimate (such as traffic court fines and certain routine or easy-to-resolve matters). The flat rate is established at the discretion of the paralegal but should reflect the industry standard in order to be competitive.

general bank account   a business bank account used by a firm for general business purposes, including depositing receipts and paying bills.

general disbursements journal   a record of payments from the general bank account by the firm to a third party. Such expenses may be incurred by the paralegal for the legal services practice or on behalf of a client, or for any other payment made by the firm to another party.

general journal   a record that tracks the day-to-day financial transactions of a firm chronologically, without any special categorization of the accounts.

general ledger   a record that posts journal entries by category in the order shown on the chart of accounts. The general ledger provides an ending balance after calculating the debits and credits for each account; this ending balance is used to prepare the trial balance.

general monetary retainer   an amount paid to a lawyer by a client to secure the availability of the lawyer for a specific period of time. The legal professional who receives a "general retainer" is not required to account for or to provide services. However, section 8(2)(2) of by-law 9 must be reviewed with caution in order to ensure that the conditions required by the Law Society of Ontario are satisfied.

general receipts journal   a record of payments received into a firm's general bank account. These may include amounts received from the paralegal, a third party, or a client.

generally accepted accounting principles (GAAP)   the common set of accounting principles and procedures that companies use to compile their financial statements. GAAP is a combination of authoritative standards set by policy boards and the commonly accepted ways of recording and reporting accounting information.

goods and services tax   see **GST/HST**.

government users   government users are interested in tax accounting, and businesses are required to submit income tax returns annually.

gross pay   the total amount of salary received before taxes or other deductions (such as health insurance) are deducted from it.

GST/HST   a tax that is added to most goods and services purchased in Canada. Each province has its own rate of tax. The HST (harmonized sales tax) is used in provinces where the federal GST (goods and services tax) and the PST (provincial sales tax) have been combined into a single value-added sales tax. In Ontario, the HST is 13 percent.

harmonized sales tax   see **GST/HST**.

historical cost   the original price paid for an item.

income   the amount received by a firm in the sale of its goods or services. Income is reported for income tax purposes and will also be used to determine the amount of deductions or credits that apply to the business or the individual; income is sometimes referred to as "revenue."

income statement   a financial statement showing the revenues and expenses for a particular accounting period; a temporary record that starts at a "zero" balance each new accounting period.

income statement account   one of two types of general ledger accounts. (Balance sheet accounts are the other type.) Income statement accounts are used to sort and store transactions involving revenues, expenses, gains, and losses. Debit all credit balances on the income account (i.e., bringing the balance to $0) and credit it to the income summary account.

income summary account   a transitional account into which all income statement revenue and expense accounts are transferred at the end of an accounting period. The net amount transferred into the income summary account equals the net profit (a credit balance) or loss (a debit balance) that the business incurred during the period. The income summary is a temporary record that must be closed (i.e., bringing the balance to $0).

income tax   a federal program that provides the government with revenue collected from all residents who are required to pay income tax. Income tax revenues are used for various programs and initiatives of the federal government. The Department of Finance sets the prescribed basic income tax rates, which vary progressively with the amount of taxable income. There are rates of tax at both the federal and the provincial levels.

information return a form filed by employers, trusts, and businesses to report to the Canada Revenue Agency about their income, source deductions, credits, and other relevant information. Each form has a number identifying its purpose. *Example:* Employers prepare a T4 slip for each employee, who in turn files it with his or her personal income tax form.

input tax credit (ITC) the amount that GST/HST registrants can recover for GST/HST paid (or payable) or owed on their purchases and expenses related to their business activities.

internal controls internal checks and balances used to create efficiency, to protect and safeguard the assets of the business, and to prevent fraud and theft. Such controls are customized for each business and process but typically follow industry standards and best practices. *Example:* having at least two signatories on any negotiable instrument, such as a cheque.

internal users a company's own stakeholders who are interested in accounting for purposes of making management decisions, such as those related to profitability or expansion.

international financial reporting standards (IFRS) a set of international accounting rules imposed on publicly accountable enterprises—for example, corporations whose shares are listed on a stock exchange, banks, etc.

journal entries a means of tracking and chronologically recording the day-to-day financial transactions of a firm, without any special categorization of the accounts. Journals document the source of the transaction and are called books of original entry. Where there is a need to specify and categorize a journal by account, this is known as a special journal.

Law Foundation of Ontario a non-profit organization, created by statute in 1974, governed by a five-person volunteer board of trustees and supported by a staff team, which funds legal programs and initiatives geared toward improving access to justice. The interest collected from the mixed trust accounts of licensees is used to fund many of these initiatives.

legal accounting software special software designed for general business and trust accounting. It provides automatic calculations, posts automatically to ledgers, and produces financial and other reports.

liabilities all the legal debts and obligations that a firm or a person owes to its creditors or customers.

licensee paralegals and lawyers who are licensed to practise by the Law Society of Ontario (LSO).

limited liability partnership a form of partnership established by professionals who are self-governed (e.g., doctors, lawyers, accountants, dentists). An LLP is not a corporation, but liability can be minimized through professional and other general liability insurance.

loss the situation in which expenses exceed income.

matching principle a basic underlying guideline in accounting that directs a firm to report an expense on its income statement in the same period as the related revenues.

matter-to-matter trust transfer journal a journal where a record of trust funds moved from one client's trust ledger account to another client's trust ledger account is recorded.

mixed or pooled trust bank account an account that holds funds for the benefit of more than one client and may be disbursed only by the rendering of an account for services or upon the authorization and direction of the client. The funds belong to the client and can be refunded or recovered by the client in the event of termination of the file or services, or where there are unused funds. (See by-law 9, section 7.)

monetary retainer   an advance payment made by a client, held in trust by a lawyer or paralegal for future services. In contrast, where services have already been rendered or billed, or disbursements already incurred on behalf of a client, the payment is not deposited in trust but is instead deposited into the general bank account. (See by-law 9, sections 7 and 8.) Monetary retainers are sometimes referred to as "unearned revenue" or "prepaid services."

multi-discipline practice (MDP) or affiliation   an arrangement among licensed legal professionals and non-licensed professionals who seek to work together through an association or partnership. MDPs are usually considered where the licensee and the non-licensee have overlapping practices or disciplines or where there is the prospect of mutual referrals. An "affiliation" is a more loosely held form of organization and may involve a larger group of professionals seeking to maximize marketing and professional support. (See by-law 7, part III.)

net income   as reported on the income statement, the situation in which income exceeds expenses, which will cause an increase in a company's equity.

net loss   as reported on the income statement, the situation in which expenses exceed income, which will cause a decrease in a company's equity.

non-billable work   work performed in relation to a file that is not billed to the client, such as a free consultation.

normal balance   the debit or credit sides of a financial statement, journal, or ledger where increases are recorded. Some accounts (such as assets) have a normal debit balance, so an entry on the debit side increases the balance in the account. Other accounts (such as liabilities) have a normal credit balance, so an entry on the credit side increases the balance in the account.

normal credit balance   *See* **normal balance**.

normal debit balance   *See* **normal balance**.

NSF cheque   a cheque that is cashed by the payee where there are insufficient funds in the payor's account to cover it. An NSF cheque is returned with a service charge. In preparing the bank reconciliation statement, the payor would credit (subtract from) the internal records the amount of the NSF cheque and the amount of the related service charge.

office supplies inventory   an asset account that reflects the value of the supplies that the firm has on hand; as office supplies are used up or consumed, this is recognized as an office supplies expense.

opening balance   the total balance for each account at the beginning of the accounting period. The total is taken from the ending or closing balance of that account from the last period.

outstanding cheque   a cheque issued by the payor that has not been cashed by the payee and therefore appears on the payor's internal records but not on the bank statement. To prepare the bank reconciliation, the payor would credit (subtract from) the bank balance the amount of the outstanding cheque (as if the transaction had been completed and the cheque paid from payor's bank account).

owner's equity   the value of assets remaining after all liabilities have been deducted; this residual value is what is received by the owner or shared by the shareholders or partners. Also called capital.

partnership   a firm managed by two or more persons who share in the profit, loss, and risk of the business. At least one partner must be a general partner, whose duty it is to manage the business; the other partners may be passive investors or take a less active role. Liability is unlimited but shared. (See by-law 7, part I.)

payee   a person to whom money, such as a cheque, is paid or is to be paid.

payor   a person who pays, especially in the case of a bill or cheque.

payroll deductions   source tax deductions, such as income tax deductions, Canada Pension Plan (CPP) contributions, and employment insurance (EI) premiums, that are deducted from an employee's income and sent regularly to the Canada Revenue Agency. Employers also contribute to some deductions and make their own CPP and EI contributions.

permanent accounts   balance sheet accounts; called "permanent" because their balances carry over from one fiscal period to the next.

personal deductions   income tax deductions that reduce tax for some taxpayers and promote certain activities considered to be beneficial, such as tuition fees and childcare expenses.

petty cash   cash on hand for a business to pay for "petty" or small expenditures such as postage, office supplies, parking, and other similar expenses. Petty cash is controlled internally by the establishment of a petty cash fund.

petty cash account   an asset account on the balance sheet, established by issuing a cheque to the custodian of the petty cash account. Each payment from the petty cash account is represented by a voucher. (See Figure 10.2.) When the petty cash account is reduced or has a zero balance, the petty cash fund is replenished to bring it back to the petty cash limit originally established, as follows:

20**		Dr.	Cr.
Jan. 1	Petty Cash	$100	
	General Bank Account		$100
	To establish (or increase) the petty cash fund ($100 limit)		

20**		Dr.	Cr.
Jan. 31	Expense Accounts (Postage, Office Supplies, Parking)	$72.50	
	General Bank Account		$72.50
	To replenish the petty cash fund ($100 limit)		

post, posting   the process of transferring information from a journal to a ledger.

post-closing trial balance   the listing of the balance sheet accounts (assets, liabilities, and owner's equity) after all adjustment and closing balances have been reduced to zero from the temporary accounts and have been transferred to update the capital account (owner's equity).

post reference (PR)   the numerical identifier for each account referenced on a chart of accounts. The PR makes it easy to cross-reference and identify journal entries.

prepaid expenses   expenses for a good or service that are paid in advance of the payment due date or before the use or consumption of the good or service. *Examples:* prepaid rent, prepaid insurance.

professional corporation   lawyers or licensed paralegals who carry on the practice of law or the provision of legal services through an incorporated entity. (See by-law 7, part II.)

profit   the situation in which income exceeds expenses.

reconciliation   the comparison of transactions recorded in a firm's internal records (the general ledger or bank account ledger) against the transactions reported on the bank statement (e.g., deposits, cheques issued, interest, bank charges) and the preparation of a bank reconciliation statement to confirm that the ending balances for the internal records and the bank statement are balanced. If the records are not balanced, the bookkeeper/accountant will need to investigate possible errors either in the firm's internal records or on the bank's part. It is good practice to reconcile both the general bank account ledger, and the trust bank account ledger, against the general bank account and the trust bank account statements.

records   documents that must be maintained by businesses and individuals to verify the information that is filed with the Canada Revenue Agency, such as account books, sales and purchase invoices, contracts, bank statements, and cancelled cheques. You must keep records at your business or residence in Canada for at least six years from the end of the last tax year to which the records relate, and the CRA must have access to these records if requested.

residual value   the estimated value of the asset at the end of its useful life.

retainer   an agreement between a client and a legal services provider for the engagement of legal services, describing the scope of services to be provided, the billing rate, and the billing practices.

revenue recognition principle   a basic guideline in the accrual approach to accounting that requires revenues to be shown on the income statement in the period in which they are earned, not in the period when the cash is collected.

separate interest-bearing trust account   a bank account that is held for each individual client who requests it, and who has large sums of money that are to be held for an extended period of time. The licensee has a duty to account for the interest on the funds in the separate interest-bearing account; interest accrues to the client. (See paragraph 2(b), "Separate Interest Bearing Trust Account," in *The Bookkeeping Guide for Paralegals* of the Law Society of Ontario.)

service charges   fees charged by a bank to manage customers' bank accounts. These fees may be regular monthly charges or charges per transaction. Service fees are expenses on the income statement and reduce the cash account.

shareholder's equity   the equity account in an incorporated company.

signature card   a card signed by anyone opening an account at a financial institution. It is kept on file to confirm the person's identity.

slide   an error resulting from incorrect placement of a decimal point in writing numbers.

small supplier   a supplier whose annual revenues from taxable supplies (before expenses) from all businesses total $30,000 or less. Once annual revenues exceed $30,000, the business must be registered and must start collecting GST/HST.

sole proprietorship   a business managed by a sole owner and operator, in his or her own name or under another, as authorized by a business name licence; liability is unlimited.

special journal   a specific journal, used instead of the general journal, to identify specific transactions by special categories. A general journal can be used but may not be helpful or efficient for reporting purposes. Special journals include trust receipts journals, general receipts journals, trust disbursements journals, general disbursements journals, and fees journals.

stakeholders   internal and external parties who rely on the information provided by a business in making decisions; these may include employees and customers.

statement of owner's equity   a financial statement used to calculate owner's equity in the firm after taking into account any profits or losses of the firm less money withdrawn by the owner; a permanent record that uses the ending balance of the last accounting period as the opening balance of the new period.

straight-line amortization method   a calculation of depreciation cost or expense at an equal amount over the life of the asset, so that the allocated monthly, quarterly, or annual costs are of equal value over time. *Example:* An asset with an original value of $3,000, a residual value of $500, and an estimated shelf life of 3 years would have an annual depreciation cost of $833 ($2,500/3 years). See Figure 8.4.

T-account   a tool used to show a particular account according to the debits and credits. *Example of a T-account for an asset account:*

Account Name

Debit	Credit
(+) increase	(−) decrease

tax year   the period for which income tax is to be paid, based on either the calendar year or the elected or designated fiscal period.

taxable benefits   benefits—such as money, or the value of goods or services—that an employer pays or provides to an employee in addition to salary or wages. *Examples:* employer contributions to a provincial health insurance plan, life insurance premiums, dental and medical benefits.

temporary accounts   income, expense, and withdrawal accounts; called "temporary" at year-end because a fresh start is needed each year.

time entry and billing   a method of tracking the time spent on billable client matters, whether manually or through the use of a computerized system. For each activity, the time and description are entered. *Best practice:* Enter the actual time (in hours and minutes, 00:00) for appointments, meetings, and telephone calls or matters where a significant amount of time is spent on an activity together with the calculated time in tenths of an hour. This approach avoids client complaints and disagreements about billing. Entering time on a daily basis, or as an activity is completed, is the best way to ensure accuracy.

transposition   the accidental reversal of digits in making a journal or ledger entry.

trial balance   A list of the closing balances of the general ledger accounts that are arranged according to the chart of account listings and categorized as either debits or credits. If the debit entries equal the credit entries, the trial balance is balanced.

trust bank account   a bank account in which a law professional (acting as an authorized custodian) holds money that belongs to clients, not to the firm. Trust funds are used for specific purposes—for example, to pay court filing fees on behalf of a client.

trust bank journal   a record of deposits to and withdrawals from a trust bank account, representing money belonging to clients and held in trust until services are rendered. Instead of using a general trust bank journal, a paralegal may wish to set up special journals for reporting purposes, called the trust receipts journal (records receipts into trust) and the trust disbursements journal (records disbursements from trust).

trust bank reconciliation   a comparison of the trust bank balance with the trust journal and trust listing balances. To obtain a reconciled balance, take the ending balance of the trust bank statement and subtract the amount of the outstanding cheques, then add any outstanding deposits.

trust comparison   a comparison of the reconciled trust bank balance with the client trust listing total. The two amounts should be equal.

trust control accounts   accounts that provide the total of the moneys received in trust from all clients and the total of moneys owed to clients. The balance sheet includes the trust bank account (e.g., funds received; an asset account) and trust funds owed (e.g., money owed to clients; a liability account). The totals in the two accounts should be equal.

undepreciated capital cost (UCC)   the balance of the capital cost left for further depreciation at any given time. The amount of CCA claimed each year will lower the UCC of the property.

valuable property record   a record of any property, other than cash, belonging to clients that is being held in trust or for safekeeping.

withdrawals   money taken out of the firm by the owner without regard to the sale of goods or services, thus reducing the equity value in the business. Money taken out of the business does not go back into the business but is used for the personal benefit of the owner. Shareholder withdrawals are known as *dividend payments*.

work in progress (WIP)   an account of work that has not been completed or services that have been performed in part but are still in progress and, therefore, not yet included as earned income or revenue. ① The account WIP Accrued (an asset account) has a debit balance; WIP Professional Fees (an income account) has a credit balance. ② When a bill is prepared, the journal entry would be: Accounts Receivable (Asset)—Dr.; Fees Earned—Cr. ③ In order to clear WIP Accrued (as a result of preparing an invoice and billing the client) for a particular period and bring it to $0 or to a value corresponding to the amount billed, the journal entry would be a reversing entry: WIP Professional Fees (Income)—Dr.; WIP Accrued (Asset)—Cr.:

Asset Accounts

WIP Accrued		Accounts Receivable	
500 ①		500 ②	
	500 ③		
Balance 0			

Income Accounts

Fees Earned		WIP Professional Fees	
	500 ②		500 ①
		500 ③	
		Balance 0	

worksheet   a form of internal reporting of the trial balance, specific adjustment entries, and adjusted trial balance showing the updated income statement and balance sheet entries. Additional columns can be used specifically for the income statement and the balance sheet. The worksheet is usually prepared in columns similar to a spreadsheet. *Example:*

Account Titles	Trial Balance		Adjustments		Adjusted Trial Balance		Income Statement		Balance Sheet	
	Dr.	*Cr.*	*Dr.*	*Cr.*	*Dr.*	*Cr.*	*Dr.*	*Cr.*	*Dr.*	*Cr.*
Office Supplies	50		35		85					
Trust Funds Owed		1,000		500		1,500				

Index

accountants, 2, 228
accounting, 3, 20, 21-22, 103, 293
  software, *see* legal
    accounting software
accounting cycle, 40, 41-43, 198, 222
accounting equation, 22, 24-25, 44, 48-49,
  see also assets; expanded accounting
  equation; liabilities; owner's equity
accounting period, 26, 40, 41, 100
accounting standards for private
  enterprises (ASPE), 21
accounts
  asset, 162, 200
  balance sheet, 226
  bank, 7-10, 13, 260-66
  categories of, 22-23
  contra-asset, 201
  dormant, 272
  drawings, 228
  expense, 226, 227
  income, 23, 226
  income summary, 227-28
  liabilities, 161, 162, 200
  payable, 125
  permanent, 226, 229
  petty cash, 256
  temporary, 43, 226
  titles, 200
  trust, *see* trust bank account
  withdrawal, 226
accounts receivable, 123,
  124-25, 128, 139, 199
accrual basis of accounting,
  21-22, 103,199, 293
accrued interest revenue, 204
accrued salaries expense, 209

adjusted trial balance, 43,
  199, 200, 206, 210
adjusting entries
  checking, 210
  in the accounting cycle, 199
  in worksheets, 42-43, 200
  preparing, 2-3, 204-10
  for tax purposes, 272
  types, 201-4
  year-end, 204, 225
adjustments, *see* adjusting entries
advertising, 13, 293
affiliation, *see* multi-discipline practice
amortization, *see* depreciation
assets
  accounts, 162, 200
  class, 201
  current, 22, 256
  defined, 29
  fixed or capital, 22
  in accounting equation, 24-25, 44
  in closing entries, 226
  in general receipts journal, 128
  on balance sheet, 100, 106-7
  prepaid, 209
  purchased, 21
  shift in, 49, 54
  trust, 169
  value of, 23
audits
  audit trail, 159
  defined, 6
  documentation for, 272
  practice audits, 171-72
  program, 285
  spot audits, 171

bad debt, 22, 199, 293; *see also* debts
balance sheet, *see also*
   financial statements
     accounts, 101, 226
     column on worksheet, 200, 210-11
     example, 169, 224
     interpreting, 108-9
     preparing, 106-8
balancing the books, 166, 199
bank, *see also* financial institutions
   charges or credits, 266, 294
   drafts, 159
   errors, 263
   memos, 263, 269
   passbooks, 272
   service charges, 261
   statements, 261
banking procedures, 259-60
barter transactions, 103
billable hours, 311
billable rate, 309
billable work, 119, 122
billing time, 118-20, 125,
   306, 308-10, 312
blank endorsement, 259
book of original entry, *see*
   general journal
book value, 201
bookkeeper, 2, 11, *see*
   also bookkeeping
bookkeeping, *see also* bookkeeper;
   electronic bookkeeping system
     as a paralegal, 3, 311
     double-entry, 24, 26,
       42, 43, 47, 161
     legal requirements, 235
     process, 118
     time to complete, 11
business entity principle, 21
business money, 159
Business Names Act, 4
business number, 11
business organization, 3-6

calculation error, 81, 82, 210
Canada Pension Plan (CPP), 288
Canada Revenue Agency (CRA)
   audits, 29, 272, 285
   payments to, 296

   recommendations, 285
   reporting to, 46
   requirements, 3, 138, 235, 312
   tax collection, 5, 299
   tax information, 103, 298
capital
   account, 26, 27, 45, 100, 105
   after posting, 229
   defined, 23, 26
   contribution, *see* investments
   gains, 298
capital cost allowance (CCA),
   199, 201, 285, 295
cash basis of accounting, 22
cash controls, 256
cash short and over, 258-59
chart of accounts, 23,
   47, 74, 131, 256
chartered professional
   accountant (CPA), 2
cheques
   bounced, 261
   cancelled, 260, 261, 267, 272, 292
   endorsement, 259-60
   NSF, 261
   outstanding, 261, 263, 267
   stale-dated, 271
   trust, 159, 172, 310
   uncashed, 271
class, 201, *see also* assets
client cost recovery journal, 312
client files, 307, 308
client ledgers
   general, 137-38
   in PCLaw®, 174
   trust, 120, 158, 161, 166
client matter, 307, *see also* matter
client number, 307
client time entries, *see* time
   entries and billing
client trust
   listing, 166, 167, 269
   obligations, 158
closing balance, 26
closing entries, 43, 224, 226-29, 228
closing the books, 43
compound entry, 44, 49, 51
conflict of interest, 308
conflict search, 308

conservatism principle, 21
consistency principle, 21
contra-asset account, 201
copying error, 81, 82
corporation, *see* professional
   corporation
cost principle, 21
CPA, *see* chartered professional
   accountant (CPA)
CPA Canada Handbook:
   Accounting, 21
CPP, *see* Canada Pension Plan (CPP)
CRA, *see* Canada Revenue
   Agency (CRA)
credit
   balance with debit, 128, 167
   column in worksheet, 200
   entries, 59, 60
   in the accounting
     equation, 24, 48
   in client general ledger
     accounts, 128
   normal balance, 44, 45, 46
   recording, 162
   rules of, 43-46
credit cards, 259
Credit Unions and Caisses
   Populaires Act, 1994, 10
creditors, 23

DEAD CLIC, 47, 210, *see also*
   assets; capital; credit; debit;
   drawings; expenses; income;
   liabilities; normal credit balance;
   normal debit balance
debit
   balance with credit, 128, 167
   cards, 259
   column in worksheet, 200
   entries, 60
   in the accounting
     equation, 24, 48
   in general bank account
     ledger sheet, 128
   memorandum, 261
   normal balance, 44, 45, 162
   recording, 162
   rules of, 43-46
debts, 22, 25; *see also* bad debt

declining balance amortization
method, 203; *see also* depreciation
deductions, 298
deposits
in transit, 260-61
to general bank account, 259
outstanding, 263, 269
records, 159
slips, 160, 259, 264-65, 310
depreciation, *see also* declining
balance amortization method
accumulated, 201
defined, 201
calculating, 199, 202, 208
rate, 295
disbursements
defined, 120
journals, 271
not incurred as agent, 299
recording, 158, 164, 311-12
trust, 161, 172, 310-11
docketing time, 119-20
documents, 46, 138, 272
dormant accounts, 272
double-entry bookkeeping,
24, 26, 42, 43, 47, 161
drawee, 260
drawer, 260
drawings, 102, 228, 229, 297

EI, *see* employment insurance (EI)
electronic bookkeeping system, 60
employer's contributions, 297
employment insurance (EI), 288
end-of-period, 312
ending balance, *see* closing balance
endorsement, 259-60
errors
bank, 263, 269
calculation, 210
detecting, 26
in adjusted trial balance, 210
in trial balance, 81-82
in trust bank journal, 167
mathematical, 82
omission, 82
overdraft, 9
posting, 82, 269
reducing, 259

slide, 82
transposition, 82
wrong column, 81, 210
exemptions, 284
expanded accounting equation,
26-29, *see also* accounting equation
expenses
accounts, 102, 226, 227
accrued, 204
advertising, 293
business, 104, 287
business use of home, 104
calculating, 295
capital, 294
classifying, 29
computer and other
equipment, 296
convention, 297
debit, 46, 200
depreciation, 199, 201
general office, 259
insurance, 294
in expanded accounting
equation, 27
living, 293
maintenance and repairs, 294
meals and entertainment, 294
motor vehicle, 295
office, 297
operating, 201, 293-98
personal, 201, 205-7, 293
prepaid, 293
recording, 21, 22, 56
recovery, 27, 120
reporting, 103
salaries, 297-98
telephone and utilities, 298
tracking, 6, 258
travelling, 293
work space in home, 296
explanation codes, 122, 308, 311
external users, 20

fees book, 118, 123-24, 271
fees journal, *see* fees book
file number, *see* client matter
financial institutions, 10, *see also*
bank; banking procedures
financial records, 158

financial statements, 3, 43, 100,
104, 108-9, 131, 211, 222
fiscal periods, 40, 103
fiscal year
adjusting entries, 204-5
defined, 40
year-end, 40, 43, 199, 209, 229-34
flat rate, 119, 309
float, 258-59
fraud, 256, 259
full endorsement, 259

general balance, 260-66
general bank account
compared with trust
account, 158-59
defined, 8, 9
ledger sheet, 128, 266
records, 271-72
withdrawals from, 259
general disbursements journal,
118, 125, 129-30, 263
general firm funds, 7
general journal
closing entries, 226, 227, 228
defined, 22, 42
entries, 47, 59, 75, 79, 130,
134, 225, 256, 257, 258
bank charges, 266
payroll, 291
example, 57
transaction details, 162
uses, 125, 199
general ledger
accounts, 74, 80, 120, 128,
167, 227, 229-34
charts, 82
client's, 131
completed, 134-37
defined, 74
in PCLaw®, 108
opening balances, 58
petty cash, 256, 258
posting in, 22, 42, 76
general monetary retainer, 7
general receipts journal,
118, 124, 125, 127-28
generally accepted accounting
principles (GAAP), 20, 21, 199, 203

GIC, *see* guaranteed investment certificate (GIC)

going concern principle, 21

goods and services tax (GST), 284, *see also* GST/HST; harmonized sales tax (HST)

government users, 20

gross pay, 288, 289

GST, *see* goods and services tax (GST)

GST/HST, *see also* goods and services tax (GST); harmonized sales tax (HST)
  barter transactions, and, 103
  filing, 292, 296, 298
  registering for, 11
  registration number, 285
  remitting, 284, 285-87, 288
  report, 311
  reporting period, 288
  returns, 235, 286, 287
  to client accounts, 299

guaranteed investment certificate (GIC), 10, 267

harmonized sales tax (HST), 9, 124, 130, 284, 299, *see also* goods and services tax (GST); GST/HST

historical cost, 201

HST, *see* harmonized sales tax (HST)

"in the red," *see* overdrawn

income
  accounts, 23, 226
  accrued, 204
  debits and credits, 46
  defined, 23
  other, 103
  reporting, 103
  sources of, 26-27, 102
  statements, 100-104, 101, 105, 108-9, 168, 199, 200, 210-11, 222, 223, *see also* financial statements
  summary account, 226, 227-28, 229
  tracking, 6

income tax, *see also* tax; *Income Tax Act*
  accounting for, 292-98
  collection, 5

deductions, 288

payable, 102

reporting, 103

returns, 3, 199, 204, 235

Income Tax Act, 5, 22, 103, 285, 287, 312, *see also* income tax

incorporated practices, *see* professional corporation

"incurred as agent," 299

information return, 292, *see also* T4 information return

input tax credit (ITC), 284, 285

insufficient funds (NSF), 9, 261

insurance, 6, 294

interest, 11, 27, 294, 296

internal controls, 24

internal users, 20

international financial reporting standards, 21

investments, 27

invoices
  example, 121
  preparing, 119-20
  recording payment, 124, 292

ITC, *see* input tax credit (ITC)

journal entries, 42

Law Foundation of Ontario (LFO), 3

Law Society Act, 2, 6, 11, 171, 272

Law Society of Ontario (LSO)
  audits, 7
  by-laws, 127, 129
    by-law 6, 6
    by-law 9, 2, 7, 9, 13, 123, 159, 160, 161, 162, 168, 169, 171, 267, 271, 306
    by-law 10, 272
  Paralegal Rules of Conduct, 299, 308
  requirements, 2, 168, 259, 272, 312
  Rules of Professional Conduct, 8, 172
  trouble with, 270

law types, 307-8

leasing costs, 296

ledgers
  balances, 48
  client, 161, 172

defined, 8

trust, 158

legal accounting software, *see also* PCLaw®
  automatization, 286
  errors, and, 26
  list of accounts, 24
  uses of, 13, 106, 122, 125, 260
  using, 306-12

legal fees, 293

letter of direction, 12

LFO, *see* Law Foundation of Ontario (LFO)

liabilities
  accounts, 161, 162, 200
  adjusting entries, 199
  defined, 23
  in accounting equation, 24-25, 44
  on balance sheet, 100, 106-7
  outstanding, 226
  trust, 169

licensee, 2, 7, 160

limited liability partnership, 4, 6

losses, 100, 105, 199

LSO, *see* Law Society of Ontario (LSO)

maintenance costs, 104

management practices, 171

matching principle, 22, 199, 201

mathematical error, 82

matters, 122, 307, 309

matter-to-matter trust transfer journal, 169-70, 272

minutes-to-decimals conversion, 119, 309

misconduct, 172

mixed trust
  balance, 269
  bank account, 8-10, 9, 11, 158-59, 161
    reconciling, 266-71, 267

monetary retainer, *see* retainers

money handling, 259-60

multi-discipline practice, 4

net income, 27, 100, 102, 105, 209

net loss, 27, 100, 102, 105, 211

net profit, 100, 211

net tax, 287
non-billable work, 119, 122
normal balance, 23, 210
normal credit balance, 44, 45, 46
normal debit balance, 44, 45, 162
"not incurred as agent," 299
NSF, *see* insufficient funds (NSF)

office supplies
    adjustment, 207
    inventory, 199
omission, 82
Ontario's Electronic Registration
  System, *see* Teraview®
opening balance, 26, 75
opening balance sheet, 26, 48, 58, 59-60
opening entries, 58, 60, 76, 307-8
overdraft, 9
overdrawn, 74
owner's equity
    accounts, 200
    defined, 23
    expanded accounting
      equation, and, 27
    in accounting equation,
      24-25, 44, 45
    on balance sheet, 100, 107
    statement of, 100, 101, 105-6,
      168, 222, 223, *see also*
      financial statements

Paralegal Annual Report, 3
paralegal–client relationship, 7
partnership
    agreement, 5
    defined, 4
    limited liability, 4, 6
    multi-discipline, 4
    recording expenses, 104
payee, 129, 260
payments
    for services rendered, 55
    method of, 128
    recording, 172-74
payor, *see* drawer
payroll, 288-92, 296
PCLaw®, 13, 24, 58, 83, 108-9,
  122, 172-74, 306, 307, *see also*
  legal accounting software

penalties, 296
period-end adjustments, 42
permanent accounts, 43, 226, 229
personal deductions, 289
personal expenses, 21, 29, 293
personal finances, 29
personal loans, 208
personal use of business assets, 297
petty cash, 13, 256-59
pooled trust bank account, *see*
  mixed trust bank account
post-closing trial balance, 41,
  229-30
post reference (PR), 59, 60, 74, 75
posting
    completed, 80
    defined, 8
    errors, 82, 269
    from general disbursements
      journal, 130
    from general receipts journal, 128
    opening entries, 76
    from special journals, 131
    from trust bank journal, 165
    to general ledger, 42, 75-80
private enterprises, 21-22
professional corporation, 4, 5, 8
professional fees, 204
profit and loss statement,
  see income statement
profits, 27, 100, 105, 199
profits and losses, 200

receipts
    cash, 160
    general, 271
    in general receipts journal, 128
    keeping, 46, 259, 292
    recording, 158, 163,
      172-74, 311-12
    trust, 161, 172, 310-11
reconciliation
    defined, 260
    general bank, 262
    trust bank, 266-71, 272
records
    bookkeeping, 21
    business, 20
    deposits, 159

electronic, 312
financial, 8, 158
general bank, 271-72
legal requirements for, 235, 292
maintenance, 6, 13, 271-72,
  285
permanent, 292
retention, 271-72
safeguarding, 60
of transactions, 161
trust bank, 272
remittances, 288, 298
reports, 12
residual value, 201
restrictive endorsement, 259
retainer agreement, 119,
  see also retainers
retainers, 7, 159, 172, 311, *see*
  also retainer agreement
revenue, *see* income
revenue recognition
  principle, 21, 203

salaries, 104, 288, 297-98
separate interest-bearing
  trust account, 10
service charges, 261
shareholders, 5
shareholder's equity, 23
signature card, 259
six-year requirement, 235, 285, 293
slide, 82
small supplier, 11, 284
software, *see* legal
  accounting software
sole proprietorship, 3-4, 5, 8,
  21, 102, 104, 199, 209, 284
special journals, 118,
  125-30, 131, 128, 312
stakeholders, 20
statement of owner's equity, *see*
  owner's equity, statement of
statements
    general bank account, 262
    of revenues and expenses,
      199
    trust, 129, 121, 268
straight-line amortization method,
  202-3, 208, *see also* depreciation

T-accounts, 48, 106
T4 information return, 40, 292, 298
T4 slips, *see* T4 information return
tax, *see also* income tax
  business, 294
  laws, 3, 5
  returns, 3, 40, 296
  year, 293
taxable benefits, 292
taxation legislation, *see* tax, laws
TD1 form, 289
temporary accounts, 43, 226
time dockets, 119
time entries and billing,
  122, 306, 308-10
time sheets, 122
transactions
  analyzing, 27, 47, 131-33
  entered and totalled, 57
  examples, 49-57
  in the accounting cycle, 42
  recording, 48-49, 125-30, 161
  source documents, 46
transposition, 82
trial balance
  accounts, 209
  column in worksheet, 200
  defined, 168
  errors in, 81
  example, 101, 139, 205
  in accounting cycle, 42
  imbalanced, 82
  preparing, 80-83
  use of, 100

trust
  account, *see* trust bank account
  assets, 169
  balance, 260-61, 269
  cheques, 159, 172, 310
  comparison, 10, 267
  control accounts, 161
  deposits from, 159
  disbursements, 172
  journal, *see* trust bank journal
  ledger, 131, 162
  liabilities, 169
  money, 169
  statement, 120, 121, 268
  withdrawals from, 159
trust bank account
  balance, 167
  defined, 158-59
  deposit slip, 160
  in trial balance, 168
  reconciliation, 270
  records, 272
  statement, 268
  withdrawals from, 259
trust bank journal
  defined, 125, 161
  entries in, 131
  example, 268
  in PCLaw®, 173
  receipts and disbursements,
    310-11
  using, 161-67
trust funds
  balance of, 310

  defined, 7
  owed, 161, 162, 168
  received, 172
trust receipts and disbursements
  journal, *see* trust bank journal
trust transfer journal, *see* matter-
  to-matter trust transfer journal

unincorporated practices, *see*
  partnership; sole proprietorship

vacation, 291-92
valuable property record, 171, 272
voucher, 257, 292
vouchers, 258

withdrawals
  accounts, 226
  defined, 26, 45, 102
  from an ATM, 259
  from trust, 159
  in expanded accounting
    equation, 26-27
work in progress, 22, 203, 204
worksheets
  adjustments in, 207, 208, 209
  completing, 211-13
  headings, 200
  in the accounting cycle,
    42-43, 198
  preparing, 199-200
wrong column error, 81, 210

year-end, *see* fiscal year